Financial Statistics and Data Analytics

Financial Statistics and Data Analytics

Editors

Shuangzhe Liu
Milind Sathye

MDPI • Basel • Beijing • Wuhan • Barcelona • Belgrade • Manchester • Tokyo • Cluj • Tianjin

Editors
Shuangzhe Liu
Faculty of Science
and Technology,
University of Canberra
Australia

Milind Sathye
Canberra Business School,
University of Canberra
Australia

Editorial Office
MDPI
St. Alban-Anlage 66
4052 Basel, Switzerland

This is a reprint of articles from the Special Issue published online in the open access journal *Journal of Risk and Financial Management* (ISSN 1911-8074) (available at: https://www.mdpi.com/journal/jrfm/special_issues/Financial_Statistics).

For citation purposes, cite each article independently as indicated on the article page online and as indicated below:

LastName, A.A.; LastName, B.B.; LastName, C.C. Article Title. *Journal Name* **Year**, *Volume Number*, Page Range.

ISBN 978-3-03943-975-1 (Hbk)
ISBN 978-3-03943-976-8 (PDF)

Contents

About the Editors

Shuangzhe Liu is an Associate Professor of Statistics in the Faculty of Science and Technology, University of Canberra, Australia. He serves as a reviewer for more than 40 mathematics, econometrics, statistics, and data science international journals and as an associate editor for four of these. He currently studies issues in matrix differential calculus, econometrics, statistics, and machine learning with applications in various fields. Jointly, he has more than 140 publications.

Milind Sathye is a Professor of Banking and Finance at the University of Canberra, Australia. Regularly consulted by Australian and global media, he has appeared on ABC 730 Report, Australia, Al Jazira, Dubai, Bloomberg Hong Kong, among others, on many occasions. Australian Parliament's Senate Economics Committees and Australian Federal Courts also consult him. His areas of research interest are banking efficiency, technology in banking, and anti-money laundering.

Preface to "Financial Statistics and Data Analytics"

This book brings state-of-art knowledge in the field of financial statistics and data analytics to the fore.

The paper by Carolina Prihandinisari et al. reviews research and theory on the important topic of labor turnover resulting from issues related to job performance and/or job satisfaction which have, in turn, been initiated by changes in work motivation.

Bahadır Yüzba and Ejaz Ahmed's paper suggests improved estimation strategies based on preliminarily test and shrinkage principles in a seemingly unrelated regression model when explanatory variables are affected by multicollinearity.

The paper by Manuel Galea et al. considers asset pricing models under the multivariate t-distribution with finite second moment. Chuxuan Jiang et al. test for multifractal scaling across several financial time series including Bitcoin and find that multifractal scaling cannot be ruled out for Bitcoin or the Nasdaq Composite Index, both technology-driven assets.

Eduardo Mineo et al. propose DCOBS with no-arbitrage restrictions, a dynamic constrained smoothing B-splines yield curve model. Maria Karadima and Helen Louri examine the evolution of competition (through market power and concentration) and credit risk (through non-performing loans) in 2005–2017 across all euro area countries (EA-19), as well as core (EA-Co) and periphery (EA-Pe) countries separately. In their second paper, they provide detailed answers to the remarks made by Tsionas on the use of stochastic frontier-based measures of market power in part of an empirical study, which examines the fragmentation and convergence dynamics of market power, concentration, and credit risk in the euro area banking sector during 2005–2017.

Danúbia R. Cunha et al. examine a general family of Birnbaum–Saunders autoregressive conditional duration (BS-ACD) models based on generalized Birnbaum–Saunders (GBS) distributions, denoted by GBS-ACD. Tronzano focuses on three "safe haven" assets (gold, oil, and the Swiss Franc) and examines the impact of recent financial crises and some macroeconomic variables on their return co-movements during the last two decades.

Juan Carlos Ruilova and Pedro Alberto Morettin study a variant of the GARCH model when we consider the arrival of heterogeneous information in high-frequency data. Ashis SenGupta and Moumita Roy obtain a simple and efficient estimator of the index parameter of symmetric stable distribution that holds universally, i.e., over the entire range of the parameter. They appeal to directional statistics on the classical result on the wrapping of a distribution in obtaining the wrapped stable family of distributions.

This book will be useful for graduate students and researchers working in any area related to financial statistics and data analytics.

Finally, we would like to thank all the authors and reviewers for their contributions, and our colleagues at the Editorial Office for their support and assistance.

Shuangzhe Liu, Milind Sathye
Editors

Journal of
Risk and Financial Management

MDPI

Article

An Universal, Simple, Circular Statistics-Based Estimator of α for Symmetric Stable Family

Ashis SenGupta [1,2,3] and Moumita Roy [4,*]

1. Applied Statistics Unit, Indian Statistical Institute, Kolkata 700108, India; amsseng@gmail.com
2. Department of Population Health Sciences, MCG, Augusta University, Augusta, GA 30912, USA
3. Department of Statistics, Middle East Technical University, 06800 Ankara, Turkey
4. Department of Statistics, Midnapore College(Autonomous), Midnapore 721101, India

* Correspondence: mouroy.roy@gmail.com

Received: 15 October 2019; Accepted: 18 November 2019 ; Published: 23 November 2019

Abstract: The aim of this article is to obtain a simple and efficient estimator of the index parameter of symmetric stable distribution that holds universally, i.e., over the entire range of the parameter. We appeal to directional statistics on the classical result on wrapping of a distribution in obtaining the wrapped stable family of distributions. The performance of the estimator obtained is better than the existing estimators in the literature in terms of both consistency and efficiency. The estimator is applied to model some real life financial datasets. A mixture of normal and Cauchy distributions is compared with the stable family of distributions when the estimate of the parameter α lies between 1 and 2. A similar approach can be adopted when α (or its estimate) belongs to (0.5,1). In this case, one may compare with a mixture of Laplace and Cauchy distributions. A new measure of goodness of fit is proposed for the above family of distributions.

Keywords: Index parameter; estimation; wrapped stable; Hill estimator; characteristic function-based estimator; asymptotic; efficiency

---

1. Introduction

Our motivation in this paper is to obtain a universal and efficient estimator of the tail index parameter α of symmetric stable distribution (explained in Section 2) Nolan (2003). This is achieved by appealing to methods available in circular statistics. We recall that there exist two popular estimators of α in the literature. The Hill estimator proposed by Hill (1975), which uses the linear function of the order statistics, however, can be used to estimate $\alpha \in [1,2]$ only. Furthermore, it is also "extremely sensitive" to the choice of k (explained in Section 6) even for other values of α. Hill (1975) and Dufour and Kurz-Kim (2010) pointed out other drawbacks of the Hill estimator. The other estimator proposed by Anderson and Arnold (1993) is based on characteristic function approach. However, this estimator cannot be obtained in a closed form and is to be solved numerically. Furthermore, neither its asymptotic distribution nor its variance and bias are available in the literature.

Our approach in this paper appeals to circular statistics and is based on the method of trigonometric moments as in SenGupta (1996) and later also discussed in Jammalamadaka and SenGupta (2001). This stems from the very useful result which presents a closed analytical form of the density of a wrapped (circular) stable distribution obtained by wrapping the corresponding stable distribution which need not have any closed form analytic representation for arbitrary α. This result shows that α is preserved as the same parameter even after the wrapping. Furthermore, this paper presents a goodness of fit test based on the wrapped probability density function, which may be used as a necessary condition to ascertain the fit of the stable distribution. We exploit this approach with the real life examples. This estimator has a simple and elegant closed form expression. It is asymptotically normally distributed with mean α and variance available in a closed analytical form. Furthermore, from extensive simulations under parameter configurations encountered in financial data, it is exhibited that this new estimator outperforms both the estimators mentioned above almost uniformly in the entire comparable support of α. In Section 2, the probability density function of the wrapped stable distribution and some associated notations are introduced. The moment estimator of the index parameter is also defined in this section. Section 3 presents the derivation of the asymptotic distribution of the moment estimator defined in Section 2. In Section 4, an improved estimator of the index parameter is obtained. Section 5 shows the derivation of the asymptotic distribution of the improved estimator using the multivariate delta method. In addition, the asymptotic variance is computed for various values of the parameters through simulation. In Section 6, comparison of the performance of the improved estimator is made with those of the Hill estimator and the characteristic function-based estimator based on their root mean square errors through simulation. In Section 7, the procedure of the various computations is presented. In Section 8, applications of the proposed estimator is made on some real life data. We also conclude with remarks on the performance of the various estimators and some comments on future scope in Section 8. Finally, the tables showing the various computations and the figures on the applications of data are given in Appendices A, B and C.

2. The Trigonometric Moment Estimator

The regular symmetric stable distribution is defined through its characteristic function given by

$$\varphi(t) = \exp(it\mu - |\sigma t|^{\alpha})$$

where μ is the location parameter; σ is the scale parameter, which we take as 1; and α is the index or shape parameter of the distribution. Here, without loss of generality, we take $\mu = 0$.

From the stable distribution, we can obtain the wrapped stable distribution (the process of wrapping explained in Jammalamadaka and SenGupta (2001)). Suppose $\theta_1, \theta_2, ..., \theta_m$ is a random sample of size m drawn from the wrapped stable (given in Jammalamadaka and SenGupta (2001)) distribution whose probability density function is given by

$$f(\theta, \rho, \alpha, \mu) = \frac{1}{2\pi}[1 + 2\sum_{p=1}^{\infty} \rho^{p^{\alpha}} \cos p(\theta - \mu)] \quad 0 < \rho \leq 1, 0 < \alpha \leq 2, 0 < \mu \leq 2\pi \tag{1}$$

It is known in general from Jammalamadaka and SenGupta (2001) that the characteristic function of θ at the integer p is defined as,

$$\psi_{\theta}(p) = E[\exp(ip(\theta - \mu))] = \alpha_p + i\beta_p$$

$$\text{where} \quad \alpha_p = E\cos p(\theta - \mu) \quad \text{and} \quad \beta_p = E\sin p(\theta - \mu)$$

Furthermore, from Jammalamadaka and SenGupta (2001), it is known that for, the p.d.f given by Equation (1),

$$\psi_{\theta}(p) = \rho^{p^{\alpha}}$$

$$\text{Hence,} \quad E\cos p(\theta - \mu) = \rho^{p^{\alpha}} \quad \text{and} \quad E\sin p(\theta - \mu) = 0 \tag{2}$$

We define

$$\bar{C_1} = \frac{1}{m}\sum_{i=1}^{m}\cos\theta_i, \quad \bar{C_2} = \frac{1}{m}\sum_{i=1}^{m}\cos 2\theta_i, \quad \bar{S_1} = \frac{1}{m}\sum_{i=1}^{m}\sin\theta_i$$

$$\text{and} \quad \bar{S_2} = \frac{1}{m}\sum_{i=1}^{m}\sin 2\theta_i$$

Then, we note that $\bar{R_1} = \sqrt{\bar{C_1}^2 + \bar{S_1}^2}$ and $\bar{R_2} = \sqrt{\bar{C_2}^2 + \bar{S_2}^2}$

By the method of trigonometric moments estimation, equating $\bar{R_1}$ and $\bar{R_2}$ to the corresponding functions of the theoretical trigonometric moments, we get the estimator of index parameter α as (see SenGupta (1996)):

$$\hat{\alpha} = \frac{1}{\ln 2} \ln \frac{\ln \bar{R_2}}{\ln \bar{R_1}}$$

Then, we define $\bar{R_j} = \frac{1}{m}\sum_{i=1}^{m} \cos j(\theta_i - \bar{\theta})$, $j = 1,2$ and $\bar{\theta}$ is the mean direction given by $\bar{\theta} = \arctan\left(\frac{\bar{S_1}}{\bar{C_1}}\right)$. Note that $\bar{R_1} \equiv \bar{R}$.

We consider two special cases.

2.1. Special Case 1 : $\mu = 0, \sigma = 1$

We now consider the case as treated by Anderson and Arnold (1993), specifically $\mu = 0$ and $\sigma = 1$, and hence the concentration parameter $\rho = \exp(-1)$ as both parameters are known. This case may arise when one has historical data or prior information on the scale parameter. In such a case, the probability density function reduces to

$$f(\theta, \alpha) = \frac{1}{2\pi}[1 + 2\sum_{p=1}^{\infty}\{\exp(-1)\}^{p^{\alpha}} \cos p\theta)], \quad 0 < \alpha \leq 2$$

In addition, by the method of trigonometric moments estimation, the estimator of index parameter α is given by

$$\hat{\alpha_1} = -\frac{\ln \bar{C_2}}{\ln 2}$$

2.2. Special Case 2 : $\mu = 0$, σ Unknown

Next, we consider a general case when $\mu = 0$ and σ, and hence the estimator of the concentration parameter is $\rho = \bar{R_1}$. This case is especially useful in many real life applications, for example, for price changes in financial data, $\mu = 0$ is a standard assumption. In such a case, the probability density function reduces to

$$f(\theta, \alpha) = \frac{1}{2\pi}[1 + 2\sum_{p=1}^{\infty} \rho^{p^{\alpha}} \cos p\theta)], \quad 0 < \alpha \leq 2$$

In addition, by the method of trigonometric moments estimation, the estimator of index parameter α is given by

$$\hat{\alpha_2} = \frac{1}{\ln 2} \ln \frac{\ln \bar{C_2}}{\ln \bar{C_1}}$$

As is also seen in Anderson and Arnold (1993), for financial data after using log-ratio transformation, the location parameter of the transformed variable becomes zero. Hence, the case of $\mu \neq 0$ was not considered by Anderson and Arnold (1993) and accordingly by us also for the comparison made in this paper.

3. Derivation of the Asymptotic Distribution of the Moment Estimator

Lemma 1.

$$\sqrt{m}(T_m - \mu) \xrightarrow{L} N_4(0, \Sigma)$$

$$where \quad T_m = (\bar{C_1}, \bar{C_2}, \bar{S_1}, \bar{S_2})',$$

μ is the mean vector given by

$$\mu = (\rho \cos \mu_0, \rho^{2^{\alpha}} \cos 2\mu_0, \rho \sin \mu_0, \rho^{2^{\alpha}} \sin 2\mu_0)'$$

and Σ is the dispersion matrix given by

$$\Sigma = \begin{pmatrix} A & B & C & D \\ B & E & F & G \\ C & F & H & I \\ D & G & I & J \end{pmatrix}$$

where

$$A = \frac{\rho^{2^\alpha} \cos 2\mu_0 + 1 - 2\rho^2 \cos^2 \mu_0}{2}$$
$$B = \frac{\rho \cos \mu_0 + \rho^{3^\alpha} \cos 3\mu_0 - 2\rho^{2^\alpha+1} \cos \mu_0 \cos 2\mu_0}{2}$$
$$C = \frac{\rho^{2^\alpha} \sin 2\mu_0 - 2\rho^2 \cos \mu_0 \sin \mu_0}{2}$$
$$D = \frac{\rho^{3^\alpha} \sin 3\mu_0 + \rho \sin \mu_0 - 2\rho^{2^\alpha+1} \cos \mu_0 \sin 2\mu_0}{2}$$
$$E = \frac{\rho^{4^\alpha} \cos 4\mu_0 + 1 - 2(\rho^{2^\alpha})^2 \cos^2 2\mu_0}{2}$$
$$F = \frac{\rho^{3^\alpha} \sin 3\mu_0 - \rho \sin \mu_0 - 2\rho^{2^\alpha+1} \cos 2\mu_0 \sin \mu_0}{2}$$
$$G = \frac{\rho^{4^\alpha} \sin 4\mu_0 - 2(\rho^{2^\alpha})^2 \cos 2\mu_0 \sin 2\mu_0}{2}$$
$$H = \frac{1 - \rho^{2^\alpha} \cos 2\mu_0 - 2\rho^2 \sin^2 \mu_0}{2}$$
$$I = \frac{\rho \cos \mu_0 - \rho^{3^\alpha} \cos 3\mu_0 - 2\rho^{2^\alpha+1} \sin \mu_0 \sin 2\mu_0}{2}$$
$$J = \frac{1 - \rho^{4^\alpha} \cos 4\mu_0 - 2(\rho^{2^\alpha})^2 \sin^2 2\mu_0}{2}$$

Proof. The derivations for the proof are given in Appendix A.

Hence, assuming large sample size, central limit theorem Feller (1971) gives $(\bar{C_1}, \bar{C_2}, \bar{S_1}, \bar{S_2})' \xrightarrow{L} N_4(\mu, \frac{\Sigma}{m})$ where μ is the mean vector given by

$$\mu = (\rho \cos \mu_0, \rho^{2^\alpha} \cos 2\mu_0, \rho \sin \mu_0, \rho^{2^\alpha} \sin 2\mu_0)'$$

and Σ is the dispersion matrix given by

$$\Sigma = \begin{pmatrix} A & B & C & D \\ B & E & F & G \\ C & F & H & I \\ D & G & I & J \end{pmatrix}$$

where $A, B, C, D, E, F, G, H, I$ and J are as defined above.

□

Theorem 1.

$$\sqrt{m}(\hat{\alpha} - \alpha) \xrightarrow{L} N(0, \gamma' \Sigma \gamma)$$

where

$$\gamma = \frac{1}{\ln 2} \left(\frac{-\cos \mu_0}{\rho \ln \rho}, \frac{\cos 2\mu_0}{\rho^{2^\alpha} \ln \rho^{2^\alpha}}, \frac{-\sin \mu_0}{\rho \ln \rho}, \frac{\sin 2\mu_0}{\rho^{2^\alpha} \ln \rho^{2^\alpha}} \right)'$$

and

$$\underline{\gamma}' \Sigma \underline{\gamma} = \frac{1}{(\ln 2)^2} \left[\frac{1 + \rho^{2^\alpha} - 2\rho^2}{2(\rho \ln \rho)^2} + \frac{1 + \rho^{4^\alpha} - 2(\rho^{2^\alpha})^2}{2(\rho^{2^\alpha} \ln \rho^{2^\alpha})^2} + \frac{2\rho^{2^\alpha+1} - \rho - \rho^{3^\alpha}}{\rho \ln \rho \rho^{2^\alpha} \ln \rho^{2^\alpha}} \right]$$

Proof. We know from Lemma 1 that $\sqrt{m}(T_m - \mu) \xrightarrow{L} N_4(0, \Sigma)$

Therefore, by delta method (given in Casella and Berger (2002)), we get

$\sqrt{m}(\hat{\alpha}-\alpha) \xrightarrow{L} N(0, \gamma'\Sigma\gamma)$ where

$$g(T_m) = \hat{\alpha} = \frac{1}{\ln 2}\ln\frac{\ln \bar{R}_2}{\ln \bar{R}_1} = \frac{1}{\ln 2}\ln\frac{\ln\sqrt{\bar{C}_2^{\,2}+\bar{S}_2^{\,2}}}{\ln\sqrt{\bar{C}_1^{\,2}+\bar{S}_1^{\,2}}}$$

$$\gamma = \begin{pmatrix} \frac{\partial g}{\partial \bar{C}_1} \\ \frac{\partial g}{\partial \bar{C}_2} \\ \frac{\partial g}{\partial \bar{S}_1} \\ \frac{\partial g}{\partial \bar{S}_2} \end{pmatrix} \text{ at } \mu
= \frac{1}{\ln 2}\begin{pmatrix} \frac{\bar{C}_1}{-(\bar{C}_1^{\,2}+\bar{S}_1^{\,2})\ln\sqrt{\bar{C}_1^{\,2}+\bar{S}_1^{\,2}}} \\ \frac{\bar{C}_2}{(\bar{C}_2^{\,2}+\bar{S}_2^{\,2})\ln\sqrt{\bar{C}_2^{\,2}+\bar{S}_2^{\,2}}} \\ \frac{\bar{S}_1}{-(\bar{C}_1^{\,2}+\bar{S}_1^{\,2})\ln\sqrt{\bar{C}_1^{\,2}+\bar{S}_1^{\,2}}} \\ \frac{\bar{S}_2}{(\bar{C}_2^{\,2}+\bar{S}_2^{\,2})\ln\sqrt{\bar{C}_2^{\,2}+\bar{S}_2^{\,2}}} \end{pmatrix} \text{ at } \mu
= \frac{1}{\ln 2}\begin{pmatrix} \frac{-\cos\mu_0}{\rho\ln\rho} \\ \frac{\cos 2\mu_0}{\rho^{2^\alpha}\ln\rho^{2^\alpha}} \\ \frac{-\sin\mu_0}{\rho\ln\rho} \\ \frac{\sin 2\mu_0}{\rho^{2^\alpha}\ln\rho^{2^\alpha}} \end{pmatrix}$$

$$\begin{aligned}
\underline{\gamma}'\Sigma\underline{\gamma} = \frac{1}{(\ln 2)^2}\Bigg[& \frac{1+\rho^{2^\alpha}\cos^2 2\mu_0 - 2\rho^2(\cos^4\mu_0+\sin^4\mu_0)}{2(\rho\ln\rho)^2} \\
& + \frac{-\rho\cos^2\mu_0\cos 2\mu_0 - \rho^{3^\alpha}\cos 3\mu_0\cos\mu_0\cos 2\mu_0 + 2\rho^{2^\alpha+1}\cos^2\mu_0\cos^2 2\mu_0}{\rho\ln\rho\rho^{2^\alpha}\ln\rho^{2^\alpha}} \\
& + \frac{\rho^{2^\alpha}\sin 2\mu_0\sin\mu_0\cos\mu_0 - 2\rho^2\cos^2\mu_0\sin^2\mu_0}{(\rho\ln\rho)^2} \\
& + \frac{-\rho^{3^\alpha}\cos\mu_0\sin 2\mu_0\sin 3\mu_0 - \rho\sin\mu_0\cos\mu_0\sin 2\mu_0 + 2\rho^{2^\alpha+1}\cos^2\mu_0\sin^2 2\mu_0}{\rho\ln\rho\rho^{2^\alpha}\ln\rho^{2^\alpha}} \\
& + \frac{\rho^{4^\alpha}\cos^2 4\mu_0 + 1 - 2(\rho^{2^\alpha})^2(\cos^4 2\mu_0+\sin^4 2\mu_0)}{2(\rho^{2^\alpha}\ln\rho^{2^\alpha})^2} \\
& + \frac{\rho^{4^\alpha}\sin 4\mu_0\sin 2\mu_0\cos 2\mu_0 - 2(\rho^{2^\alpha})^2\cos^2 2\mu_0\sin^2 2\mu_0}{(\rho^{2^\alpha}\ln\rho^{2^\alpha})^2} \\
& + \frac{-\rho^{3^\alpha}\sin 3\mu_0\cos 2\mu_0\sin\mu_0 + \rho\sin^2\mu_0\cos 2\mu_0 + 2\rho^{2^\alpha+1}\cos^2 2\mu_0\sin^2\mu_0}{\rho\ln\rho\rho^{2^\alpha}\ln\rho^{2^\alpha}} \\
& + \frac{-\rho\cos\mu_0\sin\mu_0\sin 2\mu_0 + \rho^{3^\alpha}\cos 3\mu_0\sin\mu_0\sin 2\mu_0 + 2\rho^{2^\alpha+1}\sin^2\mu_0\sin^2 2\mu_0}{\rho\ln\rho\rho^{2^\alpha}\ln\rho^{2^\alpha}}\Bigg] \\
= \frac{1}{(\ln 2)^2}\Bigg[& \frac{1+\rho^{2^\alpha}-2\rho^2}{2(\rho\ln\rho)^2} + \frac{1+\rho^{4^\alpha}-2(\rho^{2^\alpha})^2}{2(\rho^{2^\alpha}\ln\rho^{2^\alpha})^2} + \frac{2\rho^{2^\alpha+1}-\rho-\rho^{3^\alpha}}{\rho\ln\rho\rho^{2^\alpha}\ln\rho^{2^\alpha}}\Bigg]
\end{aligned}$$

(using usual trigonometric identities and formulae)

□

Lemma 2.

$$\sqrt{m}(T'_m - \mu') \xrightarrow{L} N(0, \sigma^2)$$

where

$$T'_m = \bar{C_2},$$

μ' is the mean given by

$$\mu' = \rho^{2^\alpha}$$

and σ^2 is the dispersion given by

$$\sigma^2 = \frac{\rho^{4^\alpha} + 1 - 2(\rho^{2^\alpha})^2}{2}$$

Proof. The derivations for the proof are given in Appendix B.

Hence, assuming large sample size, central limit theorem Feller (1971) gives $\bar{C_2} \xrightarrow{L} N(\mu', \frac{\sigma^2}{m})$ where μ' is the mean given by $\mu' = \rho^{2^\alpha}$ and σ^2 is the dispersion given by $\sigma^2 = mV(\bar{C_2})$, that is $\sigma^2 = \frac{\rho^{4^\alpha}+1-2(\rho^{2^\alpha})^2}{2}$. □

Theorem 2.

$$\sqrt{m}(\hat{\alpha_1} - \alpha) \xrightarrow{L} N\left(0, \sigma^2 \left(\frac{\partial g}{\partial \mu'}\right)^2\right)$$

where

$$\frac{\partial g}{\partial \mu'} = -\frac{1}{(\ln 2)\rho^{2^\alpha}} \quad \textit{and}$$

$$\sigma^2 \left(\frac{\partial g}{\partial \mu'}\right)^2 = \frac{1}{(\ln 2)^2 \rho^{2^\alpha}}$$

Proof. We know from Lemma 2 that $\sqrt{m}(T'_m - \mu') \to N(0, \sigma^2)$ in distribution

Therefore, by delta method (given in Casella and Berger (2002)), we get $\sqrt{m}(\hat{\alpha_1} - \alpha) \xrightarrow{L} N\left(0, \sigma^2 \left(\frac{\partial g(T'_m)}{\partial \mu'}\right)^2\right)$ where

$$g(T'_m) = -\frac{\ln \bar{C_2}}{\ln 2}$$

$$\frac{\partial g(T'_m)}{\partial \mu'} = -\frac{1}{\ln 2}\frac{1}{\bar{C_2}}\bigg|_{\mu'} = -\frac{1}{(\ln 2)\rho^{2^\alpha}}$$

$$\sigma^2 \left(\frac{\partial g(T'_m)}{\partial \mu'}\right)^2 = \frac{1}{(\ln 2)^2 \rho^{2^\alpha}}$$

□

Lemma 3.

$$\sqrt{m}(T''_m - \mu'') \xrightarrow{L} N_2(0, \Sigma')$$

where

$$T''_m = (\bar{C_1}, \bar{C_2})'$$

μ'' is the mean vector given by

$$\mu'' = (\rho, \rho^{2^\alpha})'$$

and Σ' is the dispersion matrix given by:-

$$\Sigma' = \begin{pmatrix} A & B \\ B & C \end{pmatrix}$$

where

$$A = \frac{\rho^{2^\alpha}+1-2\rho^2}{2}, \quad B = \frac{\rho+\rho^{3^\alpha}-2\rho^{2^\alpha+1}}{2}, \quad C = \frac{\rho^{4^\alpha}+1-2(\rho^{2^\alpha})^2}{2}$$

Proof. The derivations for the proof are given in Appendix C.

Hence, assuming large sample size, central limit theorem Feller (1971) gives

$$(\bar{C_1}, \bar{C_2})' \xrightarrow{L} N_2(\mu'', \frac{\Sigma'}{m})$$

where μ'' is the mean vector given by $\mu'' = (\rho, \rho^{2^\alpha})'$ and Σ' is the dispersion matrix given by $\Sigma' = \begin{pmatrix} A & B \\ B & C \end{pmatrix}$ where $A = \frac{\rho^{2^\alpha}+1-2\rho^2}{2}$, $B = \frac{\rho+\rho^{3^\alpha}-2\rho^{2^\alpha+1}}{2}$ and $C = \frac{\rho^{4^\alpha}+1-2(\rho^{2^\alpha})^2}{2}$. □

Theorem 3.

$$\sqrt{m}(\hat{\alpha_2} - \alpha) \xrightarrow{L} N(0, \gamma_1'\Sigma'\gamma_1)$$

where

$$\gamma_1 = \frac{1}{\ln 2}\Big(\frac{-1}{\rho \ln \rho}, \frac{1}{\rho^{2^\alpha} \ln \rho^{2^\alpha}}\Big)'$$

and

$$\underline{\gamma_1}'\Sigma'\underline{\gamma_1} = \frac{1}{(\ln 2)^2}\left[\frac{1+\rho^{2^\alpha}-2\rho^2}{2(\rho \ln \rho)^2} + \frac{1+\rho^{4^\alpha}-2(\rho^{2^\alpha})^2}{2(\rho^{2^\alpha} \ln \rho^{2^\alpha})^2} + \frac{2\rho^{2^\alpha+1}-\rho-\rho^{3^\alpha}}{\rho \ln \rho \rho^{2^\alpha} \ln \rho^{2^\alpha}}\right]$$

Proof. We know from Lemma 3 that $\sqrt{m}(T''_m - \mu'') \xrightarrow{L} N_2(0, \Sigma')$

Therefore, by delta method (given in Casella and Berger (2002)), we get

$\sqrt{m}(\hat{\alpha_2} - \alpha) \xrightarrow{L} N(0, \gamma_1'\Sigma'\gamma_1)$ where $g(T''_m) = \frac{1}{\ln 2} \ln \frac{\ln \bar{C_2}}{\ln \bar{C_1}}$

$$\gamma_1 = \begin{pmatrix} \frac{\partial g}{\partial \bar{C_1}} \\ \frac{\partial g}{\partial \bar{C_2}} \end{pmatrix} \text{ at } \mu'' = \frac{1}{\ln 2}\begin{pmatrix} \frac{-1}{\bar{C_1}(\ln \bar{C_1})} \\ \frac{1}{\bar{C_2}(\ln \bar{C_2})} \end{pmatrix} \text{ at } \mu'' = \frac{1}{\ln 2}\begin{pmatrix} \frac{-1}{\rho \ln \rho} \\ \frac{1}{\rho^{2^\alpha} \ln \rho^{2^\alpha}} \end{pmatrix}$$

$$\underline{\gamma_1}'\Sigma'\underline{\gamma_1} = \frac{1}{(\ln 2)^2}\left[\frac{1+\rho^{2^\alpha}-2\rho^2}{2(\rho \ln \rho)^2} + \frac{1+\rho^{4^\alpha}-2(\rho^{2^\alpha})^2}{2(\rho^{2^\alpha} \ln \rho^{2^\alpha})^2} + \frac{2\rho^{2^\alpha+1}-\rho-\rho^{3^\alpha}}{\rho \ln \rho \rho^{2^\alpha} \ln \rho^{2^\alpha}}\right]$$

□

The above theorems imply the estimator to be consistent. Hence, in large samples, the performance of the estimator is reasonably good. Now, assuming the sample size is large, say 100, we calculate the asymptotic variance $\underline{\gamma}'\Sigma\underline{\gamma}/100$ of $g(T_m) = \hat{\alpha}$ for different values of α ranging from 0 to 2 and different values of ρ ranging from 0 to 1 in Table 1.

Table 1. Asymptotic Variances of the moment estimator $\hat{\alpha}$ and modified truncated estimator $\widehat{\alpha^*}$.

α	ρ	$V(\hat{\alpha})$	$V(\widehat{\alpha^*})$
0.2	0.2	0.179	0.097
0.2	0.4	0.093	0.058
0.2	0.6	0.084	0.053
0.2	0.8	0.118	0.070
0.4	0.2	0.211	0.148
0.4	0.4	0.094	0.079
0.4	0.6	0.079	0.069
0.4	0.8	0.107	0.088
0.6	0.2	0.270	0.209

Table 1. *Cont.*

α	ρ	$V(\hat{\alpha})$	$V(\widehat{\alpha^*})$
0.6	0.4	0.098	0.093
0.6	0.6	0.074	0.073
0.6	0.8	0.096	0.092
0.8	0.2	0.384	0.284
0.8	0.4	0.105	0.103
0.8	0.6	0.071	0.070
0.8	0.8	0.086	0.085
1.0	0.2	0.626	0.377
1.0	0.4	0.118	0.117
1.0	0.6	0.067	0.067
1.0	0.8	0.075	0.075

4. Improvement Over the Moment Estimator

The moment estimator need not always remain in the support of the true parameter α (that is (0,2]). Hence, the moment estimators proposed above do not need to be proper estimators of α. A modified estimator free from this defect is given by

$$\begin{aligned} \hat{\alpha^*} &= \hat{\alpha} \quad if\, 0 < \hat{\alpha} < 2 \\ &= 2 \quad if\, \hat{\alpha} \geq 2 \end{aligned}$$

(since support of α excludes non-positive values).

Thus, the density function of $\hat{\alpha^*}$ is given by

$$\begin{aligned} g(\hat{\alpha^*}) &= \frac{P[\hat{\alpha} < 2]}{P[\hat{\alpha} \geq 0]} \quad ;0 < \hat{\alpha^*} < 2 \equiv -\infty < \hat{\alpha} < 2 \\ &= P[\hat{\alpha^*} = 2] \quad ;\hat{\alpha^*} = 2 \equiv \hat{\alpha} \geq 2 \\ &= \frac{P[\hat{\alpha} \geq 2]}{P[\hat{\alpha} \geq 0]} \quad ;\hat{\alpha^*} = 2 \equiv \hat{\alpha} \geq 2 \end{aligned}$$

where $f(\hat{\alpha})$ is the density function of $\hat{\alpha} \sim N(\alpha, \underline{\gamma}'\Sigma\underline{\gamma}/m)$. Therefore,

$$\begin{aligned} g(\hat{\alpha^*}) &= \frac{\Phi\left(\frac{2-\alpha}{\sqrt{\underline{\gamma}'\Sigma\underline{\gamma}/m}}\right)}{1-\Phi\left(\frac{-\alpha}{\sqrt{\underline{\gamma}'\Sigma\underline{\gamma}/m}}\right)} \quad ;0 < \hat{\alpha^*} < 2 \equiv -\infty < \hat{\alpha} < 2 \\ &= 1 - \frac{\Phi\left(\frac{2-\alpha}{\sqrt{\underline{\gamma}'\Sigma\underline{\gamma}/m}}\right)}{\Phi\left(\frac{\alpha}{\sqrt{\underline{\gamma}'\Sigma\underline{\gamma}/m}}\right)} \quad ;\hat{\alpha^*} = 2 \equiv \hat{\alpha} \geq 2 \end{aligned}$$

Thus, we get $g(\hat{\alpha^*})$ as a mixed distribution of one atomic mass function and a continuous function.

4.1. *Special Case 1 : $\mu = 0$, $\sigma = 1$*

Similar modifications can be made for the estimator $\hat{\alpha_1}$. Let it be denoted by $\hat{\alpha_1^*}$.

4.2. *Special Case 2 : $\mu = 0$, σ Unknown*

Similar modifications can be made for the estimator $\hat{\alpha_2}$. Let it be denoted by $\hat{\alpha_2^*}$.

5. Derivation of the Asymptotic Distribution of the Modified Truncated Estimators

Now, using the asymptotic normal distribution of $\hat{\alpha}$, we can derive the same results for the modified truncated estimator of the index parameter α (given as below) as we have done for the method of moment estimator of α.

The mean of $\hat{\alpha^*}$ is given by

$$E(\hat{\alpha^*}) = 0.P(\hat{\alpha} < 0) + \int_0^2 \hat{\alpha} f(\hat{\alpha}) d\hat{\alpha} + 2.P(\hat{\alpha} > 2)$$

where $\sqrt{m}(\hat{\alpha} - \alpha) \rightarrow$N(0,$\underline{\gamma}'\Sigma\underline{\gamma}$) asymptotically (as noted above) and f($\hat{\alpha}$) =probability density function of $\hat{\alpha}$.

The above is equivalent to $\tau = \frac{\hat{\alpha}-\alpha}{\sqrt{\underline{\gamma}'\Sigma\underline{\gamma}/m}}$ $\rightarrow$N(0,1) asymptotically.

Let $\phi(\tau)$ and $\Phi(\tau)$ denote the p.d.f. and c.d.f. of τ, respectively.

Let $\sigma = \sqrt{\frac{\underline{\gamma}'\Sigma\underline{\gamma}}{m}}$. Then, we get,

$$E(\hat{\alpha^*}) = aP(\tau < a^*) + \int_{a^*}^{b^*} (\tau\sigma + \alpha)\phi(\tau) d\tau + bP(\tau > b^*)$$

$$\Rightarrow E(\hat{\alpha^*}) = \sigma\left[\{\phi(a^*) - \phi(b^*)\}\right] + \alpha\left[\Phi(b^*) - \Phi(a^*)\right]$$

$$= \alpha$$

since $[\Phi(b^*) - \Phi(a^*)] \rightarrow 1, b[1 - \Phi(b^*)] \rightarrow 0$ and $\sigma \rightarrow 0$ as $m \rightarrow$ infinity where $a^* = \frac{-\alpha}{\sqrt{\frac{\underline{\gamma}'\Sigma\underline{\gamma}}{m}}}$ and $b^* = \frac{2-\alpha}{\sqrt{\frac{\underline{\gamma}'\Sigma\underline{\gamma}}{m}}}$

$E(\hat{\alpha^*}^2) = 0^2.\, P(\hat{\alpha} < 0) + \int_0^2 \hat{\alpha}^2 f(\hat{\alpha}) d\hat{\alpha} + 4.P(\hat{\alpha} > 2)$

$\Rightarrow E(\hat{\alpha^*}^2) = \sigma^2\left[\{a^*\phi(a^*) - b^*\phi(b^*) + \Phi(b^*) - \Phi(a^*)\}\right] + \alpha^2\{\Phi(b^*) - \Phi(a^*)\} + 2\alpha\sigma\{\phi(a^*) - \phi(b^*)\}$ since $b^2.\,[1 - \Phi(b')] \rightarrow 0$ as $m \rightarrow$ infinity

The asymptotic variance of $\hat{\alpha^*}$ is given by

$$V(\hat{\alpha^*}) = E(\hat{\alpha^*}^2) - [E(\hat{\alpha^*})]^2$$

Similarly, the mean of $\hat{\alpha_1^*}$ is given by

$E(\hat{\alpha_1^*}) = \frac{\sigma\left(\frac{\partial g(T'_m)}{\partial \mu'}\right)}{\sqrt{m}}\left[\{\phi(a') - \phi(b')\}\right] + \alpha\left[\Phi(b') - \Phi(a')\right]$ since $b[1 - \Phi(b')] \rightarrow 0$ as $m \rightarrow$ infinity

$E(\hat{\alpha_1^*}^2) = \frac{\sigma^2\left(\frac{\partial g(T'_m)}{\partial \mu'}\right)^2}{m}\left[\{a'\phi(a') - b'\phi(b') + \Phi(b') - \Phi(a')\}\right] + \alpha^2\{\Phi(b') - \Phi(a')\} + 2\alpha\frac{\sigma\left(\frac{\partial g(T'_m)}{\partial \mu'}\right)}{\sqrt{m}}\{\phi(a') - \phi(b')\}$ since $b^2.\,[1 - \Phi(b')] \rightarrow 0$ as $m \rightarrow$ infinity

The asymptotic variance of $\hat{\alpha_1^*}$ is given by

$$V(\hat{\alpha_1^*}) = E(\hat{\alpha_1^*}^2) - [E(\hat{\alpha_1^*})]^2$$

where $a' = -\alpha \Big/ \frac{\sigma\frac{\partial g(T'_m)}{\partial \mu'}}{\sqrt{m}}$ and $b' = (2 - \alpha) \Big/ \frac{\sigma\frac{\partial g(T'_m)}{\partial \mu'}}{\sqrt{m}}$

The mean of $\hat{\alpha_2^*}$ is given by

$$E(\hat{\alpha_2^*}) = \frac{\sqrt{\gamma_1'\Sigma'\gamma_1}}{\sqrt{m}}\left[\{\phi(a'') - \phi(b'')\}\right] + \alpha\left[\Phi(b'') - \Phi(a'')\right] \text{ since } b[1 - \Phi(b'')] \to 0 \text{ as } m \to \text{infinity}$$

$$E(\hat{\alpha_2^{*2}}) = \frac{\gamma_1'\Sigma'\gamma_1}{m}\left[\{a''\phi(a'') - b''\phi(b'') + \Phi(b'') - \Phi(a'')\}\right] + \alpha^2\{\Phi(b'') - \Phi(a'')\} + 2\alpha\sqrt{\frac{\gamma_1'\Sigma'\gamma_1}{m}}\{\phi(a'') - \phi(b'')\} \text{ since } b^2.[1 - \Phi(b'')] \to 0 \text{ as } m \to \text{infinity}$$

The asymptotic variance of $\hat{\alpha_2^*}$ is given by

$$V(\hat{\alpha_2^*}) = E(\hat{\alpha_2^{*2}}) - [E(\hat{\alpha_2^*})]^2$$

where $a'' = \frac{-\alpha}{\sqrt{\frac{\gamma_1'\Sigma'\gamma_1}{m}}}$ and $b'' = \frac{2-\alpha}{\sqrt{\frac{\gamma_1'\Sigma'\gamma_1}{m}}}$

Thus, the following theorem is established

Theorem 4.

$$(\hat{\alpha^*} - \alpha) \xrightarrow{L} N(0, V(\hat{\alpha^*}))$$

where $V(\hat{\alpha^*})$ is as derived above.

Now, assuming the sample size m is large, say 100, the asymptotic variances of the modified truncated estimator $\hat{\alpha^*}$ for different values of α and different values of ρ (ranging from 0 to 1) are displayed in Table 2.

Table 2. Comparison of RMSEs of modified truncated estimator (RMSE1) and Hill estimator (RMSE2, RMSE3, and RMSE4) with relocations of true mean, sample mean and median.

					Relocation		
					True Mean = 0	**Sample Mean**	**Sample Median**
α	ρ	**Sample Size**	**RMSE1**	k^*	**RMSE2**	**RMSE3**	**RMSE4**
1.01	0.2	100	0.483	12	0.486	0.529	0.514
1.01	0.3	100	0.468	12	0.414	0.429	0.423
1.01	0.4	100	0.412	12	0.408	0.409	0.411
1.01	0.5	100	0.320	12	0.428	0.415	0.432
1.01	0.6	100	0.277	12	0.438	0.409	0.441
1.01	0.7	100	0.272	12	0.395	0.380	0.404
1.01	0.8	100	0.299	12	0.418	0.414	0.427
1.01	0.9	100	0.403	12	0.419	0.465	0.424
1.01	0.2	250	0.395	22	0.254	0.255	0.254
1.01	0.3	250	0.353	22	0.258	0.261	0.258
1.01	0.4	250	0.242	22	0.253	0.255	0.254
1.01	0.5	250	0.189	22	0.251	0.252	0.253
1.01	0.6	250	0.168	22	0.255	0.250	0.256
1.01	0.7	250	0.165	22	0.259	0.252	0.260
1.01	0.8	250	0.179	22	0.247	0.240	0.248
1.01	0.9	250	0.238	22	0.256	0.256	0.257
1.01	0.2	500	0.360	37	0.181	0.181	0.181
1.01	0.3	500	0.251	37	0.180	0.181	0.180
1.01	0.4	500	0.161	37	0.178	0.179	0.179
1.01	0.5	500	0.131	37	0.180	0.181	0.180

Table 2. *Cont.*

					Relocation		
					True Mean = 0	Sample Mean	Sample Median
α	ρ	Sample Size	RMSE1	k^*	RMSE2	RMSE3	RMSE4
1.01	0.6	500	0.118	37	0.176	0.176	0.177
1.01	0.7	500	0.115	37	0.181	0.179	0.181
1.01	0.8	500	0.125	37	0.180	0.176	0.180
1.01	0.9	500	0.162	37	0.183	0.181	0.183
1.01	0.2	1000	0.295	64	0.131	0.131	0.131
1.01	0.3	1000	0.161	64	0.132	0.132	0.132
1.01	0.4	1000	0.113	64	0.132	0.132	0.132
1.01	0.5	1000	0.092	64	0.132	0.133	0.132
1.01	0.6	1000	0.081	64	0.131	0.131	0.131
1.01	0.7	1000	0.080	64	0.131	0.131	0.131
1.01	0.8	1000	0.086	64	0.133	0.131	0.134
1.01	0.9	1000	0.110	64	0.131	0.129	0.131
1.01	0.2	2000	0.220	83	0.114	0.114	0.114
1.01	0.3	2000	0.110	83	0.117	0.117	0.117
1.01	0.4	2000	0.078	83	0.116	0.116	0.116
1.01	0.5	2000	0.064	83	0.115	0.115	0.115
1.01	0.6	2000	0.058	83	0.114	0.114	0.114
1.01	0.7	2000	0.057	83	0.115	0.115	0.115
1.01	0.8	2000	0.062	83	0.114	0.114	0.114
1.01	0.9	2000	0.078	83	0.116	0.115	0.116
1.01	0.2	5000	0.125	193	0.074	0.074	0.074
1.01	0.3	5000	0.068	193	0.073	0.073	0.073
1.01	0.4	5000	0.049	193	0.073	0.073	0.073
1.01	0.5	5000	0.040	193	0.073	0.073	0.073
1.01	0.6	5000	0.037	193	0.073	0.073	0.073
1.01	0.7	5000	0.036	193	0.073	0.074	0.073
1.01	0.8	5000	0.039	193	0.074	0.074	0.074
1.01	0.9	5000	0.049	193	0.073	0.072	0.073
1.01	0.2	10000	0.083	282	0.060	0.060	0.060
1.01	0.3	10000	0.047	282	0.061	0.061	0.061
1.01	0.4	10000	0.035	282	0.061	0.061	0.061
1.01	0.5	10000	0.029	282	0.061	0.061	0.061
1.01	0.6	10000	0.026	282	0.061	0.061	0.061
1.01	0.7	10000	0.026	282	0.062	0.062	0.062
1.01	0.8	10000	0.027	282	0.061	0.061	0.061
1.01	0.9	10000	0.034	282	0.061	0.061	0.061
1.25	0.2	100	0.549	18	0.360	0.390	0.368
1.25	0.3	100	0.450	18	0.364	0.352	0.377
1.25	0.4	100	0.398	18	0.357	0.321	0.364
1.25	0.5	100	0.333	18	0.362	0.319	0.366
1.25	0.6	100	0.269	18	0.358	0.325	0.368
1.25	0.7	100	0.252	18	0.362	0.342	0.370
1.25	0.8	100	0.264	18	0.363	0.362	0.370
1.25	0.9	100	0.346	18	0.376	0.425	0.380
1.25	0.2	250	0.413	42	0.202	0.213	0.206
1.25	0.3	250	0.355	42	0.205	0.202	0.208
1.25	0.4	250	0.282	42	0.203	0.194	0.208
1.25	0.5	250	0.201	42	0.199	0.189	0.205
1.25	0.6	250	0.163	42	0.207	0.193	0.210
1.25	0.7	250	0.154	42	0.201	0.191	0.203
1.25	0.8	250	0.161	42	0.203	0.201	0.207
1.25	0.9	250	0.207	42	0.205	0.219	0.208
1.25	0.2	500	0.337	82	0.140	0.148	0.142
1.25	0.3	500	0.290	82	0.140	0.139	0.142
1.25	0.4	500	0.192	82	0.141	0.135	0.143

Table 2. *Cont.*

					Relocation		
					True Mean = 0	Sample Mean	Sample Median
α	ρ	Sample Size	RMSE1	k^*	RMSE2	RMSE3	RMSE4
1.25	0.5	500	0.135	82	0.141	0.134	0.144
1.25	0.6	500	0.115	82	0.141	0.134	0.143
1.25	0.7	500	0.106	82	0.140	0.134	0.142
1.25	0.8	500	0.112	82	0.139	0.137	0.141
1.25	0.9	500	0.143	82	0.140	0.147	0.143
1.25	0.2	1000	0.296	159	0.099	0.105	0.101
1.25	0.3	1000	0.222	159	0.101	0.101	0.102
1.25	0.4	1000	0.128	159	0.099	0.097	0.101
1.25	0.5	1000	0.095	159	0.099	0.095	0.100
1.25	0.6	1000	0.079	159	0.098	0.093	0.100
1.25	0.7	1000	0.075	159	0.100	0.096	0.101
1.25	0.8	1000	0.079	159	0.098	0.097	0.100
1.25	0.9	1000	0.100	159	0.100	0.104	0.102
1.25	0.2	2000	0.300	314	0.314	0.316	0.313
1.25	0.3	2000	0.219	314	0.315	0.314	0.313
1.25	0.4	2000	0.088	314	0.070	0.068	0.071
1.25	0.5	2000	0.067	314	0.071	0.068	0.072
1.25	0.6	2000	0.056	314	0.070	0.066	0.071
1.25	0.7	2000	0.053	314	0.070	0.067	0.071
1.25	0.8	2000	0.055	314	0.069	0.068	0.071
1.25	0.9	2000	0.070	314	0.070	0.072	0.071
1.25	0.2	5000	0.206	314	0.044	0.047	0.045
1.25	0.3	5000	0.087	776	0.045	0.045	0.045
1.25	0.4	5000	0.055	776	0.044	0.043	0.045
1.25	0.5	5000	0.042	776	0.044	0.043	0.045
1.25	0.6	5000	0.035	776	0.045	0.043	0.045
1.25	0.7	5000	0.034	776	0.045	0.043	0.045
1.25	0.8	5000	0.036	776	0.045	0.044	0.045
1.25	0.9	5000	0.044	776	0.045	0.046	0.045
1.25	0.2	10000	0.141	1547	0.032	0.034	0.032
1.25	0.3	10000	0.061	1547	0.032	0.032	0.032
1.25	0.4	10000	0.039	1547	0.031	0.030	0.031
1.25	0.5	10000	0.030	1547	0.031	0.030	0.032
1.25	0.6	10000	0.025	1547	0.031	0.030	0.032
1.25	0.7	10000	0.024	1547	0.031	0.030	0.032
1.25	0.8	10000	0.025	1547	0.031	0.031	0.032
1.25	0.9	10000	0.031	1547	0.031	0.032	0.032
1.5	0.2	100	0.702	21	0.413	0.435	0.408
1.5	0.3	100	0.461	21	0.393	0.341	0.394
1.5	0.4	100	0.370	21	0.404	0.332	0.396
1.5	0.5	100	0.311	21	0.382	0.326	0.378
1.5	0.6	100	0.259	21	0.402	0.342	0.393
1.5	0.7	100	0.226	21	0.386	0.350	0.385
1.5	0.8	100	0.227	21	0.398	0.374	0.390
1.5	0.9	100	0.278	21	0.379	0.393	0.376
1.5	0.2	250	0.499	51	0.222	0.228	0.221
1.5	0.3	250	0.343	51	0.223	0.203	0.221
1.5	0.4	250	0.283	51	0.221	0.196	0.220
1.5	0.5	250	0.213	51	0.221	0.196	0.220
1.5	0.6	250	0.161	51	0.222	0.198	0.219
1.5	0.7	250	0.139	51	0.221	0.201	0.219
1.5	0.8	250	0.138	51	0.219	0.208	0.219
1.5	0.9	250	0.171	51	0.219	0.223	0.218
1.5	0.2	500	0.388	101	0.151	0.155	0.152

Table 2. *Cont.*

						Relocation	
					True Mean = 0	Sample Mean	Sample Median
α	ρ	Sample Size	RMSE1	k *	RMSE2	RMSE3	RMSE4
1.5	0.3	500	0.285	101	0.152	0.140	0.151
1.5	0.4	500	0.226	101	0.152	0.137	0.152
1.5	0.5	500	0.153	101	0.155	0.139	0.156
1.5	0.6	500	0.113	101	0.150	0.136	0.151
1.5	0.7	500	0.098	101	0.152	0.140	0.151
1.5	0.8	500	0.097	101	0.152	0.147	0.153
1.5	0.9	500	0.121	101	0.153	0.156	0.152
1.5	0.2	1000	0.311	201	0.105	0.106	0.105
1.5	0.3	1000	0.245	201	0.106	0.099	0.106
1.5	0.4	1000	0.166	201	0.105	0.096	0.105
1.5	0.5	1000	0.105	201	0.106	0.095	0.105
1.5	0.6	1000	0.079	201	0.107	0.096	0.106
1.5	0.7	1000	0.069	201	0.106	0.099	0.106
1.5	0.8	1000	0.068	201	0.106	0.101	0.106
1.5	0.9	1000	0.084	201	0.106	0.109	0.107
1.5	0.2	2000	0.261	400	0.075	0.076	0.075
1.5	0.3	2000	0.204	400	0.075	0.070	0.075
1.5	0.4	2000	0.113	400	0.074	0.068	0.074
1.5	0.5	2000	0.072	400	0.075	0.068	0.075
1.5	0.6	2000	0.056	400	0.074	0.068	0.075
1.5	0.7	2000	0.048	400	0.073	0.068	0.074
1.5	0.8	2000	0.048	400	0.074	0.071	0.075
1.5	0.9	2000	0.059	400	0.075	0.076	0.075
1.5	0.2	5000	0.222	995	0.047	0.048	0.047
1.5	0.3	5000	0.133	995	0.047	0.044	0.047
1.5	0.4	5000	0.069	995	0.047	0.043	0.048
1.5	0.5	5000	0.046	995	0.047	0.042	0.047
1.5	0.6	5000	0.035	995	0.047	0.043	0.047
1.5	0.7	5000	0.031	995	0.047	0.044	0.047
1.5	0.8	5000	0.030	995	0.047	0.045	0.047
1.5	0.9	5000	0.037	995	0.047	0.048	0.047
1.5	0.2	10000	0.201	1991	0.033	0.034	0.034
1.5	0.3	10000	0.089	1991	0.033	0.031	0.033
1.5	0.4	10000	0.048	1991	0.033	0.030	0.033
1.5	0.5	10000	0.031	1991	0.033	0.030	0.033
1.5	0.6	10000	0.025	1991	0.033	0.030	0.033
1.5	0.7	10000	0.021	1991	0.033	0.031	0.033
1.5	0.8	10000	0.022	1991	0.033	0.032	0.033
1.5	0.9	10000	0.026	1991	0.033	0.033	0.033
1.75	0.2	100	0.890	22	0.469	0.478	0.443
1.75	0.3	100	0.590	22	0.471	0.388	0.448
1.75	0.4	100	0.378	22	0.489	0.378	0.457
1.75	0.5	100	0.276	22	0.479	0.378	0.441
1.75	0.6	100	0.222	22	0.493	0.399	0.446
1.75	0.7	100	0.183	22	0.470	0.408	0.449
1.75	0.8	100	0.169	22	0.491	0.430	0.463
1.75	0.9	100	0.201	22	0.466	0.439	0.442
1.75	0.2	250	0.652	54	0.264	0.253	0.252
1.75	0.3	250	0.400	54	0.265	0.225	0.255
1.75	0.4	250	0.266	54	0.263	0.219	0.252
1.75	0.5	250	0.201	54	0.260	0.219	0.249
1.75	0.6	250	0.153	54	0.262	0.226	0.251
1.75	0.7	250	0.120	54	0.258	0.229	0.250
1.75	0.8	250	0.108	54	0.264	0.239	0.251

Table 2. *Cont.*

						Relocation	
					True Mean = 0	Sample Mean	Sample Median
α	ρ	Sample Size	RMSE1	k *	RMSE2	RMSE3	RMSE4
1.75	0.9	250	0.125	54	0.263	0.250	0.251
1.75	0.2	500	0.520	107	0.181	0.173	0.173
1.75	0.3	500	0.308	107	0.181	0.154	0.173
1.75	0.4	500	0.213	107	0.179	0.152	0.172
1.75	0.5	500	0.159	107	0.180	0.152	0.172
1.75	0.6	500	0.114	107	0.180	0.156	0.174
1.75	0.7	500	0.084	107	0.179	0.157	0.171
1.75	0.8	500	0.077	107	0.179	0.164	0.173
1.75	0.9	500	0.088	107	0.180	0.171	0.171
1.75	0.2	1000	0.404	214	0.123	0.119	0.119
1.75	0.3	1000	0.242	214	0.123	0.107	0.119
1.75	0.4	1000	0.172	214	0.122	0.104	0.118
1.75	0.5	1000	0.118	214	0.125	0.107	0.120
1.75	0.6	1000	0.080	214	0.124	0.108	0.119
1.75	0.7	1000	0.060	214	0.122	0.109	0.118
1.75	0.8	1000	0.054	214	0.123	0.112	0.118
1.75	0.9	1000	0.062	214	0.123	0.118	0.118
1.75	0.2	2000	0.324	428	0.088	0.083	0.084
1.75	0.3	2000	0.199	428	0.087	0.077	0.084
1.75	0.4	2000	0.141	428	0.085	0.073	0.082
1.75	0.5	2000	0.086	428	0.086	0.074	0.082
1.75	0.6	2000	0.057	428	0.087	0.076	0.083
1.75	0.7	2000	0.043	428	0.086	0.077	0.083
1.75	0.8	2000	0.038	428	0.087	0.079	0.083
1.75	0.9	2000	0.045	428	0.087	0.083	0.084
1.75	0.2	5000	0.244	1070	0.054	0.052	0.052
1.75	0.3	5000	0.159	1070	0.055	0.047	0.053
1.75	0.4	5000	0.094	1070	0.054	0.046	0.052
1.75	0.5	5000	0.054	1070	0.055	0.047	0.053
1.75	0.6	5000	0.035	1070	0.054	0.047	0.052
1.75	0.7	5000	0.027	1070	0.054	0.048	0.052
1.75	0.8	5000	0.024	1070	0.054	0.050	0.052
1.75	0.9	5000	0.028	1070	0.055	0.052	0.053
1.75	0.2	10000	0.199	2139	0.038	0.037	0.037
1.75	0.3	10000	0.133	2139	0.039	0.034	0.037
1.75	0.4	10000	0.067	2139	0.039	0.033	0.037
1.75	0.5	10000	0.038	2139	0.038	0.033	0.037
1.75	0.6	10000	0.025	2139	0.038	0.034	0.037
1.75	0.7	10000	0.019	2139	0.038	0.034	0.037
1.75	0.8	10000	0.017	2139	0.038	0.035	0.037
1.75	0.9	10000	0.020	2139	0.038	0.037	0.037
1.9	0.2	100	1.038	22	0.568	0.542	0.504
1.9	0.3	100	0.672	22	0.563	0.432	0.507
1.9	0.4	100	0.428	22	0.531	0.416	0.488
1.9	0.5	100	0.274	22	0.549	0.430	0.498
1.9	0.6	100	0.189	22	0.562	0.449	0.510
1.9	0.7	100	0.139	22	0.586	0.460	0.492
1.9	0.8	100	0.114	22	0.585	0.493	0.512
1.9	0.9	100	0.125	22	0.566	0.502	0.511
1.9	0.2	250	0.761	55	0.287	0.267	0.264
1.9	0.3	250	0.462	55	0.287	0.232	0.264
1.9	0.4	250	0.280	55	0.292	0.232	0.268
1.9	0.5	250	0.179	55	0.287	0.233	0.264
1.9	0.6	250	0.127	55	0.288	0.238	0.264
1.9	0.7	250	0.092	55	0.292	0.247	0.268

Table 2. *Cont.*

					Relocation		
					True Mean = 0	Sample Mean	Sample Median
α	ρ	Sample Size	RMSE1	k *	RMSE2	RMSE3	RMSE4
1.9	0.8	250	0.077	55	0.288	0.253	0.265
1.9	0.9	250	0.082	55	0.288	0.262	0.268
1.9	0.2	500	0.601	110	0.193	0.179	0.177
1.9	0.3	500	0.350	110	0.196	0.162	0.182
1.9	0.4	500	0.213	110	0.197	0.162	0.184
1.9	0.5	500	0.137	110	0.195	0.162	0.181
1.9	0.6	500	0.095	110	0.192	0.163	0.180
1.9	0.7	500	0.070	110	0.193	0.168	0.181
1.9	0.8	500	0.056	110	0.193	0.172	0.180
1.9	0.9	500	0.058	110	0.192	0.176	0.180
1.9	0.2	1000	0.487	220	0.133	0.123	0.125
1.9	0.3	1000	0.272	220	0.134	0.113	0.126
1.9	0.4	1000	0.161	220	0.133	0.110	0.124
1.9	0.5	1000	0.105	220	0.134	0.112	0.125
1.9	0.6	1000	0.073	220	0.136	0.115	0.126
1.9	0.7	1000	0.052	220	0.134	0.117	0.126
1.9	0.8	1000	0.041	220	0.135	0.119	0.124
1.9	0.9	1000	0.042	220	0.136	0.124	0.128
1.9	0.2	2000	0.399	438	0.095	0.087	0.088
1.9	0.3	2000	0.212	438	0.094	0.079	0.088
1.9	0.4	2000	0.126	438	0.095	0.078	0.088
1.9	0.5	2000	0.082	438	0.093	0.078	0.087
1.9	0.6	2000	0.055	438	0.094	0.080	0.087
1.9	0.7	2000	0.038	438	0.094	0.081	0.087
1.9	0.8	2000	0.029	438	0.093	0.083	0.087
1.9	0.9	2000	0.030	438	0.095	0.086	0.088
1.9	0.2	5000	0.303	1093	0.059	0.054	0.055
1.9	0.3	5000	0.153	1093	0.059	0.050	0.056
1.9	0.4	5000	0.091	1093	0.059	0.049	0.055
1.9	0.5	5000	0.058	1093	0.059	0.049	0.055
1.9	0.6	5000	0.037	1093	0.059	0.051	0.056
1.9	0.7	5000	0.024	1093	0.059	0.051	0.056
1.9	0.8	5000	0.018	1093	0.060	0.053	0.056
1.9	0.9	5000	0.019	1093	0.059	0.054	0.055
1.9	0.2	10000	0.245	2187	0.041	0.038	0.039
1.9	0.3	10000	0.123	2187	0.042	0.035	0.040
1.9	0.4	10000	0.072	2187	0.042	0.035	0.039
1.9	0.5	10000	0.043	2187	0.041	0.035	0.039
1.9	0.6	10000	0.025	2187	0.041	0.035	0.039
1.9	0.7	10000	0.017	2187	0.041	0.036	0.039
1.9	0.8	10000	0.013	2187	0.042	0.038	0.040
1.9	0.9	10000	0.013	2187	0.041	0.038	0.039

* The value of k is obtained by linear interpolation from Dufour and Kurz-Kim (2010).

6. Comparison of the Proposed Estimator With the Hill Estimator and the Characteristic Function Based Estimator

Next, we want to compare the performance of this modified truncated estimator with that of a popular estimator known as Hill-estimator Dufour and Kurz-Kim (2010); Hill (1975), which is a simple non-parametric estimator based on order statistic. Given a sample of n observations $X_1, X_2, ... X_n$, the Hill-estimator is defined as,

$$\hat{\alpha}_H = [(k^{-1}\sum_{j=1}^{k} \ln X_{n+1-j} : n) - \ln X_{n-k:n}]^{-1}$$

with standard error

$$SD(\hat{\alpha}_H) = \frac{k\hat{\alpha}_H}{(k-1)\sqrt{k-2}}$$

where k is the number of observations which lie on the tails of the distribution of interest and is to be optimally chosen depending on the sample size, n, tail thickness α, as $k = k(n, \alpha)$ and $X_{j:n}$ denotes j-order statistic of the sample of size n.

The asymptotic normality of the Hill estimator is provided by Goldie and Richard (1987) as,

$$\sqrt{k}(\hat{\alpha_H^{-1}} - \alpha^{-1}) \xrightarrow{L} N(0, \alpha^{-2}) \tag{3}$$

Lemma 4.

$$(\hat{\alpha_H} - \alpha) \xrightarrow{L} N\Big(0, \frac{1}{\alpha^2 k}\Big)$$

Proof. Assuming $g\Big(\hat{\alpha_H^{-1}}\Big) = \frac{1}{\hat{\alpha_H^{-1}}} = \hat{\alpha_H}$ (since $g'(.)$ exists and is non-zero valued) and using Equation (3), we get

$$\begin{aligned}
&(\hat{\alpha_H^{-1}} - \alpha^{-1}) \xrightarrow{L} N\Big(0, \frac{\alpha^{-2}}{k}\Big) \\
&\Rightarrow (\hat{\alpha_H} - \alpha) \xrightarrow{L} N\Big(0, \frac{(g'^{-1}))^2\alpha^{-2}}{k}\Big) \\
&\Leftrightarrow \hat{\alpha_H} \xrightarrow{L} N\Big(\alpha, \frac{1}{\alpha^2 k}\Big)
\end{aligned}$$

□

We need this result for comparing the performances of the estimators for α.

In addition, we make a comparison of the performance of the modified truncated estimator $\hat{\alpha_2}$ with that of the characteristic function based estimator Anderson and Arnold (1993), which is obtained by minimization of the objective function (where $\mu = 0$ and $\sigma = 1$) given by

$$\hat{I}_s(\alpha) = \sum_{i=1}^{n} w_i(\hat{\eta}(z_i) - \exp(-|z_i|^{\alpha}))^2 \tag{4}$$

The performance of the modified truncated estimator $\hat{\alpha_3}$ is compared with that of the characteristic function-based estimator Anderson and Arnold (1993), which is obtained by minimization of the objective function (where $\mu = 0$ and σ unknown) given by,

$$\hat{I'}_s(\alpha) = \sum_{i=1}^{n} w_i(\hat{\eta}(z_i) - \exp(-|\sigma z_i|^{\alpha}))^2 \tag{5}$$

where

$$\hat{\eta}(t) = \frac{1}{n}\sum_j \cos(tx_j).$$

$x_1, x_2, ..., x_n$ are realizations from symmetric stable (α) distribution, z_i is the ith zero of the mth degree Hermite polynomial $H_m(z)$ and

$$w_i = \frac{2^{m-1} m! \sqrt{m}}{(m H_{m-1}(z_i))^2}$$

It is to be noted that, for the estimator of $\alpha < 1$, we do not know any explicit form of the probability density function. However, for value of the estimator between 1 and 2, i.e., for $1 < \hat{\alpha}^* < 2$, we may compare the fit with the stable family by modeling a mixture of normal and Cauchy distribution and then using the method as proposed in Anderson and Arnold (1993) by the objective function given by

$$\sum_{i=1}^{n} w_i (\hat{\eta}(z_i) - \psi_{NC})^2$$

where $\hat{\eta}(t)$ is the same as defined above with the realizations taken from the mixture distribution. ψ_{NC} denotes the corresponding theoretical characteristic function given by

$$\psi_{NC} = p \exp(-\sigma_1^2 t^2/2) + (1-p) \exp(-\sigma_2 |t|)$$

where p denotes the mixture proportion, σ_1 and σ_2 are taken as the scale parameters of the normal and Cauchy distributions, respectively (the location parameters are taken as zeros, the reason for which is mentioned above). Finally, a measure for the goodness of fit is proposed as:

Index of Objective function (I.O.) = Objective function + Number of parameters estimated

The distribution for which I.O. is minimum gives the best fit to the data.

The modified truncated estimator based on the moment estimator is free of the location parameter since it is defined in terms of $\bar{R}_j = \frac{1}{m}\sum_{i=1}^{m} \cos j(\theta_i - \bar{\theta}), j = 1, 2$, that is in terms of the quantity $(\theta_i - \bar{\theta})$, which is centered with respect to the mean direction $\bar{\theta}$, although it is not free of the nuisance parameter that is the concentration parameter ρ. The Hill estimator is scale invariant since it is defined in terms of log of ratios but not location invariant. Therefore, centering needs to be done in order to take care of the location invariance.

7. Computational Studies

The analytical variance of the untruncated moment estimator was compared with that of the modified truncated estimator, as presented in Table 1, for values of $\alpha < 1$, which is more applicable in practical situations for volatile data.

The comparison of the performances of the two estimators is shown in Table 2. The parameter configurations were chosen as given by Hill (1975) and Dufour and Kurz-Kim (2010). The simulation is presented in Table 2 for the values of α = 1.01, 1.25, 1.5, 1.75, and 1.9 each with sample size n = 100, 250, 500, 1000, 2000, 5000, and 10,000 and for different values of ρ = 0.2, 0.4, 0.6, and 0.8 when skewness parameter β = 0, location parameter μ = 0, and scale parameter $\sigma = (-\ln(\rho))^{(1/\alpha)}$, i.e., concentration parameter $\rho = e^{-\sigma^{\alpha}}$. For each combination of α and n, 10,000 replications were performed. In this simulation, the sample was relocated by three different relocations, viz. true mean = 0, estimated sample mean, and estimated sample median, and comparison of the root mean square errors (RMSEs) was made.

Next, in Table 3, comparison of the performance of the modified truncated estimator $\hat{\alpha_2}$ with that of the characteristic function-based estimator where the simulation is presented for the values of α = 0.2, 0.4, 0.6, 0.8, 1.0, 1.2, 1.4, 1.6, 1.8, and 2.0 each with sample size n = 20, 30, 40, and 50, and the values of σ were taken as 3, 5, and 10 . For each combination of α and n, 10,000 replications were performed.

Table 3. Comparison of the RMSEs of the modified truncated estimator $\hat{\alpha}_3$ (RMSE3) and the characteristic function-based estimator (RMSE4) when $\mu = 0$ and σ unknown.

α	σ	Sample Size	RMSE3	RMSE4
0.2	3.0	20	0.514	1.477
0.4	3.0	20	0.495	1.293
0.6	3.0	20	0.421	1.134
0.8	3.0	20	0.401	1.012
1.0	3.0	20	0.446	0.912
1.2	3.0	20	0.510	0.823
1.4	3.0	20	0.588	0.757
1.6	3.0	20	0.680	0.733
1.8	3.0	20	0.763	0.746
2.0	3.0	20	0.851	0.798
0.2	5.0	20	0.512	1.424
0.4	5.0	20	0.421	1.245
0.6	5.0	20	0.346	1.110
0.8	5.0	20	0.354	0.989
1.0	5.0	20	0.411	0.882
1.2	5.0	20	0.497	0.776
1.4	5.0	20	0.572	0.687
1.6	5.0	20	0.668	0.635
1.8	5.0	20	0.763	0.625
2.0	5.0	20	0.859	0.623
0.2	3.0	30	0.471	1.486
0.4	3.0	30	0.468	1.299
0.6	3.0	30	0.416	1.127
0.8	3.0	30	0.407	1.006
1.0	3.0	30	0.453	0.895
1.2	3.0	30	0.521	0.817
1.4	3.0	30	0.605	0.753
1.6	3.0	30	0.686	0.734
1.8	3.0	30	0.767	0.748
2.0	3.0	30	0.859	0.803
0.2	5.0	30	0.476	1.433
0.4	5.0	30	0.419	1.234
0.6	5.0	30	0.339	1.103
0.8	5.0	30	0.354	0.987
1.0	5.0	30	0.422	0.885
1.2	5.0	30	0.494	0.782
1.4	5.0	30	0.583	0.709
1.6	5.0	30	0.685	0.658
1.8	5.0	30	0.770	0.669
2.0	5.0	30	0.874	0.673
0.2	3.0	40	0.426	1.494
0.4	3.0	40	0.467	1.300
0.6	3.0	40	0.418	1.123
0.8	3.0	40	0.414	0.996
1.0	3.0	40	0.462	0.891
1.2	3.0	40	0.519	0.806
1.4	3.0	40	0.595	0.750
1.6	3.0	40	0.689	0.724
1.8	3.0	40	0.784	0.757
2.0	3.0	40	0.887	0.807
0.2	5.0	40	0.444	1.439
0.4	5.0	40	0.412	1.242
0.6	5.0	40	0.338	1.100
0.8	5.0	40	0.354	0.989
1.0	5.0	40	0.422	0.880
1.2	5.0	40	0.487	0.784

Table 3. *Cont.*

α	σ	Sample Size	RMSE3	RMSE4
1.4	5.0	40	0.584	0.720
1.6	5.0	40	0.680	0.674
1.8	5.0	40	0.769	0.692
2.0	5.0	40	0.881	0.711
0.2	3.0	50	0.393	1.500
0.4	3.0	50	0.447	1.292
0.6	3.0	50	0.411	1.117
0.8	3.0	50	0.414	0.989
1.0	3.0	50	0.466	0.885
1.2	3.0	50	0.530	0.805
1.4	3.0	50	0.612	0.737
1.6	3.0	50	0.698	0.719
1.8	3.0	50	0.778	0.751
2.0	3.0	50	0.870	0.828
0.2	5.0	50	0.411	1.451
0.4	5.0	50	0.402	1.235
0.6	5.0	50	0.344	1.098
0.8	5.0	50	0.357	0.983
1.0	5.0	50	0.415	0.879
1.2	5.0	50	0.502	0.788
1.4	5.0	50	0.598	0.716
1.6	5.0	50	0.677	0.691
1.8	5.0	50	0.782	0.703
2.0	5.0	50	0.858	0.729

The asymptotic variance of the characteristic function-based estimator, unlike that of the modified truncated estimator, is not available in any closed analytical form. We are thus unable to present the Asymptotic Relative Efficiency (ARE) of these estimators of α analytically. Instead, we compared these through their MSEs based on extensive simulations over all reasonable small, moderate, and large sample sizes.

8. Applications

8.1. Inference on the Gold Price Data (In US Dollars) (1980–2013)

Gold price data, say x_t, were collected per ounce in US dollars over the years 1980–2013. These were transformed as $z_t = 100(\ln(x_t) - \ln(x_{t-1}))$, which were then "wrapped" to obtain $\theta_t = z_t mod 2\pi$ and finally transformed to $\widehat{\theta} = (\theta_t - \bar{\theta}) \bmod 2\pi$, where $\bar{\theta}$ denotes the mean direction of θ_t and $\widehat{\theta}$ denotes the variable thetamod as used in the graphs. The Durbin–Watson test performed on the log ratio transformed data shows that the autocorrelation is zero. The test statistic of Watson's goodness of fit Jammalamadaka and SenGupta (2001) for wrapped stable distribution was obtained as 0.01632691 and the corresponding p-value was obtained as 0.9970284, which is greater than 0.05, indicating that the wrapped stable distribution fits the transformed gold price data (in US dollars). The modified truncated estimate $\hat{\alpha_1^*}$ is 0.3752206 while the estimate by characteristic function method is 0.401409. The value of the objective function using the characteristic function estimate is 2.218941 while that using our modified truncated estimate is 2.411018.

8.2. Inference on the Silver Price Data (In US Dollars) (1980–2013)

Data on the price of silver in US dollars collected per ounce over the same time period also underwent the same transformation. The Durbin–Watson test performed on the log ratio transformed data shows that the autocorrelation is zero. Here, the Watson's goodness of fit test for wrapped stable distribution was also performed and the value of the statistic was obtained as 0.02530653 and the corresponding p-value is 0.9639666, which is greater than 0.05, indicating that the wrapped stable distribution also fits the transformed silver price data (in US dollars). The modified truncated estimate of the index parameter α is 0.4112475 while the estimate by characteristic function method is 0.644846. The value of the objective function using the characteristic function estimate is 2.234203 while that using our modified truncated estimate is 2.234432.

8.3. Inference on the Silver Price Data (In INR) (1970–2011)

Data on the price of silver in INR were also collected per 10 grams over the same time period. The p-value for the Durbin–Watson test performed on the log ratio transformed data is 0.3437, which indicates that the autocorrelation is zero. Here, the Watson's goodness of fit test was also performed on the transformed data and the value of the statistic was obtained as 0.03382334 and the corresponding p-value is 0.8919965, which is greater than 0.05, indicating that the wrapped stable distribution also fits the silver price data (in INR). The estimate $\hat{\alpha_1^*}$ is 1.142171, which is the same as the characteristic function estimate. The value of the objective function using the characteristic function estimate is 2.813234 while that using our modified truncated estimate is 2.665166. Since the estimate of α lies between 1 and 2, a mixture of normal and Cauchy distributions is used in Anderson and Arnold (1993) to estimate the respective parameters. The initial values of the scale parameter (σ_1) for the normal distribution is taken as the sample standard deviation and that for the Cauchy distribution (σ_2) is taken as the sample quartile deviation. In addition, different initial values of the mixing parameter p yield the same estimate of the parameters, viz. $\hat{p} = 0.165$, $\hat{\sigma_1} = 14.38486$, and $\hat{\sigma_2} = 0.077$, and the value of the objective function was found to be 0.9308165. Then, the value of I.O. using modified truncated estimate (assuming stable distribution) is 4.665166 (2.665166 + 2), using the characteristic function estimate (assuming stable distribution) is 4.813234 (2.813234 + 2), and using the characteristic function estimate (assuming mixture of normal and Cauchy distribution) is 3.9308165 (0.9308165 + 3). Thus, it can be observed using the I.O. measure that a mixture of normal and Cauchy distribution gives the best fit to the data. The maximum likelihood estimate of α assuming wrapped stable distribution is 1.1421361. Akaike's information criterion (AIC) value assuming wrapped stable distribution is 153.5426 and that assuming a mixture of normal and Cauchy distribution is 201.4.

8.4. Inference on the Box and Jenkins Stock Price Data

Series B Box and Jenkins (IBM) common stock closing price data obtained from Box et al. (2016) were also transformed similarly as for the preceding one. The Durbin–Watson test performed on the log ratio transformed data shows that the autocorrelation is zero. Watson's test statistic for the goodness of fit test was obtained as 0.0554223 and the corresponding p-value was obtained as 0.6442058, which is greater than 0.05, indicating that the wrapped stable distribution fits the stock price data. The estimates of the index parameter α and the concentration parameter ρ as obtained by modified truncation method are 1.102854 and 0.4335457, respectively.

9. Findings and Concluding Remarks

It can be observed from Table 1 that the asymptotic variance of the untruncated estimator is reduced for the corresponding truncated estimator, indicating the efficiency of the truncated estimator.

It can also be noted from Table 2 that, for $\alpha = 1.01$, the RMSE of the modified truncated estimator is less than that of the Hill estimator when the sample is relocated by three different relocations, viz. true mean = 0, sample mean, and sample median, for higher values of the concentration parameter $\rho = 0.5, 0.6, 0.8$, and 0.9 for sample sizes n = 100, 250, 500, and 1000 and for $\rho = 0.3, 0.4, 0.6, 0.8$, and 0.9 for sample sizes n = 2000, 5000, and 10,000. Furthermore, it can be observed that, for $\alpha = 1.25, 1.5$, 1.75 and 1.9, the RMSE of the modified truncated is less than that of the Hill estimator for different relocations for $\rho = 0.6, 0.7, 0.8$, and 0.9 for smaller sample size and even for $\rho = 0.5$ for larger sample size. This clearly indicates the efficiency of the modified truncated estimator over the Hill estimator for higher values of the concentration parameter ρ.

It can be observed in Table 3 that the RMSE of the modified truncated estimator is less than that of the characteristic function-based estimator for almost all values of α corresponding to all values of σ.

The Hill estimator (Dufour and Kurz-Kim (2010)) is defined for $1 \leq \alpha \leq 2$, whereas the modified truncated estimator is defined for the whole range $0 \leq \alpha \leq 2$. In addition, the overall performance of the modified truncated estimator is quite good in terms of efficiency and consistency over both the Hill estimator and the characteristic function-based estimator.

Thus, we have established an estimator of the index parameter α that strongly supports its parameter space $(0, 2]$. It can be observed from the above real life data applications that the modified truncated estimator is quite close to that of the characteristic function-based estimator. In addition, it is simpler and computationally easier than that of the estimator defined in Anderson and Arnold (1993). Thus, it may be considered as a better estimator.

Again, when the estimator of α lies between 1 and 2, is attempted to model a mixture of two distributions with the value of the index parameter as that of the two extreme tails that is modeling a mixture of Cauchy ($\alpha = 1$) and normal ($\alpha = 2$) distributions when $1 < \alpha < 2$ or modeling a mixture of Double Exponential ($\alpha = \frac{1}{2}$) and Cauchy ($\alpha = 1$) distributions when $\frac{1}{2} < \alpha < 1$. Then, it is compared with that of the stable family of distributions for goodness of fit.

We could have used the usual technique of non-linear optimization as used in Salimi et al. (2018) for estimation, but it is computationally demanding and also the (statistical) consistency of the estimators obtained by such method is unknown. In contrast, our proposed methods of trigonometric moment and modified truncated estimation are much simpler, computationally easier and also possess useful consistency properties and, even their asymptotic distributions can be presented in simple and elegant forms as already proved above.

Author Contributions: Problem formulation, formal analyses and data curation, A.S.; formal and numerical data analyses, M.R.

Acknowledgments: The research of the second author of the paper was funded by the Senior Research Fellowship from the University Grants Commission, Government of India. She is also thankful to the Indian Statistical Institute and the University of Calcutta for providing the necessary facilities.

Conflicts of Interest: The authors declare no conflicts of interest.

Appendix A

Proof of Lemma 1. Putting $p = 1$ in Equation (2) and using the expansion of the characteristic function of θ, we get (henceforth, we denote $E(X)$ and $V(X)$ as expectation and variance of a random variable X, respectively, as usual)

$$E\cos\theta = \rho\cos\mu_0 \quad \text{(A1)}$$
$$\Rightarrow E(\bar{C_1}) = E\left[\frac{1}{m}\sum_{i=1}^{m}\cos\theta_i\right] = \rho\cos\mu_0$$

Again, putting $p = 2$ in Equation (2) and using the expansion of the characteristic function of θ, we get

$$E\cos 2\theta = \rho^{2^\alpha}\cos 2\mu_0 \quad \text{(A2)}$$
$$\Rightarrow E(\bar{C_2}) = E\left[\frac{1}{m}\sum_{i=1}^{m}\cos 2\theta_i\right] = \rho^{2^\alpha}\cos 2\mu_0$$

In addition, Equation (A2) implies that,

$$
\begin{aligned}
E\cos^2\theta &= \frac{(\rho^{2^\alpha}\cos 2\mu_0 + 1)}{2} \\
\Rightarrow V(\cos\theta) &= E\cos^2\theta - E^2\cos\theta \\
&= \frac{\rho^{2^\alpha}\cos 2\mu_0 + 1}{2} - \rho^2\cos^2\mu_0
\end{aligned}
$$

Hence,

$$
V(\bar{C_1}) = V\left[\frac{1}{m}\sum_{i=1}^{m}\cos\theta_i\right] \tag{A3}
$$

$$
= \frac{\rho^{2^\alpha}\cos 2\mu_0 + 1 - 2\rho^2\cos^2\mu_0}{2m} \tag{A4}
$$

Now, putting $p = 4$ in Equation (2) and using the expansion of the characteristic function of θ, we get,

$$
E\cos 4\theta = \rho^{4^\alpha}\cos 4\mu_0 \tag{A5}
$$

$$
\Rightarrow E\left[\cos^2 2\theta\right] = \frac{(\rho^{4^\alpha}\cos 4\mu_0 + 1)}{2}
$$

Hence,

$$
\begin{aligned}
V(\cos 2\theta) &= E\cos^2 2\theta - E^2\cos 2\theta \\
&= \frac{\rho^{4^\alpha}\cos 4\mu_0 + 1}{2} - (\rho^{2^\alpha})^2\cos^2 2\mu_0
\end{aligned}
$$

Therefore,

$$
V(\bar{C_2}) = V\left[\frac{1}{m}\sum_{i=1}^{m}\cos 2\theta_i\right]
$$

$$
= \frac{\rho^{4^\alpha}\cos 4\mu_0 + 1 - 2(\rho^{2^\alpha})^2\cos^2 2\mu_0}{2m} \tag{A6}
$$

Now, putting $p = 1$ in Equation (2) and using the expansion of the characteristic function of θ, we get

$$
E\sin\theta = \rho\sin\mu_0 \tag{A7}
$$

$$
\Rightarrow E(\bar{S_1}) = E\left[\frac{1}{m}\sum_{i=1}^{m}\sin\theta_i\right] = \rho\sin\mu_0
$$

Again, putting $p = 2$ in Equation (2) and using the expansion of the characteristic function of θ, we get

$$
E\sin 2\theta = \rho^{2^\alpha}\sin 2\mu_0 \tag{A8}
$$

$$
\Rightarrow E(\bar{S_2}) = E\left[\frac{1}{m}\sum_{i=1}^{m}\sin 2\theta_i\right] = \rho^{2^\alpha}\sin 2\mu_0
$$

Now, using Equation (A2),

$$E\sin^2\theta = \frac{(1-\rho^{2^\alpha}\cos 2\mu_0)}{2}$$

Hence,

$$\begin{aligned} V(\sin\theta) &= E\sin^2\theta - E^2\sin\theta \\ &= \frac{1-\rho^{2^\alpha}\cos 2\mu_0}{2} - \rho^2\sin^2\mu_0 \end{aligned}$$

Therefore,

$$\begin{aligned} V(\bar{S_1}) &= V\left[\frac{1}{m}\sum_{i=1}^{m}\sin\theta_i\right] \\ &= \frac{1-\rho^{2^\alpha}\cos 2\mu_0 - 2\rho^2\sin^2\mu_0}{2m} \end{aligned}$$

Now, using Equation (A5),

$$E\sin^2 2\theta = \frac{(1-\rho^{4^\alpha}\cos 4\mu_0)}{2}$$

Hence,

$$\begin{aligned} V(\sin 2\theta) &= E\sin^2 2\theta - E^2\sin 2\theta \\ &= \frac{1-\rho^{4^\alpha}\cos 4\mu_0}{2} - (\rho^{2^\alpha})^2\sin^2 2\mu_0 \end{aligned}$$

Therefore,

$$\begin{aligned} V(\bar{S_2}) &= V\left[\frac{1}{m}\sum_{i=1}^{m}\sin 2\theta_i\right] \\ &= \frac{1-\rho^{4^\alpha}\cos 4\mu_0 - 2(\rho^{2^\alpha})^2\sin^2 2\mu_0}{2m} \end{aligned}$$

Now, using Equations (A1), (A7) and (A8),

$$\begin{aligned} Cov(\cos\theta,\sin\theta) &= E\cos\theta\sin\theta - E\cos\theta E\sin\theta \\ &= \frac{\rho^{2^\alpha}\sin 2\mu_0}{2} - \rho\cos\mu_0\rho\sin\mu_0 \end{aligned}$$

Therefore,

$$E\sum_{i=1}^{m}\cos\theta_i\sum_{i=1}^{m}\sin\theta_i = E\sum_{i=1}^{m}\cos\theta_i\sin\theta_i + \sum_{i}^{m}\sum_{j\neq i}^{m}\cos\theta_i\sin\theta_j$$

Thus,

$$Cov(\bar{C_1}, \bar{S_1}) = Cov\left[\frac{1}{m}\sum_{i=1}^{m}\cos\theta_i, \frac{1}{m}\sum_{i=1}^{m}\sin 2\theta_i\right]$$
$$= \frac{\rho^{2^\alpha}\sin 2\mu_0 - 2\rho^2\cos\mu_0\sin\mu_0}{2m}$$

Putting $p = 3$ in Equation (2) and using the expansion of characteristic function of θ, we get

$$E(\sin 3\theta) = \rho^{3^\alpha}\sin 3\mu_0 \tag{A9}$$

Now,

$$Cov(\bar{C_1}, \bar{S_2}) = Cov\left[\frac{1}{m}\sum_{i=1}^{m}\cos\theta_i, \frac{1}{m}\sum_{i=1}^{m}\sin 2\theta_i\right]$$
$$Cov(\cos\theta, \sin 2\theta) = E\cos\theta\sin 2\theta - E\cos\theta E\sin 2\theta$$

Now, using Equations (A7) and (A9),

$$E\cos\theta\sin 2\theta = E\left[\frac{\sin 3\theta + \sin\theta}{2}\right]$$
$$= \frac{\rho^{3^\alpha}\sin 3\mu_0 + \rho\sin\mu_0}{2}$$

Thus, using Equations (A1) and (A8),

$$Cov(\cos\theta, \sin 2\theta) = \frac{\rho^{3^\alpha}\sin 3\mu_0 + \rho\sin\mu_0}{2} - \rho\cos\mu_0\rho^{2^\alpha}\sin 2\mu_0$$

Hence,

$$Cov(\bar{C_1}, \bar{S_2}) = \frac{\rho^{3^\alpha}\sin 3\mu_0 + \rho\sin\mu_0 - 2\rho^{2^\alpha+1}\cos\mu_0\sin 2\mu_0}{2m}$$

Similarly, it can be shown that,

$$Cov(\bar{C_1}, \bar{C_2}) = \frac{\rho\cos\mu_0 + \rho^{3^\alpha}\cos 3\mu_0 - 2\rho^{2^\alpha+1}\cos\mu_0\cos 2\mu_0}{2m} \tag{A10}$$

$$Cov(\bar{C_2}, \bar{S_1}) = \frac{\rho^{3^\alpha}\sin 3\mu_0 - \rho\sin\mu_0 - 2\rho^{2^\alpha+1}\cos 2\mu_0\sin\mu_0}{2m}$$

$$Cov(\bar{C_2}, \bar{S_2}) = \frac{\rho^{4^\alpha}\sin 4\mu_0 - 2(\rho^{2^\alpha})^2\cos 2\mu_0\sin 2\mu_0}{2m}$$

$$Cov(\bar{S_1}, \bar{S_2}) = \frac{\rho\cos\mu_0 - \rho^{3^\alpha}\cos 3\mu_0 - 2\rho^{2^\alpha+1}\sin\mu_0\sin 2\mu_0}{2m}$$

□

Appendix B

Proof of Lemma 2. This proof follows simply by putting $\mu_0 = 0$ into Equations (A2) and (A6) in the proof for Lemma 1. □

Appendix C

Proof of Lemma 3. This proof follows simply by putting $\mu_0 = 0$ in Equations (A1), (A2), (A3), (A6) and (A10) in the proof for Lemma 1. □

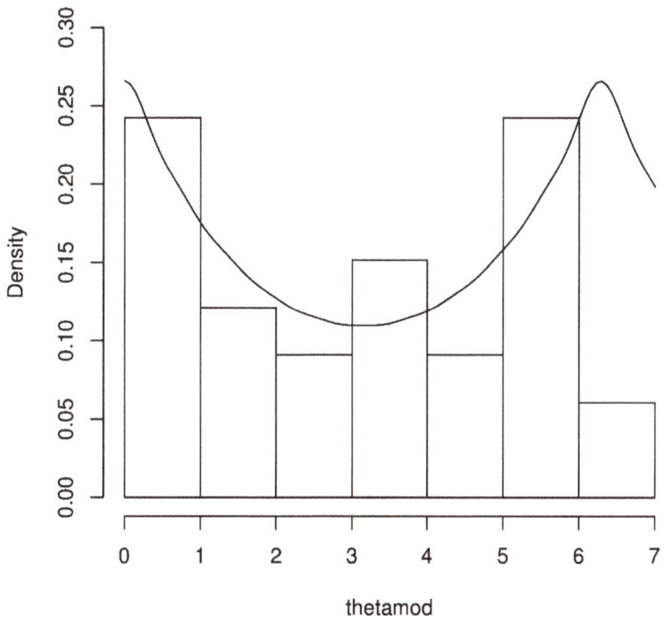

Figure A1. Histogram of wrapped log-ratio transformed gold price data (in US dollars) with wrapped stable density.

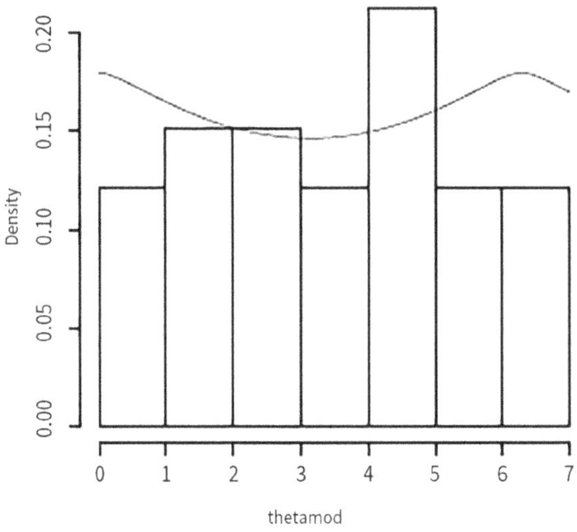

Figure A2. Histogram of wrapped log-ratio transformed silver price data(in US dollars)with wrapped stable density.

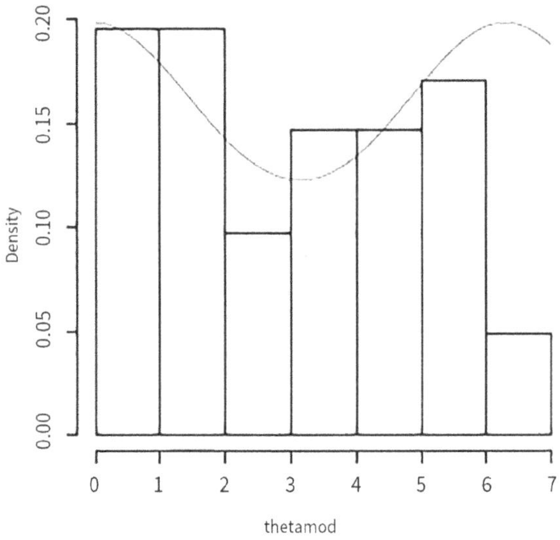

Figure A3. Histogram of wrapped log-ratio transformed gold price data(in INR)with wrapped stable density.

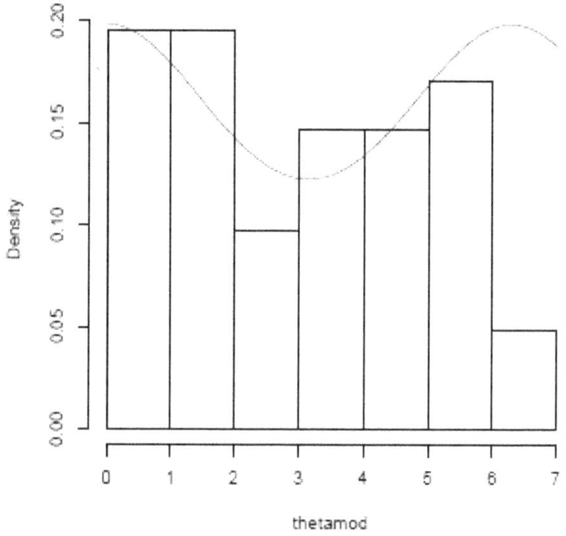

Figure A4. Histogram of wrapped log-ratio transformed silver price data (in INR) with wrapped stable density.

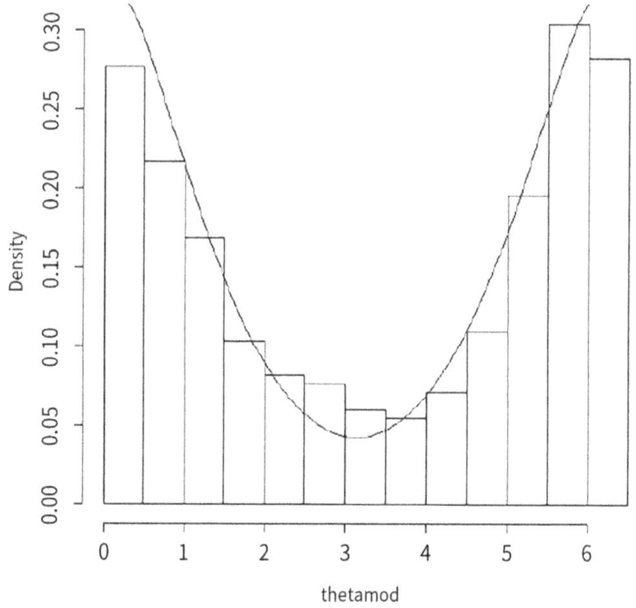

Figure A5. Histogram of wrapped log-ratio transformed Box and Jenkins data with wrapped stable density.

References

Anderson, Dale N., and Barry C. Arnold. 1993. Linnik Distributions and Processes. *Journal of Applied Probability* 30: 330–40. [CrossRef]

Box, George Edward Pelham, Gwilym M. Jenkins, Gregory C. Reinsel, and Greta M. Ljung. 2016. *Time Series Analysis: Forecasting and Control*. Hoboken: John Wiley and Sons.

Casella, George, and Roger L. Berger. 2002. *Statistical Inference*. Boston: Thomson Learning.

Dufour, Jean-Marie, and Jeong-Ryeol Kurz-Kim. 2010. Exact inference and optimal invariant estimation for the stability parameter of symmetric α-stable distributions. *Journal of Empirical Finance* 17: 180–94. [CrossRef]

Feller, Williams. 1971. *An Introduction to Probability Theory and its Applications*, 3rd ed. New York: Wiley.

Goldie, Charles M., and Richard L. Smith. 1987. Slow variation with remainder: A survey of the theory and its applications. *Quarterly Journal of Mathematics, Oxford* 38: 45–71. [CrossRef]

Hill, Bruce M. 1975. A simple general approach to inference about the tail of a distribution. *The Annals of Statistics* 3: 1163–74. [CrossRef]

Jammalamadaka, S. Rao, and Ashis SenGupta. 2001. *Topics in Circular Statistics*. Hackensack: World Scientific Publishers.

Nolan, John P. 2003. Modeling Financial Data with Stable Distributions. In *Handbook of Heavy Tailed Distributions in Finance*. Amsterdam: Elsevier, pp. 105–30.

Salimi, Mehdi, NMA Nik Long, Somayeh Sharifi, and Bruno Antonio Pansera. 2018. A multi-point iterative method for solving nonlinear equations with optimal order of convergence. *Japan Journal of Industrial and Applied Mathematics* 35: 497–509. [CrossRef]

SenGupta, Ashis. 1996. Analysis of Directional Data in Agricultural Research using DDSTAP. Invited paper. Paper presented at Indian Society of Agricultural Statistics Golden Jubilee Conference, New Delhi, India, December 19–21, pp. 43–59.

Journal of
Risk and Financial Management

MDPI

Article

Parsimonious Heterogeneous ARCH Models for High Frequency Modeling

Juan Carlos Ruilova [1] and Pedro Alberto Morettin [2,*]

[1] Itaú Bank, São Paulo 04344-902, Brazil; juan.teran@itau.com.br
[2] Department of Statistics, University of São Paulo, São Paulo 05508-090, Brazil
* Correspondence: pam@ime.usp.br

Received: 6 January 2020; Accepted: 8 February 2020; Published: 20 February 2020

Abstract: In this work we study a variant of the GARCH model when we consider the arrival of heterogeneous information in high-frequency data. This model is known as HARCH(n). We modify the HARCH(n) model when taking into consideration some market components that we consider important to the modeling process. This model, called parsimonious HARCH(m,p), takes into account the heterogeneous information present in the financial market and the long memory of volatility. Some theoretical properties of this model are studied. We used maximum likelihood and Griddy-Gibbs sampling to estimate the parameters of the proposed model and apply it to model the Euro-Dollar exchange rate series.

Keywords: GARCH model; HARCH model; PHARCH model; Griddy-Gibs; Euro-Dollar

1. Introduction

High frequency data are those measured in small time intervals. This kind of data is important to study the micro structure of financial markets and also because their use is becoming feasible due to the increase of computational power and data storage.

Perhaps the most popular model used to estimate the volatility in a financial time series is the GARCH(1,1) model; see Engle (1982), Bollerslev (1986):

$$\begin{aligned} r_t &= \sigma_t \varepsilon_t, \quad \varepsilon_t \sim \text{iid}\,(0,1)\;, \\ \sigma_t^2 &= \alpha_0 + \alpha_1 r_{t-1}^2 + \beta_1 \sigma_{t-1}^2, \end{aligned} \tag{1}$$

with $\alpha_0 > 0, \alpha_1 \geq 0, \beta_1 \geq 0, \alpha_1 + \beta_1 < 1$.

When we use high frequency data in conjunction with GARCH models, these need to be modified to incorporate the financial market micro structure. For example, we need to incorporate heterogeneous characteristics that appear when there are many traders working in a financial market trading with different time horizons.

The HARCH(n) model was introduced by Müller et al. (1997) to try to solve this problem. In fact, this model incorporates heterogeneous characteristics of high frequency financial time series and it is given by

$$\begin{aligned} r_t &= \sigma_t \varepsilon_t, \\ \sigma_t^2 &= c_0 + \textstyle\sum_{j=1}^{n} c_j \left(\sum_{i=1}^{j} r_{t-i} \right)^2, \end{aligned} \tag{2}$$

where $c_0 > 0, c_n > 0, c_j \geq 0\; \forall j = 1, \ldots, n-1$ and ε_t are identically and independent distributed (i.i.d.) random variables with zero expectation and unit variance.

However, this model has a high computational cost to fit when compared with GARCH models, due to the long memory of volatility, so the number of parameters to be estimated is usually large.

We propose a new model known as the parsimonious heterogeneous autoregressive conditional heteroscedastic model, in short-form PHARCH, as an extension of the HARCH model. Specifically, we call a PHARCH(*m*,*p*), with aggregations of different sizes $a_1, \ldots, a_m$, where m is the number of the market components, the model given by

$$\begin{aligned} r_t &= \sigma_t \varepsilon_t, \\ \sigma_t^2 &= C_0 + C_1 (r_{t-1} + \ldots + r_{t-a_1})^2 + \ldots + \\ &+ C_m (r_{t-1} + \ldots + r_{t-a_m})^2 + b_1 \sigma_{t-1}^2 + \ldots + b_p \sigma_{t-p}^2, \end{aligned} \tag{3}$$

where $\varepsilon_t \sim$ i.i.d. $(0,1)$, $C_0 > 0$, $C_j \geq 0, \forall j = 1, \ldots, m-1$, $C_m > 0$, $b_j \geq 0$, $j = 1, \ldots, p$.

HARCH models are important because they take account the natural behavior of the traders in the market. However they have some problems, mainly because they need to include several aggregations, so the number of parameters to estimate is large, because of the large memory feature of financial time series. Parsimonious HARCH includes only the most important aggregations in its structure, which makes the model more realistic. We can see some simulations in Figure 1, where the characteristics of clustering and volatility are better represented in PHARCH processes than in ARCH or HARCH processes.

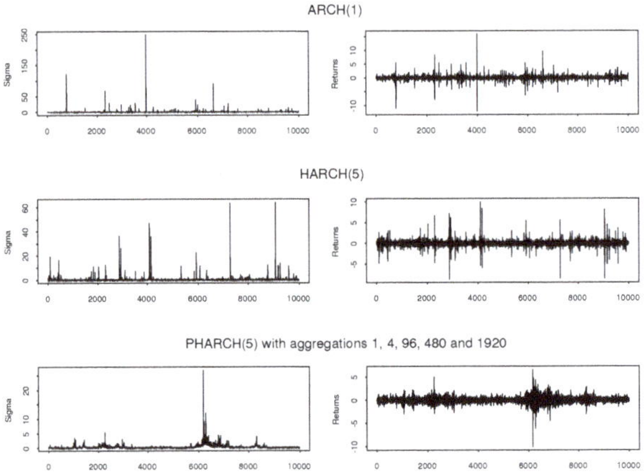

Figure 1. Simulations of ARCH, HARCH and PHARCH processes.

The organization of the paper is as follows. In Section 2 we provide some background information on Markov chains and give the necessary and sufficient conditions for the PHARCH model to be stationary. In Section 3 we obtain forecasts for the proposed model, and in Section 4 we introduce the data that will be used for illustrative purposes. The actual application is given in Section 5, and we close the paper with some conclusions in Section 6.

2. Background

In this section we provide briefly some background on Markov chains and results on stationarity of PHARCH models.

2.1. Markov Chains

Suppose that $\mathbf{X} = \{X_n, n \in \mathbb{Z}^+\}$, $\mathbb{Z}^+ := \{0, 1, 2, \ldots\}$ are random variables defined over $(\Omega, \mathcal{F}, \mathcal{B}(\Omega))$, and assume that $\mathbf{X}$ is a Markov chain with transition probability $P(x, A), x \in \Omega, A \subset \Omega$. Then we have the following definitions:

1. A function $f : \Omega \to \mathbb{R}$ is called the smallest semi-continuous function if $\liminf_{y \to x} f(y) \geq f(x),\ x \in \Omega$. If $P(\cdot, A)$ is the smallest semi-continuous function for any open set $A \in \mathcal{B}(\Omega)$, we say that (the chain) **X** is a *weak Feller chain*.
2. A chain **X** is called φ-irreducible if there exists a measure φ on $\mathcal{B}(\Omega)$ such that, for all x, whenever $\varphi(A) > 0$, we have,

   $U(x, A) = \sum_{n=1}^{\infty} P^n(x, A) > 0.$
3. The measure ψ is called maximal with respect to φ, and we write $\psi > \varphi$, if $\psi(A) = 0$ implies $\varphi(A) = 0$, for all $A \in \mathcal{B}(\Omega)$. If **X** is φ-irreducible, then there exists a probability measure ψ, maximal, such that **X** is ψ-irreducible.
4. Let $d = \{d(n)\}$ a distribution or a probability measure on $\mathbb{Z}^+$, and consider the Markov chain $\mathbf{X}_d$ with transition kernel

$$K_d(x, A) := \sum_{n=0}^{\infty} P^n(x, A) d(n).$$

   If there exits a transition kernel T satisfying

$$K_d(x, A) \geq T(x, A), \quad x \in \Omega,\ A \in \mathcal{B}(\Omega),$$

   then T is called the continuous component of K_d.
5. If **X** is a Markov chain for which there exits a (sample) distribution d such that K_d has a continuous component T, with $T(x, \Omega) > 0,\ \forall x$, then **X** is called a T-chain.
6. A measure π over $\mathcal{B}(\Omega)$, σ-finite, with the property

$$\pi(A) = \int_{\Omega} \pi(dx) P(x, A), \ A \in \mathcal{B}(\Omega),$$

   is called an *invariant measure*.

The following two lemmas will be useful. See Meyn and Tweedie (1996) for the proofs and further details. We denote by $I_A(\cdot)$ the indicator function of A.

Lemma 1. *Suppose that X is a weak Feller chain. Let $C \in \mathcal{B}(\Omega)$ be a compact set and V a positive function. If*

$$V(X_n) - E\left[V(X_{n+1}) \,|X_n\right] \geq 0, X_n \in C^c,$$

then there exists an invariant measure, finite on compact sets of Ω.

Lemma 2. *Suppose that X is a weak Feller chain. Let $C \in \mathcal{B}(\Omega)$ be a compact set, and V a positive function that is finite at some $x_0 \in \Omega$. If*

$$V(X_n) - E\left[V(X_{n+1}) \,|X_n\right] \geq 1 - bI_C(X_n), X_n \in \Omega,$$

with b a constant, $b < \infty$, then there exists an invariant probability measure π on $\mathcal{B}(\Omega)$.

Lemma 3. *Suppose that X is a ψ-irreducible aperiodic chain. Then the following conditions are equivalent:*

1. *There exists a function $f : \Omega \to [1, \infty)$, a set $C \in \mathcal{B}(\Omega)$, a constant $b < \infty$ and a function $V : \Omega \to [0, \infty)$, such that*

$$V(X_n) - E\left[V(X_{n+1}) \,|X_n\right] \geq f(X_n) - bI_C(X_n), X_n \in \Omega.$$

2. *The chain is positive recurrent with invariant probability measure π, and $\pi(f) < \infty$.*

2.2. Stationarity of PHARCH(m,p) Models

We first give a necessary condition for Model (3) to be stationary. We know that $E(r_{t-i}r_{t-j}) = 0, \forall i \neq j$, and if r_t is stationary, we must have

$$E\left(r_t^2\right) = E\left(\sigma_t^2\right) = C_0 + E\left(r_t^2\right)\sum_{i=1}^{m} a_i C_i + E\left(\sigma_t^2\right)\sum_{i=1}^{p} b_i,$$

so

$$E\left[r_t^2\right] = \frac{C_0}{1 - \left(\sum_{i=1}^{m} a_i C_i + \sum_{i=1}^{p} b_i\right)}.$$

Therefore,

$$\sum_{i=1}^{m} a_i C_i + \sum_{i=1}^{p} b_i < 1. \tag{4}$$

To prove a sufficient condition it will be necessary to represent the PHARCH(m,p) as a Markov process. We use the definitions given in the previous section, so the process

$$X_t = \left(r_{t-1}, \ldots, r_{t-a_m+1}, \sigma_t, \ldots, \sigma_{t-p+1}\right), \tag{5}$$

whose elements follow Equation (3), is also a T-chain.

The proofs of the following results are based on Dacorogna et al. (1996), and they are given in the Appendix A.

Proposition 1. *The Markov Chain X_t that represents a PHARCH(m,p) process is a T-chain.*

Proposition 2. *The Markov Chain that represents a PHARCH(m,p) process is recurrent with an invariant probability measure (stationary distribution), and its second moments are finite if the condition given in (4) is satisfied.*

Note that if $\varepsilon_t \sim t(v)$ (a Student's t distribution with ν degrees of freedom) in (3), then the necessary and sufficient condition becomes

$$\sum_{i=1}^{m} \frac{v}{v-2} a_i C_i + \sum_{i=1}^{p} b_i < 1, \quad \text{for } v > 2.$$

3. Forecasting

In this section we make some considerations about forecasting and validation of the proposed model. Usually two data bases are used for testing tha forecasting ability of a model: one (in-sample), used for estimation, and the other (out-of-sample) used for comparing forecasts with true values. There is an extra complication in the case of volatility models: there is no unique definition of volatility. Andersen and Bollerslev (1998) show that if wrong estimates of volatility are used, evaluation of forecasting accuracy is compromised. We could use the realized volatility as a basis for comparison, or use some trading system.

We could, for example, have a model for hourly returns and use the realized volatility computed from 15 min returns for comparisons. In general, we can compute $v_{h,t} = \sum_{i=1}^{a_h} r_{t-i}^2$, where a_h is the aggregation factor (4, in the case of 15 min returns). Then use some measure based on $s_h = \tilde{v}_{h,t} - v_{h,t}$, for example, mean squared error, where $\tilde{v}_{h,t}$ is the volatility predicted by the proposed model. See Taylor and Xu (1997), for example.

Now consider Model (3). The forecast of volatility at origin t and horizon ℓ is given by

$$\begin{aligned}\hat{\sigma}_t^2(l) &= E(\sigma_{t+l}^2|X_t)\\ &= E(C_0 + C_1\left(r_{t+l-1} + \ldots + r_{t+l-a_1}\right)^2 + \ldots +\\ &+ C_m\left(r_{t+l-1} + \ldots + r_{t+l-a_m}\right)^2 + b_1\sigma_{t+l-1}^2 + \ldots + b_p\sigma_{t+l-p}^2|X_t),\end{aligned}$$

where $X_t = (r_t, \sigma_t, r_{t-1}, \sigma_{t-1}, \ldots)$, for $l = 1, 2, \ldots$

Since $a_0 = 1 < a_1 < a_2 < \ldots < a_m < \infty$, then we have three cases:

(i) If $l = 1$,

$$\begin{aligned}\hat{\sigma}_t^2(l) &= E(C_0 + C_1\left(r_{t+l-1} + \ldots + r_{t+l-a_1}\right)^2 + \ldots +\\ &\quad + C_s\left(r_{t+l-1} + \ldots + r_{t+l-a_s}\right)^2 + \ldots +\\ &\quad + C_m\left(r_{t+l-1} + \ldots + r_{t+l-a_m}\right)^2 +\\ &\quad + b_1\sigma_{t+l-1}^2 + \ldots + b_p\sigma_{t+l-p}^2/X_t)\\ &= C_0 + C_1\left(r_t + \ldots + r_{t+1-a_1}\right)^2 + \ldots +\\ &\quad + C_s\left(r_t + \ldots + r_{t+1-a_s}\right)^2 + \ldots +\\ &\quad + C_m\left(r_t + \ldots + r_{t+1-a_m}\right)^2 + b_1\sigma_t^2 + \ldots + b_p\sigma_{t+1-p}^2.\end{aligned}$$

(ii) If l is such that $a_{s-1} < l < a_s$, $s = 1, 2, \ldots, m$, then we have,

$$\begin{aligned}\hat{\sigma}_t^2(l) &= E(C_0 + C_1\left(r_{t+l-1} + \ldots + r_{t+l-a_1}\right)^2 + \ldots +\\ &\quad + C_s\left(r_{t+l-1} + \ldots + r_{t+l-a_s}\right)^2 + \ldots +\\ &\quad + C_m\left(r_{t+l-1} + \ldots + r_{t+l-a_m}\right)^2 +\\ &\quad + b_1\sigma_{t+l-1}^2 + \ldots + b_p\sigma_{t+l-p}^2/X_t)\\ &= E(C_0 + \sum_{i=1}^{s-1} C_i\left(\sum_{j=1}^{a_i} r_{t+l-j}\right)^2 +\\ &\quad + \sum_{i=s}^{m} C_i\left(\sum_{j=1}^{l-1} r_{t+l-j}\right)^2 + \sum_{i=s}^{m} C_i\left(\sum_{j=l}^{a_i} r_{t+l-j}\right)^2 +\\ &\quad + \sum_{i=s}^{m} C_i\left(\sum_{j=1}^{l-1} r_{t+l-j}\right)\left(\sum_{j=l}^{a_i} r_{t+l-j}\right) +\\ &\quad + b_1\sigma_{t+l-1}^2 + \ldots + b_p\sigma_{t+l-p}^2/X_t)\\ &= E(C_0 + \sum_{i=1}^{s-1} C_i\left(\sum_{j=1}^{a_i} \sigma_{t+l-j}\varepsilon_{t+l-j}\right)^2 +\\ &\quad + \sum_{i=s}^{m} C_i\left(\sum_{j=1}^{l-1} \sigma_{t+l-j}\varepsilon_{t+l-j}\right)^2 +\\ &\quad + \sum_{i=s}^{m} C_i\left(\sum_{j=l}^{a_i} r_{t+l-j}\right)^2 +\\ &\quad + \sum_{i=s}^{m} C_i\left(\sum_{j=1}^{l-1} \sigma_{t+l-j}\varepsilon_{t+l-j}\right)\left(\sum_{j=l}^{a_i} r_{t+l-j}\right) +\\ &\quad + b_1\sigma_{t+l-1}^2 + \ldots + b_p\sigma_{t+l-p}^2/X_t),\end{aligned}$$

and given the independence of ε_t and $E(\varepsilon_t) = 0$, we have $E\left(r_{t-i}r_{t-j}\right) = 0$, $\forall i \neq j$; hence,

$$\begin{aligned}\hat{\sigma}_t^2(l) &= E(C_0 + \sum_{i=1}^{s-1} C_i \sum_{j=1}^{a_i} \sigma_{t+l-j}^2 + \sum_{i=s}^{m} C_i \sum_{j=1}^{l-1} \sigma_{t+l-j}^2 +\\ &\quad + \sum_{i=s}^{m} C_i\left(\sum_{j=l}^{a_i} r_{t+l-j}\right)^2 + b_1\sigma_{t+l-1}^2 + \ldots + b_p\sigma_{t+l-p}^2/X_t)\\ &= C_0 + \sum_{i=1}^{s-1} C_i \sum_{j=1}^{a_i} \hat{\sigma}_{t+l-j}^2 + \sum_{i=s}^{m} C_i \sum_{j=1}^{l-1} \hat{\sigma}_{t+l-j}^2 +\\ &\quad + \sum_{i=s}^{m} C_i\left(\sum_{j=l}^{a_i} r_{t+l-j}\right)^2 + b_1\tilde{\sigma}_{t+l-1}^2 + \ldots + b_p\tilde{\sigma}_{t+l-p}^2,\end{aligned}$$

where, for $i = 1, \ldots, p$, we have that $\tilde{\sigma}_{t+l-i}^2 = \begin{cases} \sigma_{t+l-i}^2, & i \geq l \\ \hat{\sigma}_{t+l-i}^2, & i < l \end{cases}$

(iii) If l is such that $l > a_m$, $s = 1, 2, \ldots, m$, then it follows

$$\tilde{\sigma}_t^2(l) = E\left(C_0 + \sum_{i=1}^{m} C_i \sum_{j=1}^{a_i} \sigma_{t+l-j}^2 + b_1\sigma_{t+l-1}^2 + \ldots + b_p\sigma_{t+l-p}^2 / X_t\right)$$
$$= C_0 + \sum_{i=1}^{m} C_i \sum_{j=1}^{a_i} \tilde{\sigma}_{t+l-j}^2 + b_1\tilde{\sigma}_{t+l-1}^2 + \ldots + b_p\tilde{\sigma}_{t+l-p}^2,$$

where for $i = 1, \ldots, p$, we have $\tilde{\sigma}_{t+l-i}^2 = \begin{cases} \sigma_{t+l-i}^2, & i \geq l \\ \tilde{\sigma}_{t+l-i}^2, & i < l \end{cases}$

4. High Frequency Data

In this section we further elaborate on high frequency data and introduce the series that will be analyzed later. High frequency data are very important in the financial environment, mainly because there exist large movements in short intervals of time. This aspect represents an interesting opportunity for trading. Furthermore, it is well known that volatilities in different frequencies have significant cross-correlation. We can even say that coarse volatility predicts fine volatility better than the inverse, as shown in Dacorogna et al. (2001).

As an example, take the tick by tick foreign exchange (FX) time series Euro-Dollar, from January First 1999 to December 31, 2002. Returns are calculated using bid and ask prices, as

$$r_t = \ln\left(\left(p_t^{bid} + p_t^{ask}\right)/2\right) - \ln\left(\left(p_{t-1}^{bid} + p_{t-1}^{ask}\right)/2\right). \quad (6)$$

We discard Saturdays and Sundays, and we replace holidays with the means of the last ten observations of the returns for each respective hour and day. After cleaning the data (see Dacorogna et al. (2001), for details) we will consider equally spaced returns, with sampling interval $\Delta t = 15$ min. This seems to be adequate, as many studies indicate.

Figure 2 shows Euro-Dollar returns calculated as above. The length of this time series is 95,317. The figure shows that the absolute returns present a seasonal pattern. This is due to the fact that physical time does not follow, necessarily, the same pattern as the business time. This is a typical behavior of a financial time series and we will use a seasonal adjustment procedure similar to that of Martens et al. (2002). However, we will use absolute returns instead of squared returns; that is, we will compute the seasonal pattern as

$$S_{d,s,h} = \frac{1}{s}\sum_{j=1}^{s} |(r_{d,j,h}|, \quad (7)$$

where $r_{d,s,h}$ is the return in the weekday d, week s and hour h, and s is the number of weeks from the beginning of the series. Therefore, $S_{d,N_s,h}$ is the rolling window mean of the absolute returns with the beginning fixed.

In Figure 3 we have the autocorrelation function of these returns and of squared returns. The seasonality pattern is no longer present.

FX data has some distinct characteristics, mainly because they are produced twenty four hours a day, seven days a week. In particular, Euro-Dollar is the most liquid FX in the world. However, there are periods where the activity is greater or smaller, causing seasonal patterns to occur, as seen above.

Let us analyze some facts about these returns that we will denote simply by r_t. We can see in Figure 4 the histogram fitted with a non-parametric density kernel estimate, using unbiased cross-validation method to estimate the bandwidth. It shows fat tails and high kurtosis, namely, 121, while its skewness coefficient is -0.079, showing almost symmetry. A normality test (Jarque-Bera) rejects the hypothesis that these returns are normal.

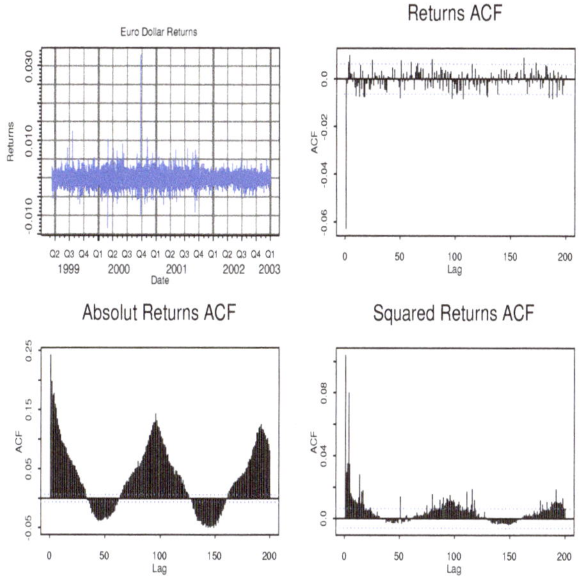

Figure 2. Euro-Dollar returns: acf of returns, acf of absolute returns and acf of squared returns.

The seasonally adjusted returns are then given by

$$\tilde{r}_t = \tilde{r}_{d,s,h} = \frac{r_{d,s,h}}{S_{d,s,h}}. \tag{8}$$

We may assume for example that the errors of a GARCH model fitted to these returns follow a Student's t distribution or a generalized error distribution, which represents better the fat tails of the distribution.

Often the optimization of the likelihood function can be a very difficult task, due mainly to the flat behavior of likelihood function, as can be seen in Zumbach (2000). Bayesian methods are an alternative, and in the next section we will use the Griddy-Gibbs sampling to estimate the parameters of a PHARCH model.

Figure 4 also shows that the Euro-Dollar series has some clusters of volatility. This is a typical behavior of financial time series. A problem is that we do not know how many clusters there are and what their sizes are. The reason for this is that the information arriving is different for each sampling frequency.

We can look these clusters as *market components* and they depend on the heterogeneity of the market. These market components are considered in our PHARCH model, as seen in Equation (3). Differently from GARCH-type models, PHARCH models have a variance equation with returns over intervals of different sizes. Therefore PHARCH models take into account the sign of the returns and not only their absolute value as GARCH models do. Two subsequent returns with similar sizes in the same direction will cause a higher impact on the variance than two subsequent returns with similar sizes but opposite signs.

Now we need to determine the number and the size of the market components for the Euro-Dollar FX series. Ruilova (2007) proposed some technical rules to determine these market components, and Dacorogna et al. (2001) proposed some empirical rules.

To help us to determine if the component sizes chosen are correct we can use the *impact of the component*.

We define the impact I_i of the ith component as,

$$I_i = a_i C_i, \forall i. \tag{9}$$

Note that the stationary condition to PHARCH(m) models can be written in terms of these impacts; namely,

$$\sum_{i=1}^{m} I_i < 1.$$

We also notice that if we consider the Student's t distribution with ν degrees of freedom, the impact should be defined as

$$I_i = \frac{v}{v-2} a_i C_i, \quad \forall i \geq 1. \tag{10}$$

As remarked above, the number of components in a financial series can vary depending how the returns are being traded in this market. That is, liquid series can have a structure with more components than a non-liquid series.

5. Application

Due to the complexity of the proposed model, the likelihod function may be flat in the neighbourhood of the maxima, so the optimization procedure using traditional procedures may fail. An alternative is to use Bayesian methods. Some references on the use of Bayesian procedures for the family of ARCH processes are Geweke (1989), Kleibergen and Dijk (1993), Geweke (1994) and Bauwens and Lubrano (1998).

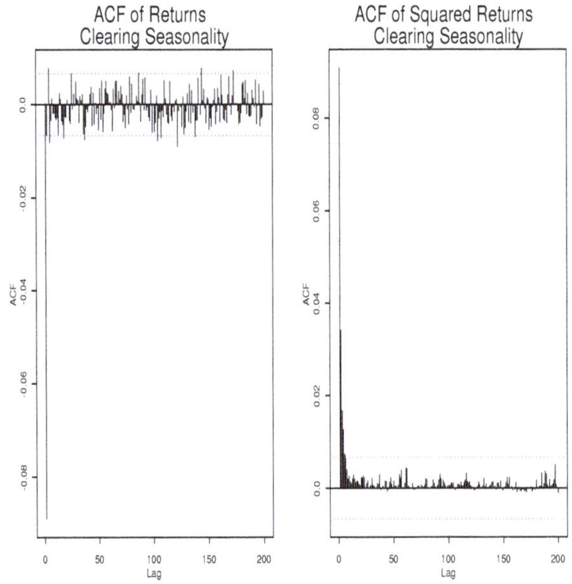

Figure 3. Autocorrelation functions of the Euro-Dollar returns and squared returns after seasonal adjustment.

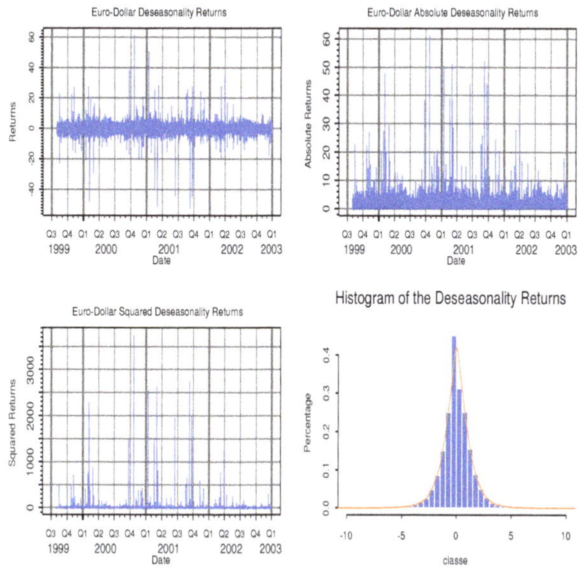

Figure 4. Euro-Dollar returns, absolute returns, squared returns and histogram after taking off seasonal pattern.

It is well known that when the analytical expressions of the full conditional distributions are known we can use Gibbs sampling. However, if the conditional distributions are not known, we need to modify the algorithm or to use another algorithm, such as the Metropolis-Hastings one. Another alternative to solve this is to use the Griddy-Gibbs sampler of Ritter and Tanner (1992).

Griddy-Gibbs sampling can be used when the joint conditional distribution of at least one parameter does not have a distribution form known but it has an analytical expression that can be evaluated on a grid of points. For that, we evaluate the analytical expressions of the joint conditional distribution function, and by numerical integration we can generate random variables of this distribution; see Davis and Rabinowitz (1975).

A problem that appears when we use Griddy-Gibbs sampling is to determine a window and the number of points where we will evaluate numerically the desired function. An inadequate determination of this grid of points could cause errors in the parameters estimation. In general it seems suitable to have 50 points in the grid for a good evaluation.

We will use a technique to reduce the variance that is to compute the conditional mean

$$\sum_{n=1}^{N} E\left(\theta_i | \theta_1^n, \ldots, \theta_{i-1}^n, \theta_{i+1}^n, \ldots, \theta_n^n, y\right) / N,$$

instead of $\sum_{n=1}^{N} \theta_i^n / N$ to estimate $E\left(\theta_i | \theta_1, \theta_2, \ldots, \theta_{i-1}, \theta_{i+1}, \ldots, \theta_n, y\right)$. Here θ_i^n denotes the value of the parameter θ_i at iteration n.

An important fact is that aggregate returns have, generally, a magnitude greater than non-aggregate returns, so the components with larger aggregations have smaller values. For this reason, we can use the impacts defined above to study the contribution of each component to the model.

In order to establish the number of components in the PHARCH model, we will use information of the financial market behavior based on the behavior of the traders. So, we consider five components, as seen in the Table 1, corresponding to information arriving at the market at the rate of 15 min, 1 h, 1 day, 1 week and 1 month.

This means that we need to estimate the parameters of a PHARCH(5) process with aggregations 1, 4, 96, 480 and 1920 as follows.

$$\begin{aligned} r_t &= \sigma_t \varepsilon_t \\ \sigma_t^2 &= C_0 + C_1 r_{t-1}^2 + C_2 \left(r_{t-1} + \ldots + r_{t-4}\right)^2 + \\ &+ C_3 \left(r_{t-1} + \ldots + r_{t-96}\right)^2 + C_4 \left(r_{t-1} + \ldots + r_{t-480}\right)^2 + \\ &+ C_5 \left(r_{t-1} + \ldots + r_{t-1920}\right)^2 \end{aligned} \quad (11)$$

where $C_j \geq 0, \quad j = 1, \ldots, 5, \quad C_0 > 0$, and $\varepsilon_t \sim t\,(0, 1, v)$.

The number of parameters to estimate is seven because we considered $\varepsilon_t \sim t\,(0, 1, v)$, $v > 2$. We use an autoregressive processes to filter the data and to take into account the information given by the acf function of the returns shown in the Figure 3.

We consider non-informative priors, that is, uniform distributions on the parametric space, as follows: $C_0, C_1, C_2, C_3, C_4, C_5 \sim U(0, 1)$ and $v \sim U(3, ct)$, where U denotes the uniform distribution and ct is a large number; in particular, we used $ct = 50$.

Estimates using maximum likelihood (ML) are shown in Table 2, and the corresponding impacts are shown in Figure 5. The optimizer used to evaluate the impacts was simulated annealing; see Belisle (1992). Several problems were faced in the process of using ML because in some situations the optimizer did not converge. Sometimes we can solve this problem, using initial values near to optimum. But this may not be a normal situation in real cases. So the need for alternative procedures.

As we can see, the impact of the components decreases for larger aggregations. This is a natural result because intraday traders are those who dominate the market. Another fact is that the weekly component has a similar impact to the monthly component, meaning that both have similar weight contributions to predicting volatility. The results show that an impact can be significant even when the parameter is small. The above estimates will serve as a comparison with Griddy-Gibbs estimates.

In the Griddy–Gibbs sampling we use a moving window: we define a new window in each iteration as a function of the mean, mode and standard deviation.

Table 1. Component description of PHARCH process for Euro-Dollar.

Component	Aggregations of Euro-Dollar	Range of Time Intervals	Description
1	1	15 min	Short term, intraday traders, market makers.
2	4	1 h	Intraday traders with few transactions per day.
3	96	1 day	Daily traders.
4	480	1 week	Medium term traders.
5	1920	1 month	Long term traders, investors, derivative traders.

Table 2. Parameter estimation by maximum likelihood using simulate annealing optimizer.

Parameter	Estimates
C_0	0.529
C_1	0.101
C_2	0.0173
C_3	0.000374
C_4	0.0000415
C_5	0.0000105
ν	3.638

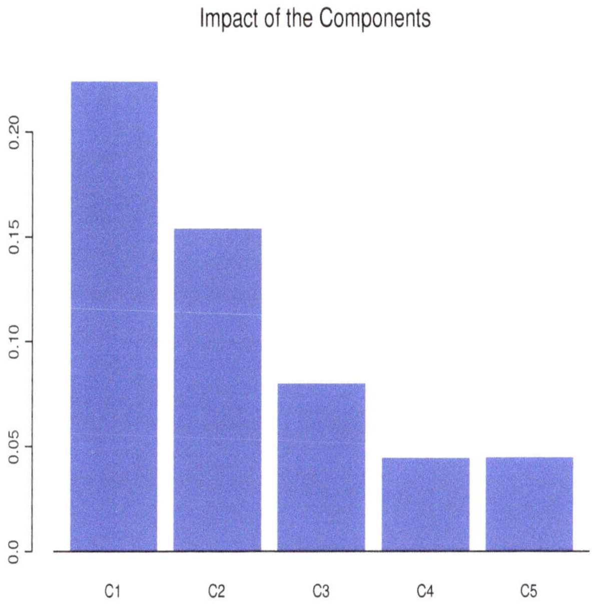

Figure 5. Impact of the components estimated by maximum likelihood.

Table 3 shows the results of the estimation of a parsimonious HARCH(5) model for the Euro-Dollar, using this criterion of selection for a moving window for each parameter, where the conditional density will be computed. The number of points where this density was evaluated was 50.

We used the non conditional and conditional mean in each step of the iteration to calculate the estimate parameters. As expected, conditional method was faster than non-conditional, but the difference was very small.

We see that the values are practically the same by both methods (maximum likelihood and Griddy-Gibbs sampling).

In Figure 6 we can see the convergence of the parameters using Griddy-Gibbs for each iteration step. We can see the fast convergence of the parameters.

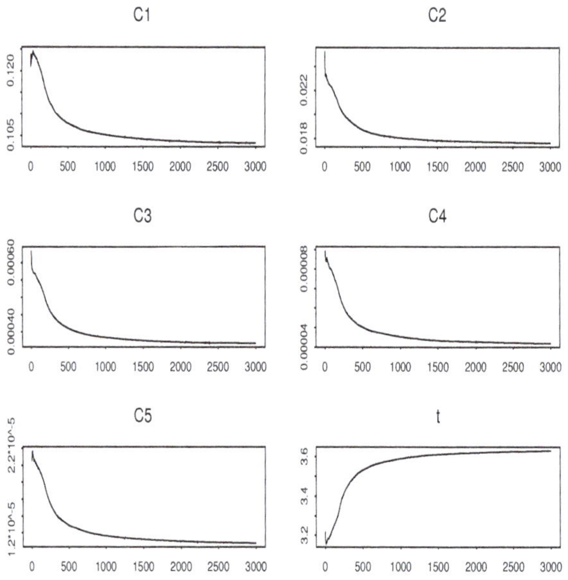

Figure 6. Convergence of the parameters using Griddy-Gibbs sampler.

Now, we compare HARCH modeling with GARCH modeling. In Figures 7–9 we present a residual analysis after the fitting of a GARCH model. In Figures 10–12 we have the corresponding graphs for the PHARCH(5) fitting. We see a slightly better fit of the PHARCH model. If we use the prediction mean squared error (PMSE) as a criterion for comparison, we obtain the values 15.58 and 15.20, for GARCH and PHARCH modeling, respectively, using the standardized residuals and 1000 values for the prediction period.

Table 3. Estimated parameters for the PHARCH(5)model with aggregations 1, 4, 96, 480 and 1920 for the Euro-Dollar series, using Griddy-Gibbs sampling.

Parameter	Non-Conditional	Conditional	Std. Dev.
C_0	0.532	0.532	0.00471
C_1	0.102	0.102	0.00321
C_2	0.0174	0.0174	0.000709
C_3	0.00359	0.000360	0.0000205
C_4	0.0000402	0.0000403	0.00000421
C_5	0.0000104	0.0000103	0.00000105
ν	3.649	3.649	0.034

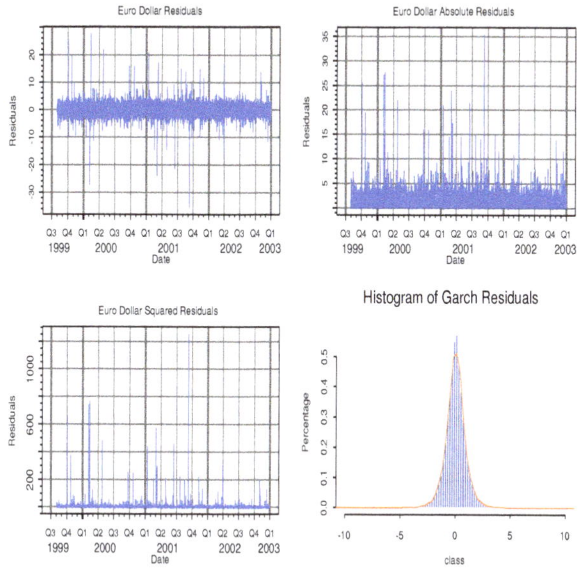

Figure 7. Euro-Dollar residuals, absolute residuals, squared residuals and histogram of the residuals after fitting a GARCH process.

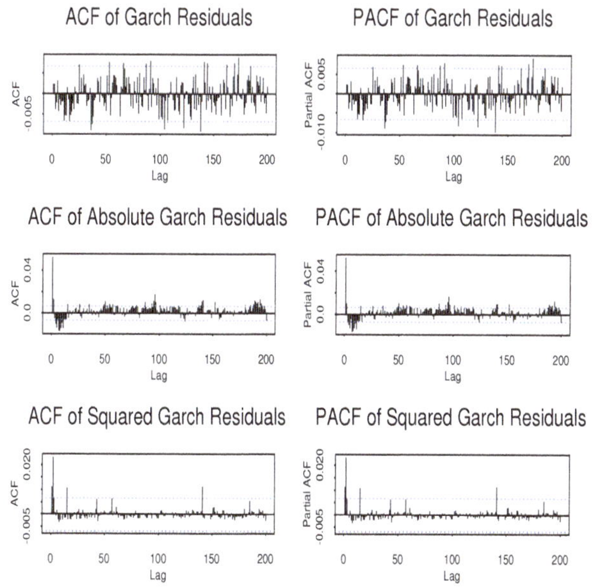

Figure 8. Autocorrelation and partial autocorrelation functions of the residuals, absolute residuals and squared residuals after GARCH fitting.

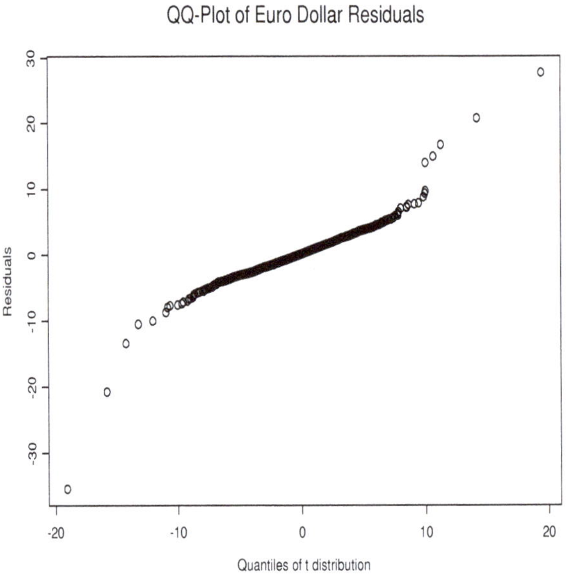

Figure 9. QQ-Plot of GARCH Residuals.

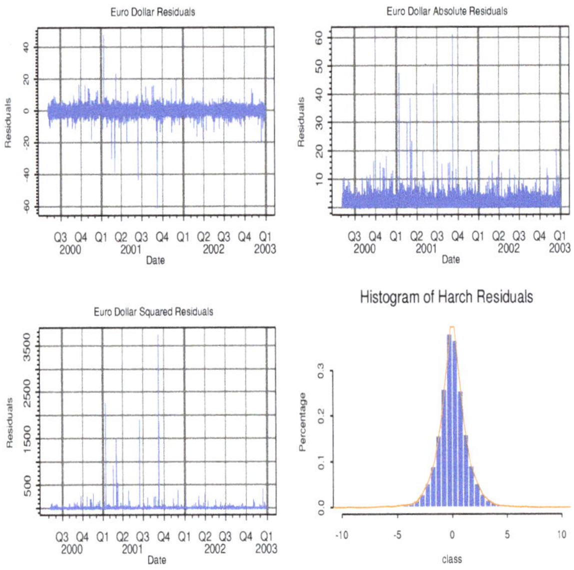

Figure 10. Euro-Dollar residuals, absolute residuals, squared residuals and histogram of the residuals after fitting a PHARCH process.

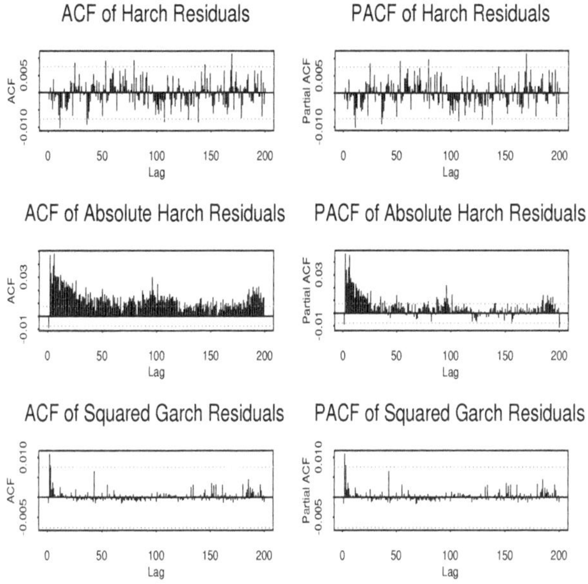

Figure 11. Autocorrelation and partial autocorrelation functions of the residuals, absolute residuals and squared residuals after PHARCH fitting.

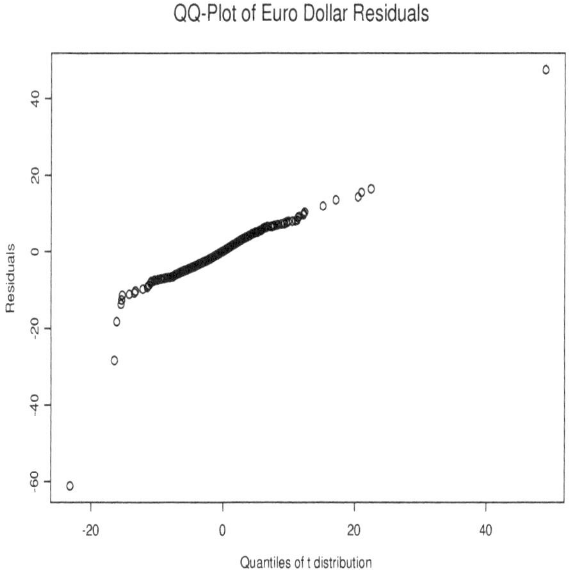

Figure 12. QQ-plot of PHARCH residuals.

6. Conclusions

PHARCH models are good models for the analysis of high frequency data, since the financial market agents behave differently, incorporating heterogeneous information to the market microstructure. Nevertheless, their use still depends on solving some issues, mainly computational ones.

One big challenge in the analysis of high frequency data is dealing with large amounts of observations, and complex models bring computational difficulties, even with the recent technological breakthroughs in computing technology. Therefore, the first issue here is to develop techniques that help us to improve the computational algorithms. Maximum likelihood estimation may collapse, as we have described earlier. Techniques such as genetic algorithms and neural networks are viable optimization alternatives.

Another possibility is to use Bayesian techniques, such as the Griddy-Gibbs samples that we have used. The disadvantage of the Griddy-Gibbs sampler lies in its high computational load. From another viewpoint, more sophisticated volatility models might be developed, taking into account the arrival of information, for example, a stochastic volatility model or stochastic duration model; or we could adapt existing models such as CHARN (conditional heteroskedasticity nonlinear autoregressive) models to heterogeneity of information characteristics. Finally, extensions similar to those proposed to GARCH models could be studied for HARCH models.

A feature of the HARCH models is that the market components are chosen in a subjective way. In the analysis of the Euro-Dollar series, we considered five components, with different aggregations. A different number of components could be proposed, depending of the degree of information one has. This is clearly a matter for further studies.

One last remark is that the performance of the different estimation methods should be evaluated. This evaluation could be done using prediction capabilities, for example. Other possibility is calculating some measure of risk. Volatility models are often established with the purpose of computing the VaR (value at risk) or other risk measure or for establishing trading strategies. In this context, an evaluation of the performance of the proposed model and several estimation procedures should be interesting. A comparison of returns of different trading systems that use a proposed model will be of fundamental importance. Further details on these aspects can be found in Acar and Satchell (2002), Dunis et al. (2003), Ghysels and Jasiak (1994) and Park and Irwin (2005).

Other models for high frequency data use the realized volatility as a basis, instead of models such as ours and models of the ARCH family, which assume that volatility is a letent variable. Among the former, we mention the autoregressive fractionally integrated moving average (ARFIMA) models, the heterogeneous autoregressive model of realized volatilidade (HAR–RV) of Corsi (2009) and the mixed data sampling regression (MIDAS) proposed by Ghysels Santa-Clara and Valkanov (2002). A comparison of the PHARCH models with HAR and MIDAS would be useful, but due to the length of the present paper, this will be the object of future research.

Author Contributions: The authors study some theoretical properties of the PHARCH models and illustrate the theory with an application to real data. All authors have read and agreed to the published version of the manuscript.

Funding: This work was partially funded by Fapesp grant 2013/00506-1.

Conflicts of Interest: The authors declare no conflict of interest.

Appendix A

Proof of Proposition 1. Let X_t following (3) and (5). Assume that the innovations distribution has a non-zero absolutely continuous component, with a positive density on a Borel set with a non-empty interior. Examples of this are the normal and Student's t distribution.

Then X_t can be written as $X_t = H(X_{t-1}, \varepsilon_t)$, where H is a non-linear continuous function for each ε_t fixed. Then, using the *Continuous Mapping Theorem* we obtain the weak convergence of X_t, namely, the conditional distribution X_t given $X_{t-1} = y_k$ converges to the conditional distribution of X_t given $X_{t-1} = y$ if $y_k \to y$. So, the Markov Chain X_t that represents the PHARCH(m,p) process is also a T-chain. □

Proof of Proposition 2. Define the function V as:

$$V\left(X_t\right) := \sum_{i=1}^{a_m-1} \alpha_i r_{t-i}^2 + 2\sum_{i=1}^{a_m-2}\sum_{j=i+1}^{a_m-1} \beta_j r_{t-i} r_{t-j} + \sum_{i=0}^{p-1} \gamma_i \sigma_{t-i}^2.$$

A simple algebraic computation gives

$$\mathbb{E}\left[\sum_{i=1}^{a_m-1} \alpha_i r_{t+1-i}^2 \,|X_t\right] = \alpha_1 \sigma_t^2 + \sum_{i=1}^{a_m-2} \alpha_{i+1} r_{t-i}^2,$$

$$\mathbb{E}\left[2\sum_{i=1}^{a_m-2}\sum_{j=i+1}^{a_m-1} \beta_j r_{t+1-i} r_{t+1-j} \,|X_t\right] = 2\sum_{i=1}^{a_m-3}\sum_{j=i+1}^{a_m-2} \beta_{j+1} r_{t-i} r_{t-j},$$

and using (4) we have,

$$\mathbb{E}\left[\sum_{i=0}^{p-1} \gamma_i \sigma_{t+1-i}^2 \,|X_t\right] = \gamma_0 \left[C_0 + \sum_{i=1}^{m} C_i \left[\sigma_t^2 + \left(\sum_{j=1}^{a_i-1} r_{t-j}\right)^2\right] + \sum_{i=1}^{p} b_i \sigma_{t+1-i}^2\right] + \\ + \sum_{i=1}^{p-1} \gamma_i \sigma_{t+1-i}^2.$$

Therefore, taking $\alpha_{a_m} = \beta_{a_m} = \gamma_p = 0$ and $a_0 = 1$ and grouping we have

$$\begin{aligned} V\left(X_t\right) - \mathbb{E}\left[V\left(X_{t+1}\right)|X_t\right] = &\sum_{k=1}^{m}\sum_{j=a_{k-1}}^{a_k-1} \left(\alpha_j - \alpha_{j+1} - \gamma_0 \sum_{i=k}^{m} C_i\right) r_{t-j}^2 + \\ &+ \sum_{l=1}^{m}\sum_{j=1}^{a_l-2}\sum_{k=a_{l-1}+j}^{a_l-1} \left(\beta_k - \beta_{k+1} - \gamma_0 \sum_{i=l}^{m} C_i\right) r_{t-j} r_{t-k} + \\ &+ \sum_{i=1}^{p-1} \left(\gamma_i - \gamma_{i+1} - \gamma_0 b_{i+1}\right) \sigma_{t-i}^2 + \\ &+ \left(\gamma_0 - \gamma_1 - \gamma_0 b_1 - \alpha_1 - \gamma_0 \sum_{i=1}^{m} C_i\right) \sigma_t^2 - \gamma_0 C_0. \end{aligned}$$

We choose $k \in \mathbb{Z}^+$, $a_{l-1} < k < a_l$, $l \in \{1, \ldots, m\}$, and $\beta_k = \beta_{k+1} + \sum_{i=l}^{m} C_i$.
If we take $\alpha_j > \beta_j$, for all j, then we have $V\left(X_t\right) \geq 0$, and we can take $\gamma_0 = 1$, so

$$\begin{aligned} V(X_t) - \mathbb{E}\left[V\left(X_{t+1}\right)|X_t\right] \;=\; &\sum_{k=1}^{m}\sum_{j=a_{k-1}}^{a_k-1} \left(\alpha_j - \alpha_{j+1} - \sum_{i=k}^{m} C_i\right) r_{t-j}^2 \\ &+ \sum_{i=1}^{p-1} \left(\gamma_i - \gamma_{i+1} - b_{i+1}\right) \sigma_{t-i}^2 \\ &+ \left(1 - \gamma_1 - b_1 - \alpha_1 - \sum_{i=1}^{m} C_i\right) \sigma_t^2 - C_0. \end{aligned} \tag{A1}$$

Similarly, we can choose $k \in \mathbb{Z}^+$, $a_{l-1} < k < a_l$, $l \in \{1, \ldots, m\}$, $\alpha_k > \alpha_{k+1} + \sum_{i=l}^{m} C_i$ and $\gamma_i > \gamma_{i+1} + b_{i+1}$.
If $\sum_{i=1}^{m} a_i C_i + \sum_{i=1}^{p} b_i < 1$, then we have for the expressions in Equation (A1):
$\xi_i = \left(\alpha_i - \alpha_{i+1} - \sum_{j=k}^{m} C_j\right) > 0$, $i = 1, \ldots, a_m - 1$ and k is chosen such that $i \in (a_{k-1}, a_k)$;
$\xi_{a_m-1+i} = \left(\gamma_i - \gamma_{i+1} - b_{i+1}\right) > 0$, $i = 1, \ldots, p-1$; and

$$\xi_{a_m+p-1} = \left(1 - \gamma_1 - b_1 - \alpha_1 - \sum_{i=1}^{m} C_i\right) > 0.$$

So, $V(X_t) - \mathbb{E}\left[V\left(X_{t+1}\right)|X_t\right]$ can be as large as we want if $X_t \in C^c$.

Then, using Lemma 1 we have that there exists an invariant measure, finite on compact sets of Ω. Choosing $\omega_{\min} = \min(\xi_i)$, for $i = 1, \ldots, a_m + p - 1$, we have,

$$V\left(X_t\right) - \mathbb{E}\left[V\left(X_{t+1}\right)|X_t\right] \geq \omega_{\min} \sum_{i=1}^{a_m-1} r_{t-j}^2 + \omega_{\min} \sum_{i=1}^{p} \sigma_{t-i}^2 - C_0$$

$$\geq 1 - \left(C_0 + 1\right) I_{B\left(0, \sqrt{\frac{C_0+1}{\omega_{\min}}}\right)},$$

where $B\left(c, r\right)$ is the ball with center c and radius r.

Therefore, the Markov chain $X_t = \left(r_{t-1}, \ldots, r_{t-a_m+1}, \sigma_t, \ldots, \sigma_{t-p+1}\right)$ that represents the PHARCH(m,p) process is recurrent, with an invariant probability measure (stationary distribution).

Now, if we consider $f\left(x_1, \ldots, x_{a_m+p-1}\right) = x_1^2 + \ldots + x_{a_m+p-1}^2$, then,

$$V\left(X_t\right) - \mathbb{E}\left[V\left(X_{t+1}\right)|X_t\right] \geq \frac{\omega_{\min}}{2} f\left(r_{t-1}, \ldots, r_{t-a_m+1}, \sigma_t, \ldots, \sigma_{t-p+1}\right) +$$
$$+ C_0 1_{B\left(0, \sqrt{\frac{2C_0}{\omega_{\min}}}\right)}.$$

We conclude, using Lemmas 2 and 3, that the process X_t is a T chain having a stationary distribution with finite second order moments. □

References

Acar, Emmanuel, and Stephen Satchell. 2002. *Adavanced Trading Rules*. Oxford: Butterworth Heinemann.

Andersen, Torben G., and Tim Bollerslev. 1998. Answering the skeptics: Yes, standard volatility models do provide accurate forecasts. *International Economic Review* 39: 885–905. [CrossRef]

Bauwens, Luc, and Michel Lubrano. 1998. Bayesian inference on GARCH models using the gibbs sampler. *Econometrics Journal* 1: 23–46. [CrossRef]

Bélisle, Claude J. 1992. Convergence theorems for a class of simulated annealing algorithms on R^d. *Journal of Applied Probability* 29: 885–95. [CrossRef]

Bollerslev, Tim. 1986. Generalized autoregressive conditional heteroskedasticity. *Journal of Econometrics* 31: 307–27. [CrossRef]

Corsi, Fulvio. 2009. A simple approximate long-memory model of realized volatility. *Journal of Financial Econometrics* 7: 174–96 [CrossRef]

Dacorogna, Michel M., Ramazan Gençay, Ulrich Muller, Richard B. Olsen, and Olivier V. Pictet. 2001. *An Introduction to High-Frequency Finance*. Amsterdam: Elsevier.

Dacorogna, Michel M., Ulrich A. Müller, Paul Embrechts, and Gennady Samorodnitsky. 1996. How heavy are the tails of a stationary HARCH(k) process? A study of the moments. In *Stochastic Processes and Related Topics*. Boston: Birkäuser.

Davis, Philip J., and Philip Rabinowitz. 1975. *Methods Of Numerical Integration*. New York: Academic Press.

Dunis, Christian L., Jason Laws, and Patrick Naïm. 2003. *Applied Quantitative Methods For Trading And Investment*. Chichester: John Wiley & Sons Ltd.

Engle, Robert F. 1982. Autoregressive conditional heteroskedasticity with estimates of the variance of u. k. inflation. *Econometrica* 50: 987–1008. [CrossRef]

Geweke, John. 1989. Exact predictive densities in linear models with ARCH disturbances. *Journal of Econometrics* 40: 63–86. [CrossRef]

Geweke, John. 1994. *Bayesian Comparison of Econometric Models*. Technical Report Working Paper 532, Research Department, Federal Reserve Bank of Minneapolis, Minneapolis, MN, USA.

Ghysels, Eric, and Joanna Jasiak. 1994. *Stochastic Volatility and Time Deformation: An Apllication to Trading Volume and Leverage Effects*. Technical report. Santa Fé: Western Finance Association Meeting.

Ghysels, Eric, Pedro Santa-Clara, and Rossen Valkanov. 2002. *The MIDAS Touch: Mixed Data Sampling Regression Models*. Working paper, UNC and UCLA, Chapel Hill, NC, USA.

Kleibergen, Frank, and Herman K. Van Dijk. 1993. Non-stationarity in GARCH models: A bayesian analysis. *Journal of Applied Econometrics* 8 (Suppl. 1): 41–61.

Martens, Martin, Yuan-Chen Chang, and Stephen J. Taylor. 2002. A comparison of seasonal adjustment methods when forecasting intraday volatility. *Journal of Financial Research* 25: 283–99. [CrossRef]

Meyn, Sean P., and Richard L. Tweedie. 1996. *Markov Chains and Stochastic Stability*. Heidelberg: Springer.

Müller, Ulricn, Michel M. Dacorogna, Rakhal D. Davé, Richard B. Olsen, Olivier V. Pictet, and Jacob E. von Weizsäcker. 1997. Volatilities of different time resolutions—Analyzing the dynamics of market components. *Journal of Empirical Finance* 4: 213–89. [CrossRef]

Park, Cheol-Ho, and Scott H. Irwin. 2005. *The Profitability of Technical Trading Rules in US Futures Markets: A Data Snooping Free Test*. Technical report, AgMAS Project Research Report. Urbana-Champaign: University of Illinois.

Ritter, Christian, and Martin A. Tanner. 1992. Facilitating the gibbs sampler: The gibbs stopper and the griddy-gibbs sampler. *Journal of the American Statistical Association* 87: 861–68. [CrossRef]

Ruilova, Juan Carlos. 2007. Modelos Arch Heterogêneos E Aplicações À Análise De Dados De Alta Freqüência. Ph.D. thesis, Institute of Mathematic and Statistics, University of São Paulo, São Paulo, Brazil.

Taylor, Stephen J., and Xinzhong Xu. 1997. The incremental volatility information in one million foreign exchange quotations. *Journal of Empirical Finance* 4: 317–40. [CrossRef]

Zumbach, Gilles. 2000. The pitfalls in fitting GARCH(1,1) processes. In *Advances in Quantitative Asset Management*. Technical report. Boston: Springer.

Journal of
Risk and Financial Management

MDPI

Article

Safe-Haven Assets, Financial Crises, and Macroeconomic Variables: Evidence from the Last Two Decades (2000–2018)

Marco Tronzano

Department of Economics, School of Social Sciences, University of Genoa, Via Vivaldi 5, 16126 Genoa, Italy; m.tronzano@mclink.it or tronzano.marco@gmail.com; Tel.: +39-10-2095226

Received: 14 January 2020; Accepted: 23 February 2020; Published: 28 February 2020

Abstract: This paper focuses on three "safe haven" assets (gold, oil, and the Swiss Franc) and examines the impact of recent financial crises and some macroeconomic variables on their return co-movements during the last two decades. All financial crises produced significant increases in conditional correlations between these asset returns, thus revealing consistent portfolio shifts from more traditional towards safer financial instruments during turbulent periods. The world equity risk premium stands out as the most relevant macroeconomic variable affecting return co-movements, while economic policy uncertainty indicators also exerted significant effects. Overall, this evidence points out that gold, oil, and the Swiss currency played an important role in global investors' portfolio allocation choices, and that these assets preserved their essential "safe haven" properties during the period examined.

Keywords: safe-haven assets; gold price; Swiss Franc exchange rate; oil price

JEL Classification: C22; G15

---

1. Introduction and Motivation

A financial asset is referred to as a "safe haven" asset if it provides hedging benefits during periods of market turbulence. In other words, during periods of market stress, "safe haven" assets are supposed to be uncorrelated, or negatively correlated, with large markets slumps experienced by more traditional financial assets (typically stock or bond prices).

The financial literature identifies various asset classes exhibiting "safe haven" features: gold and other precious metals, the exchange rates of some key international currencies against the US dollar, oil and other important agricultural commodities, and US long-term government bonds.

This paper contributes to the existing literature focusing on some of the most representative "safe haven" assets, namely gold, the Swiss Franc/US dollar exchange rate, and oil. The main motivation behind this choice is twofold.

First, empirical research on these assets have attracted major attention in recent years, both from academia and from institutional investors. Second, there are some weaknesses in the applied literature that need to be addressed.

The hedging properties of gold and its monetary role as a store of value are widely documented. Jaffe (1989) and Chua et al. (1990) find that gold yields significant portfolio diversification benefits. Moreover, the "safe haven" properties of gold in volatile market conditions are widely documented: See, among others, Baur and McDermott (2010), Hood and Malik (2013), Reboredo (2013), and Ciner et al. (2013).

The popular views of gold as a store of value and a "safe haven" asset are well described in Baur and McDermott (2010). As reported by these authors, the 17th Century British Mercantilist Sir William Petty described gold as "*wealth at all times and all places*" (Petty 1690). This popular perception of gold spreads over centuries, reinforced by its historic links to money, and even today gold is described as *"an attractive each way bet"* against risks of financial losses or inflation (Economist 2005, 2009).

Turning to the role of the Swiss Franc as a "safe haven" asset, Ranaldo and Söderlind (2010) documented that the Swiss currency yields substantial hedging benefits against a decrease in US stock prices and an increase in forex volatility. These findings corroborate earlier results (Kugler and Weder 2004; Campbell et al. 2010). More recent research documented that increased risk aversion after the 2008 global financial turmoil strengthened the "safe haven" role of the Swiss currency (Tamakoshi and Hamori 2014).

The oil hedging properties have mostly been underlined in relation to government bonds, since oil price increases are usually related to an increase in expected inflation which, in turn, negatively affects bond prices. Recent research provides strong evidence in this direction, confirming that oil qualifies as a "safe haven" financial instrument against government bonds on most international financial markets (Nguyen and Liu 2017), particularly under distressed market conditions (Ciner et al. 2013).

Although the recent literature made consistent progresses applying various econometric methodologies, there are still some notable shortcomings in existing applied work.

More specifically: (1) The effects of financial crises on time-varying correlations between these assets have rarely been explored, notwithstanding the occurrence of many crises episodes in the latest years; (2) the effects of macroeconomic and financial variables potentially affecting the degree of agents risk-aversion (and hence dynamic correlation patterns) have likewise been seldom addressed.

The former issue is almost completely neglected in recent contributions (e.g., Ding and Vo 2012; Ciner et al. 2013; Creti et al. 2013; Jain and Biswal 2016; Poshakwale and Mandal 2016; Kang et al. 2016, 2017; Nguyen and Liu 2017). Only a small number of papers explore the impact of crises episodes either on dynamic correlations (Tamakoshi and Hamori 2014) or modeling return co-movements through copula theory (Bedoui et al. 2018); these contributions, moreover, focus exclusively on the 2007/2009 global financial crisis.

A similar weakness is apparent with regards to the impact of macroeconomic and financial variables, since the bulk of applied work neglects their potential effects on dynamic correlations. One relevant exception is represented by Poshakwale and Mandal (2016), which documents a significant impact of macroeconomic, non-macroeconomic, and financial variables on "safe haven" assets co-movements.

A better understanding of factors driving time-varying conditional correlations is important both to assess the effective relevance of the hedging properties of "safe haven" assets and from an optimal asset allocation perspective.

Since "safe haven" assets are presumed to offer protection against market slumps, one would expect, during each financial crisis, a massive portfolio shift towards these assets with consequent increases in their return co-movements. As shown in Bedoui et al. (2018), this was actually the case during the 2007/2009 global financial crisis, since the dependence structures among oil, gold, and Swiss Franc returns significantly rose with respect to untroubled periods. However, how robust is this empirical evidence to financial crises occurring after the 2007/2009 turmoil? In other words, do "safe haven" assets consistently display their hedging properties during all financial crises?

Similar questions arise with regards to the influence of economic and financial variables on dynamic correlations. Poshakwale and Mandal (2016) consider three "safe haven" assets (gold, oil, 10-year US government bonds) and document a significant impact of non-macroeconomic variables on their return co-movements. How robust are these results to a change in the bundle of "safe haven" assets? How robust is this empirical evidence to different, and potentially equally relevant, economic and financial variables such as systemic stress indicators, economic policy uncertainty indicators, consumer confidence indicators, or the world equity risk premium? As discussed in Poshakwale and Mandal (2016), the forecasting performance of models explaining asset return co-movements is an important issue in asset allocation problems, and a better knowledge of variables driving correlation patterns is important for international investors and portfolio managers. Asset return co-movements, in other words, have an economic value when implementing dynamic asset allocation strategies (Guidolin and Timmermann 2007).

In light of the above discussion, this paper takes a first step towards a more accurate investigation of dynamic linkages among three important "safe haven" assets. Since the analysis does not include any traditional financial asset, the purpose of this paper is not to assess the hedging properties of gold, oil, and the Swiss franc but, more simply, to explore the underlying determinants of their correlation patterns during the last two decades.

The structure of the paper is as follows. Section 2 describes the data set and provides some descriptive statistics. Section 3 implements a standard econometric approach, i.e. the Multivariate Garch Dynamic Conditional Correlation (DCC) model of Engle (2002), in order to obtain time-varying conditional correlations estimates. On this basis, Section 4 explores the determinants of dynamic linkages among gold, oil, and the Swiss Franc, focusing on the impact of recent financial crises and of some relevant economic variables. Section 5 concludes.

2. Data and Descriptive Statistics

The analysis relies on monthly data from 1999M1 to 2018M10. All data were obtained from Thomson Reuters/Datastream.[1] Gold price is expressed in US Dollars (henceforth USD) and refers to one troy ounce gold bullion. Oil price is expressed in USD and refers to the spot price of Brent Crude Oil per barrel. With regards to the Swiss Franc/USD exchange rate, the Swiss Franc is assumed as the domestic currency (number of Swiss Franc units per one USD unit).

Increases in gold and oil prices correspond to increases in these assets returns, whereas the reverse holds for the Swiss currency. A decrease in the exchange rate corresponds to a Swiss Franc appreciation, thus capturing an increase in Swiss Franc returns.

Figures 1–3 plot the evolution of these series.

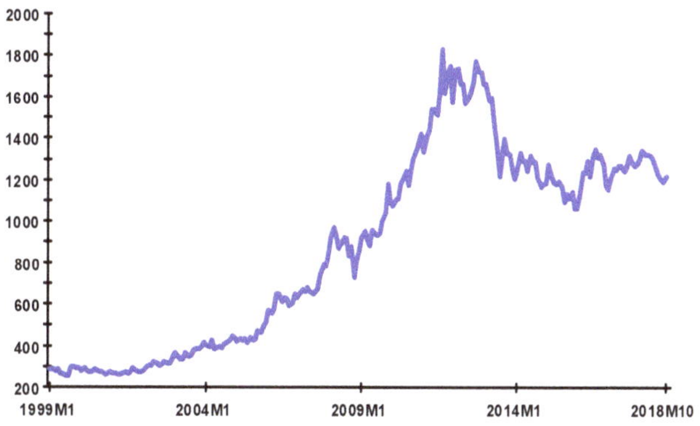

Figure 1. Gold price.

[1] The relevant references and Thomson Reuters codes are the following: Gold: Gold Bullion LBM $/t oz; Thomson Reuters code: GOLDBLN. Oil: Crude Oil-Brent Spot Price; FOB USD/BBL; Thomson Reuters code: EIACRBR. Swiss Franc: Swiss Franc/USD Exchange Rate; End-of-Month Data; Thomson Reuters code: TDCHFSP.

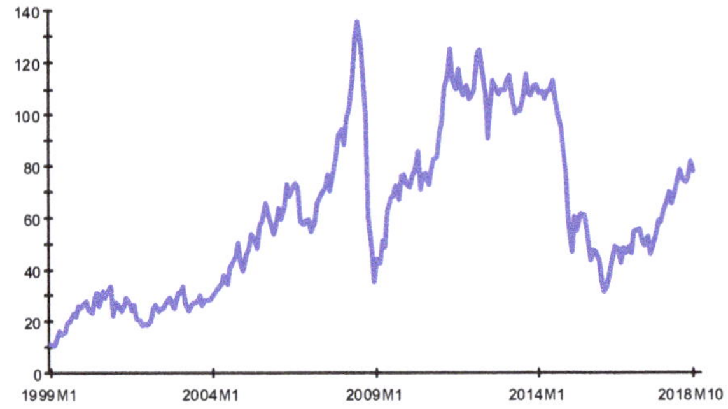

Figure 2. Oil price.

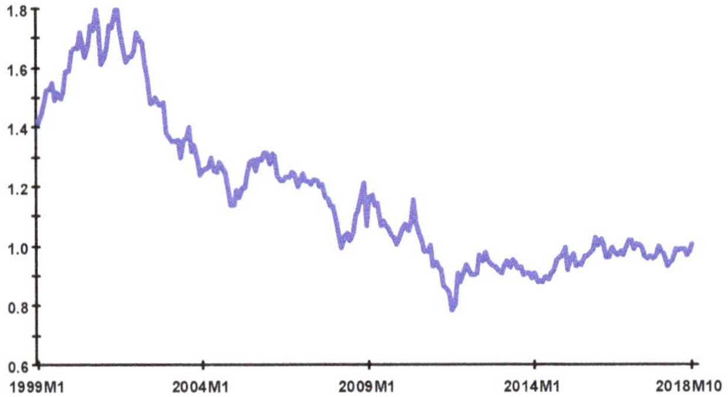

Figure 3. Swiss Franc/USD exchange rate.

The gold price exhibits a strong increasing trend during most of the sample. This trend was suddenly, but only temporarily, interrupted from the second quarter of 2008 to the end of that year. According to the consensus view, although gold market fundamentals remained favorable throughout 2008, this temporary slowdown was caused by an "investors meltdown" during the global financial crisis, which induced a massive selling of all assets (including gold and silver) by highly leveraged investors in order to cover losses in other markets. From early 2009 to November 2011 (when a record peak was reached), gold price replicated a steady and even faster increasing trend, apparently displaying its "safe haven" property during most of the Eurozone debt crisis. After a prolonged downturn in 2013, usually attributed to concomitant causes (China's weak gold demand, Cyprus Central Bank gold sales, massive ETF's sales, and bearish gold reports by major investment banks), the gold price stabilized in subsequent years oscillating around a stable trading range.

Focusing on the oil price (Figure 2), a similar increasing trend characterized the first part of the sample (1999–2008), with this series reaching an all-time-high in June 2008. The main cause was a persistent excess demand for oil induced by unprecedented growth rates in newly industrialized countries. An impressive decline occurred since the second half of 2008, with the oil price plummeting at historically low values in December 2008. This tendency was again almost entirely demand-driven, given the sharp oil demand contraction associated with the world global recession. A price rebound characterized the 2009–2012 period, with oil price increases mostly conditioned by unexpected recovery growth prospects in the earlier phase, a progressive tightening of oil supply, and other exogenous factors in 2011 (Arab spring, Libyan civil war). After an erratic lateral phase from 2013 to the first half of 2014, a further relevant downswing until end 2015 is apparent, as a consequence of a mix of supply (increased oil production) and demand factors (slower growth in major emerging market economies). A new steady oil price increase characterized the last part of the sample (2016–2018). A series of concomitant factors contributed to this process: stronger than expected economic growth, a curb in oil production, geopolitical events, and a persistent decline in inventories due to a precautionary increase in oil demand.

The Swiss Franc exchange rate (Figure 3) exhibited a lower variability. Moreover, differently from gold and oil prices, this series was characterized by two distinct long-run trends.

The former corresponds to a long-run appreciation against the USD, which, albeit with frequent short-run fluctuations, lasted for more than one decade. Starting from a peak value in October 2000, the exchange rate reached an all-time low in July 2011, generating an overall Swiss Franc appreciation of more than 50%. The final phase of this trend roughly corresponded to the global and the Eurozone debt crisis, during which the Swiss currency confirmed its role as a major "safe haven" asset. The massive Swiss Franc appreciation during this last phase forced domestic authorities to implement large expansionary unconventional monetary policy measures in order to counteract widespread deflationary pressures (Jäggi et al. 2019). The latter long-run trend corresponded to the final part of the sample (2012–2018), during which the Swiss Franc fluctuated around a 1:1 parity against the USD. This narrow trading range may be ascribed to the absence of significant shocks on the forex market, and to a temporary exchange rate floor for the Swiss currency introduced from September 2011 to December 2014.

The analysis of the next section relies on monthly returns, computed taking the first differences of the series expressed in natural logs. Standard unit root tests show that the log-levels of these series are not stationary, whereas their log-first differences are stationary. Table 1 contains some descriptive statistics on these asset returns.

Table 1. Descriptive statistics for asset returns.

Statistics	Gold	Oil	Swiss Franc
Mean	0.0061	0.0082	−0.0014
Standard Deviation	0.0479	0.1073	0.0300
Skewness	−0.1237	−0.8253	−0.2147
Excess Kurtosis	1.043	2.635	1.820
Jarque-Bera	11.35 ***	95.49 ***	34.55 ***
ARCH (1)	4.36 **	8.63 ***	6.81 ***
ARCH (2)	5.48 *	16.58 ***	7.28 **
Ljung-Box (1)	2.60	0.069	2.20
Ljung-Box (6)	5.45	2.79	7.74
Ljung-Box (12)	13.52	11.02	16.79

Jarque-Bera: Jarque and Bera (1980) test for the null hypothesis of normality. ARCH: ARCH test for the null hypothesis of homoscedasticity. Ljung-Box: Ljung-Box portmanteau test for the null hypothesis of absence of serial correlation. ***: Significant at a 1% level; **: Significant at a 5% level; *: Significant at a 10% level.

All mean returns were extremely small and not statistically different from zero. This result is consistent with a large body of empirical evidence according to which financial time series evolve like driftless random walks.

All returns displayed a high variability, as documented by standard deviations that were relatively larger than those usually recorded in the literature (see e.g., (Ciner et al. 2013) for gold and oil, and (Tamakoshi and Hamori 2014) for the Swiss Franc). This suggests that more recent financial crises played a not-negligible role in fostering assets returns variability.

All returns exhibited negative skewness, i.e., they are more likely to be far below than far above the mean, in line with an empirical regularity characterizing financial variables. Moreover, all returns displayed positive excess kurtosis, pointing out heavier tails relative to the normal distribution. This is again a typical feature of financial time series, usually displaying a higher probability of extreme outcomes. In line with the above results, the Jarque and Bera (1980) statistics strongly rejects the null of normality for all returns distributions.

ARCH tests at lags (1) and (2) always reject the null of homoscedasticity, implying that a multivariate GARCH specification is an appropriate framework to model conditional volatility. Finally, the Ljung–Box test at various lag orders (1, 6, 12) supported the absence of serial correlation. This result may be ascribed to the monthly frequency used in this paper instead of higher data frequencies usually employed in the literature. The monthly frequency is motivated by one main purpose of the present paper, i.e., the search for potential macroeconomic determinants of time-varying correlations.

Table 2 contains the (static) pair-wise correlations between assets returns.

Table 2. Correlation matrix of asset returns.

Assets	Gold	Oil	Swiss Franc
Gold	1.000		
Oil	0.157	1.000	
Swiss Franc	−0.412	−0.031	1.000

All correlation coefficients were significant at the 5% level according to the Pesaran and Timmermann (1992) nonparametric test. The highest coefficient amounted to −0.412, pointing out a positive correlation between gold and Swiss Franc returns (remember that a decrease in the Swiss/USD Dollar exchange rate corresponds to an increase in Swiss Franc returns). The lowest coefficient was −0.031, pointing out a weak positive association between oil and Swiss Franc returns. Finally, a positive correlation (0.157) between gold and oil returns is shown in Table 2. Overall, therefore, this evidence documents a positive correlation between all assets returns.

The plot of asset returns (not reported in order to save space but available upon request) revealed that the significant ARCH effects documented in Table 1 are, to a large extent, driven by the financial crises of the last two decades. Significant volatility increases characterized the central part of the sample (2008–2011), broadly corresponding to the global financial crisis and to the Eurozone debt crisis.

3. A Multivariate Garch Model of Asset Returns

This section employs a well-known approach belonging to the class of Multivariate Garch estimators, namely Engle (2002) Dynamic Conditional Correlation model, in order to compute time-varying conditional correlations between asset returns. The first sub-section provides a short outline of this econometric framework. The latter sub-section presents parameters estimates and analyzes pair-wise correlation patterns between asset returns.

3.1. Engle (2002) Dynamic Conditional Correlation Model

Let $r_t = (r_{1t}, \ldots, r_{nt})$ represent a $(n \times 1)$ vector of financial assets returns at time (t). Moreover, let $\varepsilon_t = (\varepsilon_{1t}, \ldots, \varepsilon_{nt})$ be a $(n \times 1)$ vector of error terms obtained from an estimated system of mean equations for these return series.

Engle (2002) proposes the following decomposition for the conditional variance-covariance matrix of asset returns:

$$H_t = D_t R_t D_t \tag{1}$$

where D_t is a $(n \times n)$ diagonal matrix of time-varying standard deviations from univariate Garch models, and R_t is a $(n \times n)$ time-varying correlation matrix of asset returns $(\rho_{ij,\,t})$.

The conditional variance-covariance matrix (H_t) displayed in equation [1] is estimated in two steps. In the first step, univariate Garch (1,1) models are applied to mean returns equations, thus obtaining conditional variance estimates for each financial asset ($\sigma^2{}_{it}$; for $i = 1, 2, \ldots\ldots, n$), namely:

$$\sigma^2{}_{it} = \sigma^2{}_{Uit}\,(1 - \lambda_{1i} - \lambda_{2i}) + \lambda_{1i}\,\sigma^2{}_{i,t-1} + \lambda_{2i}\,\varepsilon^2{}_{i,\,t-1} \tag{2}$$

where $\sigma^2{}_{Uit}$ is the unconditional variance of the ith asset return, λ_{1i} is the volatility persistence parameter, and λ_{2i} is the parameter capturing the influence of past errors on the conditional variance.

In the second step, the residuals vector obtained from the mean equations system (ε_t) is divided by the corresponding estimated standard deviations, thus obtaining standardized residuals (i.e., $u_{it} = \varepsilon_{it}/\sqrt{\sigma^2_{i,t}}$ for i = 1, 2, ..., n), which are subsequently used to estimate the parameters governing the time-varying correlation matrix.

More specifically, the dynamic conditional correlation matrix of asset returns may be expressed as:

$$Q_t = (1 - \delta_1 - \delta_2)\,\overline{Q} + \delta_1 Q_{t-1} + \delta_2\left(u_{t-1}\, u'_{t-1}\right) \quad (3)$$

where $\overline{Q}$ = E [$u_t\, u'_t$] is the ($n \times n$) unconditional covariance matrix of standardized residuals, and δ_1 and δ_2 are parameters (capturing, respectively, the persistence in correlation dynamics and the impact of past shocks on current conditional correlations).[2]

3.2. Model Estimation and Dynamic Conditional Correlation Patterns

The econometric framework summarized by Equations (1)–(3) was applied to gold, oil, and exchange rate returns.

After a preliminary data inspection, and in line with many contributions relying on this approach (see e.g., Ding and Vo (2012) and Jain and Biswal (2016) with regards to "safe haven" assets), a VAR(1) specification was selected to model the mean returns equation system. Alternative filtering procedures (such as an AR(1) specification for return series) produced substantially identical results.

The VAR(1) specification was selected on the basis of the Akaike Information Criterion (AIC) and of Likelihood Ratio tests against higher-order VAR models. Diagnostic tests on residuals from the VAR(1) specification never rejected the null of absence of serial correlation, while rejecting the normality assumption. This rejection was consistent with the preliminary data analysis, where the Jarque and Bera (1980) statistics turned out to be strongly significant.

These departures from normality have relevant implications on the distributional assumptions underlying the Multivariate Garch DCC model. More specifically, instead of relying on the standard Gaussian assumption (as in Engle (2002) seminal model), it is advisable to assume a Multivariate t-distribution in order to better capture the fat-tailed nature of asset returns. This is the approach taken in the present paper.[3]

With regards to parameters, conditional volatility coefficients were unrestricted, and assumed different for each asset (see Equation (2)). Conditional correlation coefficients were unrestricted as well, although a common correlation structure was imposed in model's estimation (see Equation (3)).

The Maximum Likelihood estimator converged after 48 iterations and relied on 216 observations (20 observations were used to initialize the recursions).

Table 3 contains the results.

---

2 This multivariate Garch DCC model does not consider cross influences from other related dependent variables in the conditional variance and co-variance equations. As suggested by an anonymous referee, this is a shortcoming of this econometric approach, particularly if high co-movements exist among financial assets. The concluding section outlines other potential extensions of this econometric framework related to the present empirical investigation.

3 Note that Engle's original two-step procedure is no longer applicable under this alternative distributional assumption, and the Maximum Likelihood approach relies on a more efficient algorithm involving a simultaneous estimation of all model's parameters and an additional degrees of freedom parameter referring to the Multivariate Student distribution.

Table 3. Multivariate Garch (1,1)-Dynamic Conditional Correlation (DCC) Model. Sample: 2000m11–2018m10 (216 Observations).

Parameters	Estimate	Standard Error	T-Ratio [Prob.]
λ_{1G}	0.653 ***	0.178	3.66 [0.000]
λ_{1O}	0.699 ***	0.131	5.30 [0.000]
λ_{1S}	0.799 ***	0.139	5.73 [0.000]
λ_{2G}	0.138 **	0.062	2.20 [0.028]
λ_{2O}	0.207 ***	0.077	2.67 [0.008]
λ_{2S}	0.108 **	0.054	1.99 [0.0048]
δ_1	0.978 ***	0.016	57.8 [0.000]
δ_2	0.014 **	0.006	2.16 [0.032]
df	7.423 ***	1.643	4.51 [0.000]
	Maximized Log-Likelihood: 1040.8		

***: Significant at a 1% level; **: Significant at a 5% level. λ_{1i}, λ_{2i}: Volatility parameters (assumed different for each asset) from univariate Garch equations: See Equations (2). δ_1, δ_2: Correlation parameters (assumed equal for all asset returns): See Equation (3). df: Degrees of freedom parameter for the multivariate t-distribution.

All parameters were statistically significant, in most cases at the 1% significance level. Garch (1,1) parameters for conditional variances were always positive; moreover, their sums ($\lambda_{1i} + \lambda_{2i}$) were relatively close to 1, particularly in the case of exchange rate returns (0.907) and oil returns (0.906). These results document the existence of stable time-varying volatility processes for all asset returns, although conditional volatilities displayed a high degree of persistence, particularly in the case of oil and Swiss Franc returns.

Turning to DCC parameters, in line with univariate Garch results, the common correlation structure displays a high degree of persistence. This correlation structure appeared mostly driven by lagged correlation dynamics ($\delta_1 = 0.978$). However, the positive and statistically significant estimate for δ_2 points out that also past shocks impart an appreciable effect on the time-varying correlation pattern of asset returns. The estimated degrees of freedom parameter (df = 7.42) suggests that a multivariate t distribution is appropriate to capture the not normal nature of assets returns.

Overall, these results imply that the proposed model represents an accurate description of the data generating process for filtered return series, and a reliable econometric framework to explore the nature of their pair-wise dynamic correlations.[4]

A major advantage of Multivariate Garch DCC models is to provide a straightforward framework to extract dynamic correlations for multiple assets inside a parsimonious parameter set up.

Figure 4 illustrates the estimated correlation coefficients between gold, oil, and Swiss Franc returns.

[4] Further support to this model comes from a conditional evaluation procedure based on probability integral transform estimates. Under the null hypothesis of correct model specification, these estimates are serially uncorrelated and uniformly distributed in the (0, 1) range. A Lagrange Multiplier test for serial correlation, and a Kolmogorov-Smirnov test for uniform distribution of probability transform estimates show that this is actually the case, thus supporting the validity of the estimated model (further details available on request).

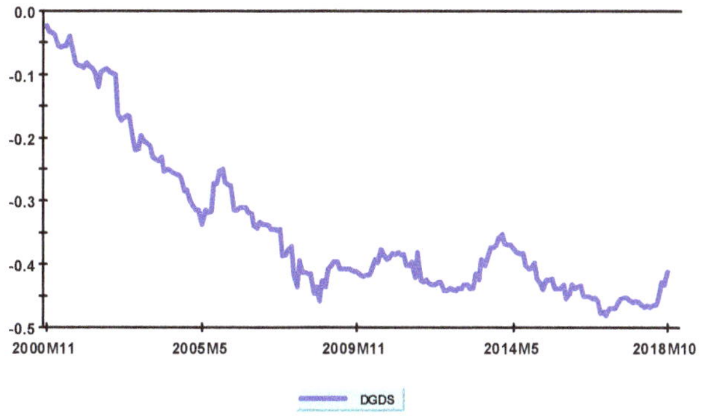

(**a**): Conditional correlation between Gold and Swiss Franc returns

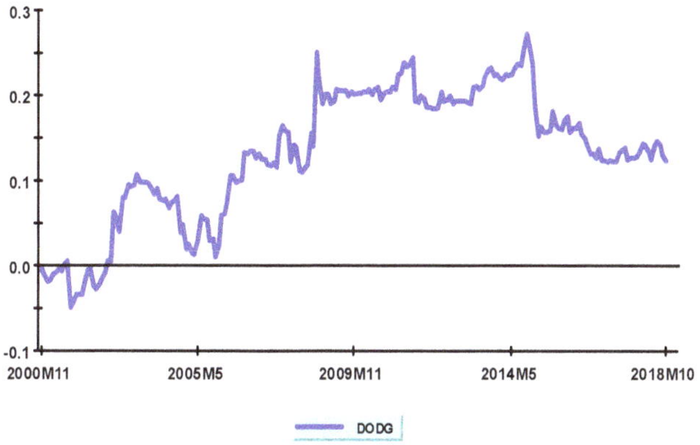

(**b**): Conditional correlation between Oil and Gold returns

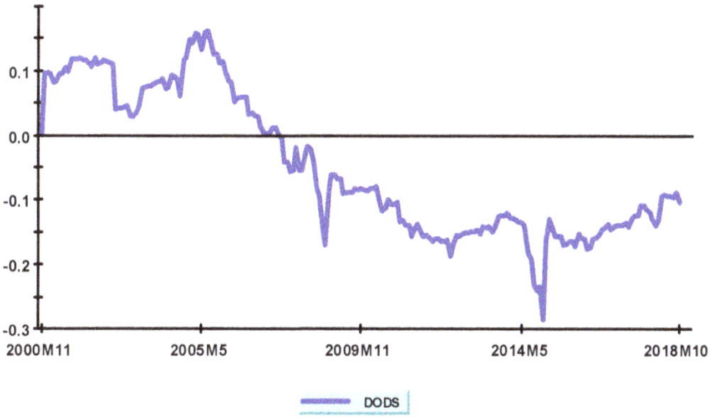

(**c**): Conditional correlation between Oil and Swiss Franc returns

Figure 4. Pair-wise dynamic conditional correlations.

Visual inspection of Figure 4 yields some interesting insights.[5] One relevant feature is that all pair-wise correlations exhibited an increasing long-run trend. This trend was stronger in the DG/DS case (starting from values around zero and reaching values around −0.4 at the end of the sample); on the other hand, this trend was relatively less intense for DO/DS and DO/DG correlations (both starting from values around zero and reaching, respectively, maximum values of −0.3 and + 0.3 during the second half of 2014).

The estimated model therefore documented a significant tendency for these "safe haven" assets to increase their return co-movements during the last two decades.

A further interesting finding is related to the short-run dynamics of time-varying correlations. The analysis included many episodes of financial crisis, both at a global or continental level, and involving single countries. Starting with the well-known global financial crisis (2007–2009) and Eurozone debt crisis (2010–2012), this period includes many other relevant episodes of financial turmoil. These further episodes comprise: The Russian financial crisis (2014–2015), driven by the sharp oil price fall in 2014, and resulting in a large Russian Ruble devaluation and a huge stock market decline; the Chinese stock market crisis (2015) caused by the burst of a domestic stock market bubble in June 2015; and the Turkish currency and debt crisis (2018), mostly generated by an excessive current account deficit, and leading to large devaluation waves of the domestic currency.

In this perspective, a closer look at Figure 4 reveals that, for all conditional correlation pairs, the tendency towards stronger assets return co-movements were notably higher during all these financial crises episodes.

Consider, for instance, the DG-DS plot (Figure 4, upper section (a)). A strong increase in the conditional correlation between gold and Swiss Franc returns was apparent during the period corresponding to the global financial crisis (2007M8–2009M5), when this variable reached a relative minimum in August 2008. After a partial recovery in subsequent months, this correlation again followed a clear downward trend (thus capturing an increase in gold/Swiss Franc returns correlation) during most of the period corresponding to the Eurozone debt crisis (2010M1–2012M6). This movement was subsequently reversed during the tranquil phase corresponding to the year 2014, whereas the Russian financial crisis (2014M2–2015M2) and the Chinese stock market crisis (2015M6–2015M10) were once again associated with strong increases in conditional correlations, as documented by the low negative values reached in 2015.

The remaining correlations (DO-DG; DO-DS) displayed similar short-run patterns, since all major spikes in these variables were systematically associated with financial crises episodes.

On the whole, this visual evidence is consistent with a basic feature characterizing "safe haven" assets, that is to provide hedging benefits in periods of market turbulence. The increased return co-movements can be interpreted in terms of global portfolio shifts from traditional asset classes towards safer financial instruments in times of particular market stress. Since these portfolio shifts simultaneously increase the demand for "safe haven" assets, this tends to increase their returns correlations during crisis episodes.

To sum up, the Multivariate Garch model estimated in this section conveys two main results:

1. The last two decades witnessed a long-run trend of increased returns correlations between major "safe haven" assets;

---

[5] With reference to Figure 4: DG-DS indicates pair-wise correlations between gold and Swiss Franc returns; DO-DS indicates pair-wise correlations between oil and Swiss Franc returns; DO-DG indicates pair-wise correlations between oil and gold returns. In order to properly interpret these plots, it must be remembered that a decrease in the Swiss Franc/USD exchange rate level corresponds to a Swiss Franc appreciation, thus generating an increase in Swiss Franc returns (see Section 2). For this reason, negative values for pair-wise correlations involving Swiss Franc returns (i.e., negative values for DO/DS and DG-DS) correspond to positive correlations between these asset returns.

2. Focusing on periods of market stress, the "safe haven" properties of these assets consistently materialized, both during global or international financial crises episodes, and during "local" financial turmoil limited to single countries.

Drawing on this evidence, the next section explores the determinants of these time-varying conditional correlations, analyzing both the influence of various financial crises episodes and that of some potentially relevant macroeconomic variables.

4. Determinants of Dynamic Conditional Correlations

This section investigates some factors potentially affecting the evolution of conditional correlations among "safe haven" assets. The analysis proceeds in two steps. First, it provides some quantitative estimates about the impact of specific crises episodes. Second, it explores to what extent dynamic conditional correlations were significantly affected by some key macroeconomic variables related to the degree of international investors' confidence.

4.1. Dynamic Conditional Correlations and Financial Crises

The impact of financial turmoil on time-varying conditional correlations is explored in various contributions. The bulk of these analyses, however, concentrates on currency and stock markets, whereas "safe haven" financial assets have rarely been investigated.

The evidence from foreign exchange markets usually points out a significant effect for all crisis episodes. Tamakoshi and Hamori (2014) explored the time-varying linkages among some outstanding exchange rates against the USD. They reported a significant impact of the global financial crisis and of the Eurozone debt crisis on most, although not all, conditional correlations. A more homogenous empirical evidence was obtained in Karfakis and Panagiotidis (2015) where the Greek debt crisis emerged as the most significant covariate in quantile regressions involving all pair-wise exchange rates correlations.

The empirical evidence is more variegated in the case of stock markets. Syllignakis and Kouretas (2011) documented a significant effect of the 2008 stock market crash for seven stock markets of Central and Eastern European countries, whereas no significant effects were detected for previous crisis episodes (Asian financial crisis, dot-com bubble). Focusing on conditional correlation between BRICS stock markets and oil/gold future prices, Kang et al. (2016) reported a relevant effect of the dot-com bubble, a non-significant effect of the global financial crisis, and a slightly significant effect of the Eurozone sovereign debt crisis.

Bedoui et al. (2018) is the only recent contribution analyzing "safe haven" financial assets. These authors proposed nested copula based Garch models to study conditional dependence structures and, in line with the visual evidence discussed in the previous section, documented significant increases in asset co-movements both during the 2007/2009 global financial crisis and in the subsequent "post crisis" period. A drawback of this paper is that the period subsequent to the global financial crisis was treated as a unified time frame, thus disregarding the impact of latest financial turmoil.

This section contributes to the literature providing a more detailed information about the impact of all financial crises occurring over the last two decades on time-varying correlations.

In line with most applied research, the analysis relies on a regression approach with crises dummies for each financial turmoil episode (see, e.g., Syllignakis and Kouretas 2011; Tamakoshi and Hamori 2014; Kang et al. 2016).

More formally, denoting the time-varying returns correlation between asset (i) and asset (j) at time t with $\rho_{ij,\,t}$, the following regression equation is estimated for each pair-wise conditional correlation:

$$\rho_{ij,t} = \varpi + \sum_{k=1}^{n} \gamma_k \, Dum_{k,t} + \varepsilon_{ij,t} \tag{4}$$

where ϖ and γ_k are parameters, $Dum_{k,t}$ is a dummy variable referring to a specific financial crisis episode, and $\varepsilon_{ij,\,t}$ is a disturbance term.

Since the estimation period includes five financial crises episodes, the k index goes from to one to five in equation [4].[6]

The dummy variables included in equation [4] are defined as follows:

- Dum1: Global Financial Crisis (1 from 2007M8 to 2009M5; 0 elsewhere);
- Dum2: Eurozone Debt Crisis (1 from 2010M1 to 2012M6; 0 elsewhere);
- Dum3: Russian Financial Crisis (1 from 2014M12 to 2015M2; 0 elsewhere);
- Dum4: Chinese Stock Market Crisis (1 from 2015M6 to 2015M10; 0 elsewhere);
- Dum5: Turkish Financial Crisis (1 from 2018M3 to 2018M8; 0 elsewhere).

These dummy variables alternate between 1 and 0 depending on the existence of "crises" and "non-crises" periods. The selection of crises periods relies on various references from the literature, and on the main events characterizing the beginning and the end of financial turmoil episodes.

With regards to the global financial crisis, August 2007 is usually regarded as its starting date (see, among others, Casarin et al. 2018), due to the first signs of trouble in the US housing market, the French bank BNL Paribas suspension of three funds investing in the US mortgage market, and the FOMC first reduction in the Fed funds rate in response to liquidity and confidence problems. The end is usually placed towards the end of the first half of 2009 (Bordo and Landon-Lane 2010), and the selection of May 2009 reflects a full stabilization of the LIBOR-OIS spread as documented in Bernanke et al. (2018).[7]

The dummy for the Eurozone debt crisis reflects the observed spreads between 10-year sovereign bond yields of European countries (France, Greece, Ireland, Italy, Portugal, Spain) against Germany. As documented in Lane (2012) (see ibid. Figure 2), significant increases in these spreads were apparent since January 2010 (thus signaling the beginning of speculative attacks on European public debts), while these tendencies disappeared at mid-2012.

The remaining financial crises displayed a shorter length.

The Russian crisis, driven by economic sanctions for the military intervention in Ukraine and sharp oil price declines in the second half of 2014, displayed its major effects on international financial markets between December 2014 and February 2015. This period was characterized by a sharp Ruble devaluation against major currencies, huge rises in domestic interest rates, large foreign reserves declines, and an all-time-low in the domestic stock price index.

The Chinese stock market crisis began in June 2015 with the burst of the domestic stock price bubble, which determined a Shangai Composite Index increase of about 150% from mid-2014 to mid-2015. This stock market crash displayed all the main features of classical financial crises described in Kindleberger (1978): irrational exuberance of investors causing share prices to progressively diverge from values consistent with market fundamentals, large presence of novice investors making highly leveraged purchases with borrowed money, and loose financial regulations (a progressive relaxation of restrictions on margin trading occurred over the preceding five years). In line with the consensus view, the end of this crisis was set at October 2015, when the Shangai Composite Index oscillated around minimum values, before exhibiting a mild recovery in subsequent months (see, Zeng et al. 2016, Figure 1, p. 413).

The Turkish financial crisis was essentially a currency and balance of payment crisis, caused by Turkey's excessive current account deficit and the large share of foreign currency denominated external

---

[6] The estimation period for Equation (4) ranges from 2000M11 to 2018M10. The dot-com financial crisis is not included since, according to the bubble monitoring approach outlined in Phillips and Shi (2018), this financial crisis originated in 1995M8 and ended in 2000M11.

[7] This document is a chart book about the global financial crisis produced under the supervision of Ben Bernanke, Timothy Geithner and Henry Paulson. It identifies three distinct phases of this crisis: increasing stress, early escalation, panic and resolution. Overall, the starting and ending dates indicated in the document (see ibid. page 17) match those corresponding to the dummy variable (Dum1) used in the present paper.

debt. This crisis manifested predominantly with large devaluation waves of the domestic currency, prompted both by Turkey's structural economic imbalances and by President Erdogan's unorthodox interest rate policy. Accordingly, the starting date was set in March 2018 (first devaluation pressures on foreign exchange markets), and the ending date was set in August 2018 (record devaluation level of the Turkish Lira against the USD).

Each financial crisis episode was expected to significantly contribute, on average, to increase conditional dependencies between "safe haven" asset returns.

The economic intuition is the following. A typical feature of "safe haven" assets is to protect investors' portfolios, particularly during financial turmoil episodes when more traditional asset classes experience severe losses due to highly negative developments in the macroeconomic and financial outlook. Therefore, during a financial crisis, when traditional asset classes are negatively affected by sequences of "bad news", massive portfolio shifts towards alternative financial instruments simultaneously pull up their prices and, hence, time-varying correlations between these asset returns. An analogous mechanism may operate in the reverse direction, again generating an increase in "safe haven" assets returns correlations.[8]

To sum up, economic intuition suggests that, although each "safe haven" asset reflects specific economic influences, return co-movements between these financial instruments may be expected to rise, on average, during financial crises episodes. The evidence reported in Bedoui et al. (2018) for the global financial crisis supports the above intuition.

Equation (4) is estimated for each pair-wise conditional correlation involving gold, oil, and Swiss Franc returns. Table 4 summarizes the empirical evidence. These results were obtained applying the Newey and West (1987) consistent covariance matrix estimator, thus making parameters estimates robust to the existence of autocorrelation and heteroscedasticity in regression residuals.

Table 4. Dynamic conditional correlations and financial crises. Sample: 2000m11–2018m10 (216 Observations).

Parameters	DGDS	DODG	DODS
ω	−0.31 ***	0.11 ***	−0.019
	(−8.47)	(5.05)	(−0.59)
γ_1	−0.098 ***	0.052 **	−0.041
	(−2.59)	(2.04)	(−1.21)
γ_2	−0.097 ***	0.096 ***	−0.113 ***
	(−2.62)	(4.22)	(−3.21)
γ_3	−0.107 ***	0.081 ***	−0.173 ***
	(−2.92)	(3.65)	(−4.94)
γ_4	−0.123 ***	0.055 **	−0.144 ***
	(−3.36)	(2.54)	(−4.43)
γ_5	−0.147 ***	0.028	−0.080 **
	(−4.05)	(1.32)	(−2.48)
R^2	0.16	0.21	0.19

Estimated equation: $\rho_{ij,\,t} = \omega + \sum_{k=1}^{n} \gamma_k\, Dum_{\,k,t} + \varepsilon_{ij,\,t}$. γ_1: Parameter relative to the effect of Global Financial Crisis; γ_2: Parameter relative to the effect of Eurozone Debt Crisis; γ_3: Parameter relative to the effect of Russian Financial Crisis; γ_4: Parameter relative to the effect of Chinese Stock Market Crisis; γ_5: Parameter relative to the effect of Turkish Financial Crisis. OLS estimation; Newey and West (1987) heteroscedasticity, and autocorrelation consistent estimates of the variance-covariance matrix of parameters. t-statistic in parentheses below estimated parameters values. ***: Significant at a 1% level; **: Significant at a 5% level.

In order to properly interpret the results, it must be remembered that in the case of DODG (oil–gold returns correlation) positive estimates of γ_k parameters point out a positive effect of financial crises

[8] During a financial crisis, a temporary sequence of "good news" may generate a reverse portfolio shift producing a temporary recovery in more traditional asset classes. In this case, massive flows of liquidity out of "safe haven" assets produce a simultaneous decrease in "safe haven" assets returns and hence, once again, an increase in their conditional correlations.

on time-varying correlations. The reverse holds in the remaining cases (DGDS, DODS): Negative γ_k estimates now point out positive effects of financial crises, given the definition of Swiss Franc returns.

The results of Table 4 confirm those obtained in Bedoui et al. (2018) for the 2007–2009 global financial crisis and are fully in line with economic intuition.

The significant increase in conditional correlations between "safe haven" assets during financial crises stands out as an important empirical regularity of the last two decades. As documented in Table 4, this regularity holds for all pair-wise correlations and all crises periods.

Although the R^2 values for estimated equations were not particularly high, the explicative power of Equation (4) was satisfactory, taking into account the nature of dependent variables and the absence of specific economic or financial variables on the right-hand side of this equation.

Focusing on Equation (4) in more detail, all estimated coefficients were statistically significant, in most cases at a 1% confidence level. All coefficients, moreover, had correct expected signs (negative for pair-wise correlations involving exchange rate returns, and positive for DODG), pointing out the significant impact of each financial crisis on the increase in conditional correlations.

The quantitative influence of various crises episodes was quite homogeneous with regards to DGDS and DODG. In these cases, the estimated γ_k coefficients were broadly similar for the two most relevant financial crises (global financial crisis, Eurozone debt crisis) and subsequent crises episodes. A greater impact of latest crises episodes, and in particular of the Russian financial crisis, was instead documented for DODS.[9]

To sum up, the empirical evidence of this section points out that gold, oil, and the Swiss Franc maintained their "safe haven" properties over the last two decades. All pair-wise correlations were significantly affected both by long-lasting and acute crises episodes and by shorter and relatively less intense financial turmoil.

Notwithstanding the significant impact of various crises episodes, hedging opportunities among alternative "safe haven" assets were still present, according to this empirical investigation.

Empirical estimates of Section 3 document that the gold–Swiss Franc correlation increased from about 0 to 0.5 during the sample period, whereas the remaining correlations never exceeded 0.3 (see Figure 4). These financial assets therefore remain de-correlated to a large extent, notwithstanding the contrarian influence exerted by various crises episodes. Therefore, for smart international investors, significant hedging opportunities persist, not only between "safe haven" and more traditional financial assets, but also with reference to the optimal portfolio allocation among alternative "safe haven" assets.

4.2. Dynamic Conditional Correlations and Macroeconomic Variables

Various contributions explore the influence of macroeconomic and financial variables on time-varying conditional correlations.

With regards to international stock markets, Cai et al. (2009) documented a significant influence of cyclical fluctuations in inflation rates and stock volatility on asset correlations of major advanced countries, while Syllignakis and Kouretas (2011) provided analogous evidence for Central and Eastern European economies. A significant influence of economic and financial variables was documented for many other financial markets (see, e.g., (Bashiri Behmiri et al. 2019) with regards to commodity futures markets).

Focusing on conditional dependencies among "safe haven" financial assets, however, existing contributions are much scarcer. Bedoui et al. (2018) reported, in line with the evidence of the present paper, that oil and gold conditional correlation increased during the global financial crisis. These

[9] The large γ_3 estimate obtained in this case is mainly explained by the large oil price drop at the end of 2014, occurred during the Russian financial crisis, and by a temporary weakness of the Swiss Franc during the same period. These movements are captured by the huge negative spike (denoting an increase in the oil/Swiss Franc returns correlation) for DODS in December 2014 (see Figure 4c).

authors suggest that *"gold and oil positively influence each other, possibly because prices move in the same way with macroeconomic variables"* (ibid., page 143), although they do not pursue further this line of research.

Poshakwale and Mandal (2016) is the only contribution systematically exploring the influence of macroeconomic and other variables on "safe haven" asset returns co-movements. These authors reported a variegated influence of macroeconomic and non-macroeconomic factors; moreover, they showed that a dynamic strategy incorporating information from these variables yielded better forecasts of future correlations, thus enhancing investor's optimal portfolio choices.

This section contributes to the applied literature on "safe haven" assets exploring the impact of some macroeconomic variables on dynamic correlations. Since the sample includes many financial crisis episodes, the variable selection concentrates on macroeconomic risk factors potentially displaying a major influence under frequent financial turbulences.

The macroeconomics risk factors considered are the following[10]:

3. World Equity Risk Premium;
4. World Economic Policy Uncertainty;
5. US Economic Policy Uncertainty;
6. ECB-Systemic Stress Composite Indicator;
7. US Consumer Confidence Index.

The realized equity risk premium is defined as the excess return of equities over risk-free securities. The expected equity risk premium represents the compensation required by investors to hold risky assets. This series represents a classical proxy to measure the degree of risk aversion in applied financial economics. The world equity risk premium used in the present paper represents an average measure for all major world economic areas and therefore captures the perspective of a representative international investor on global financial markets.[11]

Economic policy uncertainty indexes are built to reflect the degree of uncertainty surrounding future economic policy developments, both at a single-country level and considering larger economic areas. These indexes basically rely on the counting of the number of newspapers articles containing the terms "uncertain" or "uncertainty", "economic" or "economy", and one or more policy-relevant term. In the case of the US index, the component related to the newspaper coverage about economic policy uncertainty is integrated with two additional components reflecting, respectively, the number of Federal tax code provisions set to expire in future years (fiscal policy uncertainty) and the disagreement among economic forecasters (macroeconomic uncertainty). See Baker et al. (2016) fur further methodological details.

The Composite Indicator of Systemic Stress is a new indicator of contemporaneous stress in the financial system introduced by the ECB with the aim of analyzing, monitoring, and controlling systemic risk (Holló et al. 2012). From the methodological viewpoint, the main innovation of this indicator is the use of standard portfolio theory to aggregate five market-specific sub-indices into a single statistic summarizing the state of financial instability.

The US Consumer Confidence Index is an economic indicator published by the Conference Board reflecting the degree of optimism about the state of the US economy expressed through consumers saving and spending decisions. Since the US economy exerts a prominent influence on all major advanced economies, this paper focuses exclusively on this consumer confidence indicator. This index relies on monthly surveys of 5000 households with questions regarding current and short-term

---

[10] All monthly series were obtained from Thomson Reuters—Datastream. Thomson Reuters codes are the following: World Equity Risk Premium (end-of-month data): WDASERP; World Economic Policy Uncertainty (mid-month data): WDEPUCUPR; US Economic Policy Uncertainty (mid-month data): USPUPOLR; ECB-Systemic Stress Composite Indicator: EMCISSI; US Consumer Confidence Index (s.a. data): USCNFCONQ.

[11] The World Equity Premium series used in this paper ranges from very low values around 1.5% at the beginning of the sample, to record peaks above 7% during the global and Eurozone debt crises, and stabilizes around values of 4–5% thereafter.

expected business conditions, current and short-term expected employment conditions, and total family income expected for the next six months.

In line with the analysis of the previous section, a regression approach was used to investigate the effect of these macroeconomic variables on time-varying conditional correlations. The estimated equation is then specified as follows:

$$\rho_{ij,\,t} = \varpi + \phi_k\,(Macro_k) + \varepsilon_{ij,\,t} \tag{5}$$

where, as before, $\rho_{ij,}$ denotes the time-varying conditional correlation between asset (i) and asset (j), ϖ is a constant term, and ϕ_k is a coefficient relative to the impact of each single macro-variable (k).[12]

Note that, differently from Section 4.1, the impact of different variables is analyzed separately in Equation (5). Financial crises represent, to a large extent, independent events, whereas clear interdependencies exist between some macro-variables studied in the present section. Therefore, a separate analysis for each macro-variable avoids multicollinearity problems in the estimate of Equation (5).

Expected signs of ϕ_k parameters are again related to portfolio shifts between traditional financial instruments and "safe haven" assets.

An increase in the world equity risk premium captures an increase in international investor's global risk aversion. This lower risk appetite is likely to induce a simultaneous portfolio shift towards "safe haven" assets, pulling up their prices and hence increasing their returns co-movements. Therefore, other things being equal, a higher world equity risk premium is expected to increase dynamic correlations.

Analogous effects can be posited as regards economic policy uncertainty indicators. An increase in these indicators points out a greater uncertainty surrounding future economic policy developments, thus signaling a greater policymaker's difficulty to tackle complex economic problems. At the macro level, higher economic policy uncertainty foreshadows declines in investments, output, and employment, as recently documented for the US and other major economies (Baker et al. 2016). The likely effect on global financial markets is therefore a simultaneous reduction in the degree of risk exposure to more traditional financial assets, generating again an increase in "safe haven" asset returns co-movements.

An increase in the consumer confidence indicator captures a more optimistic attitude of US consumers towards future developments of the US economy. At the macro level, this boost in consumers' confidence is associated with a better future economic outlook in the US and significant positive international spillovers. The effect of an increase of this indicator on global financial markets is therefore expected to operate in the reverse direction with respect to those previously discussed. A better international macroeconomic outlook should lower dynamic correlations due to a gradual portfolio rebalancing from "safe haven" assets towards more traditional financial instruments offering increased returns prospects.[13]

With regards to the ECB-Composite Indicator of Systemic Stress, there is currently no consensus in the literature about one commonly accepted definition of systemic risk (European Central Bank 2009).[14] The intrinsic nature of this variable makes this typology of risk non-diversifiable (Ben-Horim and Levy 1980), so that previous arguments relying on portfolio shifts among alternative asset categories can

[12] ϕ_k coefficients are defined consistently with the macro-variables list provided in the main text. Therefore, ϕ_1 refers to the effect of the world equity risk premium on conditional correlations, ϕ_2 to the effect of world economic uncertainty, and so on.

[13] Lower asset returns co-movements as a consequence of better macroeconomic prospects imply a gradual, not simultaneous, liquidity outflow from "safe haven" assets towards bonds and equities. This appears as a quite realistic process in the presence of a better expected macroeconomic outlook. Differently from previously described cases, in fact, the need to quickly re-optimize portfolio allocations appears less urgent in this specific case.

[14] Theoretical and empirical research made nonetheless consistent progresses in recent years analyzing a wide set of factors triggering systemic risk, such as contagion effects, macroeconomic shocks, or endogenous builds-up of financial market unbalances. De Bandt and Hartmann (2000) provide a very accurate survey about systemic risk.

hardly be applied in this case. Strictly speaking, therefore, no significant effect of this risk indicator should be expected in the context of the present empirical investigation.

It must, however, be remembered that "safe haven" assets represent a special category of financial assets, and that this systemic risk indicator provides a real-time monitoring about the overall stability of the financial system. In this perspective, an increase in the ECB-Composite Indicator of Systemic Stress could generate some positive effect on dynamic conditional correlations, mainly as a result of "flight-to-quality" emotional reactions of global international investors in the presence of greater overall financial instability.

Table 5 summarizes the empirical evidence from OLS estimates of Equation (5). These results were again obtained applying the Newey and West (1987) consistent covariance matrix estimator.

Table 5. Dynamic conditional correlations and macro-variables. Sample: 2000m11 - 2018m10 (216 Observations).

Macrovariables	DGDS			DODG			DODS		
World Equity Risk Premium	ω −0.54 (−0.71)	ϕ_1 −0.73 *** (−4.35)	R^2 0.528	ω −0.05 (−1.59)	ϕ_1 0.48 *** (5.85)	R^2 0.574	ω 0.24 *** (5.62)	ϕ_1 −0.73 *** (−6. 99)	R^2 0. 654
World Econ. Policy Uncertainty	ω −0.22 *** (−6.07)	ϕ_2 −1.02 *** (−6.11)	R^2 0.149	ω 0.08 *** (2.76)	ϕ_2 0.39 ** (2.10)	R^2 0.054	ω 0.10 ** (2.47)	ϕ_2 −1.30 *** (−4.97)	R^2 0.292
US Economic Policy Uncertainty	ω −0.24 *** (−6.48)	ϕ_3 −0.80 *** (−3.79)	R^2 0.053	ω 0.03 (1.11)	ϕ_3 0.80 *** (3.31)	R^2 0.135	ω 0.10 * (1.77)	ϕ_3 −1.33 *** (−3.50)	R^2 0.184
Systemic Stress Comp. Indicator	ω −0.31 *** (−8.57)	ϕ_4 −0.15 ** (−2.24)	R^2 0.044	ω 0.10 *** (4.67)	ϕ_4 0.13 ** (2.74)	R^2 0.083	ω −0.02 (−0.59)	ϕ_4 −0.13 (−1.58)	R^2 0.043
US Consumer Confidence Index	ω −0.44 *** (−6.25)	ϕ_5 1.13 (1.15)	R^2 0.052	ω 0.27 *** (8.59)	ϕ_5 −1.62 *** (−3.92)	R^2 0.264	ω −0.16 ** (−2.93)	ϕ_5 1.29 * (1.77)	R^2 0.082

Estimated equation: $\rho_{ij,t} = \omega + \phi_k\,(Macro_k) + \varepsilon_{ij,t}$. OLS estimation; Newey and West (1987) heteroscedasticity, and autocorrelation consistent estimates of the variance-covariance matrix of parameters. t-statistic in parentheses below estimated parameters values; ***: Significant at a 1% level; **: Significant at a 5% level; *: Significant at a 10% level.

A proper interpretation of estimated ϕ_k parameters requires, consistently with Section 4.1, to remember the definition of Swiss Franc returns. Accordingly, in pair-wise correlations involving Swiss Franc returns (DGDS, DODS), negative ϕ_k estimates captured a positive effect of macro-variables on these conditional correlations (an increase in each macro-variable increases conditional correlations). The reverse holds in the remaining case (DODG): positive ϕ_k estimates pointed out a positive effect of macro-variables on the oil-gold returns correlation.

Almost all estimated ϕ_k coefficients were strongly significant, in most cases at the 1% confidence level. Moreover, all ϕ_k coefficients displayed their expected signs, suggesting that the economic intuition underlying the previous discussion is correct.

Let us now address the empirical evidence in more detail.

One important result is that the world equity risk premium can be singled out as the most relevant macro-variable affecting all conditional correlations (Table 5, first row). Quantitative estimates of ϕ_1 documented the positive and significant impact of this variable: an increase in the world equity risk premium significantly increased all pair-wise dynamic correlations between "safe haven" financial assets. Moreover, focusing on R-squared values, the explicative power of equations including the world equity risk premium was by far the largest than any other estimated equation. These results document that global risk aversion was the main driving force of "safe haven" assets co-movements during the period examined. A lower risk appetite during financial crises episodes induced massive simultaneous portfolio shifts towards these assets, thus increasing their return correlations. These results, together with the evidence about the impact of financial crises provided in the previous section, document that gold, the Swiss Franc, and oil retained their "safe haven" features during the last two decades.

A latter important influence stems from economic policy uncertainty indicators. Estimated ϕ_2 and ϕ_3 coefficients were always strongly significant, while the explicative power of corresponding equations remained relatively high, particularly with regards to oil/Swiss Franc return correlations (DODS). The quantitative influence exerted by these indicators was broadly similar, with a slight prevalence of the global economic policy indicator in terms of explicative power. On the whole, these findings document that uncertainty about future policy developments played a further important role in shaping global investors' asset allocation choices. Moreover, they document that the financial assets studied in this paper acted as powerful hedging instruments in the presence of increased economic policy instability.

Turning to the last two macro-variables, their influence appeared relatively more limited. With regards to US consumer confidence, the estimated coefficient (ϕ_5) was strongly significant only in the case of DODG (oil-gold correlation), whereas in the two remaining cases, it was either significant at the 10% level (DODS) or not significant (DGDS). Although the reported signs of ϕ_5 suggested that better economic prospects tend to induce a gradual portfolio rebalancing out of "safe haven" assets, the intensity of this effect was clearly weaker and less pervasive with respect to previously examined indicators.

Finally, focusing on the ECB-Composite Indicator of Systemic Stress, only a modest influence was found for systemic risk. In one case (DODS), the ϕ_4 coefficient was not statistically significant, whereas in the two remaining cases, it was significant at the 5% level. The magnitude of estimated ϕ_4 parameters for pair-wise correlations with gold returns (DGDS, DODG) was always very low and the corresponding equations displayed, on average, a low explicative power. On the whole, these results are in line with a priori expectations and support the intrinsic non-diversifiable nature of systemic risk. The modest effects documented in pair-wise correlations involving gold returns (increasing correlations as a consequence of higher systemic risk) were consistent with small flight-to-quality effects in the presence of higher global financial instability.

To sum up, this section provides interesting insights about the influence of some relevant macro-variables on co-movements between "safe haven" assets. The world equity risk premium is the most important variable affecting global investors' portfolio choices; moreover, uncertainty indicators about US and global future economic policies were also found to exert significant effects on portfolio allocation choices between traditional and "safe haven" assets. The impact of consumers' confidence and systemic risk indicators instead appeared much more limited.

5. Conclusions

This paper focuses on three "safe haven" assets which have received wide attention in the recent applied literature (gold, Swiss Franc, and oil), and explores some statistical properties of these assets with a particular focus on their time-varying correlation patterns.

The influence of financial crises and macroeconomic variables on dynamic correlations between "safe haven" assets have seldom been explored. This represents one major drawback in the literature, since the last two decades witnessed many financial crises with important international spillover effects. Moreover, the impact of macroeconomic and financial variables on co-movements between "safe haven" asset returns is likely to be substantial, particularly if these variables reflect the degree of risk aversion, economic uncertainty, or the degree of confidence of economic agents.

In this perspective, this paper fills one relevant gap in the applied literature on "safe haven" assets, providing a thorough analysis about the determinants of their return co-movements during the last two decades.

The main empirical findings may be summarized as follows.

Financial crises produced a significant increase in all pair-wise correlations between "safe haven" assets. This influence is not limited to major financial turbulences (global financial crisis, Eurozone debt crisis), but involves all subsequent crises episodes (Russian financial crisis, Chinese stock market crisis, Turkish financial crisis). This pervasive effect of financial crises implies that gold, oil, and the Swiss Franc retained their "safe haven" status during the last two decades.

A latter important result refers to the effects of some outstanding macroeconomic variables. The world equity risk premium stands out as the most relevant variable affecting return co-movements. The impact of this risk aversion indicator on "safe haven" assets return co-movements is always large, and explains a consistent fraction of correlation patterns. Another noticeable influence stems from various economic policy uncertainty indicators, which played a further relevant role in shaping global investors asset allocation choices towards "safe haven" financial assets. The effects of other macroeconomic variables, such as consumer confidence or systemic stress indicators, are instead more limited. Overall, the empirical evidence for macroeconomic variables reiterates the features of gold, oil, and the Swiss Franc as important "safe haven" assets during the period examined.

This paper can be profitably extended along many research directions.

The robustness of results may be assessed using data sampled at higher frequencies (weekly, daily, intra-daily). Moreover, this analysis can be extended to other financial assets typically included in the "safe haven" category (US long-term government bonds, the Yen exchange rate, and other precious metals).

A further interesting research area is represented by the use of more sophisticated models to compute dynamic conditional correlations. Profitable research directions are represented by some extension of Engle (2002) seminal model, allowing for asymmetric responses in conditional variance and conditional correlations to negative returns, or allowing correlation dynamics to depend on asset variances through a threshold structure.

In a more general perspective, the development of powerful econometric techniques for the analysis of conditional correlation structures of a large number of assets remains on the top of the research agenda. Although plagued by the curse of dimensionality problem, this represents a crucial condition for a more accurate assessment of the hedging properties of "safe haven" assets against traditional financial instruments and the development of efficient dynamic asset allocation strategies.

Funding: This research received no external funding.

Acknowledgments: The author is thankful to the anonymous referees for very useful comments.

Conflicts of Interest: The author declares no conflict of interest.

References

Baker, Scott R., Nicholas Bloom, and Steven J. Davis. 2016. Measuring economic policy uncertainty. *Quarterly Journal of Economics* 131: 1593–636. [CrossRef]

Bashiri Behmiri, Niaz B., Matteo Manera, and Marcella Nicolini. 2019. Understanding dynamic conditional correlation between oil, natural gas and non-energy commodity futures markets. *Energy Journal* 40: 55–76. [CrossRef]

Baur, Dirk G., and Thomas K. McDermott. 2010. Is gold a safe haven? International evidence. *Journal of Banking and Finance* 34: 1886–98. [CrossRef]

Bedoui, Rihab, Sana Braeik, Stephane Goutte, and Khaled Guesmi. 2018. On the study of conditional dependence structure between oil, gold and USD exchange rates. *International Review of Financial Analysis* 59: 134–46. [CrossRef]

Ben-Horim, Moshe, and Haim Levy. 1980. Diversifiable risk and non–diversifiable risk: A pedagogical note. *Journal of Financial and Quantitative Analysis* 15: 289–97. [CrossRef]

Bernanke, Ben, Timothy Geithner, and Henry Paulson. 2018. Charting the Financial Crisis. Hutchins Center on Fiscal and Monetary Policy at Brookings, Yale School of Management Program on Financial Stability. Available online: https://www.brookings.edu (accessed on 24 February 2020).

Bordo, Michael D., and John S. Landon-Lane. 2010. *The Global Financial Crisis of 2007–2008: Is It Unprecedented?* NBER Working n.16589. Cambridge: NBER. [CrossRef]

Cai, Jije, Ray Chou, and Dan Li. 2009. Explaining international stock correlations with CPI fluctuations and market volatility. *Journal of Banking and Finance* 33: 2026–35.

Campbell, John Y., Karine Serfaty-de Medeiros, and Luis M. Viceira. 2010. Global currency hedging. *Journal of Finance* 65: 87–121. [CrossRef]

Casarin, Roberto, Domenico Sartore, and Marco Tronzano. 2018. A Bayesian Markov–switching correlation model for contagion analysis on exchange rate markets. *Journal of Business & Economic Statistics* 36: 101–14.

Chua, Jess H., Gordon Sick, and Richard S. Woodward. 1990. Diversifying with gold stocks. *Financial Analyists Journal* 46: 76–79. [CrossRef]

Ciner, Cetin, Constantin Gurdgiev, and Brian M. Lucey. 2013. Hedges and safe havens: An examination of stocks, bonds, oil and exchange rates. *International Review of Financial Analysis* 29: 202–11. [CrossRef]

Creti, Anna, Marc Joëts, and Valerie Mignon. 2013. On the links between stock and commodity markets' volatility. *Energy Economics* 37: 16–28. [CrossRef]

De Bandt, Olivier, and Philipp Hartmann. 2000. *Systemic Risk: A Survey*. ECB Working Papers Series n. 35; Frankfurt: ECB.

Ding, Liang, and Minh Vo. 2012. Exchange rates and oil prices: A multivariate stochastic volatility analysis. *Quarterly Review of Economics and Finance* 52: 15–37. [CrossRef]

Economist. 2005. The Little yellow gold. *The Economist Newspaper Limited*, December 1.

Economist. 2009. Haring away. *The Economist Newspaper Limited*, February 29.

Engle, Robert. 2002. Dynamic conditional correlation: A simple class of multivariate generalized autoregressive conditional heteroscedasticity models. *Journal of Business & Economic Statistics* 20: 339–50.

European Central Bank. 2009. The concept of systemic risk. *Financial Stability Review*. Available online: https://www.ecb.europa.eu/pub/pdf/fsr/art/ecb.fsrart200912_02.en.pdf (accessed on 24 February 2020).

Guidolin, Massimo, and Allan Timmermann. 2007. Asset allocation under multivariate regime switching. *Journal of Economic Dynamics and Control* 31: 3503–44. [CrossRef]

Holló, Daniel, Manfred Kremer, and Marco Lo Duca. 2012. *CISS—A Composite Indicator of Systemic Stress in the Financial System*. ECB Working Papers Series n. 1426; Frankfurt: ECB.

Hood, Matthew, and Farooq Malik. 2013. Is gold the best hedge and a safe haven under changing stock market volatility? *Review of Financial Economics* 22: 47–52. [CrossRef]

Jaffe, Jeffrey. 1989. Gold and gold stocks as investments for institutional portfolios. *Financial Analysts Journal* 45: 53–59. [CrossRef]

Jäggi, Adrian, Martin Schlegel, and Attilio Zanetti. 2019. Macroeconomic surprises, market environment, and safe–haven currencies. *Swiss Journal of Economics and Statistics* 155: 1–21. [CrossRef]

Jain, Anshul, and Pratap Biswal. 2016. Dynamic linkages among oil price, gold price, exchange rate, and stock market in India. *Resources Policy* 49: 179–85. [CrossRef]

Jarque, Carlos, and Anil K. Bera. 1980. Efficient tests for normality, homoscedasticity and serial independence of regression residuals. *Economic Letters* 6: 255–59. [CrossRef]

Kang, Sang Hoon, Ron McIver, and Seong-Min Yoon. 2016. Modeling time–varying correlations in volatility between BRICS and commodity markets. *Emerging Markets Finance & Trade* 52: 1698–723.

Kang, Sang Hoon, Ron McIver, and Seong-Min Yoon. 2017. Dynamic spillover effects among crude oil, precious metal, and agricultural commodity futures markets. *Energy Economics* 62: 19–32. [CrossRef]

Karfakis, Costas, and Theodore Panagiotidis. 2015. The effects of global monetary policy and Greek debt crisis on the dynamic conditional correlations of currency markets. *Empirica* 42: 795–811. [CrossRef]

Kindleberger, Charles P. 1978. *Manias, Panic, and Crashes: A History of Financial Crises*. London: Macmillan Press.

Kugler, Peter, and Beatrice Weder. 2004. International portfolio holdings and Swiss Franc asset returns. *Swiss Journal of Economics and Statistics* 140: 301–25.

Lane, Philip R. 2012. The European sovereign debt crisis. *Journal of Economic Perspectives* 26: 49–68. [CrossRef]

Newey, Whitney K., and Kenneth D. West. 1987. A simple, positive semi–definite, heteroscedasticity and autocorrelation consistent covariance matrix. *Econometrica* 55: 703–8. [CrossRef]

Nguyen, Phong, and Wei-Han Liu. 2017. Time–varying linkage of possible safe haven assets: A cross–market and cross–asset analysis. *International Review of Finance* 17: 43–76. [CrossRef]

Pesaran, Hashem M., and Allan Timmermann. 1992. A simple nonparametric test of predictive performance. *Journal of Business & Economic Statistics* 10: 561–565.

Petty, William. 1690. Political Arithmetick. McMaster University Archive for the History of Economic Thought. Available online: https://ideas.repec.org/b/hay/hetboo/petty1690.html (accessed on 25 February 2020).

Phillips, Peter, and Shu-Ping Shi. 2018. Financial bubble implosion and reverse regression. *Econometric Theory* 34: 705–53. [CrossRef]

Poshakwale, Sunil S., and Anandadeep Mandal. 2016. Determinants of asymmetric return co–movements of gold and other financial assets. *International Review of Financial Analysis* 47: 229–42. [CrossRef]

Ranaldo, Angelo, and Paul Söderlind. 2010. Safe haven currencies. *Review of Finance* 14: 385–407. [CrossRef]

Reboredo, Juan C. 2013. Is gold a hedge or safe haven against oil price movements? *Resources Policy* 38: 130–37. [CrossRef]

Syllignakis, Manolis N., and Georgios P. Kouretas. 2011. Dynamic correlation analysis of financial contagion: Evidence from the Central and Eastern European Markets. *International Review of Economics and Finance* 20: 717–32. [CrossRef]

Tamakoshi, Go, and Shigeyuki Hamori. 2014. Co–movements among major European exchange rates: A multivariate time–varying asymmetric approach. *International Review of Economics and Finance* 31: 105–13. [CrossRef]

Zeng, Fanhua, Wei-Chiao Huang, and James Hueng. 2016. On Chinese government's stock market rescue efforts in 2015. *Modern Economy* 7: 411–18. [CrossRef]

Journal of
Risk and Financial Management

MDPI

Article

A General Family of Autoregressive Conditional Duration Models Applied to High-Frequency Financial Data

Danúbia R. Cunha [1], Roberto Vila [2], Helton Saulo [2,*] and Rodrigo N. Fernandez [3]

1 Department of Economics, Catholic University of Brasilia, 71966-700 Brasilia, Brazil; danubiarodriguess@hotmail.com
2 Department of Statistics, University of Brasilia, 70910-900 Brasilia, Brazil; rovig161@gmail.com
3 Department of Economics, Federal University of Pelotas, 96010-610 Pelotas, Brazil; rodrigo.fernandez@ufpel.edu.br
* Correspondence: heltonsaulo@gmail.com

Received: 24 December 2019; Accepted: 26 February 2020; Published: 3 March 2020

Abstract: In this paper, we propose a general family of Birnbaum–Saunders autoregressive conditional duration (BS-ACD) models based on generalized Birnbaum–Saunders (GBS) distributions, denoted by GBS-ACD. We further generalize these GBS-ACD models by using a Box-Cox transformation with a shape parameter λ to the conditional median dynamics and an asymmetric response to shocks; this is denoted by GBS-AACD. We then carry out a Monte Carlo simulation study to evaluate the performance of the GBS-ACD models. Finally, an illustration of the proposed models is made by using New York stock exchange (NYSE) transaction data.

Keywords: generalized Birnbaum–Saunders distributions; ACD models; Box-Cox transformation; high-frequency financial data; goodness-of-fit

MSC: Primary 62P20; Secondary 62F99

JEL Classification: Primary C51; Secondary C52 C53

---

1. Introduction

The modeling of high-frequency financial data has been the focus of intense interest over the last decades. A prominent approach to modeling the durations between successive events (trades, quotes, price changes, etc.) was introduced by Engle and Russell (1998). These authors proposed the autoregressive conditional duration (ACD) model, which has some similarities with the ARCH (Engle 1982) and GARCH (Bollerslev 1986) models. The usefulness of appropriately modeling duration data is stressed by the relatively recent market microstructure literature; see Diamond and Verrechia (1987), Easley and O'Hara (1992), and Easley et al. (1997). Generalizations of the original ACD model are basically based on the following three aspects, i.e., (a) the distributional assumption in order to yield a unimodal failure rate (FR) (Grammig and Maurer 2000; Lunde 1999), (b) the linear form for the conditional mean (median) dynamics (Allen et al. 2008; Bauwens and Giot 2000; Fernandes and Grammig 2006), and (c) the time series properties (Bauwens and Giot 2003; Chiang 2007; De Luca and Zuccolotto 2006; Jasiak 1998; Zhang et al. 2001); see the reviews by Pacurar (2008) and Bhogal and Variyam Thekke (2019). Bhatti (2010) proposed a generalization of the ACD model that falls into all three branches above, based on the Birnbaum–Saunders (BS) distribution, denoted as the BS-ACD model. This model has several advantages over the traditional ACD ones; in particular, the BS-ACD model (1) has a realistic distributional assumption, that is, it provides both an asymmetric probability density function (PDF) and a unimodal FR shape; (2) it provides a natural parametrization of the point process in terms of a conditional median duration which is expected to improve the model fit despite a conditional mean duration, since the median is generally considered to be a better measure of central tendency than the mean for asymmetrical and heavy-tailed distributions; and (3) has easy implementation for estimation; see Ghosh and Mukherjee (2006), Bhatti (2010), Leiva et al. (2014), and Saulo et al. (2019).

Based on the relationship between the BS and symmetric distributions, Díaz-García and Leiva (2005) introduced generalized BS (GBS) distributions, obtaining a wider class of distributions that has either lighter or heavier tails than the BS density, allowing them to provide more flexibility. This new class essentially provides flexibility in the kurtosis level; see Sanhueza et al. (2008). In addition, the GBS distributions produce models whose parameter estimates are often robust to atypical data; see Leiva et al. (2008) and Barros et al. (2008). The GBS family includes as special cases the BS, BS-Laplace (BS-LA), BS-Logistic (BS-LO), BS-power-exponential (BS-PE), and BS-Student-t (BS-t) distributions.

The main aim of this work is to generalize the BS-ACD model, which was proposed by Bhatti (2010), based on GBS distributions (GBS-ACD). The proposed models should hold with the properties of the BS-ACD model, but, in addition, they should provide further properties and more flexibility. As mentioned before, the GBS family has models that have heavier tails than the BS density, and this characteristic is very useful in the modeling of high-frequency financial durations, since duration data are heavy-tailed and heavily right-skewed. We subsequently develop a class of augmented GBS-ACD (GBS-AACD) models by using the Box-Cox transformation (Box and Cox 1964) with a shape parameter $\lambda \geq 0$ to the conditional duration process and an asymmetric response to shocks; see Fernandes and Grammig (2006). Thus, the proposed GBS-ACD and GBS-AACD models would provide greater range and flexibility while fitting data. We apply the proposed models to high-frequency financial transaction (trade duration, TD) data. This type of data has unique features absent in data with low frequencies. For example, TD data (1) inherently arrive in irregular time intervals, (2) possess a large number of observations, (3) exhibit some diurnal pattern, i.e., activity is higher near the beginning and closing than in the middle of the trading day, and (4) present a unimodal failure rate; see Engle and Russell (1998) and Bhatti (2010). In addition, TD data have a relevant role in market microstructure theory, since they can be used as proxies for the existence of information in the market, and then serve as predictors for other market microstructure variables; see Mayorov (2011).

The rest of the paper proceeds as follows. Section 2 describes the BS and GBS distributions. In addition, some propositions are presented. Section 3 derives the GBS-ACD models associated with these distributions. Section 4 derives the GBS-AACD class of models. A Monte Carlo study of the proposed GBS-ACD model is performed in Section 5. Next, Section 6 presents an application of the proposed models to three data sets of New York stock exchange (NYSE) securities, and their fits are then assessed by a goodness-of-fit test. Finally, Section 7 offers some concluding remarks.

2. The Birnbaum–Saunders Distribution and Its Generalization

In this section, we describe the BS and GBS distributions and some of their properties.

The two-parameter BS distribution was introduced by Birnbaum and Saunders (1969) for modeling failure times of a material exposed to fatigue. They assumed that the fatigue failure follows from the development and growth of a dominant crack. Let $\boldsymbol{\theta} = (\kappa, \sigma)^\top$ and

$$a(x;\boldsymbol{\theta}) = \frac{1}{\kappa}\left[\sqrt{\frac{x}{\sigma}} - \sqrt{\frac{\sigma}{x}}\right], \quad x > 0 \text{ and } \kappa, \sigma > 0. \tag{1}$$

Expressions for the first, second, and third derivatives of the function $a(\cdot;\boldsymbol{\theta})$ are, respectively, given by

$$a'(x;\boldsymbol{\theta}) = \frac{1}{2\kappa\sigma}\left[\left(\frac{\sigma}{x}\right)^{1/2} + \left(\frac{\sigma}{x}\right)^{3/2}\right], \quad a''(x;\boldsymbol{\theta}) = -\frac{1}{4\kappa\sigma x}\left[\left(\frac{\sigma}{x}\right)^{1/2} + 3\left(\frac{\sigma}{x}\right)^{3/2}\right],$$
$$a'''(x;\boldsymbol{\theta}) = \frac{3}{8\kappa\sigma x^2}\left[\left(\frac{\sigma}{x}\right)^{1/2} + 5\left(\frac{\sigma}{x}\right)^{3/2}\right]. \tag{2}$$

A random variable (RV) X has a BS distribution with parameter vector $\boldsymbol{\theta} = (\kappa, \sigma)^\top$, denoted by $\mathrm{BS}(\boldsymbol{\theta})$, if it can be expressed as

$$X = a^{-1}(Z;\boldsymbol{\theta}) = \frac{\sigma}{4}\left[\kappa Z + \sqrt{(\kappa Z)^2 + 4}\right]^2, \quad Z \sim \mathrm{N}(0,1), \tag{3}$$

where $a^{-1}(\cdot;\boldsymbol{\theta})$ denotes the inverse function of $a(\cdot;\boldsymbol{\theta})$, κ is a shape parameter, and when it decreases to zero, the BS distribution approaches the normal distribution with mean σ and variance τ, such that $\tau \to 0$ when $\kappa \to 0$. In addition, σ is a scale parameter and also the median of the distribution $F_{\mathrm{BS}}(\sigma) = 0.5$, where F_{BS} is the BS cumulative distribution function (CDF). The BS distribution holds proportionality and reciprocal properties given by $b\,X \sim \mathrm{BS}(\kappa, b\,\sigma)$, with $b > 0$, and $1/X \sim \mathrm{BS}(\kappa, 1/\sigma)$; see Saunders (1974). The probability density function (PDF) of a two-parameter BS random variable X is given by

$$f_{\mathrm{BS}}(x;\boldsymbol{\theta}) = \phi(a(x;\boldsymbol{\theta}))a'(x;\boldsymbol{\theta}), \quad x > 0, \tag{4}$$

where $\phi(\cdot)$ denotes the PDF of the standard normal distribution.

Díaz-García and Leiva (2005) proposed the GBS distribution by assuming that Z in (3) follows a symmetric distribution in $\mathbb{R}$, denoted by $X \sim \mathrm{GBS}(\boldsymbol{\theta}, g)$, where g is a density generator function associated with the particular symmetric distribution. An RV Z has a standard symmetric distribution, denoted by $Z \sim \mathrm{S}(0,1;g) \equiv \mathrm{S}(g)$, if its density takes the form $f_Z(z) = c\,g(z^2)$ for $z \in \mathbb{R}$, where $g(u)$ with $u > 0$ is a real function that generates the density of Z, and c is the normalization constant, that is, $c = 1/\int_{-\infty}^{+\infty} g(z^2)dz$. Note that $U = Z^2 \sim \mathrm{G}\chi^2(1;g)$, namely, U has a generalized chi-squared ($\mathrm{G}\chi^2$) distribution with one degree of freedom and density generator g; see Fang et al. (1990). Table 1 presents some characteristics and the values of $u_1(g)$, $u_2(g)$, $u_3(g)$, and $u_4(g)$ for the Laplace, logistic, normal, power-exponential (PE) and Student-t symmetric distributions, where $u_r(g) = \mathrm{E}[U^r]$ denotes the rth moment of U.

Table 1. Constants (c and c_{g^2}), density generators (g), and expressions of some moments $u_r(g)$ for the indicated distributions.

Dist.	c	$g = g(u), u > 0$	$u_1(g)$	$u_2(g)$	$u_3(g)$	$u_4(g)$
Laplace	$\frac{1}{2}$	$\exp(-\lvert u \rvert)$	2!	4!	6!	8!
Logistic	1	$\frac{\exp(u)}{[1+\exp(u)]^2}$	≈ 0.7957	≈ 1.5097	≈ 4.2777	≈ 16.0142
Normal	$\frac{1}{\sqrt{2\pi}}$	$\exp\left(-\frac{1}{2}u\right)$	1	3	15	105
PE	$\frac{\eta}{2^{\frac{1}{2\eta}}\Gamma\left(\frac{1}{2\eta}\right)}$	$\exp\left(-\frac{1}{2}u^\eta\right), \eta > 0$	$\frac{2^{\frac{1}{\eta}}\Gamma\left(\frac{3}{2\eta}\right)}{\Gamma\left(\frac{1}{2\eta}\right)}$	$\frac{2^{\frac{2}{\eta}}\Gamma\left(\frac{5}{2\eta}\right)}{\Gamma\left(\frac{1}{2\eta}\right)}$	$\frac{2^{\frac{3}{\eta}}\Gamma\left(\frac{7}{2\eta}\right)}{\Gamma\left(\frac{1}{2\eta}\right)}$	$\frac{2^{\frac{4}{\eta}}\Gamma\left(\frac{9}{2\eta}\right)}{\Gamma\left(\frac{1}{2\eta}\right)}$
t	$\frac{\Gamma\left(\frac{\eta+1}{2}\right)}{\sqrt{\eta\pi}\,\Gamma\left(\frac{\eta}{2}\right)}$	$\left(1 + \frac{u}{\eta}\right)^{-\frac{\eta+1}{2}}, \eta > 0$	$\frac{\eta}{(\eta-2)}$ $\eta > 2$	$\frac{3\eta^2}{(\eta-2)(\eta-4)}$ $\eta > 4$	$\frac{15\eta^3}{(\eta-2)(\eta-4)(\eta-6)}$ $\eta > 6$	$\frac{105\eta^4}{(\eta-2)(\eta-4)(\eta-6)(\eta-8)}$ $\eta > 8$

Consider an RV Z such that $Z = a(X;\boldsymbol{\theta}) \sim \mathrm{S}(g)$ so that

$$X = a^{-1}(Z;\boldsymbol{\theta}) \sim \mathrm{GBS}(\boldsymbol{\theta}, g). \tag{5}$$

The density associated with X in (5) is given by

$$f_{\text{GBS}}(x;\boldsymbol{\theta},g) = c\,g(a^2(x;\boldsymbol{\theta}))a'(x;\boldsymbol{\theta}), \quad x>0, \tag{6}$$

where, as mentioned earlier, g is the generator and c the normalizing constant associated with a particular symmetric density; see Table 1. The mean and variance of X are, respectively,

$$\text{E}[X] = \frac{\sigma}{2}(2+u_1\kappa^2), \quad \text{Var}[X] = \frac{\sigma^2\kappa^2}{4}(2\kappa^2u_2+4u_1-\kappa^2u_1^2), \tag{7}$$

where $u_r = u_r(g) = \text{E}[U^r]$, with $U \sim \text{G}\chi^2(1,g)$; see Table 1.

Based on Table 1, the expressions for the BS-LA, BS-LO, BS-PE, and BS-t densities are as follows:

$$\begin{aligned}
f_{\text{BS-LA}}(x;\boldsymbol{\theta}) &= \tfrac{1}{4\kappa\sigma}\exp\left(-\tfrac{1}{\kappa}\left|\sqrt{\tfrac{x}{\sigma}}-\sqrt{\tfrac{\sigma}{x}}\right|\right)\left[\left(\tfrac{\sigma}{x}\right)^{1/2}+\left(\tfrac{\sigma}{x}\right)^{3/2}\right],\\
f_{\text{BS-LO}}(x;\boldsymbol{\theta}) &= \tfrac{1}{2\kappa\sigma}\tfrac{\exp\left(\frac{1}{\kappa}\left[\sqrt{\frac{x}{\sigma}}-\sqrt{\frac{\sigma}{x}}\right]\right)}{\left[1+\exp\left(\frac{1}{\kappa}\left[\sqrt{\frac{x}{\sigma}}-\sqrt{\frac{\sigma}{x}}\right]\right)\right]^2}\left[\left(\tfrac{\sigma}{x}\right)^{1/2}+\left(\tfrac{\sigma}{x}\right)^{3/2}\right],\\
f_{\text{BS-PE}}(x;\boldsymbol{\theta},\eta) &= \frac{\eta}{\Gamma\left(\frac{1}{2\eta}\right)2^{\frac{1}{2\eta}+1}\kappa\sigma}\exp\left(-\tfrac{1}{2\kappa^{2\eta}}\left[\tfrac{x}{\sigma}+\tfrac{\sigma}{x}-2\right]^\eta\right)\left[\left(\tfrac{\sigma}{x}\right)^{1/2}+\left(\tfrac{\sigma}{x}\right)^{3/2}\right],\\
f_{\text{BS-}t}(x;\boldsymbol{\theta},\eta) &= \frac{\Gamma\left(\frac{\eta+1}{2}\right)}{2\sqrt{\eta\pi}\,\Gamma\left(\frac{\eta}{2}\right)\kappa\sigma}\left[1+\tfrac{1}{\eta\kappa^2}\left(\tfrac{x}{\sigma}+\tfrac{\sigma}{x}-2\right)\right]^{-\frac{\eta+1}{2}}\left[\left(\tfrac{\sigma}{x}\right)^{1/2}+\left(\tfrac{\sigma}{x}\right)^{3/2}\right],\\
&\quad x>0 \text{ and } \kappa,\sigma,\eta>0.
\end{aligned}$$

Note that if $\eta = 1$ (BS-PE) or if $\eta \to \infty$ (BS-t), then we obtain the BS distribution. It is worthwhile to point out that the BS-PE distribution has a greater (smaller) kurtosis than that of the BS distribution when $\eta < 1$ ($\eta > 1$). In addition, the BS-t distribution has a greater degree of kurtosis than that of the BS distribution for $\eta > 8$; see Marchant et al. (2013).

Let

$$b(h;\kappa,\iota,\phi) = \frac{2}{\kappa}\sinh\left(\frac{h-\iota}{\phi}\right), \quad h\in\mathbb{R},\ \kappa,\phi>0 \text{ and } \iota\in\mathbb{R}. \tag{8}$$

An alternative way to obtain GBS distributions is through sinh-symmetric (SHS) distributions. Díaz-García and Domínguez-Molina (2006) proposed SHS distributions by using the sinh-normal distribution introduced by Rieck and Nedelman (1991) in the symmetric case. They assumed the standard symmetrically distributed RV Z as follows:

$$Z = b(H;\kappa,\iota,\phi) \sim \text{S}(g). \tag{9}$$

Then,

$$H = b^{-1}(Z;\kappa,\iota,\phi) = \iota + \phi\,\text{arcsinh}\left(\tfrac{\kappa Z}{2}\right) \sim \text{SHS}(\kappa,\iota,\phi,g). \tag{10}$$

The density associated with H in (10) is given by

$$f_{\text{SHS}}(h;\kappa,\iota,\phi,g) = c\,g(b^2(h;\kappa,\iota,\phi))b'(h;\kappa,\iota,\phi), \quad h\in\mathbb{R},\ \kappa,\phi>0 \text{ and } \iota\in\mathbb{R}, \tag{11}$$

where g and c are as given in (6). A prominent result, which will be useful later on, is the following.

Proposition 1 (See Rieck and Nedelman (1991)). *If $H \sim SHS(\kappa,\iota=\ln\sigma,\phi=2,g)$, then $X=\exp(H) \sim GBS(\boldsymbol{\theta},g)$, which is denoted by $H \sim log\text{-}GBS(\kappa,\iota,g)$.*

3. The GBS-ACD Models

3.1. Existing ACD Models

Let $X_i = T_i - T_{i-1}$ denote the trade duration, i.e., the time elapsed between two transactions occurring at times T_i and T_{i-1}. Engle and Russell (1998) assumed that the serial dependence commonly found in financial duration data is described by $\psi_i = \mathrm{E}[X_i|\mathcal{F}_{i-1}]$, where ψ_i stands for the conditional mean of the ith trade duration based on the conditioning information set $\mathcal{F}_{i-1}$, which includes all information available at time T_{i-1}. The basic ACD(r,s) model is then defined as

$$\begin{aligned} X_i &= \psi_i \varepsilon_i, \\ \psi_i &= \alpha + \sum_{j=1}^{r} \beta_j \psi_{i-j} + \sum_{j=1}^{s} \gamma_j x_{i-j}, \quad i = 1, \ldots, n, \end{aligned} \tag{12}$$

where r and s refer to the orders of the lags and $\{\varepsilon_i\}$ is an independent and identically distributed nonnegative sequence with PDF $f(\cdot)$. Engle and Russell (1998) assumed a linear ACD(1,1) model defined by $\psi_i = \alpha + \beta x_{i-1} + \gamma \psi_{i-1}$, where α, β, and γ are the parameters. Note that a wide range of ACD model specifications may be defined by different distributions of ε_i and specifications of ψ_i; see Fernandes and Grammig (2006) and Pathmanathan et al. (2009).

An alternative ACD model is the Birnbaum–Saunders autoregressive conditional duration (BS-ACD) model proposed by Bhatti (2010). This approach takes into account the natural scale parameter in the BS$(\boldsymbol{\theta})$ distribution to specify the BS-ACD model in terms of a time-varying conditional median duration $\sigma_i = F_{\mathrm{BS}}^{-1}(0.5|\mathcal{F}_{i-1})$, where F_{BS} denotes the CDF of the BS distribution. This specification has several advantages over the existing ACD models, as previously mentioned, including a realistic distributional assumption—an expected improvement in the model fit as a result of the natural parametrization in terms of the conditional median duration, since the median is generally considered to be a better measure of central tendency than the mean for asymmetrical and heavy-tailed distributions—and ease of fitting.

The PDF associated with the BS-ACD(r,s) model is given by

$$f_{\mathrm{BS}}(x_i;\boldsymbol{\theta}_i) = \phi\big(a(x_i;\boldsymbol{\theta}_i)\big)a'(x_i;\boldsymbol{\theta}_i), \quad i = 1, \ldots, n, \tag{13}$$

where

$$\boldsymbol{\theta}_i = (\kappa, \sigma_i)^\top, \quad i = 1, \ldots, n,$$

with

$$\ln \sigma_i = \alpha + \textstyle\sum_{j=1}^{r} \beta_j \ln \sigma_{i-j} + \sum_{j=1}^{s} \gamma_j \big[\frac{x_{i-j}}{\sigma_{i-j}}\big]. \tag{14}$$

3.2. GBS-ACD Models

We now extend the class of BS-ACD(r,s) models by using the GBS distributions. As explained earlier, this family of distributions possesses either lighter or heavier tails than the BS density, thus providing more flexibility. From the density given in (6), the GBS-ACD(r,s) model can be obtained in a way analogous to that provided for the BS-ACD(r,s) model in (13) with an associated PDF expressed as

$$f_{\mathrm{GBS}}(x_i;\boldsymbol{\theta}_i, g) = c\, g\big(a^2(x_i;\boldsymbol{\theta}_i)\big)a'(x_i;\boldsymbol{\theta}_i), \quad i = 1, \ldots, n, \tag{15}$$

where c and g are as given in (6), $\boldsymbol{\theta}_i = (\kappa, \sigma_i)^\top$ for $i = 1, \ldots, n$, with

$$\ln \sigma_i = \alpha + \textstyle\sum_{j=1}^{r} \beta_j \ln \sigma_{i-j} + \sum_{j=1}^{s} \gamma_j \big[\frac{x_{i-j}}{\sigma_{i-j}}\big], \tag{16}$$

where $\boldsymbol{\xi} = (\kappa, \alpha, \beta_1, \ldots, \beta_r, \gamma_1, \ldots, \gamma_s)^\top$ and $\boldsymbol{\zeta} = (\zeta_1, \ldots, \zeta_k)^\top$ denotes the additional parameters required by the density function in (6).

Note that model (15) can be written as

$$X_i = \sigma_i \varphi_i, \tag{17}$$

where $\varphi_i = \exp(\varepsilon_i)$ with ε_i being positively supported independent and identically distributed RVs following the SHS$(\kappa, 0, 2, g)$ distribution, with density given by (11). Note that if $\varepsilon_i \sim$ SHS$(\kappa, 0, 2, g)$, then $\exp(\varepsilon_i) \sim$ GBS$(\kappa, 1, g)$ (see Proposition 1) with $X_i \sim$ GBS$(\boldsymbol{\theta}_i, g)$.

3.2.1. Properties

Proposition 2 (Expected value of logarithmic duration in the GBS-ACD(r,s) model)**.** *Assuming that the process $\{X_i \sim$ GBS$(\boldsymbol{\theta}_i, g) : i = 1, 2, \ldots\}$ is strictly stationary and that $E[\varepsilon_i] = \mu$, where ε_i is given in (17), we have*

$$E[\ln X_i] = \frac{2[\alpha + \mu(1+\sum_{j=1}^{r}\beta_j)] + (2+u_1\kappa^2)\sum_{j=1}^{s}\gamma_j}{2(1-\sum_{j=1}^{r}\beta_j)}, \quad \forall i,$$

whenever $\sum_{j=1}^{r}\beta_j \neq 1$. The constant (depending only on the kernel g) u_1 is given in (7).

Proposition 3 (Moments of logarithmic duration in the GBS-ACD$(1,1)$ model)**.** *If the process $\{X_i \sim$ GBS$(\boldsymbol{\theta}_i, g) : i = 1, 2, \ldots\}$ is strictly stationary and $E[\varepsilon_i] = \mu$, where ε_i is given in (17), then*

$$\left.\begin{array}{l} \bullet\ E[\ln X_i] = \frac{2[\alpha+\mu(1+\beta)]+(2+u_1\kappa^2)\gamma}{2(1-\beta)}, \quad \beta \neq 1, \\ \bullet\ E[(\ln X_i)^2] = \mu(2-\mu) + 2\mu\, E[\ln X_i] + \\ \qquad \frac{\alpha^2 - 2\alpha\beta + \frac{\gamma^2}{2}(u_2\kappa^4 + 4u_1\kappa^2 + 2) + \gamma(2+u_1\kappa^2)(\alpha - \beta\mu) + [2\alpha\beta + \gamma\beta(2+u_1\kappa^2)]\, E[\ln X_i]}{1-\beta^2}, \quad \beta \neq \pm 1, \end{array}\right\} \quad \forall i.$$

3.2.2. Estimation

Let $(X_1, \ldots, X_n)$ be a sample from $X_i \sim$ GBS$(\boldsymbol{\theta}_i, g)$ for $i = 1, \ldots, n$, and let $\boldsymbol{x} = (x_1, \ldots, x_n)^\top$ be the observed durations. Then, the log-likelihood function for $\boldsymbol{\xi} = (\kappa, \alpha, \beta_1, \ldots, \beta_r, \gamma_1, \ldots, \gamma_s)^\top$ is obtained as

$$\ell_{\mathrm{GBS}}(\boldsymbol{\xi}) = \sum_{i=1}^{n}\left[\ln(2c) - \ln\kappa - \ln\sigma_i + \ln g(a^2(x_i;\boldsymbol{\theta}_i)) + \ln\left(\left(\frac{\sigma_i}{x_i}\right)^{1/2} + \left(\frac{\sigma_i}{x_i}\right)^{3/2}\right)\right], \tag{18}$$

where the time-varying conditional median σ_i is given as in (16). The maximum-likelihood (ML) estimates can be obtained by maximizing the expression defined in (18) by equating the score vector $\dot{\ell}_{\mathrm{GBS}}(\boldsymbol{\xi})$, which contains the first derivatives of $\ell_{\mathrm{GBS}}(\boldsymbol{\xi})$, to zero, providing the likelihood equations. They must be solved by an iterative procedure for non-linear optimization, such as the Broyden–Fletcher–Goldfarb–Shanno (BFGS) quasi-Newton method. It can easily be seen that the first-order partial derivatives of $\ell_{\mathrm{GBS}}(\boldsymbol{\xi})$ are

$$\frac{\partial \ell_{\mathrm{GBS}}}{\partial u}(\boldsymbol{\xi}) = \sum_{i=1}^{n}\left[\frac{2a(x_i;\boldsymbol{\theta}_i)}{g(a^2(x_i;\boldsymbol{\theta}_i))}\frac{\partial a(x_i;\boldsymbol{\theta}_i)}{\partial u}g'(a^2(x_i;\boldsymbol{\theta}_i)) + \frac{1}{a'(x_i;\boldsymbol{\theta}_i)}\frac{\partial a'(x_i;\boldsymbol{\theta}_i)}{\partial u}\right],$$

for each $u \in \{\kappa, \alpha, \beta_1, \ldots, \beta_r, \gamma_1, \ldots, \gamma_s\}$, where

$$\left.\begin{array}{ll} \frac{\partial a(x_i;\boldsymbol{\theta}_i)}{\partial \kappa} = -\frac{a(x_i;\boldsymbol{\theta}_i)}{\kappa}, & \frac{\partial a(x_i;\boldsymbol{\theta}_i)}{\partial w} = \delta(x_i;\boldsymbol{\theta}_i)\frac{\partial \sigma_i}{\partial w} \\ \frac{\partial a'(x_i;\boldsymbol{\theta}_i)}{\partial \kappa} = -\frac{a'(x_i;\boldsymbol{\theta}_i)}{\kappa}, & \frac{\partial a'(x_i;\boldsymbol{\theta}_i)}{\partial w} = \Delta(x_i;\boldsymbol{\theta}_i)\frac{\partial \sigma_i}{\partial w} \end{array}\right\}, \quad w \in \{\alpha, \beta_1, \ldots, \beta_r, \gamma_1, \ldots, \gamma_s\}, \tag{19}$$

with $\delta(x_i;\boldsymbol{\theta}_i) = -\sqrt{x_i}(2\kappa\sqrt{\sigma_i})^{-1}(\sigma_i^{-1} - x_i^{-1})$ and $\Delta(x_i;\boldsymbol{\theta}_i) = -(4\kappa\sqrt{x_i\sigma_i})^{-1}(\sigma_i^{-1} + x_i^{-1})$, and $i = 1,\ldots,n$. Here,

$$
\begin{aligned}
\frac{\partial\sigma_i}{\partial\alpha} &= \Big(\sum_{j=1}^{r}\frac{\beta_j}{\sigma_{i-j}}\frac{\partial\sigma_{i-j}}{\partial\alpha} - \sum_{j=1}^{s}\frac{\gamma_j x_{i-j}}{\sigma_{i-j}^2}\frac{\partial\sigma_{i-j}}{\partial\alpha}\Big)\sigma_i,\\
\frac{\partial\sigma_i}{\partial\beta_l} &= \Big(\beta_l\ln\sigma_{i-l} + \sum_{j=1}^{r}\frac{\beta_j}{\sigma_{i-j}}\frac{\partial\sigma_{i-j}}{\partial\beta_l} - \sum_{j=1}^{s}\frac{\gamma_j x_{i-j}}{\sigma_{i-j}^2}\frac{\partial\sigma_{i-j}}{\partial\beta_l}\Big)\sigma_i, \quad l = 1,\ldots,r,\\
\frac{\partial\sigma_i}{\partial\gamma_m} &= \Big(\sum_{j=1}^{r}\frac{\beta_j}{\sigma_{i-j}}\frac{\partial\sigma_{i-j}}{\partial\gamma_m} + \gamma_m\Big[\frac{x_{i-m}}{\sigma_{i-m}}\Big] - \sum_{j=1}^{s}\frac{\gamma_j x_{i-j}}{\sigma_{i-j}^2}\frac{\partial\sigma_{i-j}}{\partial\gamma_m}\Big)\sigma_i, \quad m = 1,\ldots,s.
\end{aligned}
\tag{20}
$$

The asymptotic distribution of the ML estimator $\widehat{\boldsymbol{\xi}}$ can be used to perform inference for $\boldsymbol{\xi}$. This estimator is consistent and has an asymptotic multivariate normal joint distribution with mean $\boldsymbol{\xi}$ and covariance matrix $\boldsymbol{\Sigma}_{\widehat{\xi}}$, which may be obtained from the corresponding expected Fisher information matrix $\mathcal{I}(\boldsymbol{\xi})$. Then,

$$\sqrt{n}\,[\widehat{\boldsymbol{\xi}} - \boldsymbol{\xi}] \xrightarrow{\mathcal{D}} \mathrm{N}_{2+r+s}(\mathbf{0}, \boldsymbol{\Sigma}_{\widehat{\xi}} = \mathcal{J}(\boldsymbol{\xi})^{-1}),$$

as $n \to \infty$, where $\xrightarrow{\mathcal{D}}$ means "convergence in distribution" and $\mathcal{J}(\boldsymbol{\xi}) = \lim_{n\to\infty}[1/n]\mathcal{I}(\boldsymbol{\xi})$. Notice that $\widehat{\mathcal{I}}(\boldsymbol{\xi})^{-1}$ is a consistent estimator of the asymptotic variance–covariance matrix of $\widehat{\boldsymbol{\xi}}$. Here, we approximate the expected Fisher information matrix by its observed version obtained from the Hessian matrix $\ddot{\ell}_{\mathrm{GBS}}(\boldsymbol{\xi})$, which contains the second derivatives of $\ell_{\mathrm{GBS}}(\boldsymbol{\xi})$.

The elements of the Hessian are expressed as follows:

$$
\begin{aligned}
\frac{\partial^2\ell_{\mathrm{GBS}}}{\partial u\partial v}(\boldsymbol{\xi}) = \sum_{i=1}^{n}\Bigg[&\frac{\partial\Theta(x_i;\boldsymbol{\theta}_i)}{\partial v}g'(a^2(x_i;\boldsymbol{\theta}_i)) + 2\Theta(x_i;\boldsymbol{\theta}_i)a(x_i;\boldsymbol{\theta}_i)\frac{\partial a(x_i;\boldsymbol{\theta}_i)}{\partial v}g''(a^2(x_i;\boldsymbol{\theta}_i))\\
&- \frac{1}{\big(a'(x_i;\boldsymbol{\theta}_i)\big)^2}\frac{\partial a'(x_i;\boldsymbol{\theta}_i)}{\partial u}\frac{\partial a'(x_i;\boldsymbol{\theta}_i)}{\partial v} + \frac{1}{a'(x_i;\boldsymbol{\theta}_i)}\frac{\partial^2 a'(x_i;\boldsymbol{\theta}_i)}{\partial u\partial v}\Bigg],
\end{aligned}
\tag{21}
$$

for each $u, v \in \{\kappa, \alpha, \beta_1,\ldots,\beta_r,\gamma_1,\ldots,\gamma_s\}$, where

$$
\begin{aligned}
\Theta(x_i;\boldsymbol{\theta}_i) &= \frac{2a(x_i;\boldsymbol{\theta}_i)}{g(a^2(x_i;\boldsymbol{\theta}_i))}\frac{\partial a(x_i;\boldsymbol{\theta}_i)}{\partial u} \quad \text{and}\\
\frac{\partial\Theta(x_i;\boldsymbol{\theta}_i)}{\partial v} &= \frac{2}{g(a^2(x_i;\boldsymbol{\theta}_i))}\Bigg[\Big(1 - \frac{2a^2(x_i;\boldsymbol{\theta}_i)}{g(a^2(x_i;\boldsymbol{\theta}_i))}\Big)\frac{\partial a(x_i;\boldsymbol{\theta}_i)}{\partial u}\frac{\partial a(x_i;\boldsymbol{\theta}_i)}{\partial v} + a(x_i;\boldsymbol{\theta}_i)\frac{\partial^2 a(x_i;\boldsymbol{\theta}_i)}{\partial u\partial v}\Bigg].
\end{aligned}
$$

The partial derivatives $\frac{\partial a(x_i;\boldsymbol{\theta}_i)}{\partial u}$ and $\frac{\partial a'(x_i;\boldsymbol{\theta}_i)}{\partial u}$ are given in (19). Furthermore, the second-order partial derivatives of $a(x_i;\boldsymbol{\theta}_i)$ and $a'(x_i;\boldsymbol{\theta}_i)$ in (21), respectively, are given by

$$
\begin{aligned}
\frac{\partial^2 a(x_i;\boldsymbol{\theta}_i)}{\partial\kappa^2} &= \frac{2a(x_i;\boldsymbol{\theta}_i)}{\kappa^2}, & \frac{\partial^2 a(x_i;\boldsymbol{\theta}_i)}{\partial w^2} &= \frac{\sqrt{x_i}}{4\kappa\sigma_i^{3/2}}\Big(\frac{1}{\sigma_i} - \frac{1}{x_i}\Big)\Big(\frac{\partial\sigma_i}{\partial w}\Big)^2 + \delta(x_i;\boldsymbol{\theta}_i)\frac{\partial^2\sigma_i}{\partial w^2},\\
\frac{\partial^2 a'(x_i;\boldsymbol{\theta}_i)}{\partial\kappa^2} &= \frac{2a'(x_i;\boldsymbol{\theta}_i)}{\kappa^2}, & \frac{\partial^2 a'(x_i;\boldsymbol{\theta}_i)}{\partial w^2} &= \frac{2\kappa}{\sqrt{x_i}\sigma_i^{3/2}}\Big(\frac{1}{\sigma_i} + \frac{1}{x_i}\Big)\Big(\frac{\partial\sigma_i}{\partial w}\Big)^2 + \Delta(x_i;\boldsymbol{\theta}_i)\frac{\partial^2\sigma_i}{\partial w^2},
\end{aligned}
$$

for each $w \in \{\alpha, \beta_1,\ldots,\beta_r,\gamma_1,\ldots,\gamma_s\}$, with $\delta(x_i;\boldsymbol{\theta}_i) = -\sqrt{x_i}(2\kappa\sqrt{\sigma_i})^{-1}(\sigma_i^{-1} - x_i^{-1})$ and $\Delta(x_i;\boldsymbol{\theta}_i) = -(4\kappa\sqrt{x_i\sigma_i})^{-1}(\sigma_i^{-1} + x_i^{-1})$. Here,

$$
\begin{aligned}
\frac{\partial^2\sigma_i}{\partial\alpha^2} =& \Big[-\sum_{j=1}^{r}\frac{\beta_j}{\sigma_{i-j}}\Big(\frac{1}{\sigma_{i-j}}\Big(\frac{\partial\sigma_{i-j}}{\partial\alpha}\Big)^2 - \frac{\partial^2\sigma_{i-j}}{\partial\alpha^2}\Big) + \sum_{j=1}^{s}\frac{\gamma_j x_{i-j}}{\sigma_{i-j}^2}\Big(\frac{2}{\sigma_{i-j}}\Big(\frac{\partial\sigma_{i-j}}{\partial\alpha}\Big)^2 - \frac{\partial^2\sigma_{i-j}}{\partial\alpha^2}\Big)\Big]\sigma_i + \frac{1}{\sigma_i}\Big(\frac{\partial\sigma_i}{\partial\alpha}\Big)^2,\\
\frac{\partial^2\sigma_i}{\partial\beta_l^2} =& \Big[\ln\sigma_{i-l} + \frac{\beta_l}{\sigma_{i-l}}\frac{\partial\sigma_{i-l}}{\partial\beta_l} - \sum_{j=1}^{r}\frac{\beta_j}{\sigma_{i-j}}\Big(\frac{1}{\sigma_{i-j}}\Big(\frac{\partial\sigma_{i-j}}{\partial\beta_l}\Big)^2 - \frac{\partial^2\sigma_{i-j}}{\partial\beta_l^2}\Big) + \sum_{j=1}^{s}\frac{\gamma_j x_{i-j}}{\sigma_{i-j}^2}\Big(\frac{2}{\sigma_{i-j}}\Big(\frac{\partial\sigma_{i-j}}{\partial\beta_l}\Big)^2 - \frac{\partial^2\sigma_{i-j}}{\partial\beta_l^2}\Big)\Big]\sigma_i\\
&+ \frac{1}{\sigma_i}\Big(\frac{\partial\sigma_i}{\partial\beta_l}\Big)^2, \quad l = 1,\ldots,r,\\
\frac{\partial^2\sigma_i}{\partial\gamma_m^2} =& \Big[-\sum_{j=1}^{r}\frac{\beta_j}{\sigma_{i-j}}\Big(\frac{1}{\sigma_{i-j}}\Big(\frac{\partial\sigma_{i-j}}{\partial\gamma_m}\Big)^2 - \frac{\partial^2\sigma_{i-j}}{\partial\gamma_m^2}\Big) + \frac{x_{i-m}}{\sigma_{i-m}} - \frac{x_{i-m}}{\sigma_{i-m}^2}\frac{\partial\sigma_{i-m}}{\partial\gamma_m} + \sum_{j=1}^{s}\frac{\gamma_j x_{i-j}}{\sigma_{i-j}^2}\Big(\frac{2}{\sigma_{i-j}}\Big(\frac{\partial\sigma_{i-j}}{\partial\gamma_m}\Big)^2 - \frac{\partial^2\sigma_{i-j}}{\partial\gamma_m^2}\Big)\Big]\sigma_i\\
&+ \frac{1}{\sigma_i}\Big(\frac{\partial\sigma_i}{\partial\gamma_m}\Big)^2, \quad m = 1,\ldots,s;\ i = 1,\ldots,n.
\end{aligned}
$$

Note that the functions $a(x_i; \boldsymbol{\theta}_i)$ and $a'(x_i; \boldsymbol{\theta}_i)$ have continuous second-order partial derivatives at a given point $\boldsymbol{\theta}_i \in \mathbb{R}^4$, $i = 1, \ldots, n$. Then, by Schwarz's Theorem, it follows that the partial differentiations of these functions are commutative at that point, that is, $\frac{\partial^2 a(x_i;\boldsymbol{\theta}_i)}{\partial u \partial v} = \frac{\partial^2 a(x_i;\boldsymbol{\theta}_i)}{\partial v \partial u}$ and $\frac{\partial^2 a'(x_i;\boldsymbol{\theta}_i)}{\partial u \partial v} = \frac{\partial^2 a'(x_i;\boldsymbol{\theta}_i)}{\partial v \partial u}$, for each $u \neq v \in \{\kappa, \alpha, \beta_1, \ldots, \beta_r, \gamma_1, \ldots, \gamma_s\}$. With this in mind, the mixed partial derivatives of $a(x_i; \boldsymbol{\theta}_i)$ and $a'(x_i; \boldsymbol{\theta}_i)$ in (21) have the following form:

$$
\begin{aligned}
\frac{\partial^2 a(x_i;\boldsymbol{\theta}_i)}{\partial \kappa \partial w_1} &= -\frac{1}{\kappa} \frac{\partial a(x_i;\boldsymbol{\theta}_i)}{\partial w_1}, \\
\frac{\partial^2 a(x_i;\boldsymbol{\theta}_i)}{\partial \alpha \partial w_2} &= \frac{\sqrt{x_i}}{4\kappa \sigma_i^{3/2}} \Big(\frac{1}{\sigma_i} - \frac{1}{x_i}\Big) \frac{\partial \sigma_i}{\partial \alpha} \frac{\partial \sigma_i}{\partial w_2} + \delta(x_i; \boldsymbol{\theta}_i) \frac{\partial^2 \sigma_i}{\partial \alpha \partial w_2}, \\
\frac{\partial^2 a(x_i;\boldsymbol{\theta}_i)}{\partial \beta_l \partial \gamma_m} &= \frac{\sqrt{x_i}}{4\kappa \sigma_i^{3/2}} \Big(\frac{1}{\sigma_i} - \frac{1}{x_i}\Big) \frac{\partial \sigma_i}{\partial \beta_l} \frac{\partial \sigma_i}{\partial \gamma_m} + \delta(x_i; \boldsymbol{\theta}_i) \frac{\partial^2 \sigma_i}{\partial \beta_l \partial \gamma_m}, \\
\frac{\partial^2 a'(x_i;\boldsymbol{\theta}_i)}{\partial \kappa \partial w_1} &= -\frac{1}{\kappa} \frac{\partial a'(x_i;\boldsymbol{\theta}_i)}{\partial w_1}, \\
\frac{\partial^2 a'(x_i;\boldsymbol{\theta}_i)}{\partial \alpha \partial w_2} &= \frac{2\kappa}{\sqrt{x_i} \sigma_i^{3/2}} \Big(\frac{1}{\sigma_i} + \frac{1}{x_i}\Big) \frac{\partial \sigma_i}{\partial \alpha} \frac{\partial \sigma_i}{\partial w_2} + \Delta(x_i; \boldsymbol{\theta}_i) \frac{\partial^2 \sigma_i}{\partial \alpha \partial w_2}, \\
\frac{\partial^2 a'(x_i;\boldsymbol{\theta}_i)}{\partial \beta_l \partial \gamma_m} &= \frac{2\kappa}{\sqrt{x_i} \sigma_i^{3/2}} \Big(\frac{1}{\sigma_i} + \frac{1}{x_i}\Big) \frac{\partial \sigma_i}{\partial \beta_l} \frac{\partial \sigma_i}{\partial \gamma_m} + \Delta(x_i; \boldsymbol{\theta}_i) \frac{\partial^2 \sigma_i}{\partial \beta_l \partial \gamma_m},
\end{aligned}
$$

for each $w_1 \in \{\alpha, \beta_1, \ldots, \beta_r, \gamma_1, \ldots, \gamma_s\}$, $w_2 \in \{\beta_1, \ldots, \beta_r, \gamma_1, \ldots, \gamma_s\}$, and $l = 1, \ldots, r$; $m = 1, \ldots, s$, where $\delta(x_i; \boldsymbol{\theta}_i)$ and $\Delta(x_i; \boldsymbol{\theta}_i)$ are as before. In the above identities, the mixed partial derivatives $\frac{\partial^2 \sigma_i}{\partial \alpha \partial w_2}$ and $\frac{\partial^2 \sigma_i}{\partial \beta_l \partial \gamma_m}$, respectively, are given by

$$
\begin{aligned}
\frac{\partial^2 \sigma_i}{\partial \alpha \partial w_2} &= \Big[-\sum_{j=1}^{r} \frac{\beta_j}{\sigma_{i-j}} \Big(\frac{1}{\sigma_{i-j}} \frac{\partial \sigma_{i-j}}{\partial \alpha} \frac{\partial \sigma_{i-j}}{\partial w_2} - \frac{\partial^2 \sigma_{i-j}}{\partial \alpha \partial w_2}\Big) + \sum_{j=1}^{s} \frac{\gamma_j x_{i-j}}{\sigma_{i-j}^2} \Big(\frac{2}{\sigma_{i-j}} \frac{\partial \sigma_{i-j}}{\partial \alpha} \frac{\partial \sigma_{i-j}}{\partial w_2} - \frac{\partial^2 \sigma_{i-j}}{\partial \alpha \partial w_2}\Big)\Big] \sigma_i + \frac{1}{\sigma_i} \frac{\partial \sigma_i}{\partial \alpha} \frac{\partial \sigma_i}{\partial w_2}, \\
\frac{\partial^2 \sigma_i}{\partial \beta_l \partial \gamma_m} &= \Big[\frac{\beta_l}{\sigma_{i-l}} \frac{\partial \sigma_{i-l}}{\partial \gamma_m} - \sum_{j=1}^{r} \frac{\beta_j}{\sigma_{i-j}} \Big(\frac{1}{\sigma_{i-j}} \frac{\partial \sigma_{i-j}}{\partial \beta_l} \frac{\partial \sigma_{i-j}}{\partial \gamma_m} - \frac{\partial^2 \sigma_{i-j}}{\partial \beta_l \partial \gamma_m}\Big) + \sum_{j=1}^{s} \frac{\gamma_j x_{i-j}}{\sigma_{i-j}^2} \Big(\frac{2}{\sigma_{i-j}} \frac{\partial \sigma_{i-j}}{\partial \beta_l} \frac{\partial \sigma_{i-j}}{\partial \gamma_m} - \frac{\partial^2 \sigma_{i-j}}{\partial \beta_l \partial \gamma_m}\Big)\Big] \sigma_i \\
&\quad + \frac{1}{\sigma_i} \frac{\partial \sigma_i}{\partial \beta_l} \frac{\partial \sigma_i}{\partial \gamma_m}, \quad l = 1, \ldots, r;\ m = 1, \ldots, s \text{ and } i = 1, \ldots, n.
\end{aligned}
$$

3.2.3. Residual Analysis

We carry out goodness-of-fit through residual analysis. In particular, we consider the generalized Cox–Snell residual, which is given by

$$
r^{\text{cs}} = -\ln \hat{S}(x_i | \mathcal{F}_{i-1}), \tag{22}
$$

where $\hat{S}(x_i|\mathcal{F}_{i-1})$ denotes the fitted conditional survival function. When the model is correctly specified, the Cox–Snell residual has a unit exponential (EXP(1)) distribution; see Bhatti (2010).

4. The GBS-AACD Models

Now, we introduce a generalization of the linear form for the conditional median dynamics based on the Box-Cox transformation; see Box and Cox (1964) and Fernandes and Grammig (2006) for pertinent details. Hereafter, we use the log-linear form σ_i given in (16) with $r = 1$ and $s = 1$ (i.e., the GBS-ACD($r = 1, s = 1$) model, which we abbreviate as the GBS-ACD model, since a higher-order model does not increase the distributional fit of the residuals (Bhatti 2010)). Therefore, (16) results in

$$
\ln \sigma_i = \alpha + \beta \ln \sigma_{i-1} + \gamma \Big[\frac{x_{i-1}}{\sigma_{i-1}}\Big]. \tag{23}
$$

The asymmetric version of the GBS-ACD model—GBS-AACD model—is given by

$$
\sigma_i = \alpha + \beta \sigma_{i-1} + \gamma \sigma_{i-1} \big(|\varphi_{i-1} - b| + c(\varphi_{i-1} - b)\big), \tag{24}
$$

where b and c are the shift and rotation parameters, respectively. By applying the Box-Cox transformation with parameter $\lambda \geq 0$ to the conditional duration model process σ_i and introducing the parameter ν, we can write (24) as

$$\frac{\sigma_i^\lambda - 1}{\lambda} = \alpha_* + \beta \frac{\sigma_{i-1}^\lambda - 1}{\lambda} + \gamma_* \sigma_{i-1}^\lambda \big(|\varphi_{i-1} - b| + c(\varphi_{i-1} - b)\big)^\nu. \tag{25}$$

The parameter λ determines the shape of the transformation, i.e., concave ($\lambda \leq 1$) or convex ($\lambda \geq 1$), and the parameter ν aims to transform the (potentially shifted and rotated) term $\big(|\varphi_{i-1} - b| + c(\varphi_{i-1} - b)\big)$. Setting $\alpha = \lambda\alpha_* - \beta + 1$ and $\gamma = \lambda\gamma_*$, we obtain

$$\sigma_i^\lambda = \alpha + \beta\sigma_{i-1}^\lambda + \gamma\sigma_{i-1}^\lambda \big(|\varphi_{i-1} - b| + c(\varphi_{i-1} - b)\big)^\nu. \tag{26}$$

We present below the forms of GBS-AACD models obtained from different specifications. Note that the Logarithmic GBS-ACD type II is equivalent to (23).

- Augmented ACD (GBS-AACD):

$$\sigma_i^\lambda = \alpha + \beta\sigma_{i-1}^\lambda + \gamma\sigma_{i-1}^\lambda \big(|\varphi_{i-1} - b| + c(\varphi_{i-1} - b)\big)^\nu.$$

- Asymmetric power ACD (GBS-A-PACD) ($\lambda = \nu$):

$$\sigma_i^\lambda = \alpha + \beta\sigma_{i-1}^\lambda + \gamma\sigma_{i-1}^\lambda \big(|\varphi_{i-1} - b| + c(\varphi_{i-1} - b)\big)^\lambda.$$

- Asymmetric logarithmic ACD (GBS-A-LACD) ($\lambda \to 0$ and $\nu = 1$):

$$\ln\sigma_i = \alpha + \beta\ln\sigma_{i-1} + \gamma\big(|\varphi_{i-1} - b| + c(\varphi_{i-1} - b)\big).$$

- Asymmetric ACD (GBS-A-ACD) ($\lambda = \nu = 1$):

$$\sigma_i = \alpha + \beta\sigma_{i-1} + \gamma\sigma_{i-1}\big(|\varphi_{i-1} - b| + c(\varphi_{i-1} - b)\big).$$

- Power ACD (GBS-PACD) ($\lambda = \nu$ and $b = c = 0$):

$$\sigma_i^\lambda = \alpha + \beta\sigma_{i-1}^\lambda + \gamma x_{i-1}^\lambda.$$

- Box-Cox ACD (GBS-BCACD) ($\lambda \to 0$ and $b = c = 0$):

$$\ln\sigma_i = \alpha + \beta\ln\sigma_{i-1} + \gamma\varphi_{i-1}^\nu.$$

- Logarithmic ACD type I (GBS-LACD I) ($\lambda, \nu \to 0$ and $b = c = 0$):

$$\ln\sigma_i = \alpha + \beta\ln\sigma_{i-1} + \gamma\ln x_{i-1}.$$

- Logarithmic ACD type II (GBS-LACD II) ($\lambda \to 0$, $\nu = 1$ and $b = c = 0$):

$$\ln\sigma_i = \alpha + \beta\ln\sigma_{i-1} + \gamma\varphi_{i-1}.$$

5. Numerical Results for the GBS-ACD Models

In this section, we perform two simulation studies, one for evaluating the behavior of the ML estimators of the GBS-ACD models, and another for examining the performance of the residuals. We have focused on the GBS-ACD models because similar results were obtained for the GBS-AACD models.

5.1. Study of ML Estimators

Through a Monte Carlo (MC) study, we evaluate here the finite sample behavior of the ML estimators of the GBS-ACD model parameters presented in Section 3. The sample sizes considered were $n = 500$, 1000, and 3000. The number of MC replications was $B = 1000$. The data-generating process for each of the realizations is

$$X_i = \psi_i \epsilon_i, \quad \ln \psi_i = 0.10 + 0.90 \ln \psi_{i-1} + 0.10\left[\frac{x_{i-1}}{\psi_{i-1}}\right], \tag{27}$$

where the distribution of ϵ_i is a generalized gamma with density $f(x;\mu,\sigma,\nu) = \theta^\theta z^\theta \nu \exp(-\theta z)/(\Gamma(\theta)x)$ with $z = (x/\mu)^\mu$ and $\theta = 1/\sigma^2|\nu|^2$. Note that stationarity conditions only require $|\beta| < 1$, and in (27), $\beta = 0.9$; see Bauwens and Giot (2000).

We estimate the GBS-ACD model parameters through the following two-step algorithm:

- Estimate only the ACD parameters (α, β, γ) by the Nelder and Mead (1965) (NM) approach, with starting values for (α, β, γ) fixed at $(0.01, 0.70, 0.01)$, σ_0 being the unconditional sample median, and the value of κ being fixed at $\kappa_0 = \sqrt{2\left[\overline{x}/\text{Med}[x] - 1\right]}$, where $\overline{x}$ and $\text{Med}[x]$ are the sample mean and median based on observations (data) $\boldsymbol{x} = (x_1, \ldots, x_n)^\top$, respectively;
- Estimate all of the ACD model parameters using the Broyden–Fletcher–Goldfarb–Shanno (BFGS) quasi-Newton approach, with starting values obtained from the estimates obtained in the anterior step.

The estimation results from the simulation study are presented in Table 2. The following sample statistics for the ML estimates are reported: Mean, coefficients of skewness (CS) and kurtosis (CK), relative bias (the RB, in absolute values, is defined as $|\text{E}(\widehat{\tau}) - \tau|/\tau$, where $\widehat{\tau}$ is an estimator of a parameter τ), and root mean squared error ($\sqrt{\text{MSE}}$). The sample CS and CK are, respectively, given by

$$\text{CS}(\boldsymbol{x}) = \frac{\sqrt{n[n-1]}}{[n-2]} \frac{n^{-1}\sum_{i=1}^n [x_i - \bar{x}]^3}{\left[n^{-1}\sum_{i=1}^n (x_i - \bar{x})^2\right]^{3/2}} \quad \text{and} \quad \text{CK}(\boldsymbol{x}) = \frac{n^{-1}\sum_{i=1}^n [x_i - \bar{x}]^4}{\left[n^{-1}\sum_{i=1}^n (x_i - \bar{x})^2\right]^2},$$

where $\boldsymbol{x} = (x_i, \ldots, x_n)^\top$ denotes an observation of the sample. This definition of kurtosis is the raw measure, not excess kurtosis, which subtracts three from this quantity. From Table 2, we note that, as the sample size increases, the RBs and $\sqrt{\text{MSE}}$ become smaller. We can also note that both $\widehat{\beta}$ and $\widehat{\gamma}$ are persistently skewed and somewhat unstable; nonetheless, they remain close to a normal distribution in terms of their skewness and kurtosis values.

Table 2. Results of the Monte Carlo (MC) experiments based on the generalized gamma distribution.

		BS-ACD	BS-LA-ACD	BS-LO-ACD	BS-PE-ACD	BS-t-ACD
		$n = 500$				
$\widehat{\beta}$	Mean	0.8893	0.8920	0.8932	0.8919	0.8931
	SD	0.0455	0.0607	0.0430	0.0447	0.0432
	CS	−1.2311	−2.6638	−1.4726	−1.5005	−1.4408
	CK	5.5554	16.9123	6.9795	6.8696	6.8782
	RB	0.0118	0.0088	0.0074	0.0089	0.0075
	$\sqrt{\text{MSE}}$	0.0467	0.0612	0.0435	0.0454	0.0438
$\widehat{\gamma}$	Mean	0.1210	0.1135	0.1147	0.1165	0.1146
	SD	0.0277	0.0291	0.0241	0.0252	0.0243
	CS	0.3561	0.3929	0.2769	0.3364	0.2823
	CK	3.2213	3.2985	3.2425	3.2974	3.2485
	RB	0.2108	0.1354	0.1470	0.1655	0.1461
	$\sqrt{\text{MSE}}$	0.0348	0.0321	0.0282	0.0302	0.0283
		$n = 1000$				
$\widehat{\beta}$	Mean	0.8925	0.8960	0.8953	0.8945	0.8955
	SD	0.0309	0.0364	0.0287	0.0292	0.0287
	CS	−0.8445	−1.0195	−0.7789	−0.8251	−0.7971
	CK	4.2081	4.7648	3.9145	4.0728	4.0305
	RB	0.0082	0.0043	0.0051	0.0060	0.0049
	$\sqrt{\text{MSE}}$	0.0318	0.0366	0.0291	0.0297	0.0291
$\widehat{\gamma}$	Mean	0.1089	0.1052	0.1059	0.1068	0.1058
	SD	0.0182	0.0196	0.0164	0.0168	0.0164
	CS	0.2838	0.2560	0.2254	0.2605	0.2493
	CK	3.2734	3.1051	3.2301	3.2127	3.2768
	RB	0.0892	0.0525	0.0590	0.0685	0.0581
	$\sqrt{\text{MSE}}$	0.0203	0.0203	0.0174	0.0181	0.0174
		$n = 2000$				
$\widehat{\beta}$	Mean	0.8959	0.8986	0.8972	0.8967	0.8971
	SD	0.0218	0.0250	0.0203	0.0206	0.0203
	CS	−0.6096	−0.8894	−0.6294	−0.6631	−0.6345
	CK	3.7129	4.7915	3.9189	3.9201	3.8773
	RB	0.0045	0.0015	0.0030	0.0035	0.0031
	$\sqrt{\text{MSE}}$	0.0222	0.0251	0.0204	0.0208	0.0205
$\widehat{\gamma}$	Mean	0.1024	0.1017	0.1015	0.1019	0.1014
	SD	0.0123	0.0136	0.0113	0.0114	0.0113
	CS	0.0999	0.0920	0.0696	0.1094	0.0880
	CK	2.8660	2.8964	2.9778	2.9514	2.9710
	RB	0.0241	0.0173	0.0157	0.0192	0.0146
	$\sqrt{\text{MSE}}$	0.0125	0.0137	0.0114	0.0116	0.0114

5.2. Study of Residuals

We now carry out an MC simulation study to examine the performance of the Cox–Snell residual r^{cs} defined in (22). To do so, we use the estimation procedure presented in Section 5.1 and consider only the BS-PE-ACD model, as it provides greater flexibility in relation to other models, that is, it has either less or greater (lighter or heavier tails) than the BS distribution. The BS-PE-ACD samples are generated using the transformation in (5). We simulate $B = 1000$ MC samples of size $n = 500$. The empirical autocorrelation function (ACF) of the residual r^{cs} is plotted in Figure 1a. This plot indicates that the BS-PE-ACD model is well specified, since the residual r^{cs} mimics a sequence of independent and identically distributed RVs and there is no indication of serial correlation. Moreover, the empirical mean of the residual r^{cs}, whose value was expected to be 1, was 0.9836. Finally, using a quantile-against-quantile (QQ) plot with a simulated envelope (see Figure 1b), we note that the

Cox–Snell residual has an excellent agreement with the EXP(1) distribution, which supports the adequacy and flexibility of the BS-PE-ACD model. It is then possible to conclude that the residual r^{cs} seems adequate to assess the adjustment of the proposed models.

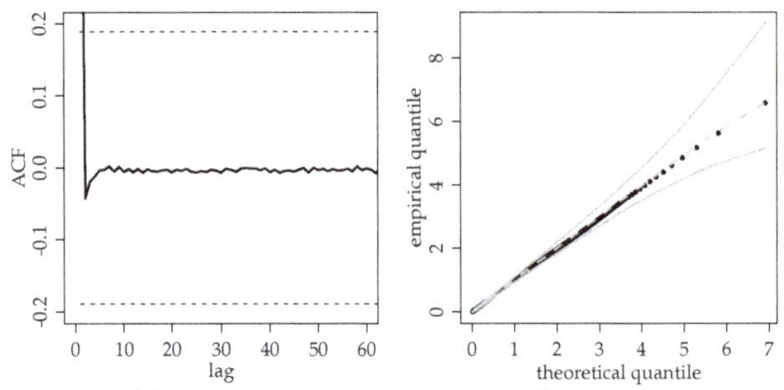

(**a**) ACF plot (**b**) QQ plot

Figure 1. Autocorrelation function (ACF) plot and quantile-against-quantile (QQ) plot with envelope for the residuals.

6. Application to Analysis of Financial Transaction Data

In this section, our objective is to assess the GBS-ACD and GBS-AACD models using TD data. In particular, we consider here three TD data sets studied in Bhatti (2010), corresponding to the time elapsed (in seconds) between two consecutive transactions, which cover forty trading days from January 1, 2002 to February 28, 2002: International Business Machines (IBM), Johnson and Johnson Company (JNJ), and The Proctor and Gamble Company (PG). Note that, as mentioned before, these types of data exhibit some diurnal patterns, so that the final data sets are constructed from adjusted TD $\bar{x}_i = x_i/\hat{\phi}$, where $\hat{\phi} = \exp(\hat{s})$ and $\hat{s}$ denotes a set of quadratic functions and indicator variables for each half-hour interval of the trading day from 9:30 am to 4:00 pm; for more details, see Giot (2000), Tsay (2002), and Bhatti (2010).

6.1. Exploratory Data Analysis

Table 3 provides some descriptive statistics for both plain and diurnally adjusted TD data, which include central tendency statistics and coefficients of variation (CV), of skewness (CS), and of kurtosis (CK), among others. These measures indicate the positively skewed nature and the high kurtosis of the data. Figure 2 shows graphical plots of the ACF and partial ACF for the IBM, JNJ, and PG data sets, which indicate the presence of serial correlation.

Table 3. Summary statistics for the International Business Machines (IBM), Johnson and Johnson Company (JNJ), and The Proctor and Gamble Company (PG) data sets.

	Data	Min.	Max.	Median	Mean	SD	CV	CS	CK
Plain data	IBM	1	166	5	6.768	6.234	92.10%	3.106	20.368
	JNJ	1	225	7	10.391	11.737	109.45%	3.187	18.706
	PG	1	172	7	10.904	12.066	110.66%	2.973	14.339
Adjusted data	IBM	0.169	32.523	1.038	1.384	1.252	90.43%	3.023	19.802
	JNJ	0.131	33.973	0.976	1.557	1.680	107.91%	3.135	18.463
	PG	0.121	26.327	0.985	1.582	1.718	108.58%	2.865	13.311

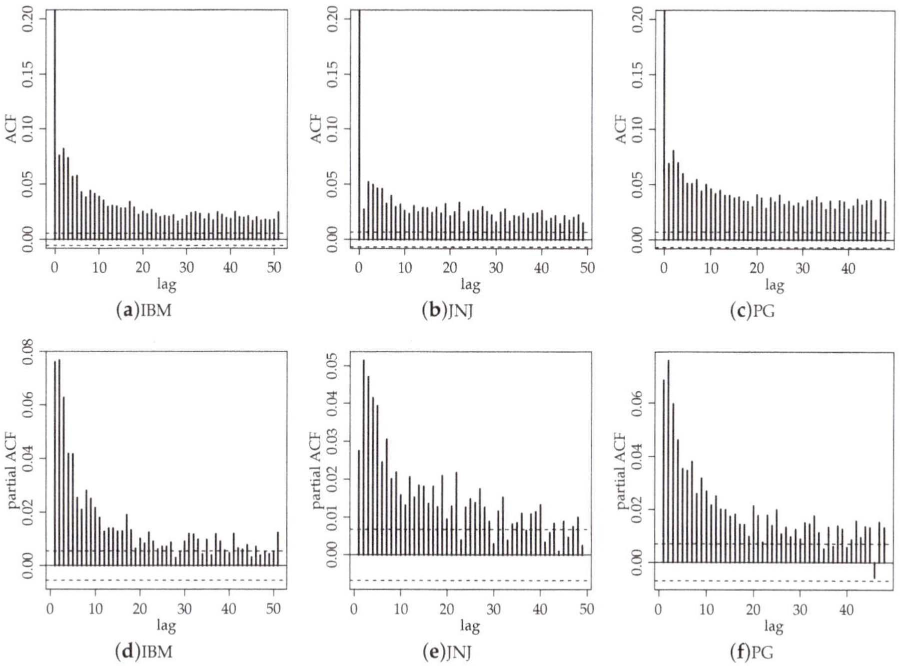

Figure 2. Autocorrelation and partial autocorrelation functions for the indicated data sets.

The hazard function of a positive RV X is given by $h_X(t) = f_X(x)/(1 - F_X(x))$, where $f_X(\cdot)$ and $F_X(\cdot)$ are the PDF and CDF of X, respectively. A useful way to characterize the hazard function is by the scaled total time on test (TTT) function, namely, we can detect the type of hazard function that the data have and then choose an appropriate distribution. The TTT function is given by $W_X(u) = H_X^{-1}(u)/H_X^{-1}(1)$ for $0 \leq u \leq 1$, where $H_X^{-1}(u) = \int_0^{F_X^{-1}(u)}[1 - F_X(y)]\mathrm{d}y$, where $F_X^{-1}(\cdot)$ is the inverse CDF of X. By plotting the consecutive points $(k/n, W_n(k/n))$ with $W_n(k/n) = [\sum_{i=1}^{k} x_{(i)} + (n - k)x_k]/\sum_{i=1}^{n} x_{(i)}$ for $k = 0, \ldots, n$, and $x_{(i)}$ being the ith-order statistic, it is possible to approximate $W_X(\cdot)$; see Aarset (1987) and Azevedo et al. (2012).

From Figure 3, we observe that the TTT plots suggest a failure rate with a unimodal shape. We also observe that the histograms suggest a positive skewness for the data density. This supports the results obtained in Table 3. However, Huber and Vanderviere (2008) pointed out that, in cases where the data follow a skewed distribution, a significant number of observations can be classified as atypical when they are not. The boxplots depicted in Figure 3 suggest such a situation, i.e., most of the observations considered as potential outliers by the usual boxplot are not outliers when we consider the adjusted boxplot.

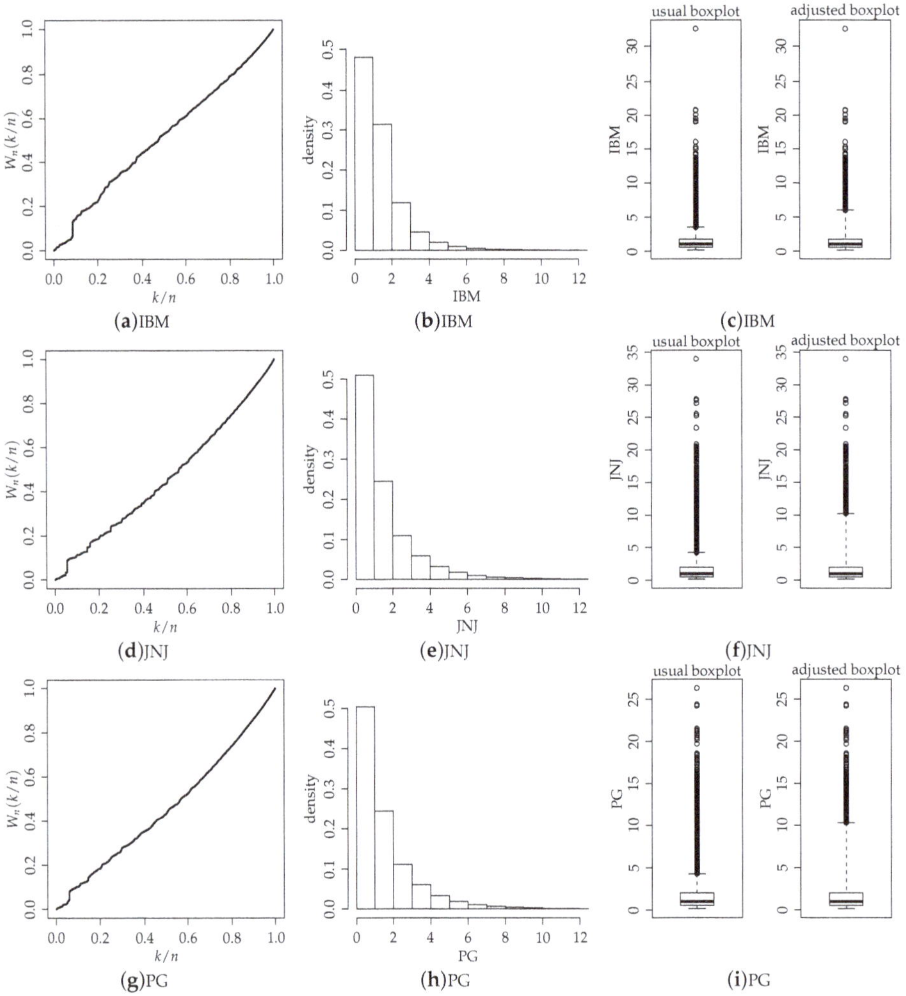

Figure 3. Total time on test (TTT) plot (**a**), histogram (**b**), and usual and adjusted boxplots (**c**) for the indicated data sets.

6.2. Estimation Results and Analysis of Goodness-of-Fit for the GBS-ACD Models

We now estimate the GBS-ACD models by the maximum likelihood method using the steps described in Section 5.1. Tables 4–6 present the estimation results for the indicated models. The standard errors (SEs) are reported in parentheses and ℓ stands for the value of the log-likelihood function, whereas AIC $= -2\ell + 2k$ and BIC $= -2\ell + k \ln n$ denote, respectively, the Akaike information and Bayesian information criteria, where k stands for the number of parameters and n for the number of observations. The maximum and minimum values of the sample autocorrelations (ACF) from order 1 to 60 are also reported. Finally, $\bar{\gamma}$ denotes the mean magnitude of autocorrelation for the first 15 lags, namely, $\bar{\gamma} = 1/15 \sum_{i=1}^{15} |\gamma_k|$, where $\gamma_k = \text{cor}(x_i, x_{i+k})$. The mean magnitude of autocorrelation $\bar{\gamma}$ is relevant for separating the influence of the sample size on the measure of the degree of autocorrelation in the residuals.

From Tables 4–6, we observe that all of the parameters are statistically significant at the 1% level. It is also interesting to observe that, in general, the ACD parameter estimates are very similar across the models independently of the assumed distribution. In terms of AIC values, the BS-PE-ACD model outperforms all other models. Based on the BIC values, we note that the BS-PE-ACD model once again outperforms the remaining models, except for the JNJ data set. However, in this case, there does not exist one best model, since the BIC values for the BS-ACD and BS-PE-ACD models are very close.

In order to check for misspecification, we look at the sample ACF from order 1 to 60. Tables 4–6 report that there is no sample autocorrelation greater than 0.05 (in magnitude) throughout the models and residuals. Figure 4 shows the QQ plots of the Cox–Snell residual with the IBM, JNJ, and PG data sets. The QQ plot allows us to check graphically if the residual follows the EXP(1) distribution. These graphical plots show an overall superiority in terms of fit of the BS-PE-ACD model. Moreover, the empirical means of the residual r^{cs} for the BS-PE-ACD model with the IBM, GM, and PG data sets were 1.0271, 0.9990, and 1.0153, respectively. Thus, the BS-PE-ACD model seems to be more suitable for modeling the data considered. It must be emphasized that this model provides greater flexibility in terms of kurtosis compared to the BS-ACD model.

Table 4. Estimation results based on the generalized Birnbaum–Saunders autoregressive conditional duration (GBS-ACD) models for IBM trade durations.

	BS-ACD	BS-LA-ACD	BS-L0-ACD	BS-PE-ACD	BS-t-ACD
α	−0.0454	−0.0495	−0.0503	−0.0473	−0.0470
	(0.00164)	(0.00199)	(0.00174)	(0.00168)	(0.00168)
β	0.9393	0.9387	0.9367	0.9373	0.9383
	(0.00381)	(0.00436)	(0.00389)	(0.00389)	(0.00384)
γ	0.0324	0.0385	0.0372	0.0342	0.0336
	(0.00116)	(0.00158)	(0.00128)	(0.00121)	(0.00119)
κ	0.8736	0.6862	0.4949	0.7934	0.8575
	(0.00173)	(0.00192)	(0.00115)	(0.00532)	(0.00266)
η				0.9019	54.4022
				(0.00582)	(7.05075)
ℓ	−153644.7	−157875.7	−154274.3	−153519.2	−153625.1
AIC	307297.4	315759.4	308556.6	307048.4	307260.2
BIC	307336.4	315798.4	308595.6	307097.2	307309
max ACF	0.0253	0.0293	0.0258	0.0341	0.0251
min ACF	−0.0075	−0.0100	−0.0089	−0.0052	−0.0079
$\bar{\gamma}$	0.0060	0.0061	0.0057	0.0074	0.0059

Table 5. Estimation results based on the GBS-ACD models for JNJ trade durations.

	BS-ACD	BS-LA-ACD	BS-L0-ACD	BS-PE-ACD	BS-t-ACD
α	−0.0174	−0.0168	−0.0503	−0.0174	−0.0179
	(0.00080)	(0.00070)	(0.00174)	(0.00081)	(0.00078)
β	0.9744	0.9830	0.9367	0.9744	0.9769
	(0.00207)	(0.00138)	(0.00389)	(0.00209)	(0.00171)
γ	0.0113	0.0108	0.0372	0.0113	0.0115
	(0.00051)	(0.00044)	(0.00128)	(0.00051)	(0.00050)
κ	1.0427	0.8296	0.4949	1.0195	1.0395
	(0.00256)	(0.00288)	(0.00115)	(0.00749)	(0.00256)
η				0.9747	334.0810
				(0.00755)	(12.93302)
ℓ	−112581.4	−116353.4	−154274.3	−112575.8	−112582.8
AIC	225170.8	232714.8	308556.6	225161.6	225175.6
BIC	225208.1	232752.1	226547.4	225208.3	225222.1
max ACF	0.0197	0.0191	0.0182	0.0157	0.0189
min ACF	−0.0103	−0.0144	−0.0134	−0.0111	−0.0112
$\bar{\gamma}$	0.0075	0.0071	0.0072	0.0061	0.0070

Table 6. Estimation results based on the GBS-ACD models for PG trade durations.

	BS-ACD	BS-LA-ACD	BS-L0-ACD	BS-PE-ACD	BS-t-ACD
α	−0.0182 (0.00066)	−0.0313 (0.00281)	−0.0181 (0.00086)	−0.0189 (0.00070)	−0.0231 (0.00101)
β	0.9859 (0.00101)	0.9744 (0.00396)	0.9748 (0.00223)	0.9856 (0.00105)	0.9810 (0.00150)
γ	0.0115 (0.00041)	0.0202 (0.00180)	0.0117 (0.00055)	0.0120 (0.00044)	0.0146 (0.00063)
κ	1.0636 (0.00267)	0.8404 (0.00299)	0.5944 (0.00171)	1.0058 (0.00814)	1.0596 (0.00286)
η				0.9401 (0.00770)	267.2753 (67.87919)
ℓ	−108461.2	−111511.8	−113251	−108433	−108464.8
AIC	216930.4	223031.6	226510	216876	216939.6
BIC	216967.5	223068.7	218064	216922.4	216986.1
max ACF	0.0396	0.0309	0.0341	0.0326	0.0352
min ACF	−0.0143	−0.0133	−0.0140	−0.0101	−0.0132
$\bar{\gamma}$	0.0112	0.0067	0.0080	0.0114	0.0087

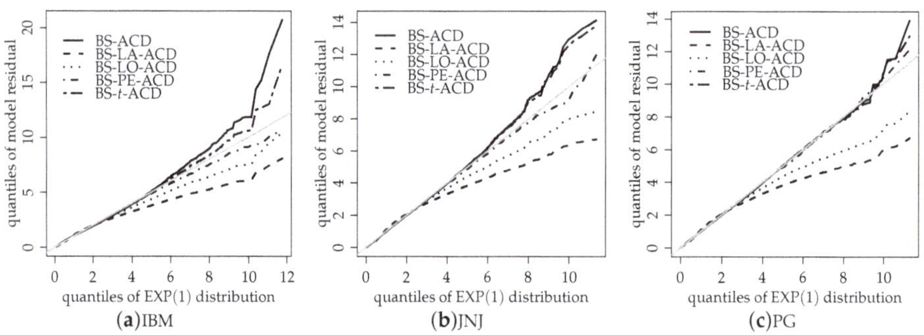

Figure 4. QQ plot for the Cox–Snell residual with the indicated data sets.

6.3. Estimation Results for the BS-PE-AACD Models

We estimate here different ACD specifications (see Section 4) assuming a BS-PE PDF and using JNJ TD data. We focus on the BS-PE-AACD models (in short, AACD models), since, as observed in Section 6.2, this model fits the data adequately to provide effective ML-based inference. The estimation is performed using the steps presented in Section 5.1.

Tables 7 and 8 report the estimation results for different specifications. It is important to point out that the estimates of the BS-PE parameters κ and η are quite robust throughout the specifications. The Box-Cox ACD result (see column BCACD) shows that allowing ν of φ_{i-1} to freely vary in the logarithm ACD processes (LACD I and LACD II) increases the log-likelihood value, indicating that ν may play a role. In fact, $\hat{\nu}$ is significantly different from zero and one, thus supporting the BCACD model against its logarithm counterparts, i.e., LACD I and LACD II. The AIC values show that the BCACD, LACD I, and AACD are best models. From the BIC values, the LACD I, BCACD, and AACD models are the best ones. Note, however, that the BIC values for the LACD I and BCACD models are quite close. Tables 4–6 also show that there is no sample autocorrelation greater than 0.05 (in magnitude) throughout the models and residuals.

Table 7. Estimation results for ACD specifications of JNJ trade durations. A star (∗) indicates that the parameter estimate is not significantly different from zero.

	LACD I	LACD II	BCACD	PACD
α	7.2771e-05	−0.0174	−0.2719	0.0449
	(0.00165)	(0.00126)	(0.06500)	(0.01096)
β	0.9638	0.9744	0.9817	0.9266
	(0.02594)	(0.00294)	(0.00464)	(0.01604)
γ	0.0189	0.0113	0.2713	0.0258
	(0.00166)	(0.00081)	(0.06526)	(0.00893)
λ				0.4606 *
				(0.40488)
ν			0.0713	
			(0.02436)	
κ	1.0190	1.0195	1.0189	1.0126
	(0.01245)	(0.00753)	(0.00748)	(0.00752)
η	0.9746	0.9747	0.9748	0.9678
	(0.03448)	(0.00758)	(0.00753)	(0.00754)
ℓ	−112544.7	−112575.8	−112539.5	−112558.6
AIC	225099.4	225161.6	225091	225129.2
BIC	225146	225208.3	225146.9	225185.1
max ACF	0.0175	0.0156	0.0158	0.0119
min ACF	−0.0130	−0.0113	−0.0134	−0.0188
$\bar{\gamma}$	0.0057	0.0061	0.0055	0.0045

Table 8. Estimation results for ACD specifications of JNJ trade durations. A star (∗) indicates that the parameter estimate is not significantly different from zero.

	A-ACD	A-LACD	A-PACD	AACD
α	0.0267	−0.0167	0.1358	0.0319
	(0.00122)	(0.00344)	(0.00728)	(0.00881)
β	0.9537	0.9745	0.7975	0.8241
	(0.00601)	(0.00239)	(0.00077)	(0.00599)
γ	0.0139	0.0140	0.0632	0.1329
	(0.00100)	(0.00046)	(0.00918)	(0.00730)
λ			0.1118	0.5896
			(0.01008)	(0.08903)
ν				0.1348
				(0.01590)
b	−0.1060 *	0.0610 *	−0.6393	−0.4250
	(0.69799)	(0.35477)	(0.21157)	(0.10707)
c	−0.1493	−0.1949	−0.1395 *	0.1229
	(0.05026)	(0.03656)	(1.82254)	(0.06525)
κ	1.0187	1.0195	1.0188	1.0182
	(0.00749)	(0.00749)	(0.00750)	(0.00749)
η	0.9740	0.9747	0.9737	0.9746
	(0.00754)	(0.00755)	(0.00755)	(0.00756)
ℓ	−112574.5	−112575.8	−112681.5	−112543.1
AIC	225163	225165.6	225379	225104.2
BIC	225228.3	225230.9	225453.6	225188.2
max ACF	0.0148	0.0157	0.0171	0.0137
min ACF	−0.0114	−0.0111	−0.0253	−0.0147
$\bar{\gamma}$	0.0057	0.0061	0.0081	0.0049

7. Concluding Remarks

We have introduced a general class of ACD models based on GBS distributions. These distributions possess either lighter or heavier tails than the BS distribution, thus providing a wider class of positively skewed densities with nonnegative support. In addition, we have proposed a wider class of GBS-ACD models based on the Box-Cox transformation with a shape parameter to the conditional duration process and an asymmetric response to shocks. We then investigated the performance of the maximum likelihood estimates of the GBS-ACD models by means of an MC study. We also compared the proposed GBS-ACD and GBS-AACD models through an analysis with real financial data sets, which has shown the superiority of the BS-PE-ACD and BS-PE-BCACD models. A future line of research may be the out-of-sample forecast abilities of these models, as well as their application to other types of irregularly time-spaced data (besides TD data).

Author Contributions: All authors contributed equally to this manuscript. All authors have read and agreed to the published version of the manuscript

Funding: This research received no external funding.

Conflicts of Interest: The authors declare no conflict of interest.

Appendix A

Mathematical Proofs

Proof of Proposition 2. Since $\mu = \mathrm{E}[\varepsilon_i]$ and the process $\eta_i = (\ln X_i - \mu) - \ln \sigma_i$ is a martingale difference sequence, $\mathrm{E}[\eta_i|\mathcal{F}_{i-1}] = 0$ almost surely (a.s.). Replacing (16) in the equation $\ln X_i = \ln \sigma_i + \eta_i + \mu$, note that the GBS-ACD$(r,s)$ model can be written as

$$\ln X_i = \alpha + \mu(1 + \textstyle\sum_{j=1}^{r} \beta_j) - \sum_{j=1}^{r} \beta_j \eta_{i-j} + \sum_{j=1}^{s} \gamma_j \left[\frac{X_{i-j}}{\sigma_{i-j}}\right] + \sum_{j=1}^{r} \beta_j \ln X_{i-j} + \eta_i. \tag{A1}$$

Note that

$$\mathrm{E}\left[\frac{X_{i-j}}{\sigma_{i-j}}\right] = \mathrm{E}[\varphi_{i-j}] = \tfrac{1}{2}(2 + u_1\kappa^2), \tag{A2}$$

where, in the first equality, we use the relation $X_i = \sigma_i \varphi_i$; in the second equality, the identity $\mathrm{E}[\varphi_i] = (2 + u_1\kappa^2)/2$ is used, where $u_r = u_r(g) = \mathrm{E}[U^r]$ with $U \sim \mathrm{G}\chi^2(1, g)$, because $\varphi_i = \exp(\varepsilon_i) \sim \mathrm{GBS}(\kappa, 1, g)$.

Provided that $\{X_i\}$ is a strictly stationary process, the transformed process $\{\ln X_i\}$ is always strictly stationary, too. Using this fact, taking expectation on both sides in (A1), and using the identity (A2), we obtain, after some algebra, that

$$\mathrm{E}[\ln X_i] = \frac{2[\alpha + \mu(1 + \sum_{j=1}^{r} \beta_j)] + (2 + u_1\kappa^2) \sum_{j=1}^{s} \gamma_j}{2(1 - \sum_{j=1}^{r} \beta_j)},$$

whenever $\sum_{j=1}^{r} \beta_j \neq 1$. The proof is complete. □

Proof of Proposition 3. From Proposition 2 follows the expression for $\mathrm{E}[\ln X_i]$. In what follows, we find the expression for $\mathrm{E}[(\ln X_i)^2]$. Indeed, since $X_i = \sigma_i \varphi_i$, σ_i is $\mathcal{F}_{i-1}$-measurable and $\varphi_i \sim \mathrm{GBS}(\kappa, 1, g)$, it follows that

$$\begin{aligned}
&\mathrm{E}[\ln X_i] = \mu + \mathrm{E}[\ln \sigma_i], \\
&\mathrm{E}[(\ln X_i)^2] = \mu(2 + \mu) + \mathrm{E}[(\ln \sigma_i)^2] + 2\mu \mathrm{E}[\ln \sigma_i], \\
&\mathrm{E}\left[\ln \sigma_i \left(\tfrac{X_i}{\sigma_i}\right)\right] = \mathrm{E}\left[\ln \sigma_i \, \mathrm{E}[\varphi_i|\mathcal{F}_{i-1}]\right] = \tfrac{1}{2}(2 + u_1\kappa^2)\mathrm{E}[\ln \sigma_i], \\
&\mathrm{E}\left[\tfrac{X_{i-1}}{\sigma_{i-1}}\right] = \tfrac{1}{2}(2 + u_1\kappa^2) \\
&\mathrm{E}\left[\left(\tfrac{X_{i-1}}{\sigma_{i-1}}\right)^2\right] = \mathrm{Var}[\varphi_{i-1}] + \mathrm{E}^2[\varphi_{i-1}] \overset{(7)}{=} \tfrac{1}{2}(u_2 k^4 + 4u_1 k^2 + 2).
\end{aligned} \tag{A3}$$

Taking the square of $\ln \sigma_i$ in (23) and after the expectation, by a strictly stationary process, we have

$$\begin{aligned} \mathrm{E}[(\ln \sigma_i)^2] &= \alpha^2 + \beta^2 \mathrm{E}[(\ln \sigma_i)^2] + 2\alpha\beta \mathrm{E}[\ln \sigma_i] \\ &\quad + \gamma^2 \mathrm{E}\big[(\tfrac{X_{i-1}}{\sigma_{i-1}})^2\big] + 2\gamma\alpha \mathrm{E}\big[\tfrac{X_{i-1}}{\sigma_{i-1}}\big] + 2\gamma\beta \mathrm{E}\big[\ln \sigma_{i-1}(\tfrac{X_{i-1}}{\sigma_{i-1}})\big]. \end{aligned} \tag{A4}$$

Combining the Equation (A3) with (A4),

$$(1-\beta^2)\mathrm{E}[(\ln \sigma_i)^2] = \alpha^2 - 2\alpha\beta + \tfrac{\gamma^2}{2}(u_2\kappa^4 + 4u_1\kappa^2 + 2) + \gamma\alpha(2 + u_1\kappa^2) - \gamma\beta(2 + u_1\kappa^2)\{\mathrm{E}[\ln X_i] - \mu\}.$$

Using this identity and Proposition 2 in the second identity for $\mathrm{E}[(\ln X_i)^2]$ in (A3), the proof follows. □

References

Aarset, M. V. 1987. How to identify a bathtub hazard rate. *IEEE Trans. Rel.* 36: 106–08. [CrossRef]

Allen, D., F. Chan, M. McAleer, and S. Peiris. 2008. Finite sample properties of the QMLE for the log-ACD model: Application to Australian stocks. *J. Econometrics* 147: 163–83. [CrossRef]

Azevedo, C., V. Leiva, E. Athayde, and N. Balakrishnan. 2012. Shape and change point analyses of the Birnbaum-Saunders-*t* hazard rate and associated estimation. *Comp. Statist. Data Anal.* 56: 3887–97. [CrossRef]

Barros, M., G. A. Paula, and V. Leiva. 2008. A new class of survival regression models with heavy-tailed errors: Robustness and diagnostics. *Lifetime Data Anal.* 14: 316–32. [CrossRef]

Bauwens, L., and P. Giot. 2000. The logarithmic ACD model: An application to the bid-ask quote process of three NYSE stocks. *Ann. Econ. Statist.* 60: 117–49. [CrossRef]

Bauwens, L., and P. Giot. 2003. Asymmetric ACD models: Introducing price information in ACD models. *Empir. Econ.* 28: 709–31. [CrossRef]

Bhatti, C. R. 2010. The Birnbaum-Saunders autoregressive conditional duration model. *Math. Comp. Simul.* 80: 2062–78. [CrossRef]

Bhogal, S. K., and R. Variyam Thekke. 2019. Conditional duration models for high-frequency data: A review on recent developments. *J. Econ. Surv.* 33: 252–73. [CrossRef]

Birnbaum, Z. W., and S. C. Saunders. 1969. A new family of life distributions. *J. Appl. Prob.* 6: 319–27. [CrossRef]

Bollerslev, T. 1986. Generalized autoregressive conditional heteroskedasticity. *J. Econometrics* 31: 307–27. [CrossRef]

Box, G. E. P., and D. R. Cox. 1969. An analysis of transformations. *J. R. Statist. Soc. B* 26: 211–43. [CrossRef]

Chiang, M. 2007. A smooth transition autoregressive conditional duration model. *Stud. Nonlinear Dyn. E.* 11: 108–44. [CrossRef]

De Luca, G., and P. Zuccolotto. 2006. Regime-switching Pareto distributions for ACD models. *Comp. Statist. Data Anal.* 51: 2179–91. [CrossRef]

Diamond, D. W., and R. E. Verrechia. 1987. Constraints on short-selling and asset price adjustments to private information. *J. Finan. Econ.* 18: 277–311. [CrossRef]

Díaz-García, J. A., and J. R. Domínguez-Molina. 2006. Some generalisations of Birnbaum-Saunders and sinh-normal distributions. *Int. Math. Forum* 1: 1709–27. [CrossRef]

Díaz-García, J. A., and V. Leiva. 2005. A new family of life distributions based on the contoured elliptically distributions. *J. Statist. Plann. Infer.* 128: 445–57. [CrossRef]

Engle, R. F. 1982. Autoregressive conditional heteroscedasticity with estimates of the variance of United Kingdom inflation. *Econometrica* 50: 987–1008. [CrossRef]

Engle, R., and J. Russell. 1998. Autoregressive conditional duration: A new method for irregularly spaced transaction data. *Econometrica* 66: 1127–62. [CrossRef]

Easley, D., and M. O'Hara. 1992. Time and the process of security price adjustment. *The Journal of Finance* 47: 577–605. [CrossRef]

Easley, D., N. M. Kiefer, and M. O'Hara. 1997. The information content of the trading process. *Journal of Empirical Finance* 4: 159–86. [CrossRef]

Fang, K. T., S. Kotz, and K. W. Ng. 1990. *Symmetric Multivariate and Related Distributions*. London: Chapman & Hall.

Fernandes, M., and J. Grammig. 2006. A family of autoregressive conditional duration models. *J. Econometrics* 130: 1–23. [CrossRef]

Ghosh, Y. N., and B. Mukherjee. 2006. On probabilistic properties of conditional median and quantiles. *Statist. Prob. Letters* 76: 1775–80. [CrossRef]

Giot, P. 2000. Time transformations, intraday data and volatility models. *J. Comp. Finance* 4: 31–62. [CrossRef]

Grammig, J., and K. Maurer. 2000. Non-monotonic hazard functions and the autoregressive conditional duration model. *Economet. J.* 3: 16–38. [CrossRef]

Hubert, M., and E. Vandervieren. 2008. An adjusted boxplot for skewed distributions. *Comp. Statist. Data Anal.* 52: 5186–201. [CrossRef]

Jasiak, J. 1998. Persistence in intertrade durations. *Finance* 19: 166–95. [CrossRef]

Leiva, V., M. Barros, G. A. Paula, and A. Sanhueza. 2008. Generalized Birnbaum-Saunders distributions applied to air pollutant concentration. *Environmetrics* 19: 235–49. [CrossRef]

Leiva, V., H. Saulo, J. Leão, and C. Marchant. 2014. A family of autoregressive conditional duration models applied to financial data. *Comp. Statist. Data Anal.* 79: 175–91. [CrossRef]

Lunde, A. 2008. *A Generalized Gamma Autoregressive Conditional Duration Model*. Discussion Paper. Denmark: Aalborg University.

Marchant, C., K. Bertin, V. Leiva, and H. Saulo. 2013. Generalized Birnbaum-Saunders kernel density estimators and an analysis of financial data. *Comp. Statist. Data Anal.* 63: 1–15. [CrossRef]

Mayorov, K. 2011. Modelling Trade Durations with the Birnbaum-Saunders Autoregressive Model. M.Sc. thesis, McMaster University, Hamilton, ON, Canada.

Nelder, J. A., and R. Mead. 1965. A simplex method for function minimization. *Comp. J.* 7: 308–13. [CrossRef]

Pacurar, M. 2008. Autoregressive conditional durations models in finance: A survey of the theoretical and empirical literature. *J. Econ. Surv.* 22: 711–51. [CrossRef]

Pathmanathan, D., K. H. Ng, and M. S. S. Peiris. 2009. On estimation of autoregressive conditional duration (ACD) models based on different error distributions. *S. Lankan J. Appl. Statist.* 10: 251–69.

Rieck, J., and J. Nedelman. 1991. A log-linear model for the Birnbaum-Saunders distribution. *Technometrics* 33: 51–60.

Sanhueza, A., Leiva, V., Balakrishnan, N. 2008. The generalized Birnbaum–Saunders distribution and its theory, methodology and application. *Comm. Statist. Theor. Meth.* 37: 645–70. [CrossRef]

Saulo, H., J. Leão, V. Leiva, and R. G. Aykroyd. 2019. Birnbaum-Saunders autoregressive conditional duration models applied to high-frequency financial data. *Stat. Pap.* 60: 1605–29. [CrossRef]

Saunders, S. C. 1974. A family of random variables closed under reciprocation. *J. Amer. Statist. Assoc.* 69: 533–39. [CrossRef]

Tsay, R. S. 2002. *Analysis of Financial Time Series*. New York: John Wiley & Sons.

Zhang, M. Y., J. R. Russell, and R. S. Tsay. 2001. A nonlinear autoregressive conditional duration model with applications to financial transaction data. *J. Econometrics* 104: 179–207. [CrossRef]

Journal of
Risk and Financial Management

MDPI

Article

Bank Competition and Credit Risk in Euro Area Banking: Fragmentation and Convergence Dynamics

Maria Karadima [1,*] and Helen Louri [1,2]

1 Department of Economics, Athens University of Economics and Business, 76 Patission Street, GR-10434 Athens, Greece; elouri@aueb.gr
2 European Institute/Hellenic Observatory, London School of Economics, Houghton Street, London WC2A 2AE, UK
* Correspondence: karadimam@aueb.gr

Received: 9 February 2020; Accepted: 12 March 2020; Published: 16 March 2020

Abstract: Consolidation in euro area banking has been the major trend post-crisis. Has it been accompanied by more or less competition? Has it led to more or less credit risk? In all or some countries? In this study, we examine the evolution of competition (through market power and concentration) and credit risk (through non-performing loans) in 2005–2017 across all euro area countries (EA-19), as well as core (EA-Co) and periphery (EA-Pe) countries separately. Using Theil inequality and convergence analysis, our results support the continued existence of fragmentation as well as of divergence within and/or between core and periphery with respect to competition and credit risk, especially post-crisis, in spite of some partial reintegration trends. Policy measures supporting faster convergence of our variables would be helpful in establishing a real banking union.

Keywords: banking competition; credit risk; NPLs; Theil index; convergence analysis

JEL Classification: C23; G21

1. Introduction

Financial integration has been one of the major goals of the European Union (EU) because of its significant capability to offer more opportunities for risk sharing, better allocation of capital, and higher economic growth (Baele et al. 2004). Financial integration may be defined as "a situation whereby there are no frictions that discriminate between economic agents in their access to—and their investment of—capital, particularly on the basis of their location" (European Central Bank, ECB 2003). A related concept is financial fragmentation, which is often used to indicate some forms of imperfect integration (Claessens 2019). Fragmentation generally refers to financial markets, which fragment either by type of product/participant or geographically (Financial Stability Board, FSB 2019).

From the establishment of the European Monetary Union (EMU) up to the outbreak of the global financial crisis, the euro area witnessed a rapidly growing financial integration, which was evident in terms of both volume and prices (De Sola Perea and Van Nieuwenhuyze 2014). Financial integration was also expected to promote competition in the euro area banking sector (Casu and Girardone 2009), due inter-alia to increased disintermediation and cross-border competition (De Bandt and Davis 2000). Nevertheless, the financial crisis of 2008 reversed some advances in competitive pressure, which had been achieved until then (Maudos and Vives 2019).

Financial fragmentation peaked during the euro area debt crisis (2011–2012) and declined afterwards due to the measures taken by the ECB. According to Al-Eyd and Berkmen (2013), the unconventional monetary policy undertaken by the ECB was instrumental in reducing the overall degree of financial market fragmentation. Berenberg-Gossler and Enderlein (2016) confirm that after the ECB announcement of the Outright Monetary Transactions (OMT) program in 2012 there was a gradual, but often fragile, decline of financial fragmentation across all markets. After a temporary correction between late 2015 and 2016, the aggregate post-crisis reintegration trend in the euro area resumed with respect to prices. In contrast, the post-crisis reintegration trend with respect to quantities stalled in 2015, partly due to the supply of excess reserves from the ECB, which had reduced the need for counterparties to trade across borders (ECB 2018).

In this study, we test the hypothesis of the existence of fragmentation in the euro area (EA) as a whole (EA-19 group—19 countries of the Euro Area from 1 January, 2015), as well as in core countries (EA-Co group) and periphery countries (EA-Pe group), with respect to bank competition (through market power and concentration) and credit risk over the period 2005–2017. The group of core countries includes eleven countries (Austria, Belgium, Estonia, Germany, Finland, France, Latvia, Lithuania, Luxembourg, Netherlands, and Slovakia), while the periphery group includes eight countries (Cyprus, Greece, Ireland, Italy[1], Malta, Portugal, Slovenia, and Spain). The periphery countries were hit by the 2008 financial crisis more severely than the core countries, while some of them (namely, Cyprus, Greece, Ireland, Slovenia, and Spain) received state aid through various impaired asset measures or direct state recapitalization. The classification of countries into each group is based on a prior identification from the European Commission of distinct groups of EU Member States, according to their levels of non-performing loans (NPLs) (Magnus et al. 2017). More specifically, the hypothesis of the existence of fragmentation is tested through the investigation of inequalities among the country-members of each group, as well as between EA-Co and EA-Pe, with respect to bank competition, bank concentration and credit risk. In total, four types of inequality—with respect to a given variable—are considered: (a) inequality between banks in a given country (within-country inequality), (b) inequality between banks of different countries belonging to the same group (between-country inequality), (c) inequality between banks or countries in a given group (within-group inequality), and (d) inequality between banks or countries of different groups (between-group inequality).

A second hypothesis, which is tested in this study, refers to the presence of β-convergence and σ-convergence[2] among the country-members of each group, with respect to bank competition, bank concentration, and credit risk. It should be noted, however, that a possible convergence of the variables under examination is only a necessary but not a sufficient condition for the achievement of financial integration in the euro area.

The Lerner index for market power, used in our study as an inverse proxy for bank competition, has been calculated following the innovative stochastic frontier estimator of market power, suggested by Kumbhakar et al. (2012). Bank concentration, which also indicates the degree of competitive pressure, is measured by the Herfindahl–Hirschman Index (HHI) and the market share of the five largest banks (CR5). Credit risk is approximated by non-performing loans (NPLs). Finally, we use the Theil inequality index for the four variables to examine the evolution of inequality either within/between countries or within/between groups.

To the best of our knowledge, this is the first time in the empirical literature that the evolution and convergence of bank competition, concentration and credit risk are examined across EA-19, EA-Co and EA-Pe to test for continued fragmentation and converging or diverging trends. Our analysis, which employs a panel dataset of euro area banks from 2005 to 2017, extends beyond the period of financial crisis, thereby taking into account the non-standard measures adopted by the ECB to support further integration. By using data from all the 19 euro area countries, which have a common currency and a single bank supervisory mechanism, a possible bias that might stem from the use of

---

1 While Italy should in principle be considered as a core country since it has been one of the EU founding members, it is classified in this study as a periphery country because of its high levels of NPLs during the crisis. A classification of Italy as a periphery country has also been made in other studies (see Al-Eyd and Berkmen 2013; Anastasiou et al. 2019; Louri and Migiakis 2019).

2 In the case of competition, for example, β-convergence would apply if countries with lower levels of competition were found to tend to catch up with countries characterized by higher levels of competition, while σ-convergence would apply if the dispersion of competition levels across countries showed a tendency to decline over time.

either heterogeneous data or data coming from only a subset of euro area countries was eliminated. In addition to uncovering the evolution of financial integration a major aim of our study was to provide substantiated clues to policy makers about the progress of integration and underline the need for further measures required to achieve a real banking union.

The use of an alternative measure of credit risk, such as the loan loss provisions (LLPs), was prohibited by the lack of non-available comparable data. In addition, the lack of bank-level data on total assets and NPLs did not facilitate the breakdown of total inequality in both bank concentration and credit risk into their within-country and between-country components, an issue that remains open for future research. Finally, since a limitation of this study is that countries with possibly different characteristics form a group on the basis of a priori classification, future research could use novel methods (e.g., Phillips and Sul 2007) to identify groups of countries that exhibit convergence ("convergence clubs").

The rest of the study is organized as follows. Section 2 describes the evolution of competitive conditions in EU banking. Sections 3–5 examine the evolution of bank competition, concentration and credit risk, respectively. Section 6 investigates the Theil inequality for bank competition, concentration and credit risk. Section 7 displays the convergence analysis, while Section 8 concludes.

2. Evolution of Competitive Conditions in EU Banking

2.1. Before the Introduction of the Euro

We classify the literature review on the evolution of competition in the European Union into three groups, according to the period examined by each study: (1) before the introduction of the euro in 1999, (2) around the introduction of the euro, and (3) after the introduction of the euro. The above classification has been made in order to facilitate the comparison of the results.

The first group of studies examines the degree of competition before the introduction of the euro in 1999. The major milestones of this period were: (1) the adoption of the Second Banking Directive (Directive 89/646/ European Economic Community (EEC) of 15 December, 1989), which entered into force on 1 January, 1993, providing a "passport" to European banks, which allowed a bank licensed in an EU country to establish branches or provide financial services in any of the other Member States, while the prudential supervision of a bank remained the responsibility of the home Member State; (2) the start of Stage One (1990–1993) of the EMU on 1 July, 1990, a date on which the restrictions on the free movement of goods, persons, capital and services between the EMU Member States were removed; (3) the establishment of the European Union with the signing of the Treaty on the European Union (the "Maastricht Treaty") on 7 February, 1992; and (4) the start of Stage Two (1994–1998) of the EMU on 1 January, 1994, with the establishment of the European Monetary Institute (EMI), whose task was to coordinate monetary policy among the central banks of the Member States and make all the necessary preparations for the introduction of the euro in Stage Three, starting from 1 January, 1999.

Bikker and Haaf (2002) examine the competitive conditions and concentration in 23 European and non-European industrialized countries over the period 1988–1998. Using the H-statistic, they find that all the banking markets under examination were characterized by monopolistic competition. Perfect competition could not be excluded for a number of European large-bank markets, while competition appeared to be higher in Europe than in Canada, Japan and the US. De Bandt and Davis (2000) investigate the effects of the EMU on the competitive conditions in France, Germany and Italy over the period 1992–1996. The H-statistic indicates that large banks in Germany and France operated in an environment of monopolistic competition, in contrast to small banks, which seemed to have some monopoly power. In Italy, both large and small banks operated under monopolistic competition. The H-statistic, calculated for the same period on a sample of US banks, indicates that the US banking system was more competitive than those of France, Germany and Italy.

Some other studies of this group use cross-country data from the EU area only. Fernandez de Guevara et al. (2007) investigate the progress of financial integration in 15 EU countries. The study reveals the existence of convergence in interest rates during the period 1993–2001, which is attributed to the convergence of inflation rates and the decrease in nominal interest rates. By examining the evolution of the levels of competition, measured by the Lerner index, they find that market power increased about 10% on average in 10 of the 15 countries during the period 1993–2000. They also constructed a Theil inequality index for the Lerner index, which helped them to identify an increase in market power inequality in the 15 countries under examination. The decomposition of the Theil index into a within-country and a between-country component suggests that the main part of the market power inequality was within countries themselves (within-country inequality).

The rest of the studies in this group examine the case of one EU country only. Hondroyiannis et al. (1999) assess the competitive conditions in Greece over the period 1993–1995. The results, based on the use of the H-statistic, indicate that Greek banks operated in an environment characterized by monopolistic competition. These competitive conditions were formed as a result of the enactment of the EU Second Banking Directive, the lifting of controls on foreign exchange, and the liberalization of capital movements. Angelini and Cetorelli (2003) examine the banking competitive conditions in Italy over the period 1984–1997. Using the Lerner index for each of five geographical banking markets in Italy (i.e., Nationwide, North-East, North-West, Center, and South), they find that competitive conditions across the five areas remained relatively unchanged until 1992, before starting to improve thereafter as a result of the implementation of the EU Second Banking Directive in 1993. Another finding is that the large-scale bank consolidation in Italy during the 1990s not only did not worsen competitive conditions, but actually improved banks' efficiency. Coccorese (2004) examines the banking competitive conditions in Italy during the period 1997–1999. Using the H-statistic, he finds that banks operated under conditions of monopolistic competition at a national level. When banks are classified into four macro-regions (North-West, North-East, Center, and South and Islands), the results indicate that banks in both the North-West and the North-East regions operated in an environment characterized by perfect competition.

The conclusion that can be drawn from the first group of studies is that euro area banks operated under conditions of monopolistic competition during the pre-EMU period, while contradictory results have been derived regarding the sign of the change in competition levels.

2.2. *Around the Introduction of the Euro*

The second group of studies examines the competitive conditions in the EU during a period including a few years both before and after the introduction of the euro, which was introduced in 1999 but entered into circulation in 2002. For this reason, some studies (Apergis et al. 2016; Sun 2009) consider 2000 as the end year of the pre-EMU period and 2001 as the start year of the after-EMU period.

Some of the studies of this group employ data not only from the EU area but also from other geographical regions for comparison purposes. Bikker and Spierdijk (2008) examine the developments in bank competition in 101 countries worldwide during the period 1986–2004. Using the H-statistic, they find that the EU-15 (15 EU Member States from 1 January, 1995) experienced a major break in competitive conditions around 2001–2002, followed by a decrease of about 60% in competition. In contrast, nine Eastern European countries that have joined the EU since 2004 experienced a modest decrease of about 10% in competition during the years 1994–2004. Sun (2009) assesses the degree of bank competition in the US, the UK and 10 euro area countries over the period 1995–2009. The results of the study indicate that the euro area experienced convergence of competition levels across member countries, as well as a decrease in competition, measured by the H-statistic, after the introduction of the EMU (period 2001–2007). Competition also decreased during the crisis period (2008–2009), especially in countries where large credit and housing booms had been observed pre-crisis.

Some other studies of this group examine countries belonging to the EU area only, making in some cases a comparison between euro area and non-euro area countries. Staikouras and Koutsomanoli-Filippaki (2006) assess the competitive conditions in the EU-15 and EU-10 (10 EU Member States that joined in 2004) countries over the period 1998–2002. The results of the study, based on three different H-statistic specifications, indicate that banks in both the EU-15 and the EU-10 countries operated in an environment of monopolistic competition. Goddard et al. (2013) examine the convergence of bank profits in eight EU countries (Belgium, Denmark, France, Germany, Italy, Netherlands, Spain and the UK) over the period 1992–2007. They find that the average profitability was lower for banks that had a higher capital level, while banks that were more efficient and diversified were characterized by higher average profitability. Another finding is that excess profit presented weaker persistence during the years 1999–2007 than in the previous period 1992–1998, indicating that the introduction of the EU financial integration, especially with the adoption of the euro and the implementation of the Financial Services Action Plan (FSAP), intensified bank competition. Apergis et al. (2016) assess the level of bank competition across three EU economic blocks (EU-27—27 EU Member States from 1 January, 2007; EA-17—17 EA Member States from 1 January, 2011; and the remaining 12 EU countries) over the period 1996–2011. The H-statistic, calculated on the basis of three alternative specifications of both scaled and unscaled reduced-form revenue equations, indicates the presence of conditions of monopolistic competition across all the above economic blocks. Competition levels seemed to be lower in the EA-17 countries than in the EU-27 countries, which could be due to the increasing mergers and acquisitions in the EA-17 countries. The results also show that the competition level in the EA-17 countries decreased slightly in the post-EMU period (2001–2007), compared to the pre-EMU period (1996–2000), while the competition levels in the EA-17 countries showed a slight decline during the post-crisis period (2008–2011). The development of banking competition policy in the EU area, as well as the trends in bank competition and concentration, during the 25-year period 1992–2017, are examined by Maudos and Vives (2019). They find that the recent global financial crisis interrupted the process of normalization of the banking competition policy in the EU, which had started in the 1980s, and reversed the advances that had been made in competitive pressures due to the implementation of the Single Market initiative and the introduction of the euro. After the crisis, competition policy in the EU focused on limiting the distortions in competition created by the massive state aid granted to banks. They also find that the crisis accelerated the pace of bank concentration in the countries that had been hit most severely by the crisis and whose banking systems had been subject to restructuring.

Regarding studies that examine the case of only one country, Gischer and Stiele (2008) examine the banking competitive conditions in Germany over the period 1993–2002. Using the H-statistic on a dataset of more than 400 cooperative banks (Sparkassen), they find that these banks operated under conditions of monopolistic competition. In addition, the H-statistic for small cooperative banks was lower than for large cooperative banks, suggesting that smaller cooperative banks seemed to enjoy more market power than larger ones.

In summary, the second group of studies suggests that banks in the euro area operated under conditions of monopolistic competition during the period around the introduction of the euro. The results regarding the impact of the introduction of the euro on bank competition are contradictory, with most studies suggesting a decline in competition during the post-EMU period.

2.3. *After the Introduction of the Euro*

The third group of studies examines the evolution of competition well after the introduction of the euro. Some of these studies examine the case of more than one EU country. Casu and Girardone (2009) assess the effects of the EU deregulation and competition policies on bank concentration and competition in the five largest EU banking markets (France, Germany, Italy, Spain, and the UK) over the period 2000–2005. Using the HHI and CR5 concentration indices, they observe an increasing degree of bank concentration during the period under examination, with the exception of Spain. Furthermore, the values of concentration indices vary significantly across countries. Their findings are confirmed when a sub-sample of only commercial banks is taken into account. The use of the Lerner index did not provide any evidence that competition increased until 2005, while the results derived from the estimation of H-statistics indicate conditions of monopolistic competition in all five countries. Weill (2013) investigates whether economic integration in the European Union banking industries has favored bank competition over the period 2002–2010, by following two different approaches. First, he examines the evolution of competition in the EU-27 countries, as measured by the Lerner index and the H-statistic. The results do not confirm a general improvement of bank competition over the entire period under examination. In contrast, a small increase of the Lerner index was observed during the pre-crisis period, which, however, slowed down after the outbreak of the global financial crisis, in particular in the case of the twelve new EU member countries. Second, he employs β-convergence and σ-convergence tests on the Lerner index and the H-statistic, which suggest that during the period 2002–2010 the least competitive banking systems had experienced a greater improvement in competition than the most competitive banking systems, while the disparity in competition levels among the EU-27 countries was reduced. The impact of the 2008 global crisis on the fragmentation of the banking system in 11 euro area countries over the period 1999–2011 was examined by Lucotte (2015) who uses ten different harmonized banking indicators covering the areas of concentration and competition, efficiency, stability, development, and activity. Using a hierarchical cluster analysis, he indicates the existence of large dissimilarities since the creation of the euro area between Greece and Italy on the one hand, and the other nine countries on the other. The nine countries were split after 2008 into two different clusters with large dissimilarities. The first cluster comprises Austria, Belgium, Finland, France, and Germany, while Ireland, Netherlands, Portugal, and Spain belong to the other. Cruz-Garcia et al. (2017) investigate the impact of financial market integration on the evolution of disparities among European banks' market power. They use bank-specific data for the EA-12 countries (12 EA Member States from 1 January, 2001) over the period 2000–2014, and find that the Lerner index of bank market power increased in 10 of the 12 countries. Using a Theil inequality index for the Lerner index, they find that while the differences in market power between European banks decreased significantly over the period 2000–2014, significant and persistent differences in market power existed between banks in the same country.

Regarding studies of this group that examine the case of only one country, Moch (2013) investigates the competition conditions in Germany over the period 2001–2009. Using the H-statistic on a dataset comprising data from 1888 private, savings and cooperative banks, the study finds that interpretations about competitive conditions that are based on H-statistic calculated at a national level can be distorted when the banking market is fragmented, as in Germany. When examining separately the three banking pillars in Germany (i.e., private, savings, and cooperative banks), the hypothesis for the presence of monopoly power in any of these pillars was definitely rejected. Savings and cooperative banks seemed to operate either under monopolistic conditions in a long-run equilibrium or under long-run competitive conditions with flat average cost functions, while the private banks operated in a long-run competitive equilibrium.

In summary, the third group of studies suggests that monopolistic competition has been the dominant form of bank competition in the euro area after the introduction of the euro. The results regarding the evolution of competition are either inconclusive or suggest a decrease in competition levels after the 2008 global financial crisis.

A conclusion that can be drawn from all the studies presented in this section is that there is general agreement in the literature that banks in the euro area operated under conditions of monopolistic competition during the last 25 years. On the other hand, contradictory results are obtained regarding the impact of the introduction of the euro on the level of bank competition. This lack of consensus may be due to differences in the competition measures used, as well as to differences in the data employed with respect to geographical and time coverage.

3. Bank Competition in the Euro Area

3.1. Measuring Bank Competition through Market Power

The literature on the measurement of competition follows two major approaches: the structural and the non-structural. The structural approach, which has its roots in the traditional Industrial

Organization theory, embraces the Structure-Conduct-Performance (SCP) paradigm and the Efficiency Structure Hypothesis (ESH). The SCP paradigm states that a higher degree of concentration is likely to cause collusive behavior among the larger banks, resulting in superior market performance. Because of their ability to capture structural features of a market, concentration ratios are often used to proxy for competition. The most frequently used concentration ratios are the Herfindahl-Hirschman Index (HHI) and the k-bank concentration ratios (CRk). The HHI index is the sum of the squares of the market shares in total banking assets of all banks in a banking system, while the CRk concentration ratio is the sum of the shares of the k largest banks. The Efficiency Structure Hypothesis (ESH) investigates the relationship between the efficiency of larger banks and their performance. A widely used ESH indicator is the Boone indicator (Boone 2008), which is calculated as the elasticity of profits or market share to marginal costs. The idea underlying the Boone indicator is that competition improves the performance or market share of efficient firms and weakens the performance or market share of inefficient ones.

The non-structural approach developed on the basis of the New Empirical Industrial Organization (NEIO) theory assesses the competitive behavior of firms without having to rely on information about the structure of the market. The H-statistic, developed by Panzar and Rosse (1987), and the Lerner index, developed by Lerner (1934), are the most well-known non-structural measures of competition. The Panzar and Rosse's model employs firm-level data to investigate the degree to which a change in input prices is reflected in equilibrium revenues. This model uses the H-statistic, which takes a negative value to indicate a monopoly, a value between 0 and 1 to indicate monopolistic competition and the value 1 to indicate perfect competition. The Lerner index is a direct measure of a bank's market power. It represents the markup of prices over marginal cost and its value theoretically ranges between 0 (perfect competition) and 1 (pure monopoly). In practice, however, negative values may be observed for banks that face problems.

In our study, bank market power is measured by the Lerner index (L), which identifies the degree of monopoly power as the difference between the price (P) of a firm and its marginal cost (MC) at the profit-maximizing rate of output:

$$L = \frac{P - MC}{P} \tag{1}$$

A zero value of the Lerner index indicates competitive behavior, while a bigger distance between price and marginal cost is associated with greater market power.

In contrast to P, the value of MC is not directly observable, so we derive its value from the estimation of the following translog cost function:

$$\begin{aligned} lnTC_{it} &= \alpha_0 + \alpha_Q lnQ_{it} + 0.5\alpha_{QQ}(lnQ_{it})^2 + \sum_{k=1}^{3} \alpha_k lnW_{k,it} + \sum_{k=1}^{3} \alpha_{Qk} lnQ_{it} lnW_{k,it} \\ &+ 0.5 \sum_{j=1}^{3}\sum_{k=1}^{3} \alpha_{jk} lnW_{j,it} lnW_{k,it} + \alpha_E lnE_{it} + 0.5\alpha_{EE}(lnE_{it})^2 + \sum_{k=1}^{3} \alpha_{Ek} lnE_{it} lnW_{k,it} \\ &+ \alpha_{EQ} lnE_{it} lnQ_{it} + \alpha_T T + 0.5\alpha_{TT} T^2 + \alpha_{TQ} T lnQ_{it} + \sum_{k=1}^{3} \alpha_{Tk} T lnW_{k,it} + \varepsilon_{it} \end{aligned} \tag{2}$$

where TC is total cost (sum of total interest and non-interest expenses), Q is total assets (proxy for bank output), W_1 is the ratio of other operating expenses to total assets (proxy for input price of capital), W_2 is the ratio of personnel expenses to total assets (proxy for input price of labor), W_3 is the ratio of total interest expenses to total funding (proxy for input price of funds), T is a time trend variable, E is total equity and ε_{it} is the error term. The subscripts i and t denote bank i and year t, respectively.

The time trend (T) has been included in (2) to account for advances in banking technology. We have also included in (2) the level of Total Equity (E), since it can be used in loan funding as a substitute for deposits or other borrowed funds.

Symmetry conditions have been applied to the translog portion of (2), while the restriction of linear homogeneity in input prices is imposed by dividing in (2) both total cost and input prices by one of the input prices.

$$\begin{aligned}\ln\left(\frac{TC_{it}}{W_{3,it}}\right) &= \alpha_0 + \alpha_Q lnQ_{it} + 0.5\alpha_{QQ}(lnQ_{it})^2 + \sum_{k=1}^{2} \alpha_k \ln\left(\frac{W_{k,it}}{W_{3,it}}\right) \\ &+ \sum_{k=1}^{2} \alpha_{Qk} lnQ_{it} \ln\left(\frac{W_{k,it}}{W_{3,it}}\right) + 0.5 \sum_{j=1}^{2}\sum_{k=1}^{2} \alpha_{jk} \ln\left(\frac{W_{j,it}}{W_{3,it}}\right)\ln\left(\frac{W_{k,it}}{W_{3,it}}\right) \\ &+ \alpha_E lnE_{it} + 0.5\alpha_{EE}(lnE_{it})^2 + \sum_{k=1}^{2} \alpha_{Ek} lnE_{it} \ln\left(\frac{W_{k,it}}{W_{3,it}}\right) + \alpha_{EQ} lnE_{it} lnQ_{it} \\ &+ \alpha_T T + 0.5\alpha_{TT}T^2 + \alpha_{TQ} TlnQ_{it} + \sum_{k=1}^{2} \alpha_{Tk} Tln\left(\frac{W_{k,it}}{W_{3,it}}\right) + \varepsilon_{it}\end{aligned} \tag{3}$$

3.2. Calculation of a Lerner Index Using a Stochastic Frontier Methodology

The traditional approach of first estimating Equation (3) and then using the derived coefficient values to calculate marginal cost (*MC*) is based on the unrealistic assumption that all firms are profit maximizers. This approach may also produce negative values for the Lerner index, although this should normally be expected to be non-negative. These problems can be solved by employing the innovative procedure suggested by Kumbhakar et al. (2012) who draw on a stochastic frontier methodology from the efficiency literature to estimate the mark-up for each observation.

Starting from the fact that a profit-maximizing behavior of a bank *i* at time *t* requires that

$$P_{it} \geq MC_{it} \equiv \frac{\partial TC_{it}}{\partial Q_{it}} \tag{4}$$

where *P* is defined as the ratio of total revenues (total interest and non-interest income) to total assets, and after doing some mathematics, we arrive at the following equation:

$$\frac{TR_{it}}{TC_{it}} = \frac{\partial lnTC_{it}}{\partial lnQ_{it}} + v_{it} + u_{it} \tag{5}$$

where *TR* denotes the total revenues, v_{it} is a symmetric two-sided noise term, which is included in (5) to capture the possibility that the total revenue share in total cost might by affected by other unobserved variables, and u_{it} is a non-negative term, which captures the mark-up. This way, Equation (5) becomes a stochastic frontier function, where

$$\frac{\partial lnTC_{it}}{\partial lnQ_{it}} + v_{it}$$

represents the stochastic frontier of *TRit/TCit*, i.e., the minimum level that *TRit/TCit* can reach.

Taking the partial derivative in (3), we get:

$$\frac{\partial lnTC_{it}}{\partial lnQ_{it}} = \alpha_Q + \alpha_{QQ} lnQ_{it} + \sum_{k=1}^{2} \alpha_{Qk} \ln\left(\frac{W_{k,it}}{W_{3,it}}\right) + \alpha_{EQ} lnE_{it} + \alpha_{TQ} T \tag{6}$$

Substituting (6) into (5), we get:

$$\frac{TR_{it}}{TC_{it}} = \alpha_Q + \alpha_{QQ} lnQ_{it} + \sum_{k=1}^{2} \alpha_{Qk} \ln\left(\frac{W_{k,it}}{W_{3,it}}\right) + \alpha_{EQ} lnE_{it} + \alpha_{TQ} T + v_{it} + u_{it} \tag{7}$$

Using the maximum likelihood method, Equation (7) is estimated separately for each country in order to account for different banking technologies per country. The estimation procedure is based on the distributional assumption that the non-negative term u_{it} is independently half-normally distributed with mean 0 and variance σ_u^2, while v_i is independently normally distributed with mean 0 and variance

σ_v^2. The estimation of (7) also allows to calculate the Jondrow et al. (1982) conditional mean estimator of u_{it}.

The estimated parameters from (7) are substituted into (6) to calculate $(\partial lnTC_{it})/(\partial lnQ_{it})$ and, after omitting v_{it} from (5) and doing some calculations, we finally get:

$$\frac{P_{it} - MC_{it}}{MC_{it}} = u_{it}\frac{1}{\frac{\partial lnTC_{it}}{\partial lnQ_{it}}} \quad (8)$$

The left part of (8) contains a definition of mark-up, labelled by Kumbhakar et al. (2012) as Θ_{it}, where the distance between price and marginal cost is a fraction of the marginal cost. Then, the Lerner index is calculated from Θ_{it} as follows:

$$L_{it} = \frac{\Theta_{it}}{1 + \Theta_{it}} \quad (9)$$

3.3. Evolution of the Lerner Index of Bank Market Power

The evolution of the Lerner index, which is calculated using an unbalanced panel dataset containing 13,890 observations from the unconsolidated balance sheets of 1442 commercial, savings, and mortgage banks from all euro area countries, is presented in Table 1 and in Figure 1. The data have been collected from the Orbis BankFocus (BankScope) Database provided by Bureau van Dijk.

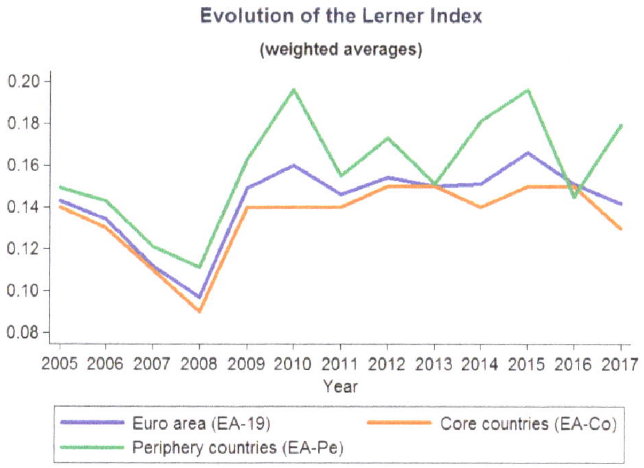

Figure 1. Evolution of the Lerner index of market power. Source: BankScope database, own calculations.

The country-level reported values have been obtained by taking the weighted average of the Lerner index values of individual banks, using as weights the country-level shares of individual banks in terms of total assets[3]. The total assets of banks per country and year have been obtained from the ECB Statistical Data Warehouse (ECB 2019a).

[3] In this study, we preferred the weighted euro area averages to unweighted ones, because it is only the weighted averages that can take into account the large differences between euro area countries with regard to total banking assets.

Table 1. Evolution of the Lerner index of market power.

Country	2005	2006	2007	2008	2009	2010	2011	2012	2013	2014	2015	2016	2017	Total Change	Coeff. Var (%)
Euro Area Core Countries (EA-Co)															
Austria	0.142	0.112	0.096	0.096	0.117	0.128	0.125	0.116	0.139	0.133	0.150	0.136	0.189	0.047	18.9
Belgium	0.194	0.213	0.129	0.099	0.113	0.159	0.153	0.112	0.135	0.123	0.170	0.146	0.147	−0.047	22.6
Estonia	0.107	0.133	0.201	0.110	0.046	0.090	0.114	0.137	0.223	0.167	0.205	0.240	0.242	0.135	40.4
Finland	0.129	0.165	0.135	0.124	0.225	0.255	0.220	0.257	0.199	0.209	0.285	0.321	0.174	0.045	29.7
France	0.185	0.177	0.119	0.100	0.190	0.154	0.138	0.168	0.162	0.137	0.178	0.200	0.141	−0.044	18.7
Germany	0.111	0.085	0.085	0.071	0.100	0.113	0.131	0.128	0.121	0.118	0.115	0.108	0.108	−0.003	16.5
Latvia	0.211	0.182	0.166	0.158	0.183	0.163	0.165	0.196	0.218	0.215	0.232	0.243	0.185	−0.026	14.4
Lithuania	0.164	0.162	0.128	0.097	0.121	0.118	0.071	0.108	0.137	0.178	0.112	0.193	0.186	0.022	27.3
Luxembourg	0.160	0.175	0.143	0.145	0.245	0.250	0.215	0.260	0.296	0.298	0.329	0.287	0.253	0.093	26.5
Netherlands	0.084	0.088	0.121	0.100	0.101	0.166	0.153	0.091	0.153	0.155	0.108	0.071	0.068	−0.016	30.3
Slovakia	0.116	0.126	0.109	0.105	0.137	0.157	0.168	0.118	0.126	0.128	0.146	0.174	0.080	−0.036	20.3
Coeff. Var (%)	27.8	28.0	24.7	22.3	41.9	32.7	28.5	38.7	31.4	32.0	39.3	39.5	37.1		
EA-Co average	**0.140**	**0.130**	**0.107**	**0.091**	**0.142**	**0.144**	**0.142**	**0.145**	**0.149**	**0.139**	**0.154**	**0.153**	**0.128**	**−0.012**	**13.4**
Euro Area Periphery Countries (EA-Pe)															
Cyprus	0.102	0.236	0.233	0.103	0.146	0.167	0.103	0.154	0.184	0.295	0.331	0.318	0.216	0.114	40.4
Greece	0.159	0.127	0.086	0.085	0.091	0.075	0.101	0.119	0.056	0.067	0.080	0.111	0.128	−0.031	29.2
Ireland	0.036	0.016	0.016	0.068	0.153	0.224	0.209	0.140	0.217	0.224	0.285	0.141	0.194	0.158	60.1
Italy	0.142	0.138	0.109	0.098	0.110	0.117	0.109	0.129	0.126	0.145	0.142	0.103	0.138	−0.004	13.5
Malta	0.178	0.192	0.215	0.209	0.217	0.196	0.161	0.237	0.219	0.224	0.212	0.251	0.166	−0.012	12.9
Portugal	0.163	0.193	0.147	0.128	0.154	0.179	0.118	0.109	0.088	0.130	0.192	0.159	0.233	0.070	25.9
Slovenia	0.120	0.128	0.142	0.074	0.121	0.158	0.145	0.172	0.156	0.154	0.122	0.145	0.106	−0.014	19.4
Spain	0.207	0.202	0.181	0.143	0.237	0.295	0.207	0.251	0.187	0.240	0.264	0.202	0.231	0.024	18.1
Coeff. Var (%)	38.1	44.4	50.3	40.8	32.9	37.7	30.9	32.5	38.7	39.7	42.5	41.5	27.9		
EA-Pe average	**0.150**	**0.144**	**0.122**	**0.111**	**0.163**	**0.196**	**0.155**	**0.174**	**0.151**	**0.181**	**0.196**	**0.145**	**0.179**	**0.030**	**16.4**
All Euro Area Countries (EA-19)															
Coeff. Var (%)	31.4	35.1	37.6	30.7	37.2	34.5	28.7	35.2	33.8	35.0	40.0	39.3	32.6		
EA-19 average	**0.143**	**0.134**	**0.112**	**0.097**	**0.149**	**0.160**	**0.146**	**0.154**	**0.150**	**0.151**	**0.166**	**0.151**	**0.142**	**−0.001**	**13.3**

Notes: Total change is the difference between the value for 2017 and the value for 2005. Coeff. Var (%) stands for the percent Coefficient of Variation measure. All average values are weighted by total banking assets. Source: BankScope database, own calculations.

As shown in Table 1 and in Figure 1, the weighted average of market power in EA-19 initially followed a decreasing path arriving at a minimum value in 2008. Afterwards it started increasing, reaching a peak in 2015. It started falling in 2016, reaching in 2017 a value that is close to its corresponding value for 2005. On the other hand, the row-wise and column-wise coefficients of variation[4] in Table 1 show that there are significant disparities in market power not only between countries for each year but also between different years for the same country. In Ireland, market power increased between 2005 and 2017 by about 16 percentage points, while the biggest decrease of about 5 percentage points was observed in Belgium.

Regarding the other two country groups under examination, the weighted average of market power in EA-Pe has been persistently higher, also presenting more fluctuation, than market power in EA-Co during almost all years of the period under study. From 2009 onwards, as it is shown in Table 1 and in Figure 2, the disparities between EA-Co countries, measured by the coefficient of variation, have been moving almost in parallel with those between EA-Pe countries, both fluctuating between 30% and 40%.

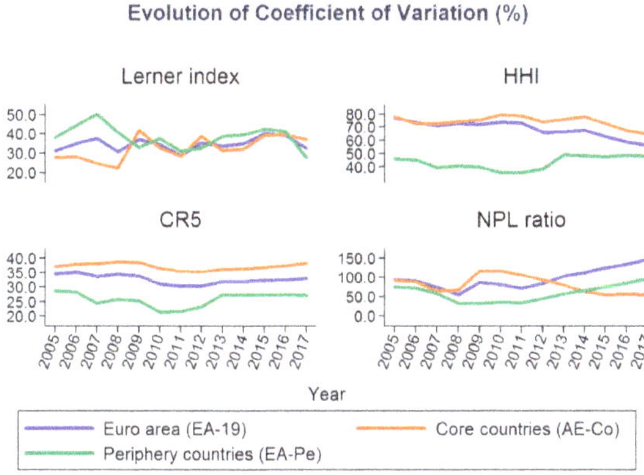

Figure 2. Evolution of the Coefficient of Variation (%). Source: BankScope database, European Central Bank (ECB), World Bank, own calculations.

Unfortunately, the evolution of market power disparities in each group (EA-Co and EA-Pe) separately does not provide adequate information on which part of the disparities is due to differences inside each group (within-group inequality), and which part comes from differences between these two groups (between-group inequality). This task was accomplished by employing the Theil index and the relevant results are presented in Section 6.2.

4. Bank Concentration in the Euro Area

4.1. The Evolution of the Herfindahl–Hirschman Index (HHI)

The Herfindahl-Hirschman Index (HHI) is defined as the sum of the squares of the market shares in total banking assets of all banks in a banking system. An HHI value below 1000 indicates low concentration, a value between 1000 and 1800 indicates moderate concentration, and a value above 1800 indicates high concentration. The HHI evolution for the three country groups under examination is presented in Table 2 and in Figure 3. Country-level data from the ECB Statistical Data Warehouse (ECB 2019b) are used.

4 The coefficient of variation is defined as the ratio of the standard deviation to the mean. It shows the degree of variability in relation to the mean.

Table 2. Evolution of concentration (Herfindahl–Hirschman Index, HHI).

Country	2005	2006	2007	2008	2009	2010	2011	2012	2013	2014	2015	2016	2017	Total Change	Coeff. Var (%)
Euro Area Core Countries (EA-Co)															
Austria	560	534	527	454	414	383	423	395	405	412	397	358	374	−186	18.9
Belgium	2112	2041	2079	1881	1622	1439	1294	1061	979	981	998	1017	1102	−1010	22.6
Estonia	4039	3593	3410	3120	3090	2929	2613	2493	2483	2445	2409	2406	2419	−1620	40.4
Finland	3130	3010	2970	3490	3480	3830	3880	3250	3410	3630	3160	2300	1700	−1430	29.7
France	727	726	679	681	605	610	600	545	568	584	589	572	574	−153	18.7
Germany	174	178	183	191	206	301	317	307	266	300	273	277	250	76	16.5
Latvia	1176	1270	1158	1205	1181	1005	929	1027	1037	1001	1033	1080	1235	59	14.4
Lithuania	1838	1913	1827	1714	1693	1545	1871	1749	1892	1818	1939	1938	2189	351	27.3
Luxembourg	373	333	316	309	310	343	346	345	357	330	321	260	256	−117	26.5
Netherlands	1796	1822	1928	2167	2034	2049	2067	2026	2105	2131	2104	2097	2087	291	30.3
Slovakia	1076	1131	1082	1197	1273	1239	1268	1221	1215	1221	1250	1264	1332	256	20.3
Coeff. Var (%)	77.8	73.0	72.9	74.3	75.7	79.5	78.5	73.9	75.9	78.1	73.1	67.3	65.0		
EA-Co average	**711**	**714**	**733**	**757**	**713**	**742**	**767**	**713**	**705**	**746**	**724**	**695**	**663**	**−48**	**3.8**
Euro Area Periphery Countries (EA-Pe)															
Cyprus	1029	1056	1089	1017	1085	1125	1030	1007	1645	1445	1443	1366	1962	933	40.4
Greece	1096	1101	1096	1172	1183	1214	1278	1487	2136	2195	2254	2332	2307	1211	29.2
Ireland	600	600	700	661	714	700	645	630	671	673	672	636	658	58	60.1
Italy	230	220	328	307	298	410	407	410	406	424	435	452	519	289	13.5
Malta	1330	1171	1177	1236	1250	1181	1203	1313	1458	1648	1620	1602	1599	269	12.9
Portugal	1154	1134	1098	1114	1150	1207	1206	1191	1197	1164	1215	1181	1220	66	25.9
Slovenia	1369	1300	1282	1268	1256	1160	1142	1115	1045	1026	1077	1147	1133	−236	19.4
Spain	487	442	459	497	507	528	596	654	719	839	896	937	965	478	18.1
Coeff. Var (%)	46.0	45.4	39.6	40.6	40.0	35.8	35.9	38.4	49.4	48.6	47.9	48.7	48.0		
EA-Pe average	**480**	**462**	**520**	**526**	**540**	**594**	**604**	**626**	**681**	**726**	**754**	**765**	**812**	**332**	**18.6**
All Euro Area Countries (EA-19)															
Coeff. Var (%)	77.2	73.5	71.3	72.8	72.2	74.1	73.2	66.5	66.6	67.9	63.4	58.9	56.6		
EA-19 average	**647**	**640**	**669**	**685**	**657**	**696**	**717**	**686**	**698**	**740**	**733**	**714**	**703**	**56**	**4.5**

Notes: Total change is the difference between the value for 2017 and the value for 2005. Coeff. Var (%) stands for the percent Coefficient of Variation measure. All average values are weighted by total banking assets. Source: ECB, own calculations.

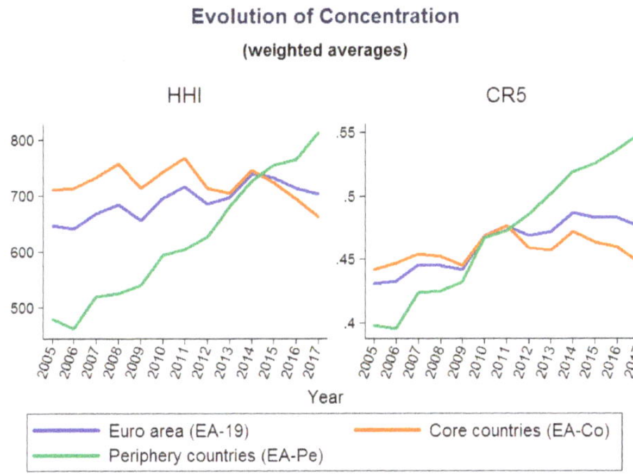

Figure 3. Evolution of bank concentration. Source: ECB, own calculations.

The weighted average of HHI in EA-19 peaked in 2014, when it started following a decreasing path arriving in 2017 at a value that is 56 points bigger than the HHI value for 2005. The weighted average of HHI in EA-Co reached a peak in 2011, and started declining thereafter, in contrast to the EA-Pe countries whose weighted average of HHI followed an increasing path reaching a peak in 2017.

On the other hand, the row-wise and column-wise coefficients of variation in Table 2 show that there are significant disparities among the HHI values not only between countries within each year but also between different years for the same country. The biggest decline in HHI values was observed in Belgium, Estonia, and Finland, in contrast to Cyprus and Greece, which presented the biggest increase in HHI values during the period under examination.

As it is shown in Table 2 and in Figure 2, the disparities in HHI values between EA-Co countries, measured by the coefficient of variation, reached a peak of about 80% in 2010. Afterwards they remained at high levels (74%–79%) until 2015 when they started decreasing, arriving at a minimum of 65% in 2017. In contrast, the disparities between EA-Pe countries, started increasing in 2011, after having followed a decreasing path since 2005. In 2013, the disparities between EA-Pe countries reached a peak of 50%, staying very close to this level thereafter. The decomposition of the HHI disparities into within-group and between-group components, using the Theil inequality index, is presented in Section 6.3.

4.2. The Evolution of the CR5 Concentration Ratio

The CR5 concentration ratio is the sum of the shares of the five largest banks in a banking system. The CR5 evolution for the three country groups under examination is presented in Table 3 and in Figure 3. The weighted average of CR5 in EA-19 peaked in 2014, when it started following a decreasing path arriving in 2017 at a value that is 4.5% bigger than the CR5 value for 2005. The weighted average of CR5 in EA-Co reached a peak in 2011, and started declining thereafter, in contrast to EA-Pe whose weighted average of CR5 followed an increasing path since 2007.

On the other hand, the row-wise and column-wise coefficients of variation in Table 3 show that there are significant disparities among the CR5 values not only between countries for each year but also between different years for the same country. The biggest positive evolution for CR5 was observed in Greece, Cyprus, and Spain, in contrast to Belgium and Finland, which presented the biggest decrease in the CR5 value between 2005 and 2017.

Table 3. Evolution of concentration (market share of the five largest banks, CR5).

Country	2005	2006	2007	2008	2009	2010	2011	2012	2013	2014	2015	2016	2017	Total Change	Coeff. Var (%)
Euro Area Core Countries (EA-Co)															
Austria	0.450	0.438	0.428	0.390	0.372	0.359	0.384	0.365	0.367	0.368	0.358	0.345	0.361	−0.089	8.8
Belgium	0.853	0.844	0.834	0.808	0.771	0.749	0.708	0.663	0.640	0.658	0.655	0.662	0.688	−0.165	10.9
Estonia	0.981	0.971	0.957	0.948	0.934	0.923	0.906	0.896	0.897	0.899	0.886	0.880	0.903	−0.078	3.6
Finland	0.871	0.868	0.861	0.877	0.875	0.892	0.869	0.859	0.871	0.897	0.880	0.805	0.735	−0.136	5.0
France	0.519	0.523	0.518	0.512	0.472	0.474	0.483	0.446	0.467	0.476	0.472	0.460	0.454	−0.065	5.5
Germany	0.216	0.220	0.220	0.227	0.250	0.326	0.335	0.330	0.306	0.321	0.306	0.314	0.297	0.081	16.8
Latvia	0.673	0.692	0.672	0.702	0.693	0.604	0.596	0.641	0.641	0.636	0.645	0.665	0.735	0.062	6.0
Lithuania	0.806	0.825	0.809	0.813	0.805	0.788	0.847	0.836	0.871	0.857	0.868	0.871	0.901	0.095	4.0
Luxembourg	0.345	0.315	0.306	0.297	0.293	0.311	0.312	0.331	0.337	0.320	0.313	0.276	0.262	−0.083	7.5
Netherlands	0.845	0.851	0.863	0.867	0.851	0.842	0.836	0.821	0.838	0.850	0.846	0.847	0.838	−0.007	1.4
Slovakia	0.677	0.669	0.682	0.716	0.721	0.720	0.722	0.707	0.703	0.707	0.723	0.727	0.745	0.068	3.1
Coeff. Var (%)	37.3	37.9	38.1	38.8	38.7	36.5	35.4	35.4	36.3	36.4	36.9	37.5	38.3		
EA-Co average	**0.442**	**0.447**	**0.454**	**0.452**	**0.445**	**0.468**	**0.477**	**0.459**	**0.457**	**0.472**	**0.464**	**0.460**	**0.447**	**0.005**	**2.4**
Euro Area Periphery Countries (EA-Pe)															
Cyprus	0.598	0.639	0.649	0.638	0.647	0.642	0.607	0.626	0.641	0.634	0.675	0.658	0.842	0.244	9.2
Greece	0.656	0.663	0.677	0.696	0.692	0.706	0.720	0.795	0.940	0.941	0.952	0.973	0.970	0.314	16.7
Ireland	0.478	0.490	0.504	0.503	0.526	0.499	0.467	0.464	0.478	0.476	0.459	0.443	0.455	−0.023	4.9
Italy	0.268	0.262	0.331	0.312	0.310	0.398	0.395	0.397	0.396	0.410	0.410	0.430	0.434	0.166	16.6
Malta	0.753	0.709	0.702	0.728	0.728	0.713	0.720	0.744	0.765	0.815	0.813	0.803	0.809	0.056	5.6
Portugal	0.688	0.679	0.678	0.691	0.701	0.709	0.708	0.699	0.703	0.692	0.723	0.712	0.731	0.043	2.3
Slovenia	0.630	0.620	0.595	0.591	0.597	0.593	0.593	0.584	0.571	0.556	0.592	0.610	0.615	−0.015	3.3
Spain	0.420	0.404	0.410	0.424	0.433	0.443	0.481	0.514	0.544	0.583	0.602	0.618	0.637	0.217	17.3
Coeff. Var (%)	28.6	28.3	24.4	25.8	25.4	21.5	21.7	23.2	27.4	27.4	27.3	27.3	27.3		
EA-Pe average	**0.398**	**0.395**	**0.424**	**0.425**	**0.432**	**0.467**	**0.473**	**0.486**	**0.502**	**0.519**	**0.526**	**0.537**	**0.549**	**0.151**	**11.3**
All Euro Area Countries (EA-19)															
Coeff. Var (%)	34.7	35.1	33.8	34.5	33.9	31.2	30.5	30.4	32.0	32.0	32.3	32.6	33.1		
EA-19 average	**0.431**	**0.433**	**0.446**	**0.445**	**0.442**	**0.469**	**0.477**	**0.469**	**0.472**	**0.487**	**0.483**	**0.483**	**0.476**	**0.045**	**4.4**

Notes: Total change is the difference between the value for 2017 and the value for 2005. Coeff. Var (%) stands for the percent Coefficient of Variation measure. All average values are weighted by total banking assets. Source: ECB, own calculations.

As it is shown in Table 3 and in Figure 2, the disparities in CR5 values between EA-Co countries, measured by the coefficient of variation, reached a peak of about 39% in 2008, after a continuous increase from 2005. After a temporary decrease during 2010–2012, they remained at levels ranging between 36 and 38%. After having followed a decreasing path since 2005, the disparities between EA-Pe countries increased in 2013, remaining afterwards close to 27%. The decomposition of the CR5 disparities into within-group and between-group components, using the Theil inequality index, is presented in Section 6.3.

5. Credit Risk in the Euro Area

Although several years have passed since the onset of the global financial crisis of 2008, many euro area banks still have high levels of non-performing loans (NPLs) on their balance sheets. The non-performing loans to total gross loans ratio (NPL ratio) reached 3.4% in September 2019 for the euro area as whole (ECB 2020), following a downward trend after 2012, when it reached an all-time high of around 8%. However, despite this positive evolution for the euro area in total, large dispersions remain across euro area countries (ratios between 0.9% and 37.4%). Such a large stock of NPLs puts serious constraints on many banks' lending capacity and their ability to build further capital buffers, thus exerting a strong negative influence on economic growth through the reduction of credit supply.

Bank competition is one of the factors that have been extensively investigated in the past as one of the major determinants of credit risk, as well as of bank risk in general. In a recent study, Karadima and Louri (2019) reached the conclusion that competition exerts a statistically significant and positive impact on NPLs, supporting the "competition-stability" view in banking. This motivated us to extend the scope of the present study, by investigating the evolution and convergence of NPLs in the euro area during the period 2005–2017. The investigation is based on country-level data collected mainly from the World Bank (2019a, 2019b).

The evolution of NPL ratios for the three country groups under examination is presented in Table 4 and in Figure 4. The weighted average of the NPL ratio in EA-19 peaked in 2013, when it started following a decreasing path arriving in 2017 at a value 1.6% higher than that of 2005. The weighted average of the NPL ratio in EA-Co reached a maximum of 3.4% in 2009 and 2013, and started declining thereafter, reaching in 2017 a value 0.9% smaller than that of 2005. In contrast, after a very sharp and continuous increase, which started in 2008, the weighted average of NPL ratio in EA-Pe reached a maximum of 15.6% in 2014, when it started decreasing arriving in 2017 at a value 8.5% higher than that of 2005.

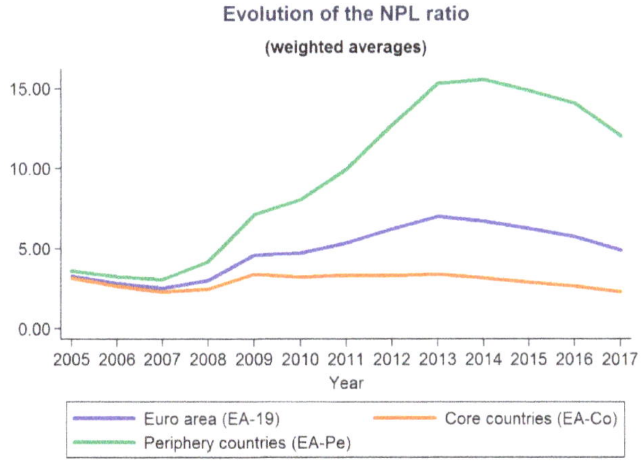

Figure 4. Evolution of the NPL ratio. Source: World Bank, own calculations.

Table 4. Evolution of credit risk (non-performing loan (NPL) ratio).

Country	2005	2006	2007	2008	2009	2010	2011	2012	2013	2014	2015	2016	2017	Total change	Coeff. Var (%)
Euro area core countries (EA-Co)															
Austria	2.60	2.74	2.24	1.90	2.25	2.83	2.71	2.81	2.87	3.47	3.39	2.70	2.37	−0.23	16.3
Belgium	2.00	1.28	1.16	1.65	3.08	2.80	3.30	3.74	4.24	4.18	3.79	3.43	2.92	0.92	36.6
Estonia	0.20	0.20	0.50	1.94	5.20	5.38	4.05	2.62	1.47	1.39	0.98	0.87	0.70	0.50	92.6
Finland	0.30	0.20	0.30	0.40	0.60	0.60	0.50	0.50	0.67	1.30	1.34	1.52	1.67	1.37	66.7
France	3.50	3.00	2.70	2.82	4.02	3.76	4.29	4.29	4.50	4.16	3.98	3.64	3.08	−0.42	16.5
Germany	4.05	3.41	2.65	2.85	3.31	3.20	3.03	2.86	2.70	2.34	1.97	1.71	1.50	−2.55	26.2
Latvia	0.70	0.50	0.80	2.10	14.28	15.93	14.05	8.72	6.41	4.60	4.64	6.26	5.51	4.81	82.0
Lithuania	0.60	1.00	1.00	6.08	23.99	23.33	18.84	14.80	11.59	8.19	4.95	3.66	3.18	2.58	90.4
Luxembourg	0.20	0.10	0.40	0.60	0.67	0.25	0.38	0.15	0.21	0.21	0.21	0.90	0.79	0.59	67.7
Netherlands	1.20	0.80	1.50	1.68	3.20	2.83	2.71	3.10	3.23	2.98	2.71	2.54	2.31	1.11	34.2
Slovakia	5.00	3.20	2.50	2.49	5.29	5.84	5.61	5.22	5.14	5.35	4.87	4.44	3.70	−1.30	25.6
Coeff. Var (%)	92.4	88.5	65.4	67.3	117.2	117.1	106.6	93.2	81.0	64.0	55.6	56.7	55.2		
EA-Co average	**3.15**	**2.63**	**2.28**	**2.45**	**3.38**	**3.20**	**3.32**	**3.30**	**3.38**	**3.14**	**2.88**	**2.62**	**2.28**	**−0.87**	**14.4**
Euro area periphery countries (EA-Pe)															
Cyprus	7.10	5.40	3.40	3.59	4.51	5.82	9.99	18.37	38.56	44.97	47.75	48.68	40.17	33.07	89.5
Greece	6.30	5.40	4.60	4.67	6.95	9.12	14.43	23.27	31.90	33.78	36.65	36.30	45.57	39.27	75.7
Ireland	0.48	0.53	0.63	1.92	9.80	13.05	16.12	24.99	25.71	20.65	14.93	13.61	11.46	10.98	75.6
Italy	7.00	6.57	5.78	6.28	9.45	10.03	11.74	13.75	16.54	18.03	18.06	17.12	14.38	7.38	39.5
Malta	8.21	6.47	5.31	5.01	5.78	7.02	7.09	7.75	8.95	9.05	6.77	5.32	4.07	−4.14	23.2
Portugal	1.50	1.30	2.85	3.60	5.13	5.31	7.47	9.74	10.62	11.91	17.48	17.18	13.27	11.77	67.7
Slovenia	2.50	2.50	2.50	4.22	5.79	8.21	11.81	15.18	13.31	11.73	9.96	5.07	3.20	0.70	61.7
Spain	0.79	0.70	0.90	2.81	4.12	4.67	6.01	7.48	9.38	8.45	6.16	5.64	4.46	3.67	60.4
Coeff. Var (%)	75.9	72.5	58.9	33.7	33.3	35.4	34.2	44.7	58.4	66.2	75.5	85.5	97.0		
EA-Pe average	**3.58**	**3.22**	**3.05**	**4.15**	**7.14**	**8.07**	**9.95**	**12.71**	**15.32**	**15.56**	**14.86**	**14.08**	**12.03**	**8.45**	**51.6**
All euro area countries (EA-19)															
Coeff. Var (%)	93.4	91.7	75.6	55.9	87.4	82.6	72.7	84.1	103.7	113.6	126.0	134.6	147.3		
EA-19 average	**3.27**	**2.80**	**2.51**	**2.98**	**4.59**	**4.72**	**5.35**	**6.23**	**7.02**	**6.72**	**6.26**	**5.76**	**4.90**	**1.63**	**32.0**

Notes: Total change is the difference between the value for 2017 and the value for 2005. Coeff. Var (%) stands for the percent Coefficient of Variation measure. All average values are weighted by total banking assets. Source: World Bank, own calculations.

On the other hand, the row-wise and column-wise coefficients of variation in Table 4 show that there are significant disparities among the NPL ratios not only between countries within each year but also between different years for the same country. The biggest decline in NPL ratio values was observed in Germany and Malta, in contrast to Cyprus and Greece, which presented the biggest increase in NPL ratios during the period under examination.

After having followed a decreasing path until 2008, as it is shown in Table 4 and Figure 2, the disparities between EA-Co countries, measured by the coefficient of variation, increased sharply in 2009 to a level of about 117%. They started decreasing thereafter, arriving a minimum of 55% in 2017; thus, presenting a clear tendency to converge to lower levels. After having followed a decreasing path until 2011, in 2012 the disparities between EA-Pe countries started increasing continuously, arriving at an all-time peak of 97% in 2017; thus, not showing, in contrast to EA-Co, any sign of convergence to lower levels. By employing the Theil inequality index (see Section 6.4), more information on which part of the disparities is due to differences inside each group (within-group inequality), and which part comes from differences between these two groups (between-group inequality) is provided.

6. Theil Inequality for Bank Competition, Concentration, and Credit Risk

6.1. Theil Inequality Index

An inequality index that belongs to the entropy class has the following general form:

$$GE(\alpha) = \frac{1}{n(a^2 - a)} \sum_{i=1}^{n} [(\frac{y_i}{\bar{y}})^{\alpha} - 1] \tag{10}$$

where n is the size of the sample, y_i is the i-th observation and $\bar{y}$ is the mean value of the sample. The parameter α represents the weight given to distances between values at different parts of the distribution. For smaller values of α, $GE(\alpha)$ is more sensitive to changes in the bottom tail of the distribution. For higher values of α, $GE(\alpha)$ is more sensitive to changes in the upper tail of the distribution. The most commonly used values of α are −1, 0, 1 and 2. The most well-known member of the entropy class of inequality indices is the $GE(1)$ index, called Theil index (T), by the name of Henri Theil who introduced it in 1967. All the members of the entropy class of inequality indices have the advantage of being perfectly decomposable (i.e., with a zero residual part).

Following Fernandez de Guevara et al. (2007), the Theil index for bank market power can be calculated from Equation (11):

$$T = \sum_{g=1}^{G} sh_g T_{w,g} + T_b \tag{11}$$

where T is the total market power inequality, G is the number of observation groups in the sample, sh_g is the share in the sample (in terms of total assets) of a group g, $T_{w,g}$ is the within-group inequality in group g and T_b is the between-group inequality.

The within-group inequality in group g is defined by Equation (12):

$$T_{w,g} = -\sum_{i=1}^{N_g} (\frac{sh_i}{sh_g}) ln(\frac{x_i}{\mu_g}) \tag{12}$$

where N_g is the number of entities (e.g., countries or banks) in group g, sh_i is the share in the sample (in terms of total assets) of an entity i belonging to group g and μ_g is the weighted average of the Lerner index of entities belonging to group g.

The between-group inequality is defined by Equation (13):

$$T_b = -\sum_{g=1}^{G} sh_g ln(\frac{\mu_g}{\mu}) \quad (13)$$

where μ is the weighted average of the Lerner index (variable x_i) in the sample.

6.2. Theil Inequality for Market Power

The results from the calculation of the total Theil inequality index for the Lerner index of market power and its within-group and between-group components are presented in Table 5, as well as in Figures 5 and 6.

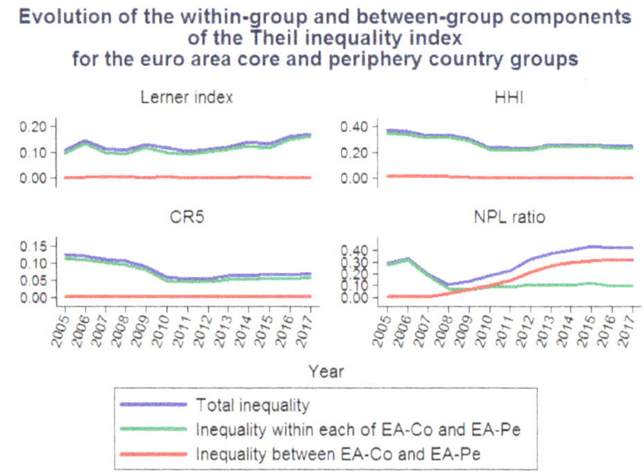

Figure 5. Evolution of the within-group and between-group components of the Theil inequality index for the euro area core and periphery country groups. Source: BankScope database, ECB, World Bank, own calculations.

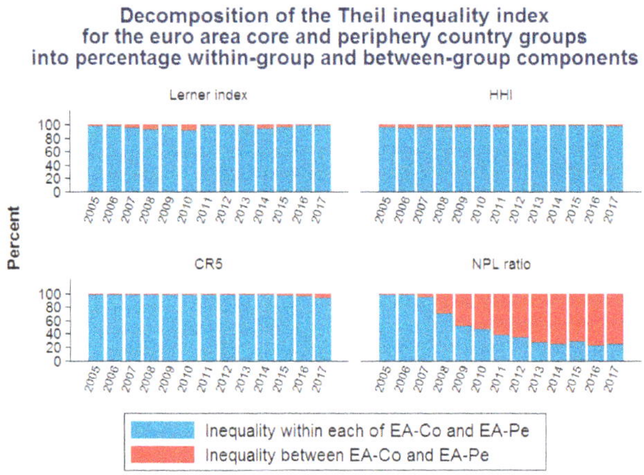

Figure 6. Decomposition of the Theil inequality index for the euro area core and periphery country groups into percentage within-group and between-group components. Source: BankScope database, ECB, World Bank, own calculations.

Table 5. Evolution and decomposition of the Theil inequality index for the euro area core and periphery country groups into within-group and between-group components.

Year	Market Power (Lerner Index)			Concentration (HHI)			Concentration (CR5)			Credit Risk (NPL Ratio)		
		Inequality			Inequality			Inequality			Inequality	
	Total	Within-Group	Between-Group	Total	Within-Group	Between-Group	Total	Within-Group	Between-Group	Total	Within-Group	Between-Group
2005	0.099	0.097 (98%)	0.002 (2%)	0.365	0.350 (96%)	0.015 (4%)	0.116	0.115 (99%)	0.001 (1%)	0.280	0.278 (99%)	0.002 (1%)
2006	0.136	0.133 (98%)	0.003 (2%)	0.354	0.336 (95%)	0.018 (5%)	0.112	0.110 (98%)	0.002 (2%)	0.322	0.318 (99%)	0.004 (1%)
2007	0.105	0.100 (95%)	0.005 (5%)	0.323	0.311 (96%)	0.012 (4%)	0.102	0.101 (99%)	0.001 (1%)	0.194	0.185 (95%)	0.009 (5%)
2008	0.099	0.092 (93%)	0.007 (7%)	0.331	0.318 (96%)	0.013 (4%)	0.097	0.096 (99%)	0.001 (1%)	0.108	0.077 (71%)	0.031 (29%)
2009	0.121	0.119 (98%)	0.002 (2%)	0.299	0.291 (97%)	0.008 (3%)	0.081	0.080 (99%)	0.001 (1%)	0.135	0.069 (51%)	0.066 (49%)
2010	0.110	0.101 (92%)	0.009 (8%)	0.229	0.224 (98%)	0.005 (2%)	0.049	0.048 (98%)	0.001 (2%)	0.187	0.087 (47%)	0.100 (53%)
2011	0.095	0.094 (99%)	0.001 (1%)	0.227	0.221 (97%)	0.006 (3%)	0.045	0.044 (98%)	0.001 (2%)	0.229	0.088 (38%)	0.141 (62%)
2012	0.103	0.102 (99%)	0.001 (1%)	0.218	0.216 (99%)	0.002 (1%)	0.045	0.044 (98%)	0.001 (2%)	0.325	0.110 (34%)	0.215 (66%)
2013	0.112	0.111 (99%)	0.001 (1%)	0.249	0.247 (99%)	0.002 (1%)	0.054	0.053 (98%)	0.001 (2%)	0.372	0.102 (27%)	0.270 (73%)
2014	0.134	0.126 (94%)	0.008 (6%)	0.243	0.241 (99%)	0.002 (1%)	0.053	0.052 (98%)	0.001 (2%)	0.400	0.100 (25%)	0.300 (75%)
2015	0.124	0.119 (96%)	0.005 (4%)	0.249	0.247 (99%)	0.002 (1%)	0.059	0.057 (97%)	0.002 (3%)	0.437	0.123 (28%)	0.314 (72%)
2016	0.153	0.152 (99%)	0.001 (1%)	0.237	0.235 (99%)	0.002 (1%)	0.057	0.055 (96%)	0.002 (4%)	0.423	0.097 (23%)	0.326 (77%)
2017	0.164	0.162 (99%)	0.002 (1%)	0.236	0.232 (98%)	0.004 (2%)	0.062	0.058 (94%)	0.004 (6%)	0.421	0.104 (25%)	0.317 (75%)
Total change	**0.065**	**0.065**	**0.000**	**−0.129**	**−0.118**	**−0.011**	**−0.054**	**−0.057**	**0.003**	**0.141**	**−0.174**	**0.315**

Notes: Total change is the difference between the value for 2017 and the value for 2005. The figures in parentheses denote percentages of within-group and between-group inequality over total inequality. Source: BankScope database, ECB, World Bank, own calculations.

As it is shown in Table 5, as well as in Figures 5 and 6, the disparities in market power are due, almost exclusively, to differences inside each group (EA-Co or EA-Pe). The differences between the EA-Co and EA-Pe are negligible. This evolution suggests that there is a clear convergence between the EA-Co and EA-Pe country groups with respect to competition, as measured by the Lerner index of market power. In addition, it is also clear that we need higher granularity, which can be obtained by investigating whether differences in market power stem from inequalities between different countries (between-country inequality) or from inequalities between banks in a given country (within-country inequality). This desired level of granularity can be obtained by the calculation of a Theil inequality index and its decomposition into within-country and between-country components.

The results from the calculation of the total Theil inequality index and its within-country and between-country components are presented in Table 6[5], as well as in Figures 7 and 8. Figure 7 shows that in 2008 the level of total inequality in bank market power in EA-19 was close to its 2005 level, after a sharp increase of the between-country inequality in 2006. The increase of the Theil inequality index in 2009 indicates that the financial crisis reversed the progress towards lower disparities across countries, suggested by the lower values of the between-country component in the period 2007–2008. In 2011, total inequality was close to its 2008 level, since an increase in within-country inequality in 2011 was accompanied by a decrease in between-country inequality in that year. Total inequality started increasing in 2012, mainly due to an increase in its within-country component, reaching a peak in 2017. The persistence of significant within-country inequalities in market power has also been shown by Cruz-Garcia et al. (2017), who investigate the impact of financial market integration on the evolution of disparities among European banks' market power using bank-specific data for the EA-12 countries over the period 2000–2014.

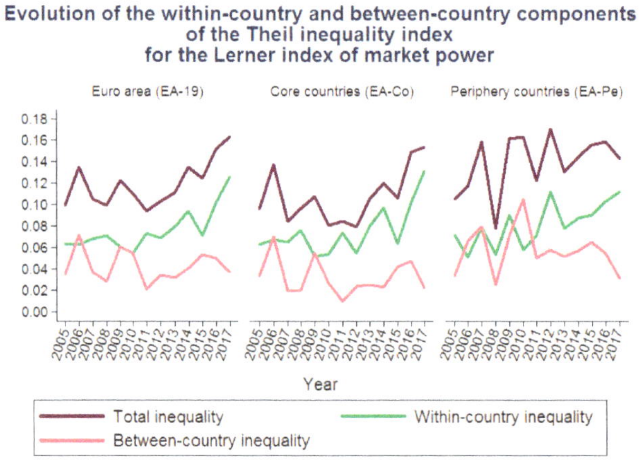

Figure 7. Evolution of the within-country and between-country components of the Theil inequality index for the Lerner index of market power. Source: BankScope database, own calculations.

The level of total inequality in bank market power in periphery countries was generally higher, presenting also more fluctuations than that of the core countries during almost all years of the period under study, mainly due to the higher between-country inequality among periphery countries.

---

5 It should be noted that some expected minor differences (at the third decimal place) in total inequality between Tables 5 and 6 are due to different data grouping (19 countries vs EA-Co/EA-Pe) and weighting.

Table 6. Evolution and decomposition of the Theil inequality index for the Lerner index of market power into within-country and between-country components

Year	Euro Area (EA-19)			Core Countries (EA-Co)			Periphery Countries (EA-Pe)		
		Inequality			Inequality			Inequality	
	Total	Within-Country	Between-Country	Total	Within-Country	Between-Country	Total	Within-Country	Between-Country
2005	0.099	0.064 (65%)	0.035 (35%)	0.096	0.063 (66%)	0.033 (34%)	0.105	0.072 (69%)	0.033 (31%)
2006	0.135	0.063 (47%)	0.072 (53%)	0.137	0.067 (49%)	0.070 (51%)	0.117	0.051 (44%)	0.066 (56%)
2007	0.105	0.068 (65%)	0.037 (35%)	0.084	0.065 (77%)	0.019 (23%)	0.158	0.079 (50%)	0.079 (50%)
2008	0.099	0.071 (72%)	0.028 (28%)	0.096	0.076 (79%)	0.020 (21%)	0.078	0.053 (68%)	0.025 (32%)
2009	0.122	0.061 (50%)	0.061 (50%)	0.107	0.052 (49%)	0.055 (51%)	0.161	0.090 (56%)	0.071 (44%)
2010	0.110	0.055 (50%)	0.055 (50%)	0.081	0.054 (67%)	0.027 (33%)	0.163	0.058 (36%)	0.105 (64%)
2011	0.094	0.073 (78%)	0.021 (22%)	0.084	0.074 (88%)	0.010 (12%)	0.122	0.072 (59%)	0.050 (41%)
2012	0.103	0.069 (67%)	0.034 (33%)	0.079	0.055 (70%)	0.024 (30%)	0.170	0.112 (66%)	0.058 (34%)
2013	0.111	0.079 (71%)	0.032 (29%)	0.105	0.080 (76%)	0.025 (24%)	0.130	0.078 (60%)	0.052 (40%)
2014	0.135	0.094 (70%)	0.041 (30%)	0.120	0.097 (81%)	0.023 (19%)	0.144	0.087 (61%)	0.057 (39%)
2015	0.124	0.071 (57%)	0.053 (43%)	0.106	0.064 (60%)	0.042 (40%)	0.155	0.090 (58%)	0.065 (42%)
2016	0.152	0.102 (67%)	0.050 (33%)	0.149	0.102 (68%)	0.047 (32%)	0.158	0.103 (65%)	0.055 (35%)
2017	0.163	0.126 (77%)	0.037 (23%)	0.153	0.131 (86%)	0.022 (14%)	0.143	0.112 (78%)	0.031 (22%)
Total change	**0.064**	**0.062**	**0.002**	**0.057**	**0.068**	**−0.011**	**0.038**	**0.040**	**−0.002**

Notes: Total change is the difference between the value for 2017 and the value for 2005. The figures in parentheses denote percentages of within-country and between-country inequality over total inequality. Source: BankScope database, own calculations.

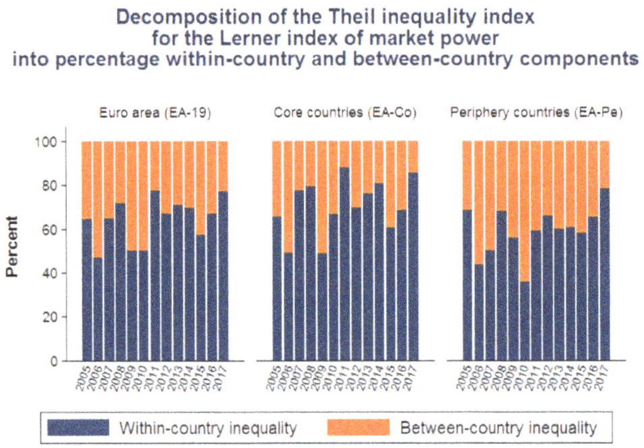

Figure 8. Decomposition of the Theil inequality index for the Lerner index of market power into percentage within-country and between-country components. Source: BankScope database, own calculations.

As shown in Figure 8, from 2011 to 2017 the between-country inequality was generally much smaller than the within-country inequality across all the three country groups under examination, indicating a decrease in fragmentation in the euro area with respect to market power.

The values of the Lerner index and the Theil inequality index, presented in Tables 1 and 6, respectively, could be biased due to the unbalanced nature of the underlying panel dataset, so we also considered a fully balanced subset of the unbalanced dataset. After the deletion of countries with less than five banks per year, the balanced subset contains 7605 observations from 585 banks from nine euro area countries (Austria, Belgium, France, Germany, Italy, Latvia, Lithuania, Luxembourg, and Slovakia). The results obtained for this group of nine countries were generally in line with the results obtained for EA-19.

6.3. Theil Inequality for Concentration

The results from the calculation of the total Theil inequality index for HHI and its within-group and between-group components are presented in Table 5, as well as in Figures 5 and 6. As it is shown in Table 5, as well as in Figures 5 and 6, the disparities in HHI values are due, almost exclusively, to differences inside each group (EA-Co or EA-Pe). This evolution suggests that there is a clear convergence between the EA-Co and EA-Pe country groups with respect to concentration, as measured by the HHI structural measure. In contrast to the case of the Lerner index, the lack of availability of the bank-level underlying determinants of HHI did not let us to go deeper in order to investigate whether the above-described differences stem from inequalities between different countries (between-country inequality) or from inequalities between banks in a given country (within-country inequality).

The results from the calculation of the total Theil inequality index for CR5 and its within-group and between-group components are presented in Table 5, as well as in Figures 5 and 6. As it is shown in Table 5, as well as in Figures 5 and 6, the disparities in CR5 values are due, almost exclusively, to differences inside each group (EA-Co or EA-Pe). This evolution suggests that there is a clear convergence between the EA-Co and EA-Pe country groups with respect to concentration, as measured by the CR5 structural measure. The lack of availability of the bank-level underlying determinants of CR5 did not let us to go deeper in order to investigate whether these differences stem from inequalities between different countries (between-country inequality) or from inequalities between banks in a given country (within-country inequality).

6.4. Theil Inequality for Credit Risk (NPL Ratio)

The results from the calculation of the total Theil inequality index for the NPL ratio and its within-group and between-group components are presented in Table 5, as well as in Figures 5 and 6. As it is shown in Table 5, as well as in Figures 5 and 6, the between-group component of the Theil index (disparities due to differences between EA-Co and EA-Pe) presented a sharp increase in 2008, when it started following a continuously increasing path until 2013, afterwards fluctuating slightly to the end of 2017. This evolution shows that there is a clear divergence between the EA-Co and EA-Pe country groups with respect to credit risk, as measured by the NPL ratio. The lack of availability of the underlying bank-level NPL data did not let us to go deeper in order to investigate whether the above-described differences stem from inequalities between different countries (between-country inequality) or from inequalities between banks in a given country (within-country inequality).

7. Convergence Analysis

The evolution of the coefficient of variation, presented in Table 1 and in Figure 2, provides useful information about changes of inequality in Lerner index values across countries and/or years. However, the visual inspection of these changes cannot always provide safe results regarding the existence of convergence or divergence in terms of the Lerner index across euro area countries during a given period, especially when the Lerner index has presented significant ups and downs along this period. The same situation holds in the case of the two concentration measures (HHI/CR5) and the NPL ratio.

To overcome these problems, we employ two concepts of convergence, namely β-convergence and σ-convergence (Barro and Sala-i-Martin 1991), which have been prevailing for many years in the growth literature. β-convergence applies if poor countries tend to catch up with rich ones in terms of per capita income or product levels. In the case of competition, β-convergence would apply if countries with lower levels of competition were found to tend to catch up with countries with higher levels of competition. On the other hand, σ-convergence applies if the dispersion of per capita income or product across countries declines over time. The existence of β-convergence is a necessary but not sufficient condition for σ-convergence. Regarding competition, σ-convergence would apply if the dispersion of competition levels across countries showed a tendency to decline over time.

In the case of competition, the β-convergence test is performed through the estimation of Equation (14).

$$\ln\left(\frac{C_{it}}{C_{i,t-1}}\right) = \alpha + \beta lnC_{i,t-1} + \sum Country_i + \varepsilon_{it} \quad (14)$$

where C_{it} is the level of competition, as expressed by the (inverse of) the Lerner index, in country i in year t, α and β are parameters to be estimated, $Country_i$ are dummy variables to control for possible country effects, and ε_{it} is a random error term. There is β-convergence when the coefficient β in (14) is statistically significant and negative. A higher absolute value of the coefficient β corresponds to a greater tendency towards β-convergence.

Following Lapteacru (2018), the σ-convergence test is performed through the estimation of Equation (15):

$$D_{it} = \alpha + \sigma T + \sum Country_i + \varepsilon_{it} \quad (15)$$

where D_{it} is the absolute value of the difference between the competition in country i in year t and the average competition in year t, T is a time trend, α and σ are parameters to be estimated, $Country_i$ are dummy variables to control for possible country effects, and ε_{it} is a random error term. There is σ-convergence when the coefficient σ in (15) is statistically significant and negative. A higher absolute value of the coefficient σ corresponds to a greater tendency towards σ-convergence.

The estimation of Equations (14) and (15) is performed by applying Ordinary Least Squares (OLS) regressions. A same type convergence analysis, as that described for competition, was also performed for concentration (HHI/CR5) and NPLs. The results, which are presented in Table 7, cover the total period under study (i.e., 2005–2017), as well as two important sub-periods: (a) the period 2008–2012, which includes the years of the financial and debt crisis in the euro area, and (b) the period 2013–2017. This division was based on the evolution of financial integration in the euro area. As Berenberg-Gossler and Enderlein (2016) note, financial integration reached a minimum in July 2012. After the ECB announcement of the OMT program on 26 July, 2012, there was a gradual, but often fragile, decline of financial market fragmentation across all markets. It should also be noted that the sub-period 2005–2007 was not included in the regression analysis, due to its limited time coverage that might possibly provide biased estimations.

Table 7. Regression results for β-convergence and σ-convergence.

Variable	Period	EA-19		EA-Co		EA-Pe	
		β	σ	β	σ	β	σ
Lerner index	2008–2012	−0.9976 *** (0.1001)	0.0031 * (0.0017)	−1.0405 *** (0.1450)	0.0043 * (0.0022)	−0.9490 *** (0.1367)	0.0016 (0.0028)
	2013–2017	−0.8851 *** (0.1436)	0.0012 (0.0022)	−0.9229 *** (0.2177)	0.0026 (0.0026)	−0.8542 *** (0.1930)	−0.0014 (0.0035)
	2005–2017	−0.4072 *** (0.0548)	0.0018 *** (0.0005)	−0.5367 *** (0.0834)	0.0023 *** (0.0006)	−0.3551 *** (0.0781)	0.0011 (0.0008)
HHI	2008–2012	−0.4009 *** (0.1003)	−0.0018 ** (0.0008)	−0.4112 *** (0.1203)	−0.0022 * (0.0012)	−0.3711 * (0.1924)	−0.0004 (0.0007)
	2013–2017	−0.1257 (0.1524)	−0.0025 * (0.0014)	0.1707 (0.1714)	−0.0048 ** (0.0022)	−0.8280 *** (0.2513)	0.0007 (0.0010)
	2005–2017	−0.1210 *** (0.0363)	−0.0005 (0.0004)	−0.1531 *** (0.0478)	−0.0018 *** (0.0005)	−0.0914 (0.0558)	0.0013 *** (0.0004)
CR5	2008–2012	−0.4466 *** (0.0953)	−0.0056 *** (0.0020)	−0.4785 *** (0.1099)	−0.0070 *** (0.0024)	−0.3822 ** (0.1805)	−0.0027 (0.0029)
	2013–2017	−0.1709 (0.1672)	0.0030 (0.0022)	0.0201 (0.1848)	0.0042 (0.0026)	−0.4191 (0.3000)	0.0035 (0.0033)
	2005–2017	−0.1415 *** (0.0356)	−0.0002 (0.0009)	−0.2044 *** (0.0486)	−0.0008 (0.0008)	−0.0941 * (0.0530)	0.0017 (0.0013)
NPL ratio	2008–2012	−0.7191 *** (0.0829)	1.0584 *** (0.1872)	−1.0430 *** (0.0974)	0.2944 (0.2230)	−0.3218 *** (0.0927)	0.9931 *** (0.1779)
	2013–2017	−0.2679 ** (0.1012)	0.2008 * (0.1771)	−0.3747 *** (0.1347)	−0.2758 *** (0.0910)	−0.0174 (0.1426)	0.8723 ** (0.3450)
	2005–2017	−0.2009 *** (0.0325)	0.7479 *** (0.0793)	−0.2817 *** (0.0519)	−0.0245 (0.0545)	−0.1304 *** (0.0369)	1.0566 *** (0.1243)

Notes: Standard errors are reported in parentheses. *, ** and *** indicate statistical significance at the 10%, 5% and 1% levels respectively. Country dummies are not reported for brevity. Source: BankScope database, ECB, World Bank, own calculations.

According to the regression results of Table 7, the Lerner index of market power presented β-convergence in all country groups across all the three periods examined. These results are generally in accordance with the results of β-convergence tests, performed by Weill (2013), which suggest that during the period 2002–2010 the least competitive banking systems in the EU-27 experienced a greater improvement in competition than the most competitive banking systems. Regarding σ-convergence, the related regression coefficient for the period 2008–2012 for both the EA-19 and the EA-Co groups is positive and statistically significant, thus indicating a diverging trend. This coefficient remains positive for the period 2013–2017, however having lost its statistical significance. Regarding the EA-Pe group, its related regression coefficient for the period 2008–2012 was found to be positive, but not statistically significant. In the period 2013–2017, it became negative, but still not statistically significant. According to the regression results for the total period 2005–2017, both the EA-19 and the EA-Co groups experienced a diverging trend of market power, while the regression coefficient for the EA-Pe group is positive, but not statistically significant.

The adverse evolution of the σ-convergence of market power during the period under examination may be attributed to the 2008 crisis, which led to distortions in competition created by the state aid granted to banks, while mergers were allowed without taking into account their effects on market power (Maudos and Vives 2019).

The σ-convergence related regression coefficient of the HHI concentration measure for both the EA-19 and the EA-Co groups in the period 2008–2012 is negative and statistically significant; thus, indicating a converging trend. The corresponding regression coefficient for the EA-Pe group is also negative, but not statistically significant. Its sign turned to positive in the period 2013–2017, with the coefficient remaining not statistically significant. In addition, the HHI concentration measure did not present β-convergence in the case of both the EA-19 and the EA-Co groups during this period. Finally, the EA-Co group was the only one that experienced σ-convergence during the total period 2005–2017. From 2008 to 2012, both the EA-19 and the EA-Co groups experienced σ-convergence of the CR5 concentration measure, in contrast to the EA-Pe group, the regression coefficient of which was found to be negative, but not statistically significant. The CR5 concentration measure did not present β-convergence during the period 2013–2017 in any of the three country groups under examination. The regression results also show that none of the three groups experienced σ-convergence during the total period 2005–2017, with the situation being worse in the case of EA-Pe group.

The observed diverging trends in concentration, measured by the HHI and CR5 concentration indices, were caused by the global financial crisis of 2008, which accelerated the pace of bank concentration in the countries that had been hit most severely by the crisis and whose banking systems had been subject to restructuring (Maudos and Vives 2019). Concentration in Cyprus and Greece, which were already characterized by highly concentrated banking systems, increased further during the crisis period, widening the gap with Italy, which has the lowest bank concentration in the EA-Pe group, including strong cooperative and savings banking sectors (ECB 2016). Regarding the EA-Co group, which was affected less than the EA-Pe group by the global financial crisis, the observed diverging trends in concentration during the period 2013–2017 may be attributed to the fact that in countries, such as Austria, France, and Luxembourg, which were already characterized by very low bank concentration, concentration decreased further, widening the gap with other more concentrated banking systems in the EA-Co group.

During the period 2008–2012, both the EA-19 and the EA-Pe groups experienced lack of σ-convergence with respect to the NPL ratio, while the related regression coefficient for the EA-Co group was found to be positive, but not statistically significant. The situation for the EA-Co group changed in the period 2013–2017, since the related regression coefficient not only changed to negative but also became statistically significant; thus, suggesting a clear convergence. In the case of the EA-19 group, the related regression coefficient remained positive. Finally, the NPL ratio did not present β-convergence in the case of the EA-Pe group during the period 2013–2017. Regarding the total period 2005–2017, both the EA-19 and the EA-Pe groups experienced a clear divergence, in contrast to the EA-Co group, the regression coefficient of which was found to be negative, albeit not statistically significant.

The convergence of the NPL ratio in the EA-Co group during the period 2013–2017 may be attributed to the fact that the countries of this group are characterized by low or relatively low levels of NPLs. Although the NPL levels increased enormously in Latvia and Lithuania at the outburst of the crisis, they entered into a very sharp decreasing path afterwards. On the contrary, the divergence of the NPL ratio in the EA-Pe countries may be attributed to the fact that these countries experienced higher levels of NPLs than the EA-Co countries during the crisis, which remain very high in the case of Cyprus and Greece.

8. Conclusions

In this study, we examined the evolution of competition (through market power and concentration) and credit risk (through non-performing loans) across euro area core (EA-Co), periphery (EA-Pe) and all 19 countries (EA-19) in the period 2005–2017, as well as in two sub-periods, 2008–2012 and 2013–2017. Furthermore, we tested two hypotheses with respect to competition, concentration and credit risk: (a) the existence of fragmentation in the euro area as a whole (EA-19), as well as in core countries (EA-Co) and periphery countries (EA-Pe), and (b) the presence of β-convergence and σ-convergence among the country-members of each of the three groups.

Our analysis extends beyond the period of financial crisis, thereby taking into account the non-standard measures adopted by the ECB to support further integration. By using data from all the 19 euro area countries, which have a common currency and a single bank supervisory mechanism, a possible bias that might stem from the use of either heterogeneous data or data coming from only a subset of euro area countries was eliminated, allowing for robust testing of fragmentation and converging or diverging trends. In addition to uncovering the evolution of bank competition and risk, providing substantiated clues to policy makers about the progress of integration was a major aim of our research.

Competition (as expressed by the inverse of the Lerner index of market power) reached a minimum in 2015 and increased afterwards in all three country groups under examination (EA-19, EA-Co and EA-Pe), in line with a gradual but fragile post-crisis reintegration trend. This is supported by the Theil inequality index for market power, which reveals a decrease of the between-country inequality from 2011 onwards in each of the three groups. This evolution was also confirmed by means of β-convergence and σ-convergence tests, which showed a decrease in divergence of competition. Another finding is that the global financial crisis reversed the advances in competitive pressure that had been observed during the preceding few years.

With respect to concentration, as measured by the HHI and CR5 concentration indices, the average concentration in EA-19 and EA-Co started decreasing in 2015 and 2012, respectively, in contrast to EA-Pe, where concentration has followed a continuously increasing path since 2007. The progress that had been made during the period 2008–2012 with the achievement of β-convergence and σ-convergence in the whole euro area and the core countries was reversed in the period 2013–2017. Periphery countries did not experience convergence of concentration in either of the two periods 2008–2012 and 2013–2017.

Regarding credit risk, NPL ratios have always been higher in EA-Pe. Moreover, while the weighted average of the NPL ratio in EA-Co peaked in 2013 at 3.38%, in EA-Pe the peak of 15.56% was in 2014. The decrease thereafter has not been proportional between the two groups, in line with the β-convergence and σ-convergence tests, which indicate that the EA-Co group experienced β-convergence and σ-convergence in the period 2013–2017, while the EA-Pe group has been characterized by divergence. The Theil inequality index confirms the divergence between the two groups, indicating that the inequality between the EA-Co and the EA-Pe groups has been continuously increasing since 2008. This evolution suggests that the presence of persistent large stocks of NPLs remains a pressing challenge, which contributes to fragmentation between euro area countries. Hence, more effective measures, such as the creation of asset management companies, NPL transaction platforms, securitization, or state guarantees schemes, should be introduced in order not only to reduce the existing NPL volumes, but also to prevent their increase in the future.

All in all, the persistence of fragmentation, in spite of some partial reintegration trends, suggests that policy measures accelerating convergence of our variables would not only strengthen financial integration, but also help in establishing a real euro area banking union.

Author Contributions: Conceptualization, M.K. and H.L.; methodology, M.K. and H.L.; software, M.K.; validation, M.K.; formal analysis, M.K.; investigation, M.K.; resources, M.K.; data curation, M.K.; writing—original draft preparation, M.K.; writing—review and editing, M.K. and H.L.; visualization, M.K. and H.L.; supervision, H.L.; project administration, H.L.; funding acquisition, H.L. All authors have read and agreed to the published version of the manuscript.

Funding: Financial assistance from the Research Centre of the Athens University of Economics and Business.

Acknowledgments: The authors would like to thank participants at the ASSET Conference (Athens 2019), FEBS Conferences (Athens 2019; Prague 2019), JIMF Conference (Marrakech 2019), and EBES Conference (Kuala Lumpur 2020), for discussing and commenting on many of the research questions and approaches of this paper.

Conflicts of Interest: The authors declare no conflict of interest.

References

Al-Eyd, Ali, and Pelin Berkmen. 2013. Fragmentation and Monetary Policy in the Euro Area. Working Paper No. 13/208, International Monetary Fund, Washington, DC, USA.

Anastasiou, Dimitrios, Helen Louri, and Mike Tsionas. 2019. Non-Performing Loans in the Euro-area: Are Core-Periphery Banking Markets Fragmented? *International Journal of Finance and Economics* 24: 97–112. [CrossRef]

Angelini, Paolo, and Nicola Cetorelli. 2003. The Effects of Regulatory Reform on Competition in the Banking Industry. *Journal of Money, Credit and Banking* 35: 663–84. [CrossRef]

Apergis, Nicholas, Irene Fafaliou, and Michael L. Polemis. 2016. New evidence on assessing the level of competition in the European Union banking sector: A panel data approach. *International Business Review* 25: 395–407. [CrossRef]

Baele, Lieven, Annalisa Ferrando, Peter Hördahl, Elizaveta Krylova, and Cyril Monnet. 2004. *Measuring Financial Integration in the Euro Area*. Occasional Paper No. 14. Frankfurt: European Central Bank.

Barro, Robert J., and Xavier Sala-i-Martin. 1991. Convergence across states and regions. *Brookings Papers on Economic Activity* 1: 107–82. [CrossRef]

Berenberg-Gossler, Paul, and Henrik Enderlein. 2016. *Financial Market Fragmentation in the Euro Area: State of Play*. Policy Paper No. 177. Berlin: Jacques Delors Institut.

Bikker, Jacob A., and Katharina Haaf. 2002. Competition, concentration and their relationship: An empirical analysis of the banking industry. *Journal of Banking and Finance* 26: 2191–214. [CrossRef]

Bikker, Jacob A., and Laura Spierdijk. 2008. How Banking Competition Changed over Time. Working Paper No. 167, De Netherlandsche Bank, Amsterdam, The Netherlands.

Boone, Jan. 2008. A new way to measure competition. *Economic Journal* 118: 1245–61. [CrossRef]

Casu, Barbara, and Claudia Girardone. 2009. Competition issues in European banking. *Journal of Financial Regulation and Compliance* 17: 119–33. [CrossRef]

Claessens, Stijn. 2019. Fragmentation in Global Financial Markets: Good or Bad for Financial Stability? BIS Working Papers No. 815, Bank for International Settlements, Basel, Switzerland.

Coccorese, Paolo. 2004. Banking competition and macroeconomic conditions: A disaggregate Analysis. *Journal of International Financial Markets, Institutions and Money* 14: 203–19. [CrossRef]

Cruz-Garcia, Paula, Juan Fernandez de Guevara, and Joaquin Maudos. 2017. The evolution of market power in European banking. *Finance Research Letters* 23: 257–62. [CrossRef]

De Bandt, Olivier, and E. Philip Davis. 2000. Competition, contestability and market structure in European banking sectors on the eve of EMU. *Journal of Banking and Finance* 24: 1045–66. [CrossRef]

De Sola Perea, Maite, and Christophe Van Nieuwenhuyze. 2014. *Financial integration and fragmentation in the euro area. Economic Review, 99-125, June*. Brussels: National Bank of Belgium.

ECB. 2003. *The Integration of Europe's Financial Markets*. European Central Bank Monthly Bulletin. Frankfurt: European Central Bank.

ECB. 2016. *Report on Financial Structures*. Frankfurt: European Central Bank.

ECB. 2018. *Financial integration in Europe*. Frankfurt: European Central Bank.

ECB. 2019a. Statistical Data Warehouse: Balance Sheet Items Statistics. Available online: https://sdw.ecb.europa.eu/browse.do?node=1491 (accessed on 3 September 2019).

ECB. 2019b. Statistical Data Warehouse: Banking Structural Financial Indicators Statistics. Available online: https://sdw.ecb.europa.eu/browseSelection.do?node=9689719 (accessed on 3 September 2019).

ECB. 2020. *Supervisory Banking Statistics—Third Quarter 2019*. Frankfurt: European Central Bank.

Fernandez de Guevara, Juan, Joaquin Maudos, and Francisco Perez. 2007. Integration and competition in the European financial markets. *Journal of International Money and Finance* 26: 26–45. [CrossRef]

FSB. 2019. *FSB Report on Market Fragmentation*. Basel: Financial Stability Board.

Gischer, Horst, and Mike Stiele. 2008. Competition Tests with a Non-Structural Model: The Panzar–Rosse Method Applied to Germany's Savings Banks. *German Economic Review* 10: 50–70. [CrossRef]

Goddard, John, Hong Liu, Phil Molyneux, and John O. S. Wilson. 2013. Do Bank Profits Converge? *European Financial Management* 19: 345–65. [CrossRef]

Hondroyiannis, George, Sarantis Lolos, and Evangelia Papapetrou. 1999. Assessing competitive conditions in the Greek banking system. *Journal of International Financial Markets, Institutions and Money* 9: 377–91. [CrossRef]

Jondrow, James, C. A. Knox Lovell, Ivan S. Materov, and Peter Schmidt. 1982. On the estimation of technical inefficiency in the stochastic frontier production function model. *Journal of Econometrics* 19: 233–38. [CrossRef]

Karadima, Maria, and Helen Louri. 2019. Non-Performing Loans in the Euro Area: Does Market Power Matter? Working Paper No. 271, Bank of Greece, Athens, Greece.

Kumbhakar, Subal C., Sjur Baardsen, and Gudbrand Lien. 2012. A new method for estimating market power with an application to Norwegian sawmilling. *Review of Industrial Organization* 40: 109–29. [CrossRef]

Lapteacru, Ion. 2018. Convergence of bank competition in Central and Eastern European countries: do foreign and domestic banks go hand in hand? *Post-Communist Economies* 30: 588–616. [CrossRef]

Lerner, Abba P. 1934. The concept of monopoly and the measurement of monopoly power. *Review of Economic Studies* 1: 157–75. [CrossRef]

Louri, Helen, and Petros Migiakis. 2019. Bank lending margins in the euro area: Funding conditions, fragmentation and ECB's policies. *Review of Financial Economics* 37: 482–505. [CrossRef]

Lucotte, Yannick. 2015. Euro area banking fragmentation in the aftermath of the crisis: A cluster analysis. *Applied Economics Letters* 22: 1046–50. [CrossRef]

Magnus, Marcel, Alienor Margerit, Benoit Mesnard, and Christina Katopodi. 2017. *Non-Performing Loans in the Banking Union—Stocktaking and Challenges*. European Parliament Briefing, 13 July. Brussels: European Parliament.

Maudos, Joaquin, and Xavier Vives. 2019. Competition Policy in Banking in the European Union. *Review of Industrial Organization* 55: 27–54. [CrossRef]

Moch, Nils. 2013. Competition in fragmented markets: New evidence from the German banking industry in the light of the subprime crisis. *Journal of Banking and Finance* 37: 2908–19. [CrossRef]

Panzar, John C., and James N. Rosse. 1987. Testing for "monopoly" equilibrium. *Journal of Industrial Economics* 35: 443–56. [CrossRef]

Phillips, Peter, and Donggyu Sul. 2007. Transition modeling and econometric convergence tests. *Econometrica* 75: 1771–855. [CrossRef]

Staikouras, Christos K., and Anastasia Koutsomanoli-Filippaki. 2006. Competition and Concentration in the New European Banking Landscape. *European Financial Management* 12: 443–82. [CrossRef]

Sun, Yu. 2009. Recent Developments in European Bank Competition. Working Paper No. 11/146, International Monetary Fund, Washington, DC, USA.

Weill, Laurent. 2013. Bank competition in the EU: How has it evolved? *Journal of International Financial Markets, Institutions and Money* 26: 100–12. [CrossRef]

World Bank. 2019a. World Development Indicators Database. Available online: https://databank.worldbank.org/source/world-development-indicators (accessed on 28 October 2019).

World Bank. 2019b. Global Financial Development Database. Available online: https://datacatalog.orldbank.org/dataset/global-financial-development (accessed on 28 October 2019).

Journal of
Risk and Financial Management

MDPI

Article

Forecasting the Term Structure of Interest Rates with Dynamic Constrained Smoothing B-Splines

Eduardo Mineo [1,*], Airlane Pereira Alencar [1], Marcelo Moura [2] and Antonio Elias Fabris [1]

1 Instituto de Matemática e Estatística, University of São Paulo USP, São Paulo 05508-090, Brazil; lane@ime.usp.br (A.P.A.); fabris@usp.br (A.E.F.)

2 Moura Madalozzo Consultoria Econômica, São Paulo 04560-010, Brazil; marcelommce@gmail.com

* Correspondence: eduardo.mineo@usp.br

Received: 27 February 2020; Accepted: 30 March 2020; Published: 3 April 2020

Abstract: The Nelson–Siegel framework published by Diebold and Li created an important benchmark and originated several works in the literature of forecasting the term structure of interest rates. However, these frameworks were built on the top of a parametric curve model that may lead to poor fitting for sensible term structure shapes affecting forecast results. We propose DCOBS with no-arbitrage restrictions, a dynamic constrained smoothing B-splines yield curve model. Even though DCOBS may provide more volatile forward curves than parametric models, they are still more accurate than those from Nelson–Siegel frameworks. DCOBS has been evaluated for ten years of US Daily Treasury Yield Curve Rates, and it is consistent with stylized facts of yield curves. DCOBS has great predictability power, especially in short and middle-term forecast, and has shown greater stability and lower root mean square errors than an Arbitrage-Free Nelson–Siegel model.

Keywords: interest rates; yeld curve; no-arbitrage; bonds; B-splines; time series

1. Introduction

Forecast methods applied to a term structure of interest rates are important tools not only for banks and financial firms, or governments and policy makers, but for society itself, helping to understand the movements of markets and flows of money. Several works have been done during the past few decades in order to predict the dynamics of term structure of interest rates. This paper presents a dynamic version of the constrained smoothing B-splines model to forecast the yield curve with no-arbitrage restrictions.

A complete term structure of interest rates does not exist in the real world. Observable market data are discrete points that relate interest rates to maturity dates. Since it is unlikely that there will be an available contract in the market for every maturity needed by practitioners, a continuous curve model is necessary. The importance of these models is crucial for pricing securities, for instance. The first modeling technique that comes to mind is interpolation. With interpolation, one can indeed obtain an adherent fit, but it can easily lead to unstable curves since market data are subject to many sources of disturbance.

The literature describes two approaches for estimating the term structure of interest rates: a statistical approach and an equilibrium approach. The equilibrium approach makes use of theories that describe the overall economy in terms of state variables and its implications on short-term interest rates Cox et al. (1985); Duffie and Kan (1996); Vasicek (1977). In the statistical approach, the construction of the yield curve relies on data observed in the market Heath et al. (1992); Hull and White (1990). This observed data can be smoothed with parametric or nonparametric methods. Parametric methods have functional forms and their parameters can have economic interpretations such as a Nelson–Siegel model Nelson and Siegel (1987) or the Svensson model Svensson (1994). One advantage is that restrictions on parameters can be added so it copes with convenient economic theories such as the arbitrage-free set. However, its functional form makes parametric methods less flexible to fit observed data. This lack of adherence to data can make its practical usage inappropriate, especially in asset pricing and no-arbitrage applications due to misspecification Laurini and Moura (2010). The model can produce yield curves with theoretical integrity but without reflecting the reality. On the other hand, nonparametric methods do not assume any particular functional form and consequently they are very flexible and can be very robust if combined with appropriate conditions.

After almost 50 years since the publication of the first yield curve models McCulloch (1971), just recently the yield curve dynamics became an essential topic. With the publication of the Dynamic Nelson–Siegel (DNS) model by Diebold and Li (2003), the subject became established. Even though the dynamics of term structure play a vital role in macroeconomic studies, Diebold and Li argued that until then little attention had been paid to forecasting term structures. They gave two reasons for this lack of interest. Firstly, they stated that no-arbitrage models had little to say about term structure dynamics. Secondly, based on the work of Duffee (2002), they assumed that affine equilibrium models[1] forecast poorly. Therefore, there was a belief that the dynamics of yield curves could not be forecast with parsimonious models.

In order to challenge this idea, Diebold and Li proposed the DNS model using a Nelson–Siegel yield curve fitting to forecast its dynamics. This model became very popular among financial market users and even central banks around the world. It is parsimonious and stable. In addition, the Nelson–Siegel model imposes some desired economic properties such as discount function approaching zero as maturity evolves and its factors representing short-, medium-, and long-term behaviors.

In practice, the forecast results of DNS are remarkable, but, despite its both theoretical and empirical success, DNS does not impose restrictions for arbitrage opportunities. Consequently, practitioners could be exposed to critical financial risks, as the pricing of assets that depends on interest rates relies on arbitrage-free theory. In order to mitigate these risks, Christensen et al. (2011) introduce a class of Arbitrage-Free Nelson–Siegel (AFNS) models. They are affine term structure models that keep the DNS structure and incorporate no-arbitrage restrictions. Tourrucôo et al. (2016) list several appealing features of AFNS. Namely, they keep the desired economic properties of the three-factors model of the original structure of DNS. They also ensure lack of arbitrage opportunities with a more simple structure compared to those affine arbitrage-free models published previously by Duffie and Kan (1996) and Duffee (2002). This is achieved by adding a yield-adjustment term to the Nelson–Siegel yield curve model described as an ordinary differential system of equations to ensure no-arbitrage. Tourrucôo et al. (2016) argue that, in long forecast horizons, the AFNS model with uncorrelated factors delivers the most accurate forecasts. Their conclusion is that no-arbitrage is indeed helpful, but only for longer forecasting horizons. Barzanti and Corradi (2001) published earlier works on the use of constrained smoothing B-splines to overcome some difficulties while estimating term structures of interest rates with ordinary cubic splines. They computed the B-splines coefficients as a least squares problem. However, Laurini and Moura (2010) proposed constrained smoothing B-splines with a different methodology. This methodology was initially proposed by He and Shi (1998) and He and Ng (1999) as a general tool to smooth data with certain qualitative properties such as monotonicity and concavity or convexity constraints. Roughly, the methodology builds the yield curve as a L_1 projection of a smooth function into the space of B-splines. It is achieved by estimating a conditional median function as described in quantile regression theory of Koenker and Bassett (1978). A great advantage is that, being a conditional median function, it is robust to outliers. In addition, its formulation as a linear programming problem allows us to impose several constraints without a substantial increase in computational costs.

---

1 The expression "affine term structure model" describes any arbitrage-free model in which bond yields are affine (constant-plus-linear) functions of some state vector x. For further reading, we recommend Piazzesi (2010).

Our present work proposes DCOBS, a dynamic constrained smoothing B-splines model to forecast the term structure of interest rates. DCOBS describes the coefficients of the yield curve model proposed by Laurini and Moura (2010) as processes evolving over time. Even though constrained smoothing B-splines specification provides full automation in knot mesh selection, we could not use it in a dynamic framework setting. In order to build a common ground and observe curve shapes evolving over time, knots were fixed to capture short-, medium- and long-term behavior according to observed data. These knots were distributed equally in the dataset, so there was the same amount of coefficients on each daily curve, and it was possible to run a statistical regression. DCOBS has shown great predictability in the short-term, and remained stable in the long-term.

In Sections 2–4, we present a brief introduction to the fundamental concepts of dynamic Nelson–Siegel models. In Section 5, we introduce the DCOBS model. Section 6 presents the dataset used for fitting and forecasting the US Daily Treasury Yield Curve Rates. In Section 7, we study the outputs from a time series of fitted yield curves. Finally, in Section 8, we finish the work pointing the conclusions we made.

The main contributions of this paper are:

- A complete formulation of no-arbitrage constrained smoothing B-splines in terms of objective functions and linear constraint equations;
- A dynamic framework of constrained smoothing B-splines (DCOBS) described as AR(1) processes for each coefficient;
- Automatic selection of the best smoothing parameter λ for fitting yield curves;
- Yield curves estimated as conditional median functions robust to outliers;
- Evaluation of the DCOBS framework compared to the Arbitrage-Free Nelson–Siegel for ten years of US Daily Treasury Yield Curve Rates;
- Yield curves with better adherence to data compared to Nelson–Siegel family curves.
- A software program that fits several curve fitting models, including no-arbitrage constrained smoothing B-splines.

2. Term Structure of Interest Rates

In this paper, interest rates are treated as a multidimensional variable that represents the return on investment expressed by three related quantities: spot rate, forward rate, and the discount value.

Each of these quantities depends on several economical, political, and social information, such as supply and demand of money and the expectation of its future value, risk, and trust perception, consequences of political acts, etc. The term structure of interest rates is a valuable tool not only for banks and financial firms, or governments and policy makers, but, for society itself, helping to understand the movements of markets and flows of money.

It is assumed that fixed income government bonds can be considered risk-free so we can define a special type of yield that is the *spot interest rate*, $s(\tau)$. This function is the return of a fixed income zero-coupon risk-free bond that expires in τ periods. Today's price of such financial instrument whose future value is \$1.00, assuming that its interest rate is continuously compounded, is given by the *discount function*, $d(\tau)$, represented by

$$d(\tau) = e^{-s(\tau)\times\tau}. \tag{1}$$

The relationship between the discount value and the spot rate can be recovered by

$$s(\tau) = -\frac{log(d(\tau))}{\tau}.$$

Based on the available bonds in the market with different maturities, it is possible to plan at an instant a financial transaction that will take place in another future instant, starting at the maturity of the shorter bond and expiring at the maturity of the longer bond. The interest rate of this future transaction is called the *forward rate*.

Consider a forward contract traded at the present day at $\tau_P = 0$. This contract arranges an investment in the future that starts at the settlement date at time τ. This investment will be kept until the maturity date, at time $\tau_M > \tau$. Then, the implied continuously compounded forward rate is related to the spot rate according to

$$f(\tau, \tau_M) = \frac{s(\tau_M) \times \tau_M - s(\tau) \times \tau}{\tau_M - \tau}.$$

The instantaneous forward rate or short rate $f(\tau)$ is defined by

$$f(\tau) = \lim_{\tau_M \to \tau} f(\tau, \tau_M).$$

That is, the short rate $f(\tau)$ is the forward rate for a forward contract with an infinitesimal investment period after the settlement date. The forward rate can be seen as the marginal increase in the total return from a marginal increase in the length of the investment Svensson (1994). The spot rate $s(\tau)$ is defined by

$$s(\tau) = \frac{1}{\tau} \int_0^\tau f(x)\,\mathrm{d}x. \quad (2)$$

Note that the spot rate is the average of the instantaneous forward rates with settlement between the trade date 0 and the maturity date τ. From (1) and (2), the discount function and forward rate may be written as

$$d(\tau) = e^{-\int_0^\tau f(x)\,\mathrm{d}x}$$

and

$$f(\tau) = -\frac{d'(\tau)}{d(\tau)}.$$

Yield curve is a function of the interest rates of bonds that share the same properties except by their maturities. A yield curve of spot rates is called *term structure of interest rates* Cox et al. (1985).

Yield curves of coupon-bearing bonds are not equivalent to yield curves of zero-coupon bonds with same maturity dates Svensson (1994). Therefore, yield curves for coupon-bearing bonds should not be used as direct representations of the term structure of interest rates.

In the real world, the term structure of interest rates has a discrete representation. Using interpolation techniques, we can represent the term structure of interest rates in a continuous way. Such a continuous representation provides a valuable tool for calculating the spot rate at any given interval.

As pointed out by Diebold and Li (2003), the classical approaches to model the term structure of interest rates are equilibrium models and no-arbitrage models.

Equilibrium models Cox et al. (1985); Duffie and Kan (1996); Vasicek (1977) construct the term structure of interest rates from economic variables to model a stochastic process for the short rate dynamic. Then, spot rates can be obtained under risk premium assumptions, that is, considering what investors expect as an extra return relative to risk-free bonds.

On the other hand, *no-arbitrage models* focus on perfectly fitting the term structure of interest rate on observed market spot rates so that there is no arbitrage opportunity. A major contribution to no-arbitrage models was given by Hull and White (1990) and Heath et al. (1992).

In the work of Diebold and Li (2003), neither the equilibrium model nor the no-arbitrage model are used to model the term structure of interest rates. Instead, they use the Nelson and Siegel exponential components framework Nelson and Siegel (1987). They do so because they claim their model produces encouraging results for out-of-sample forecasting. In addition, at that time, little attention had been paid in the research of both no-arbitrage and equilibrium models regarding the dynamics and forecasting of interest rates.

3. Dynamic Nelson–Siegel

Diebold and Li (2003) proposed the following dynamic version of Nelson–Siegel yield curve model

$$NS(\tau) = \beta_1 L_1(\tau) + \beta_2 L_2(\tau) + \beta_3 L_3(\tau), \tag{3}$$

where

$$L_1(\tau) = 1,$$
$$L_2(\tau) = \frac{1-e^{-\lambda\tau}}{\lambda\tau},$$
$$L_3(\tau) = \frac{1-e^{-\lambda\tau}}{\lambda\tau} - e^{-\lambda\tau}$$

and the parameter λ is a constant interpreted as the conductor of the curve exponential decay rate.

A yield curve is fitted according to the Nelson–Siegel model to relate yields and maturities of available contracts for a specific day. We will refer to such yield curve as the Nelson–Siegel *static yield curve*. Let θ be $\{\beta_1, \beta_2, \beta_3\}$. The curves are fitted by constructing a simplex solver which computes appropriate values for θ to minimize the distance between $NS(\tau)$ and market data points. The coefficients β_1, β_2, and β_3 are interpreted as three latent dynamic factors. The loading on β_1 is constant and do not change in the limit; then, β_1 can be viewed as a long-term factor. The loading on β_2 starts at 1 and decays quickly to zero; then, β_2 can be viewed as a short-term factor. Finally, the loading on β_3 starts at zero, increases, and decays back to zero; then, β_3 can be viewed as a medium term factor.

The Dynamic Nelson–Siegel (DNS) model is defined by

$$s_t(\tau) = \beta_{1,t} L_1(\tau) + \beta_{2,t} L_2(\tau) + \beta_{3,t} L_3(\tau) + \epsilon_t \qquad t = 1, ..., T, \tag{4}$$

where the coefficients $\beta_{i,t}$ are AR(1) processes defined by

$$\beta_{i,t} = c_i + \phi_i \beta_{i,t-1} + \eta_{i,t} \qquad i = 1, 2, 3.$$

The parameters c_i and ϕ_i are estimated with the maximum likelihood for the ARIMA model. The coefficients $\beta_{i,t}$ are predicted as AR(1) over a dataset of T daily market observations. Furthermore, $\epsilon_t \sim \mathcal{N}(0, \sigma_\epsilon^2)$ and $\eta_{i,t} \sim \mathcal{N}(0, \sigma_i^2)$ are independent errors. Since the yield curve model depends only on $\beta_{1,t}, \beta_{2,t}, \beta_{3,t}$, then forecasting the yield curve is equivalent to forecasting $\beta_{1,t}$, $\beta_{2,t}$, and $\beta_{3,t}$.

Conversely, the factors for long-term, short-term, and medium-term can also be interpreted, respectively, in terms of level, slope, and curvature of the model. Diebold and Li (2003) use these interpretations to claim that the historical stylized facts of the term structure of interest rates can be replicated by fitting the three factors, which means that the model can replicate yield curve geometric shapes.

For the US market, Diebold and Li (2003) show that the DNS model outperforms traditional benchmarks such as the random walk model, even though Vicente and Tabak (2008) state that the model does not outperform a random walk for short-term forecasts (one-month ahead).

4. Arbitrage-Free Nelson–Siegel

The Arbitrage-Free Nelson–Siegel (AFNS) static model for daily yield curve fitting was derived by Christensen et al. (2011) from the standard continuous-time affine Arbitrage-Free formulation of Duffie and Kan (1996). The AFNS model almost matches the NS model except by the yield-adjustment term $-\frac{C(\tau,\tau_M)}{\tau_M-\tau}$. In fact, the definition of the AFNS static model in Christensen et al. (2011) is given by

$$AFNS(\tau) = \beta_1 L_1(\tau) + \beta_2 L_2(\tau) + \beta_3 L_3(\tau) - \frac{C(\tau,\tau_M)}{\tau_M-\tau}. \quad (5)$$

The AFNS model built by Christensen et al. (2011) considers the mean levels of the state variable under the Q-measure at zero, i.e., $\Theta^Q = 0$. Thus, $-\frac{C(\tau,\tau_M)}{\tau_M-\tau}$ have the form

$$-\frac{C(\tau,\tau_M)}{\tau_M-\tau} = -\frac{1}{2}\frac{1}{\tau_M-\tau} \sum_{j=1}^{3}\int_{\tau}^{\tau_M} \left(\Sigma' B(s,\tau_M) B(s,\tau_M)'\Sigma\right)_{j,j} ds.$$

Considering a general volatility matrix (not related to the dynamic model for forecasting the yield curve)

$$\Sigma = \begin{pmatrix} \sigma_{11} & \sigma_{12} & \sigma_{13} \\ \sigma_{21} & \sigma_{22} & \sigma_{23} \\ \sigma_{31} & \sigma_{32} & \sigma_{33} \end{pmatrix},$$

Christensen et al. (2011) show that an analytical form of the yield-adjustment term can be derived as

$$\frac{C(\tau,\tau_M)}{\tau_M-\tau} = \frac{1}{2}\frac{1}{\tau_M-\tau}\int_{\tau}^{\tau_M} \sum_{j=1}^{3} \left(\Sigma' B(s,\tau_M) B(s,\tau_M)'\Sigma\right)_{j,j} ds.$$

They also estimated the general volatility matrix for maturities measured in years as

$$\hat{\Sigma} = \begin{pmatrix} 0.0051 & 0 & 0 \\ 0 & 0.0110 & 0 \\ 0 & 0 & 0.0264 \end{pmatrix}$$

and $\hat{\lambda} = 0.5975$ for independent factors AFNS model, solving the yield-adjustment equation for arbitrage-free conditions.

Note that the adjustment-term $C(\tau,\tau_M)$ is only time-independent. In other words, it is a deterministic function that depends only on the maturity of the bond. Thus, let the auxiliary function $\Gamma(\tau)$ be

$$\Gamma(\tau) = -\frac{C(0,\tau)}{\tau}.$$

As in the Dynamic Nelson–Siegel model, the Dynamic AFNS model describes the AFNS static model evolving over time. The Dynamic AFNS model is defined by

$$\begin{aligned} s_t(\tau) = {} & \beta_{1,t} L_1(\tau) \\ & + \beta_{2,t} L_2(\tau) \\ & + \beta_{3,t} L_3(\tau) + \Gamma(\tau) + \epsilon_t \\ t = {} & 1, \ldots, T \end{aligned} \quad (6)$$

where the loadings $L_1(\tau)$, $L_2(\tau)$ and $L_3(\tau)$ are the usual functions of (3) and the coefficients $\beta_{i,t}$ are autoregressive processes described by

$$\beta_{i,t} = c_i + \phi_i \beta_{i,t} + \eta_{i,t} \qquad i = 1,2,3 \quad (7)$$

where the parameters c_i and ϕ_i and the coefficients $\beta_{i,t}$ are estimated and predicted as described in Section 3.

If $\beta_{i,t}$ is a linear function of $\beta_{j,t}$ where $i \neq j$, or there is a cointegration, the component $\beta_{i,t}$ can be predicted as a linear function of $\beta_{j,t}$, and the model can be simplified.

5. Dynamic Constrained Smoothing B-Splines

Constrained Smoothing B-Splines is a methodology first proposed by He and Shi (1998) and then formalized by He and Ng (1999) as a proper algorithm. Constrained Smoothing B-Splines extends smoothing splines to a conditional quantile function estimation and then formulates the model as a linear programming problem that can incorporate constraints such as monotonicity, convexity, and boundary conditions. Laurini and Moura (2010) applied this methodology as a static model to fit daily yield curves along with no-arbitrage constraints. The estimation of the daily term structure of interest rates is set to be a conditional median estimation that is robust to outliers. This model produces yield curves as L_1 projection into the space of B-splines. The flexible nature of B-splines and the arbitrage-free constraints makes the model a powerful tool that creates balance between financial meaning and adherence to data avoiding overfitting.

Our main contribution is the proposal of the Dynamic Constrained Smoothing B-splines (DCOBS) model that describes the static model evolving over time.

DCOBS is estimated by the Penalized Least Absolute Deviation

$$\min_{\theta \in \mathbb{R}^C} \sum_{i=1}^{n} \left| y_i - \sum_{j=1}^{C} a_j B_j(\tau_i) \right| + \Lambda \max_{\tau} \sum_{j=1}^{C} a_j (B_j(\tau))'', \tag{8}$$

where n is the number of contracts available in the reference day, y_i are market yields of the contracts, $C = N + m$ is the number of coefficients, N is the number of internal knots, $\theta = (a_1, \ldots, a_C)$ is the coefficient vector to be estimated, B_j are the B-splines basis, and τ_i are distinct maturities of the contracts. As in Laurini and Moura (2010), the model is configured with $m = 3$ as the order for quadratic B-Splines basis. The selection of the smoothing parameter Λ is automated with generalized cross validation (Leave-One-Out GCV) method of Fisher et al. (1995).

The formulation in (8) can be rewritten as

$$\min_{\theta \in \mathbb{R}^C} \sum_{i=1}^{n} \left| y_i - \sum_{j=1}^{C} a_j B_j(\tau_i) \right| + \Lambda \omega,$$

such that

$$-\omega \quad \leq \quad \sum_{j=1}^{C} a_j (B_j(t_k))'' \quad \leq \quad \omega,$$

where $k = 1, \ldots, N$ and t_k is an internal knot position.

The static model defined by (8) can be implemented as an equivalent linear programming problem that minimizes the objective function z such that

$$\min z = \sum_{i=1}^{n} |e_i| + |\omega| \, .$$

Each yield observed in the market will produce five linear constraint equations: two constraints for fitting the curve, one constraint for smoothing, and two constraints for no-arbitrage conditions.

The fitting constraints are

$$\sum_{j=1}^{C} a_j B_j(\tau_i) + |e_i| \geq y_i,$$
$$\sum_{j=1}^{C} a_j B_j(\tau_i) - |e_i| \leq y_i,$$

where all $B_j(\tau_i)$ are quadratic B-splines basis.

The smoothing constraint is

$$\Lambda \sum_{j=1}^{C} a_j (B_j(\tau_i))'' - |\omega| \leq 0.$$

Finally, the no-arbitrage constraints are

$$\sum_{j=1}^{C} a_j B_j(\tau_i) > 0,$$
$$\sum_{j=1}^{C} a_j (B_j(\tau_i))' < 0.$$

The resulting fitted yield curve

$$\hat{s}(\tau) = \sum_{j=1}^{C} \hat{a}_j B_j(\tau)$$

is a conditional median function represented by quadratic smoothing B-splines.

Now, we propose the Dynamic Constrained Smoothing B-Splines model by

$$s_t(\tau) = \sum_{j=1}^{C} a_{j,t} B_j(\tau) + \epsilon_t, \quad t = 1, ..., T, \tag{9}$$

where the coefficients $a_{j,t}$ are autoregressive processes described by

$$a_{j,t} = c_j + \phi_j a_{j,t-1} + \eta_{j,t} \qquad j = 1 \ldots C,$$

where the parameters c_i and ϕ_i and the coefficients $\beta_{i,t}$ are estimated and predicted as described in Sections 3 and 4.

If $a_{i,t}$ is a linear function of $a_{j,t}$ where $i \neq j$, or there is a cointegration, the component $a_{i,t}$ can be predicted as linear function of $a_{j,t}$ and the model can be simplified.

The DCOBS model extends the static model and extrapolates the temporal axis creating a surface of fitted curves.

Figure 1 displays a visual idea of the differences between each yield curve model and the superiority of fitting of DCOBS over AFNS.

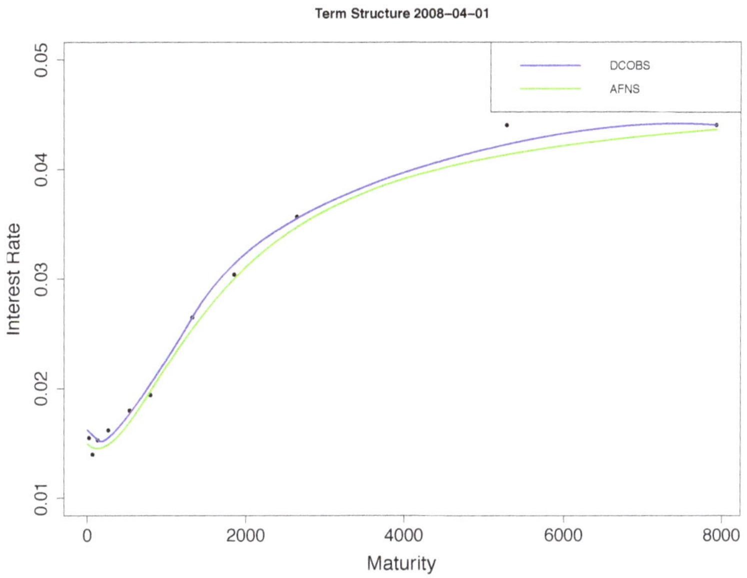

Figure 1. Dynamic Constrained B-Splines compared to Arbitrage-Free Nelson–Siegel.

6. Descriptive Analysis

This work used 10 years (2007–2017) of public historical data of US Daily Treasury Yield Curve Rates[2]. The data were partitioned so 2007–2016 was the sample data set and 2017 was the test data set. A US federal holidays dataset was built for auxiliary calculations of business days.

The sample data set had 27,544 data points in 2504 reference dates spanning between 2 January 2007 and 30 December 2016. The term structure horizon spans between 22 and 7920 business days. The sample data set originated 5008 yield curves, with 2504 AFNS and 2504 DCOBS.

By the nature of parametric models, there is no challenge in relating the coefficients in a time-dependent process. Thus, Arbitrage-Free Nelson–Siegel yield curves are fitted using the raw sample data.

On the other hand, nonparametric B-Splines models depend on its knots and data points position. Therefore, a two-step normalization procedure was applied and so the coefficients could be related in a time-dependent process. The first step normalizes the horizon length. The second step normalizes the data point positions.

In the first step, the Nelson–Siegel model is applied to extrapolate the horizon and calculate the yields on the boundaries of the term structure. The largest curve was picked from the dataset with a horizon of 7920 days.

For the second step, an auxiliary DCOBS curve was built with knots being equally distributed across the horizon. With the resulting fitted curve, we calculated the normalized term structure by evaluating the auxiliary curve at the points $(0, s(132), s(594), s(1320), s(7920))$. Theses knots were selected based on observed data and the overall fitting quality it produced[3].

In this analysis, 2504 yield curves were generated by our computational program using both methods AFNS and the DCOBS. For each curve, the AFNS method produced three coefficients while

---

2 For more information: https://www.treasury.gov/resource-center/data-chart-center/interest-rates/Pages/TextView.aspx?data=yield.

3 For more information: https://www.gnu.org/software/gsl/manual/html_node/Evaluation-of-B_002dspline-basis-functions.html.

DCOBS produced five coefficients. The resulting DCOBS yield curves had a better performance compared to AFNS considering Root Mean Square Error in every year of a sample data set as shown in Table 1. The difference of fitting both methods can be seen in Figure 1 for the yield curve on 2 January 2008.

Table 1. Root of Mean Squared Errors for the AFNS and DCOBS.

Year	AFNS RMSE	DCOBS RMSE
2007	0.02	0.02
2008	0.06	0.02
2009	0.08	0.02
2010	0.09	0.03
2011	0.09	0.03
2012	0.07	0.04
2013	0.08	0.03
2014	0.07	0.02
2015	0.05	0.01
2016	0.04	0.01
Total	0.65	0.23

7. Results

The time series for AFNS coefficients can be seen in Figure 2. Coefficients $\beta_{1,t}$ and $\beta_{3,t}$ may be cointegrated, so we run a two-step Engle–Granger cointegration test Engle and Granger (1987). The linear regression of $\beta_{3,t}$ explained by $\beta_{1,t}$ returned an intercept of -0.10 and a coefficient of 0.84. Applying the Augmented-Dickey–Fuller Unit Root Test on regression residuals yielded a statistic of -2.68. Such statistics, confronting the critical values for the co-integration test of Engle and Yoo (1987) leads us to reject the unitary root hypothesis because the residuals are stationary. The conclusion is that there is cointegration between $\beta_{1,t}$ and $\beta_{3,t}$.

In economic terms, the cointegration describes a strong relationship between long- and medium-term contracts, which can be a result of a political measure or some market characteristics that stimulated the emission of long-term contracts based on the price of medium-term contracts and vice versa.

The time series for $\beta_{1,t}$ and $\beta_{2,t}$ in (7) are modeled as AR(1) processes with one differentiation. The estimated ϕ for $\beta_{1,t}$ is -0.04 and for $\beta_{2,t}$ is 0.13.

As seen in AFNS coefficients time series, DCOBS estimated coefficients $a_{2,t}$ and $a_{3,t}$ seem to cointegrate in Figure 3, as well as coefficients $a_{4,t}$ and $a_{5,t}$, so we run a two-step Engle-Granger cointegration test. The linear regression of $a_{3,t}$ explained by $a_{2,t}$ returned an estimated intercept of -7.61 and a coefficient of 8.60. The linear regression of $a_{5,t}$ explained by $a_{4,t}$ returned an estimated intercept of 0.11 and an estimated coefficient of 0.43. Applying the Augmented-Dickey–Fuller Unit Root Test on regression residuals yielded the statistics -5.48 for estimated coefficients $a_{2,t}$ and $a_{3,t}$. The same test yielded the statistics -2.41 for estimated coefficients $a_{4,t}$ and $a_{5,t}$. Confronting these statistics with the critical values in Engle and Yoo (1987) implied the unitary root hypothesis because the residuals are stationary. The conclusion is that there is a cointegration between $a_{2,t}$ and $a_{3,t}$ as well as between $a_{4,t}$ and $a_{5,t}$.

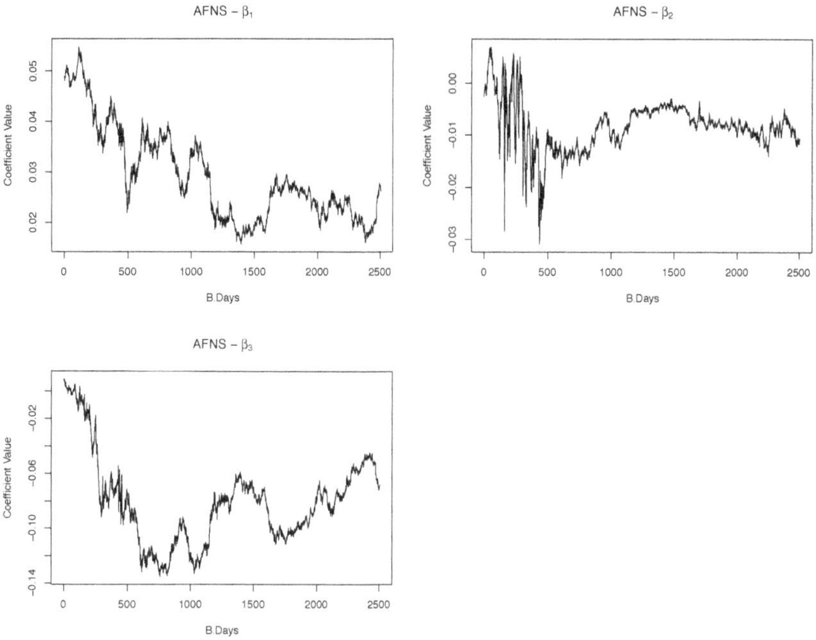

Figure 2. AFNS coefficient series.

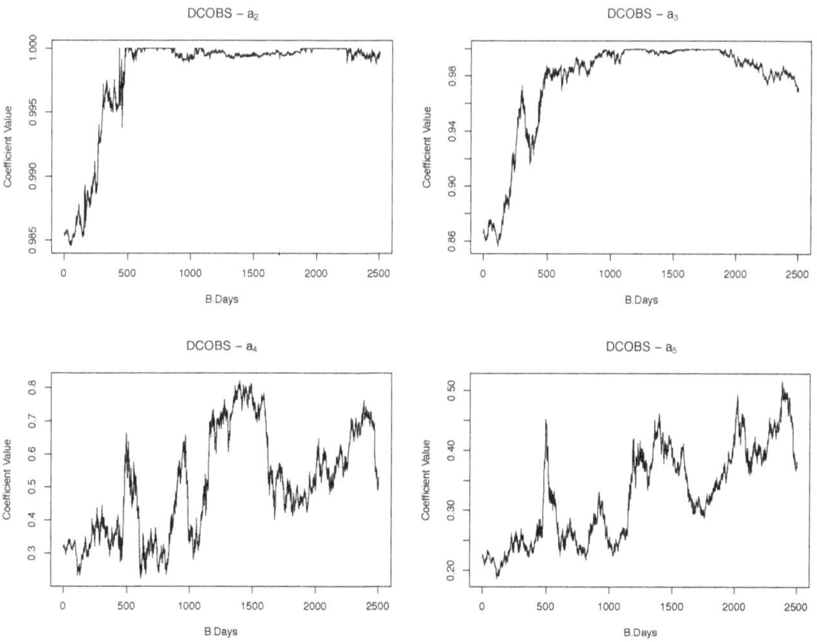

Figure 3. DCOBS estimated coefficient series.

Since B-Splines coefficients have a more local specific behavior, these cointegrations give a more detailed analysis than the AFNS model. It reveals the binding between short- and medium-term contracts on one side and medium- and long-term contracts on the other side. Like the economic interpretation of the AFNS model, this is an important feature of the model because it shows to investors and policy makers the magnitude of how the supply and demand on a type of contract can influence the price of another type of contract.

The time series for $a_{2,t}$ and $a_{4,t}$ are modeled as AR(1) processes with one differentiation. The estimated ϕ of $a_{2,t}$ is 0.02 and for $a_{4,t}$ is -0.03. Then, $a_{3,t}$ and $a_{5,t}$ are linear functions of $a_{2,t}$ and $a_{4,t}$, respectively.

The time series modeled as AR(1) processes above were used to make the out-of-sample forecast with a horizon of 250 business days, the amount of business days in a test dataset of 2017. Three reference dates were considered for evaluation: 1 month (short-term), 6 months (medium-term), and 12 months (long-term). Figure 4 shows short-, medium- and long-term forecasts for AFNS and DCOBS curves.

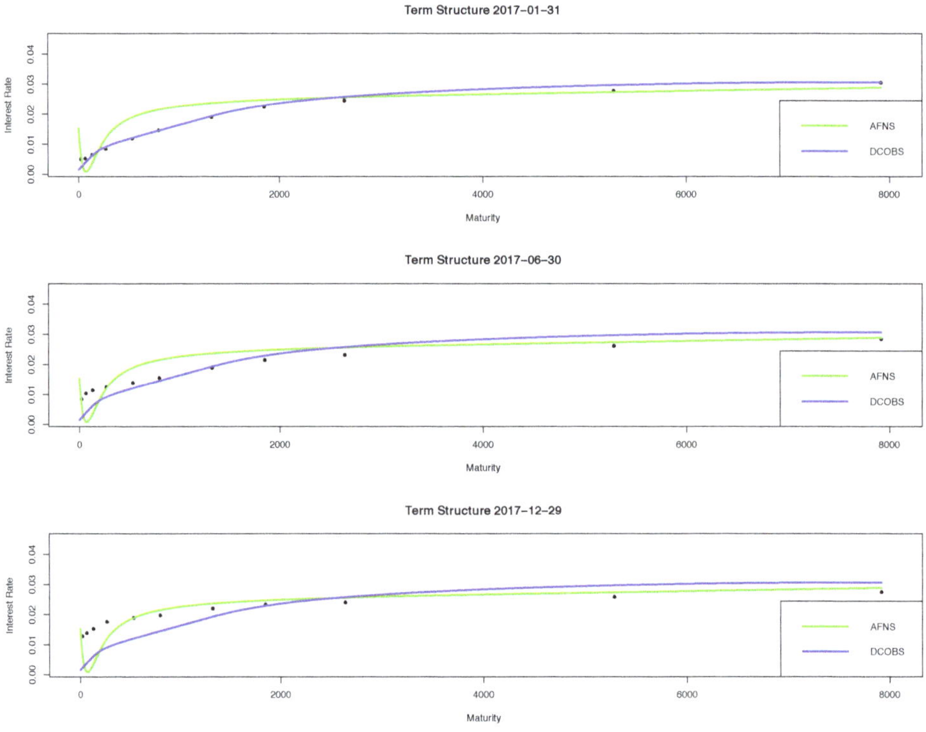

Figure 4. Short-, medium- and long-term forecasts for AFNS and DCOBS curves.

In a 1-month forecast, DCOBS performs a good fit to the term structure both in the short-term as in a long-term horizon, as the curve follows the data points. AFNS shows a heavy instability in the beginning of the curve in all forecasting, although, in the long-term, it performs well.

We compared both forecast techniques using the Diebold–Mariano accuracy test Diebold and Mariano (1995) with an alternative hypothesis being DCOBS outperforming AFNS prediction. As stated before, DCOBS outperforms AFNS in the short-term prediction. The absolute value of Diebold–Mariano statistics for a one-month forecast is greater than 1.96, so the null hypothesis that both techniques have the same accuracy is rejected. On the other hand, for 6-month and 12-month forecasts, the absolute value of Diebold–Mariano statistics stays lower than 1.96, which means that both techniques may have the same predictive accuracy. Table 2 shows forecasts' root mean square errors, and Table 3 shows Diebold–Mariano statistics results.

Table 2. Forecast root mean square errors.

Method	1-Month	6-Months	12-Months
AFNS	0.02	0.02	0.023
DCOBS	0.01	0.01	0.029

Table 3. Diebold–Mariano Test Statistics.

Method	1-Month	6-Months	12-Months
DM	2.60	1.64	−0.38
p-value	0.01	0.06	0.64

8. Conclusions

In this work, we have proposed DCOBS, a methodology for forecasting the dynamics of the term structure of interest rates extending the Constrained Smoothing B-Splines curve model.

The results have shown a great predictability power of the DCOBS model on the short- and middle-term, which are extremely important for traders and other financial market specialists. In comparison, the AFNS model has shown poor fitting as seen in Figure 1 and lack of stability in the beginning of the curves. Even though the accuracy of DCOBS in the middle and long-term is statistically equivalent to AFNS, the stability of the DCOBS can certainly be explored in future works to improve its predictability quality.

Finally, DCOBS can be a powerful tool to be applied in other areas like biology, physics, earth sciences, etc.

Author Contributions: E.M. and A.E.F. stated the real problem; E.M. obtained and processed the data, wrote all the programs and obtained the results; E.M., A.P.A., M.M. and A.E.F. analyzed the results; E.M. prepared the first draft manuscript; E.M., A.P.A., M.M. and A.E.F. revised the text and contributed to the conclusions. Authorship must be limited to those who have contributed substantially to the work reported. All authors have read and agreed to the published version of the manuscript.

Funding: This research was funded by FAPESP 18/04654-9.

Conflicts of Interest: The authors declare no conflict of interest.

References

Barzanti, Luca, and Corrado Corradi. 2001. A note on interest rate term structure estimation by monotonic smoothing splines. *Statistica (Bologna)* 61: 205–12.

Christensen, Jens H.E., Francis X. Diebold, and Glenn D. Rudebusch. 2011. The affine arbitrage-free class of Nelson-Siegel term structure models. *Journal of Econometrics* 164: 4–20. [CrossRef]

Cox, John C., Jonathan E. Ingersoll, and Stephen A. Ross. 1985. A Theory of the Term Structure of Interest Rates. *Econometrica* 53: 385–407. [CrossRef]

Diebold, Francis X., and Robert S. Mariano. 1995. Comparing Predictive Accuracy. *Journal of Business and Economic Statistics* 13: 253–63.

Diebold, Francis X., and Canlin Li. 2003. *Forecasting the Term Structure of Government Bond Yields*. Working Paper 10048. Cambridge: National Bureau of Economic Research.

Duffie, Darrell, and Rui Kan. 1996. A yield-factor model of interest rates. *Mathematical Finance* 6: 379–406. [CrossRef]

Duffee, Gregory. R. 2002. Term Premia and Interest Rate Forecasts in Affine Models. *The Journal of Finance* 57: 405–43. [CrossRef]

Engle, Robert, and Clive W.J. Granger. 1987. Co-integration and Error Correction: Representation, Estimation, and Testing. *Econometrica* 55: 251–76. [CrossRef]

Engle, Robert, and Byung S. Yoo. 1987. Forecasting and testing in co-integrated systems. *Journal of Econometrics* 35: 143–59. [CrossRef]

Fisher, Mark, Douglas Nychka, and David Zervos. 1995. *Fitting the Term Structure of Interest Rates with Smoothing Splines*. Finance and Economics Discussion Series 95-1. Washington, DC: Board of Governors of the Federal Reserve System (U.S.).

Heath, David R., Robert Jarrow, and Andrew Morton. 1992. Bond Pricing and the Term Structure of Interest Rates: A New Methodology for Contingent Claims Valuation. *Econometrica* 60: 77–105. [CrossRef]

He, Xuming, and Peide Shi. 1998. Monotone B-Spline Smoothing. *Journal of the American Statistical Association* 93: 643–50. [CrossRef]

He, Xuming, and Pin Ng. 1999. COBS: Qualitatively constrained smoothing via linear programming. *Computational Statistics* 14: 315–37. [CrossRef]

Hull, John, and Alan White. 1990. Pricing Interest-Rate-Derivative Securities. *Review of Financial Studies* 3: 573–92. [CrossRef]

Koenker, Robert W., and Gilbert Bassett. 1978. Regression Quantiles *Econometrica* 46: 33–50. [CrossRef]

Laurini, Marcio, and Marcelo Moura. 2010. Constrained smoothing B-splines for the term structure of interest rates. *Insurance: Mathematics and Economics* 46: 339–50.

McCulloch, J. Huston. 1971. Measuring the term structure of interest rates. *The Journal of Business* 44: 19–31. [CrossRef]

Nelson, Charles R., and Andrew F. Siegel. 1987. Parsimonious Modeling of Yield Curves. *The Journal of Business* 60: 473–89. [CrossRef]

Piazzesi, Monika. 2010. CHAPTER 12—Affine Term Structure Models. In *Handbook of Financial Econometrics: Tools and Techniques*. Handbooks in Finance. San Diego: North-Holland, vol. 1, pp. 691–766.

Svensson, Lars. 1994. *Estimating and Interpreting Forward Interest Rates: Sweden 1992–1994*. Working Paper 4871. Cambridge: National Bureau of Economic Research.

Tourrucôo, Fabricio, João A.F. Caldeira, Guilherme Moura, and André Santos. 2016. Forecasting the yield curve with the arbitrage-free dynamic Nelson–Siegel model: Brazilian evidence. In *Anais do XLII Encontro Nacional de Economia [Proceedings of the 42nd Brazilian Economics Meeting]*. Niterói: ANPEC - Associação Nacional dos Centros de Pós Graduação em Economia [Brazilian Association of Graduate Programs in Economics].

Vicente, José, and Benjamin M. Tabak. 2008. Forecasting bond yields in the Brazilian fixed income market. *International Journal of Forecasting* 24: 490–97. [CrossRef]

Vasicek, Oldrich. 1977. An equilibrium characterization of the term structure. *Journal of Financial Economics* 5: 177–88. [CrossRef]

Journal of
Risk and Financial Management

MDPI

Article

A Hypothesis Test Method for Detecting Multifractal Scaling, Applied to Bitcoin Prices

Chuxuan Jiang, Priya Dev and Ross A. Maller *

School of Finance & Applied Statistics, Australian National University, Canberra ACT 0200, Australia; chuxuan.jiang@anu.edu.au (C.J.); priya.dev@anu.edu.au (P.D.)
* Correspondence: ross.maller@anu.edu

Received: 2 March 2020; Accepted: 14 May 2020; Published: 20 May 2020

Abstract: Multifractal processes reproduce some of the stylised features observed in financial time series, namely heavy tails found in asset returns distributions, and long-memory found in volatility. Multifractal scaling cannot be assumed, it should be established; however, this is not a straightforward task, particularly in the presence of heavy tails. We develop an empirical hypothesis test to identify whether a time series is likely to exhibit multifractal scaling in the presence of heavy tails. The test is constructed by comparing estimated scaling functions of financial time series to simulated scaling functions of both an iid Student t-distributed process and a Brownian Motion in Multifractal Time (BMMT), a multifractal processes constructed in Mandelbrot et al. (1997). Concavity measures of the respective scaling functions are estimated, and it is observed that the concavity measures form different distributions which allow us to construct a hypothesis test. We apply this method to test for multifractal scaling across several financial time series including Bitcoin. We observe that multifractal scaling cannot be ruled out for Bitcoin or the Nasdaq Composite Index, both technology driven assets.

Keywords: multifractal processes; fractal scaling; heavy tails; long range dependence; financial models; Bitcoin

1. Introduction

The cryptocurrency market is an emerging market comprised of thousands of digital assets including Bitcoin. A cryptocurrency is a digital asset that uses cryptography and decentralised governance to secure a ledger of transactions. Cryptocurrencies can also be used as a medium of exchange; for background, refer to the review article by Milutinović (2018). Bitcoin, introduced in Nakamoto (2009), is an example of the world's first cryptocurrency; its core innovation established digital scarcity, regulated and audited via a novel decentralised governance mechanism. Financial analysts, chartists and the news media often report on Bitcoin's fractal features (Chambers 2019); however, academic research has shown mixed evidence for multifractal or monofractal scaling with Mensi et al. (2019); Lahmiri and Bekiros (2018); Stavroyiannis et al. (2019) presenting a case for multifractal scaling, while Nadarajah and Chu (2017); Bariviera (2017); Bariviera et al. (2017); Zhang et al. (2018) presenting a case for monofractal scaling. The inconclusive evidence of fractal scaling could be a result of the different detection methods along with varied assumptions. Salat et al. (2017) emphasise that implementation of existing multifractal detection methods can be a perilous undertaking. Moreover, Sly (2006) and Grahovac and Leonenko (2014) demonstrate that attempts to use the scaling function to detect multifractality may mistakenly give rise to false positive results, due to heavy-tailed effects. This calls into question the reliability of the above-mentioned results. Therefore, a detailed examination of scaling functions in the presence of heavy tails is required to bridge the gap between the theory and empirical realities. As an application of the new method we present here, we seek to understand Bitcoin's scaling properties to assist practitioners with model selection for the purpose of risk management and volatility forecasting.

Given the novel nature of digital assets, it is also of interest to observe similarities in scaling behaviour between Bitcoin and other asset classes. In this paper, we address the central research question: Do Bitcoin prices exhibit multifractal scaling? To answer this question, we investigate the effect of heavy-tails on the scaling function and study scenarios in which false positive[1] detection occurs. If multifractal scaling is plausible, it could indicate the need to incorporate more complex scaling behaviour into pricing models. In the case of Bitcoin, capturing complex scaling behaviour could result in better volatility forecasting. This paper develops an empirical method that tests for multifractal scaling in the presence of heavy tails. Its application is not limited to financial time series, however. This paper is structured as follows. In the rest of this section, we introduce multifractal stochastic processes and their simulation methods. We then explain how the multifractal scaling function is distorted by the presence of heavy tails. In Section 2, we propose a new empirical hypothesis test and construct the look-up table to form rejection and acceptance regions. Then, in Section 3, we apply our hypothesis test to detect multifractal scaling in Bitcoin prices and compare the scaling behaviour of Bitcoin to other financial assets, including the S&P500 index, the Nasdaq Composite Index, the USD/JPY exchange rate, and Gold Futures. Our method detects more complex scaling behaviour in emerging technology asset classes such as Bitcoin and the Nasdaq Composite Index.

1.1. Monofractal vs. Multifractal Processes

The multifractal system was introduced as a generalisation of the fractal system to describe more complicated dynamics in time series. Multifractals are common in nature and have enjoyed great application in finance and science, e.g., modelling the turbulence in fluid dynamics (Sreenivasan 1991). In the finance field, multifractal processes are able to capture many stylised characteristics of high-volatility financial assets.

Multifractal processes are defined based on the scaling property of their moments, when they are finite, in Mandelbrot et al. (1997).

Definition 1. *(Multifractal Stochastic Process) A stochastic process $\{X(t), t \geq 0\}$ is multifractal if it has stationary increments and there exist functions $c(q) > 0$ and $\tau(q) > 0$ and positive constants $\mathcal{Q}$ and $\mathcal{T}$ such that*

$$\mathbb{E}|X(t)|^q = c(q)t^{\tau(q)}, \text{for all } q \in [0, \mathcal{Q}] \text{ and } t \in [0, \mathcal{T}]. \tag{1}$$

The function $\tau(q)$ is called the scaling function.

The multifractal processes are said to be *multiscaling* when the scaling function is nonlinear. For a multifractal process, the scaling function $\tau(q)$ is always concave when $q > 0$ on a bounded interval as is shown in Sly (2006).

In contrast, the multifractal process is called *uniscaling* or a monofractal process when the scaling function is linear, $\tau(q) = Hq$. Monofractal processes enjoy a self-similarity.[2]

Theorem 1 (Lamperti (1962)). *If $\{X(t), t \geq 0\}$ is self-similar and stochastically continuous at t = 0, then there exists a unique $H > 0$ such that for all $a > 0$,*

$$\{X(at)\} \stackrel{d}{=} \{a^H X(t)\} \tag{2}$$

where equality is of finite dimensional distributions.

1 "False positive" corresponds to the scenario that we mistakenly detect multifractality when the underlying process does not possess the multifractal property.

2 For convenience, in the rest of this paper, we call uniscaling multifractal processes *monofractal processes* while referring to multiscaling multifractal processes as *multifractal processes*.

Here, $H \geq 0$ is a constant known as the *Hurst parameter*. H measures in some way the persistence of a process. Given all moments of the process are finite, the process is long-range dependent if $H \in (\frac{1}{2}, 1)$, while anti-persistence occurs if $H \in (0, \frac{1}{2})$ (Embrechts and Maejima 2000). Typical examples of monofractal processes are the fractional Brownian motions and the stable Lévy processes. The fractional Brownian motion $B_H(t)$ introduced in Mandelbrot et al. (1997) is a unique class of self-similar Gaussian process with stationary increments possessing a dependence structure described by the following covariance equation. When $H = \frac{1}{2}$, the fractional Brownian motion becomes Brownian motion with independent increments.

1.2. Examination of Multifractality

Copious methods have been proposed to examine the multifractality in a certain process $\{X(t), 0 \leq t \leq T\}$, including the *multifractal detrended fluctuation analysis method* (MF-DFA) by Kantelhardt et al. (2002) and the *wavelet transform modulus maxima method* (WTMM). In this paper, we employ the *standard partition method* introduced by Mandelbrot et al. (1997). This method attempts to detect multifractality based on concavity in the scaling function. From Definition 1, one can easily derive

$$\log \mathbb{E}|X(t)|^q = \log c(q) + \tau(q) \log t, \text{ for all } q \in [0, \mathcal{Q}] \text{ and } t \in [0, T], \tag{3}$$

where the q-th moment of the process $X(t)$, $\mathbb{E}|X(t)|^q$, can be estimated by the sample statistic

$$S_q(T, \Delta t) = \frac{1}{N} \sum_{i=1}^{N} |X((i-1)\Delta t) - X(i\Delta t)|^q, \tag{4}$$

with $N = \lfloor T/\Delta t \rfloor$.

The scaling function can be derived by fitting a linear regression between $\log S_q(T, \Delta t)$ and $\log t$ with various values of $q \in [0, \mathcal{Q}]$. For a fixed value of q, we obtain an estimate $\hat{\tau}(q)$, the slope of our linear regression. A plot of $\hat{\tau}(q)$ against q then provides visual display of the scaling function. The function of $\ln S_q(T, \Delta t)$ for various values of $\ln \Delta t$ is called *the partition function*. If the scaling function shows concavity, we have evidence that multifractality is present in the process of interest.

1.3. Simulation of Multifractal Processes

The Brownian motion in multifractal time (BMMT) $B_H(\theta(t))$ introduced in Mandelbrot et al. (1997) is employed to simulate a multifractal process. The BMMT model shows appealing features that coincide with some stylised features of financial time series. It displays heavy-tails while not necessarily implying infinite variance. It also implies long-term dependence in absolute values of returns while the price increments themselves can remain uncorrelated. By construction, the BMMT is defined as the subordinate model of a fractional Brownian motion $B_H(t)$ with a multifractal process $\theta(t)$.

Definition 2 (Brownian Motion in Multifractal Time)**.** *Brownian motion in multifractal time is defined as*

$$X(t) = B_H(\theta(t)),\ t \in [0, T],$$

where $\theta(t)$ is a positive multifractal stochastic process and B_H is an independent fractional Brownian motion with Hurst parameter H.

$\theta(t)$ can also be seen as a trading time where the index t denotes clock time. We assume the activity time $\theta(t)$ to be the cumulative density function of a random multifractal measure μ defined on $[0, T]$. That is, $\theta(t)$ is a multifractal process with continuous, non-decreasing paths, and stationary increments.

The *multiplicative multifractal measure* is implemented for simulation. Without loss of generality, we assume that the time series of interest is defined on a compact interval $[0,1]$. A multiplicative measure is constructed as follows:

1. In Stage 1, divide the time interval $[0,1]$ into $b > 1$ non-overlapping subintervals with equal length $1/b$. Assign multipliers $M_{1,\beta}$ $(0 \leq \beta \leq b-1)$ to each subinterval, where the $M_{1,\beta}$ are random variables with distributions that are not necessarily discrete. For computational convenience, we assume the $M_{1,\beta}$ to be identically distributed with a common distribution M.
2. In Stage 2, each of the b intervals is further divided into b subintervals of length $1/b^2$. Again, we assign multipliers $M_{2,\beta}$ $(0 \leq \beta \leq b-1)$ to each subinterval. The $M_{2,\beta}$ are assumed to be identically distributed with distribution M. Thus, after the second stage, the mass on an interval, for example $[0,1/b^2]$, will be $\mu_2[0,1/b^2] = m_0 m_1$ if $M_{1,0} = m_0$ and $M_{2,0} = m_1$ with probability
$$\mathbb{P}(\mu_2[0,1/b^2] = m_0 m_1) = \mathbb{P}(M = m_0)P(M = m_1),$$
since the multipliers at different stages are independent. The measure μ_2 represents the multiplicative measure at Stage 2.
3. Repetition of this scheme generates a sequence of measures $(\mu_k)_{k\in\mathbb{N}}$ which converges to our desired multiplicative measure μ as $k \to \infty$.

Remark 1. *To preserve the mass at each stage, some restrictions are required on the values of the $M_{l,\beta}, 1 \leq l \leq k$. If we strictly assume that $\sum_{\beta=0}^{b-1} M_{l,\beta} = 1$ at each stage, the resulting measure is called microcanonical or micro-conservative. If we loosen the assumption so that the mass at each stage is only conserved "on average", that is, $\mathbb{E}(\sum_{\beta=0}^{b-1} M_{l,\beta}) = 1, \forall 1 \leq l \leq k$, the resulting measure is called canonical.*

In this paper, we only consider canonical measures, as they impose less restriction on the distribution of M. Let

$$t = 0.\eta_1...\eta_k = \sum_{i=1}^{k} \eta_i b^{-i}$$

be a b-adic number and set $\Delta t = b^{-k}$. The mass on the b-adic cell $[t, t+\Delta t]$ for a canonical measure at Stage k is

$$\mu(\Delta t) = \mu[t, t+\Delta t] = \Omega(\eta_1, ..., \eta_k)M(\eta_1)M(\eta_1, \eta_2)...M(\eta_1, ..., \eta_k),$$

where the random variable Ω represents the total mass. The high-frequency component $\Omega(\eta_1, ..., \eta_k)$ is assumed to have the same distribution as Ω. It captures changes in total mass of the interval caused by stages beyond k. As μ here is a canonical measure, we assume the multipliers $M_{l,\beta}$ $(0 \leq \beta \leq b-1)$ satisfy $\mathbb{E}(\sum M_{l,\beta}) = 1$ or equivalently $\mathbb{E}M = 1/b$.

Since multipliers at different stages of subdivision are independent, $\mathbb{E}[\mu(\Delta t)^q] = \mathbb{E}(\Omega^q)[\mathbb{E}(M^q)]^k$, for all q. Defining $\tau(q) = -\log_b \mathbb{E}(M^q)$ and recalling $\Delta t = b^{-k}$, we have

$$\mathbb{E}[\mu(\Delta t)^q] = \mathbb{E}(\Omega^q)(\Delta t)^{\tau(q)}. \tag{5}$$

Consequently, the constructed multiplicative measure μ is multifractal according to Definition 1. Because Equation (5) only holds for $\Delta t = b^{-k}$ and $t = 0.\eta_1...\eta_k = \sum_{i=1}^{k} \eta_i b^{-i}$ being a b-adic number, these multiplicative measures are said to be *grid-bound multifractal measures*.

The relation between the distribution of M and the scaling function can be inferred from the following theorem.

Theorem 2 (Calvet et al. 1997). *Define $p(\alpha)$ to be the continuous density of $V = -\log_b M$, and $p_k(\alpha)$ to be the density of the k-th convolution product of p. The scaling function of a multiplicative measure satisfies*

$$\tau(q) = \inf_{\alpha}[\alpha q - \lim_{k\to\infty} \frac{1}{k} \log_b[kp_k(k\alpha)]. \tag{6}$$

In this paper, we have estimated sample scaling functions using the BMMT with a log-normal multiplicative measure. We have chosen this measure because its multifractal spectrum is a better fit for financial time series[3]. When V follows a normal distribution, $\mathcal{N}(\lambda, \sigma^2)$ where $\lambda > 1$, then $M = b^{-V}$ follows a log-normal distribution that is, $\log_b M \stackrel{d}{=} \mathcal{N}(-\lambda, \sigma^2)$. We then have

$$\mathbb{E}M = \mathbb{E}(e^{-V\log b}) = \exp\left(-\lambda \log b + \frac{(\log b)^2\sigma^2}{2}\right),$$

As $M \in (0, \infty)$, we need the constraint $\mathbb{E}(M) = 1/b$ to make M a canonical measure. This constraint gives a relationship between λ and σ^2, namely $\log b = \frac{2(\lambda-1)}{\sigma^2}$.

Based on Theorem 2, the scaling function for the log-normal multiplicative cascade is derived as follows:

$$\tau(q) = \inf_{\alpha}\left(\alpha q - \lim_{k\to\infty} \frac{1}{k} \log_b[kp_\alpha(k\alpha)]\right) = \lambda q - \frac{\sigma^2 \log b}{2} q^2. \tag{7}$$

This quadratic form reaches its maximum at $q = \frac{\lambda}{\sigma^2 \log b}$.

The cumulative distribution of the simulated multiplicative measures μ gives a multifractal multiplicative cascade, which is taken to be the trading time $\theta(t) = \int_0^t \mu([0,s])ds$ in a BMMT model $B_H(\theta(t))$.

1.4. Multifractality and Heavy Tails

While a concave scaling function is necessary for multifractality, it is not sufficient. Several papers have explored other potential drivers of concavity in the scaling function. One is heavy-tailedness (Sly 2006; Heyde 2009 and Grahovac and Leonenko 2014). Sly (2006) has shown that, after removing the extreme values of the S&P500 price process, the scaling function approaches linearity. He proceeded further to study the asymptotic behaviour of the estimated scaling functions and proved the following theorem.

Theorem 3 (Sly 2006). *Let X be a random variable with $\mathbb{E}(X) = 0$ such that the distribution function of $|X|$ has a regularly varying tail of order $-\alpha$ where $\alpha > 2$; that is,*

$$P(|X| > x) = x^{-\alpha}L(x),$$

where $L(x)$ is slowly varying. Then, for an i.i.d. sequence with distribution X and $q > \alpha$, for each $s \in (0,1)$, with S_q as defined in Equation (4) and the time increment $\Delta t = n^s$,

$$\frac{\ln S_q(n, n^s)}{\ln n} \xrightarrow{p} \max\left(s + \frac{q}{\alpha} - 1, \frac{sq}{2}\right) \tag{8}$$

as $n \to \infty$, where $\xrightarrow{p}$ stands for convergence in probability.

[3] We compared the scaling functions of the Bitcoin and other financial assets with the ones of BMMTs simulated using multiplicative cascades with Poisson distribution, Gamma distribution and Normal distribution. The scaling function of the BMMT simulated through log-Normal multiplicative cascade displays the most similar behaviour.

Grahovac and Leonenko (2014) generalised this result to a type $\mathcal{E}$ set of stochastic processes and extended Sly's (2006) work by investigating the relationship between the asymptotic behaviour of scaling functions and tail indices.

Definition 3 (*Type $\mathcal{E}$ stochastic processes*). *A stochastic process $\{X(t), t \geq 0\}$ is said to be of type $\mathcal{E}$ if $Y(t) = X(t) - X(t-1)$, $t \in \mathbb{N}$, is a strictly stationary sequence having heavy-tailed marginal distribution with index α, satisfying the strong mixing property with an exponentially decaying rate and such that $\mathbb{E}Y(t) = 0$ when $\alpha > 1$.*

Theorem 4 (Grahovac and Leonenko 2014). *Suppose $\{X(t), 0 \leq t \leq T\}$ is of type $\mathcal{E}$ and suppose Δt_i is of the form $T^{\frac{i}{N}}$ for $i = 1, ..., N$. Then, for every $q > 0$ and $s \in (0,1)$*

$$\lim_{N\to\infty} \underset{T\to\infty}{\text{plim}} \hat{\tau}_{N,T}(q) = \tau_\infty(q), \tag{9}$$

where plim *stands for limit in probability and*

$$\tau_\infty(q) = \begin{cases} \frac{q}{\alpha} & \text{if } 0 < q \leq \alpha \text{ and } \alpha \leq 2 \\ 1 & \text{if } q > \alpha \text{ and } \alpha \leq 2 \\ \frac{q}{2} & \text{if } 0 < q \leq \alpha \text{ and } \alpha > 2 \\ \frac{q}{2} + \frac{2(\alpha-q)^2(2\alpha+4q-3\alpha q)}{\alpha^3(q-2)^2} & \text{if } q > \alpha \text{ and } \alpha > 2. \end{cases} \tag{10}$$

Besides the heavy-tailed effects, other factors are discussed in a number of papers. Matia et al. (2003) concludes that price fluctuations can contribute to concavity of scaling function. Bouchaud et al. (2000) states that another factor is the long range nature of the volatility correlations. Nevertheless, neither of these scenarios excludes the effect of heavy-tailedness. Therefore, we regard the heavy-tailedness as a main contributor to the possible misdetection of multifractality in this paper.

Figure 1 displays the situation considered in Theorem 4. To illustrate the heavy-tailed effect, the estimated scaling functions for both S&P500 Index and 20 Student t_4-distributed processes before and after truncating heavy tails are shown in Figure 2.[4]

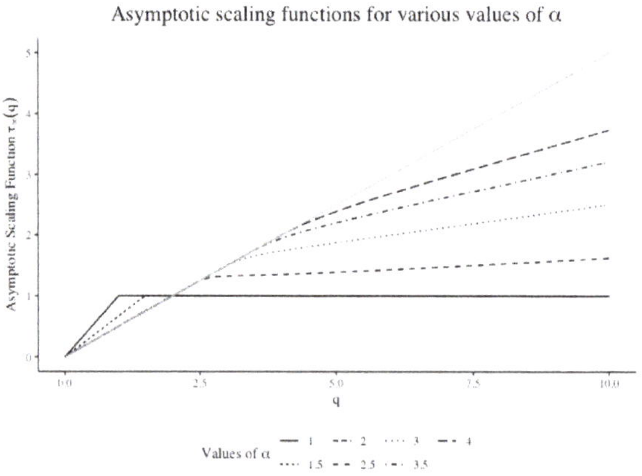

Figure 1. Asymptotic scaling functions for various values of α. The grey line is the $q/2$ reference line.

[4] The choice of Student's t-distribution with 4 degrees of freedom is suggested by the findings of Platen and Rendek (2008).

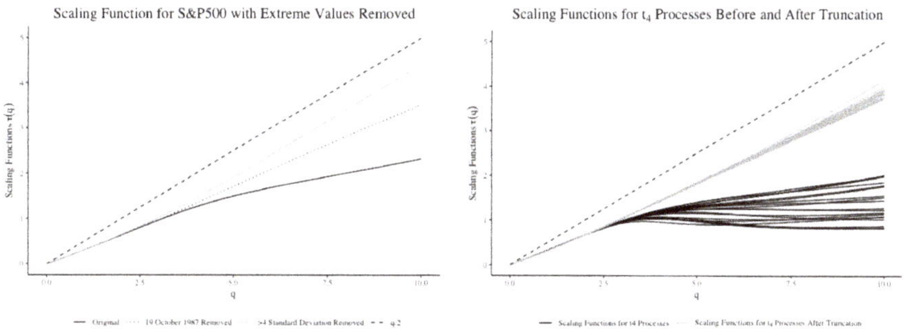

Figure 2. Left—Scaling Functions of the original S&P 500 open price data (black solid line), the S&P 500 open price data after removing 19 October 1987 (dotted line), the S&P 500 open price data after truncating any return larger than 4 standard deviations from the mean (grey solid line). **Right**—Scaling Functions of the Student t-distributed processes before (black lines) and after truncation (grey lines). For comparison, the reference lines $q/2$ (black dashed line) are included.

2. Methodology

Our hypothesis test aims to identify multifractal scaling in the presence of heavy tails. It is constructed based on the different distributions of concavity measures for various tail indices:

H_0: The process of interest is not multifractal.

vs.

H_A: The process of interest is multifractal.

In this section, we first introduce the measure of concavity and tail index implemented in this paper. Then, we examine the distributions of concavity measures with regard to various tail indices for different processes. The following four instances are chosen: monofractal process (Brownian motion and fractional Brownian motion); Student t-distributed processes with degrees of freedom between 1 and 20; and a multifractal process simulated using BMMT with a log-Normal multiplicative measure.

2.1. Measure of Concavity

The global and localised *simplex statistics* proposed in Abrevaya and Jiang (2005) are employed. These loosen the assumption of normality and homoscedasticity of the error disturbances, which is required for most other concavity measures.

Definition 4 (Global Simplex Statistics). *Assume that*

1. *there is an iid sample* $\{(x_i, \epsilon_i)\}_{i=1}^n$ *drawn from the joint distribution of the random variables* (x, ϵ), *where* ϵ *is symmetrically distributed about 0 (conditional on x), so that* $\mathbb{E}(\epsilon_i|x_i) = 0, i = 1, ..., n$;
2. *the observed sample is* $\{(y_i, x_i)\}_{i=1}^n$, *where* y_i *is generated by* $y_i = f(x_i) + \epsilon_i$, $i = 1, ..., n$, *and the functional form of f is left unspecified.*

Then, for a sample of size n, the global simplex statistic is defined as

$$U_n = \binom{n}{3}^{-1} \sum_{1 \le t_1 \le t_2 \le t_3 \le n} sign(a_1 y_{[t_1]} + a_2 y_{[t_2]} - y_{[t_3]}), \tag{11}$$

where $t_1, t_2, t_3 \in \{1, \ldots, n\}$,

$$sign(q) = \begin{cases} 1 & if\, q > 0, \\ -1 & if\, q < 0, \\ 0 & if\, q = 0. \end{cases} \tag{12}$$

and a_1, a_2 are non-negative numbers with $a_1 + a_2 = 1$.

Abrevaya and Jiang (2005) proves the asymptotic normality for the global simplex statistic. An interval is considered to be a concave interval if its standardised global simplex statistics $\tilde{U_n}$ is less than $Z_{\alpha/2}$, where $Z_{\alpha/2}$ is the $(\alpha/2)$-th percentile of the standard normal distribution, vice versa for a convex interval.

For the localised simplex statistic, calculation starts with dividing the time interval $[0, T]$ into $G = \lfloor T/2h \rfloor$ subintervals, where $2h$ is the window width. Let $x_1^*, x_2^*, ..., x_G^*$ denote evaluation points. In this case, they are assumed to be the mid-points of each sub-interval. Then, the sub-population for which the x values fall in a local window is defined to be

$$V_h(x^*) = \{(y, x) : x^* - h < x < x^* + h\}.$$

Definition 5. *Let $p_h(x^*)$ be the number of observations in the set $V_h(x^*)$. The localised simplex statistic at a given x^* is then defined as*

$$U_{n,h}(x^*) = \binom{p_h(x^*)}{3}^{-1} \sum_{t_1<t_2<t_3} \left(sign(a_1 y_{[t_1]} + a_2 y_{[t_2]} - y_{[t_3]}) \times \prod_{k=1}^{3} K_h(x_{t_k} - x^*) \right), \tag{13}$$

where $a_1 + a_2 = 1$ and $K_h(v) = K(v/h)$ where the kernel function K is to be specified.

In this paper, we assume a uniform kernel function since no addition information is given. Asymptotic normality also holds for the localised simplex statistics. A sub-interval is defined to be concave if $U_{n,h} < Z_{\alpha/2}$, vice versa for the convex case. We define a concavity measure (localised) as the difference in the proportions of the concave intervals and the convex intervals:

$$L_{n,h} = \text{proportion of convex intervals} - \text{proportion of concave intervals}.$$

Here, $L_{n,h} \in [-1, 1]$ measures the level of concavity (convexity). Convexity is concluded for the overall interval when $L_{n,h} \in [0, 1]$, while we report strict concavity when $L_{n,h} \in [-1, 0)$.

As a measure of tail index, the classic Hill's estimator is implemented. If $X_1, X_2, ..., X_n$ is a sequence of independent and identically distributed random variables with distribution function F and n is the sample size, let $X_{(i,n)}$ be the i-th order statistic of $X_1, X_2, ..., X_n$. The Hill's estimator is

$$h^{\text{Hill}}_{(k(n),n)} = \left(\frac{1}{k(n)} \sum_{i=n-k(n)+1}^{n} \log(X_{(i,n)}) - \log(X_{(n-k(n)+1,n)}) \right)^{-1}, \tag{14}$$

where $k(n) \in \{1, 2, ..., n-1\}$ is a sequence to be specified. Under these assumptions, $h^{\text{Hill}}_{(k(n),n)}$ converges in probability to the true tail index, and is asymptotically normal when $k(n) \to \infty$.

2.2. Simulation Results

We explore the possible range of behaviours for scaling functions for simulated multifractal processes. The findings are compared with some simulated monofractal processes (e.g., Brownian motions and fractional Brownian motions) and Student t-distributed processes. Both Brownian motion and fractional Brownian motion yield convex scaling functions only, which puts them out of consideration in the case of multifractality detection. The distributions of the concavity measures of the simulated multifractal processes and Student t-distributed processes are found to differ significantly in terms of their ranges and skewness. This provides us with a way to design a hypothesis test. As a result of these simulations, we construct a look-up table for a multifractality hypothesis test.

The simulated distributions of both the global and localised[5] simplex statistics are quite similar. Here, we only present the simulation results based on the global simplex statistics. The simulation results are shown in Figures 3 and 4. The distributions for the Student t-distributed process and a simulated multifractal process both span $[-1, 1]$ but display different characteristics. A detailed comparison for the specific tail index $= 3.06$ is shown in Figure 4. For the simulated BMMTs, more than 20% of the scaling functions have global simplex statistics of exactly -1 indicating strict concavity. For the Student t-distributed process, the concavity statistic spans $[-1, 1]$ with its median at around -0.36 in comparison to the one for the simulated BMMTs, -0.45.

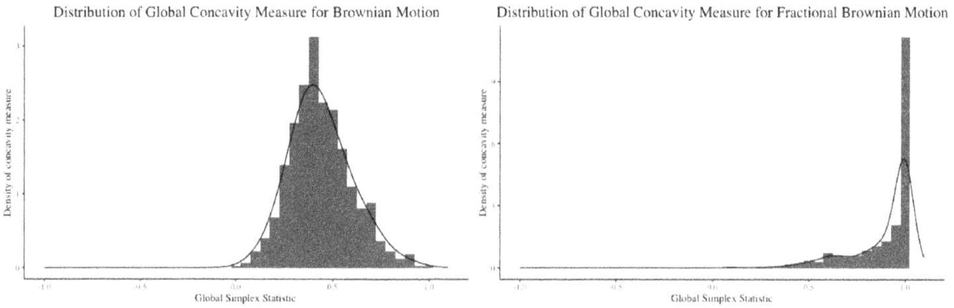

Figure 3. Distribution of global simplex statistics for Brownian motion (**left**) and fractional Brownian motion (**right**).

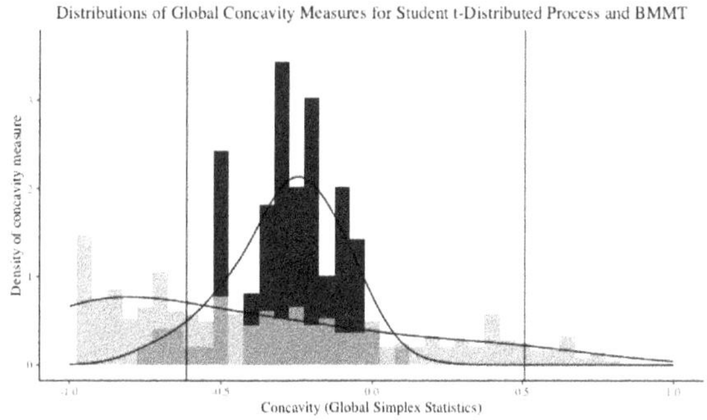

Figure 4. Distributions of global simplex statistics for Student t-distributed process (black) and the simulated BMMT with log-normal multiplicative cascade (grey) around tail index 3.06. The two vertical lines represent the 95th percentile for the simulated BMMTs (**left**) and 5th percentiles for the Student t-distributed processes, respectively (**right**).

If the concavity of the observed scaling function for a given process is more severe than for the Student t-distributed processes, we are led to conclude that the concavity is driven by multifractality instead of heavy tails. Therefore, hypothesis tests can be constructed using the concavity measures as the test statistic.

2.3. Look-Up Table

To perform this hypothesis test on a given set of data, we firstly estimate the heaviness of tail using Hill's estimator h^{Hill}. Then, the null distribution of concavity measures is constructed by

[5] Knots were chosen so that the function is evaluated on 18 equal sub-intervals. This gave the best approximation considering computational efficiency.

simulating from Student t-distributed processes corresponding to tail indices ranging over the interval $[h^{\text{Hill}} - 0.5, h^{\text{Hill}} + 0.5]$. A larger range of tail index is used to allow for variation in our tail index estimation, while allowing more observations for constructing the concavity measure distribution.[6] The 5th percentile of this distribution is the critical value for the hypothesis test.

The null hypothesis is rejected if the observed test statistic is less than the calculated critical value. To carry out the hypothesis test, a look-up table is generated to summarise the tail indices and the corresponding critical values based on both the localised and global concavity measures. A simplified version of the look-up table is presented in Appendix A. The critical values are presented for tail indices 0.5, 1.0, 1.5, ..., with the largest tail index being 10.

3. Results

3.1. Application to Bitcoin

In this section, we apply our proposed hypothesis test to Bitcoin prices in order to address our research question: Do Bitcoin prices exhibit multifractal scaling? Both the global simplex statistic and the localised concavity measures are employed and reported. Two Bitcoin data sets are used in this paper:

1. the daily Bitcoin open price, daily data (in USD) from 28 April 2013 to 3 September 2019 with 2,320 observations, retrieved from CoinMarketCap (2019); and
2. the high frequency Bitcoin open price data minute-by-minute (in USDT) covering the period 22 May 2018 14:00 to 1 March 2019 11:00 with 406,089 observations, retrieved from Binance (2019).

Let $\{P(t), t = 0, 1, ..., T\}$ denote the open prices of Bitcoin. We define $X(t)$ to be the mean-centered log-prices

$$X(t) = \ln P(t) - \ln P(0) - \mu t,$$

where $\mu = \frac{1}{T}\sum_{i=1}^{T} \ln \frac{P(i)}{P(i-1)}$. The mean-centered log-returns are then defined as

$$r(t) = X(t) - X(t-1).$$

3.1.1. Daily Bitcoin Price Data

Mean-centered log-prices $X(t)$ and the log-returns for daily Bitcoin price are displayed in Figure 5. Two bull runs followed by two bear runs are observed in late 2013 and late 2017 represented by two prominent spikes. These two price surges are believed to be results of the increases in Bitcoin's popularity and media coverage. A price drop is spotted in early 2018 followed by the price falls of most cryptocurrencies. This period is known as 'the 2018 cryptocurrency crash' (Popken 2018). The Bitcoin price collapsed by 80% from January to September 2018, which is reported to be worse than the dot-com bubble's 78% collapse (Patterson 2018). Subsequently, a price hike on a smaller scale is observed between early 2019 and 3 September 2019.

A stylised feature check gives uncorrelated and stationary return increments but correlations in the absolute value of returns.

The estimation of $\tau(q)$ exhibits a relatively linear scaling function, as is shown in Figure 6. However, both concavity measures are less than 0, indicating the presence of concavity. A global simplex statistic of value -0.2222 and a localised concavity measure of value -0.6256 are obtained. The hypothesis tests based on these two measures indicate that the null hypothesis should be rejected in favour of the alternative; see Table 1.

---

[6] For example, if Hill's estimator takes value $h^{\text{Hill}} = 2$, we generate simulated student t-distributed processes with 2 degrees of freedom, select those with tail indices in the interval $[1.5, 2.5]$, and construct the null distribution using the empirical distribution of their concavity measures.

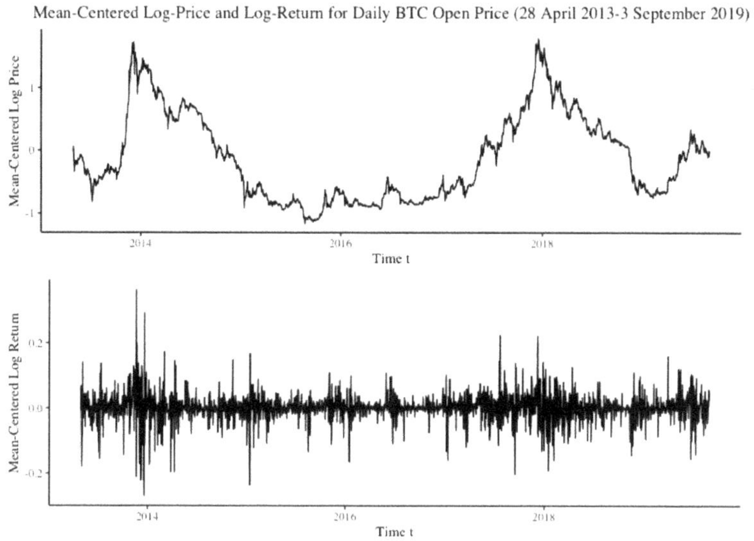

Figure 5. Daily mean-centered log Bitcoin open price process (**top**) and mean-centered log returns process (**bottom**).

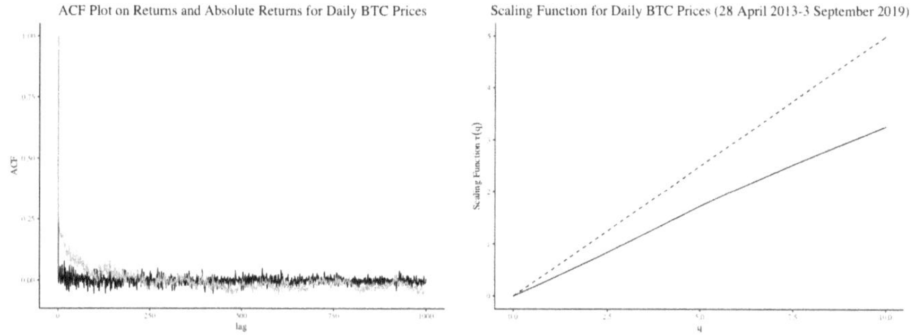

Figure 6. Left—Autocorrelations of mean-centered log-returns (black) and absolute returns (grey) for daily Bitcoin open price (28 April 2013–3 April 2019). **Right**—Scaling function for daily Bitcoin open price (28 April 2013–3 September 2019). The dashed line is the $q/2$ reference line (same for all the scaling function figures).

Table 1. Hypothesis test results on daily Bitcoin open prices (28 April 2013–3 September 2019).

Tail Index	**3.0630**			
	Sample Size [1]	**Test Statistic**	**Rejection Region**	**Test Result**
Localised Test	1479	−0.2222	$[-1, -0.0556)$	Multifractal
Global Test	99	−0.6256	$[-1, -0.6148)$	Multifractal

Sample size refers to the number of student t-distributed processes used in estimating the distribution of concavity measures under H_0. In the case of Bitcoin open prices from 28/04/2013 to 03/09/2019, there are 1479 student t-distributed processes with tail indices ranging in the interval [2.5630, 3.5630] when constructing the distribution of localised concavity measures. 99 student t-distributed processes are used in the construction of the distributions of global simplex statistics.

Thus, despite appearances in Figure 6, we have preliminary evidence that Bitcoin may follow a multifractal process.

To observe whether different results appear when the sample changes, the log-price time series is broken down into smaller time periods. The same hypothesis tests are performed to examine multifractality. Some literature indicates that 2017 is a turning point for Bitcoin's price behaviour. Zhang et al. (2018) concluded an increase in market inefficiency from late 2016, which is believed to be a result of an increase in speculation. Consequently, we break the daily price process into two parts,

- $X_1(t)$ from 28 April 2013 to 16 July 2017 with 1541 observations; and,
- $X_2(t)$ from 17 July 2017 to 3 September 2019 with 779 observations.

The corresponding scaling functions are shown in Figure 7 with hypothesis test results in Tables 2 and 3. The hypotheses tests for $X_1(t)$ give various results. This may be a result of a smaller data set or it could indicate a change to the way Bitcoin prices scale.

Table 2. Hypothesis test results on daily Bitcoin open prices (28 April 2013–16 July 2017).

Tail Index	**3.2791**			
	Sample Size	**Test Statistic**	**Rejection Region**	**Test Result**
Localised Test	1403	−0.4444	$[-1, -0.1111)$	Multifractal
Global Test	98	−0.5378	$[-1, -0.7014)$	Non-Multifractal

Table 3. Hypothesis test results on daily Bitcoin open prices (17 July 2017–3 September 2019).

Tail Index	**1.6528**			
	Sample Size	**Test Statistic**	**Rejection Region**	**Test Result**
Localised Test	1992	−0.8333	$[-1, -0.6111)$	Multifractal
Global Test	75	−0.9950	$[-1, -0.8703)$	Multifractal

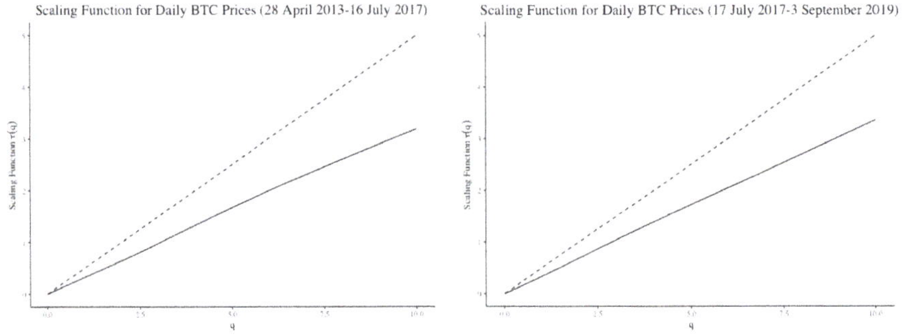

Figure 7. Scaling functions for Daily Bitcoin open price from 28 April 2013 to 16 July 2017 (**left**) vs. from 17 July 2017 to 3 September 2019 (**right**).

3.1.2. High-Frequency Bitcoin Price Data

Multifractality tests are performed on the high-frequency minute-by-minute data of Bitcoin open prices from 22 May 2018 14:00 to 1 March 2019 11:00 with 406,089 observations. Its mean-centered log-prices and log-returns are displayed in Figure 8. Similar to other financial assets, a lack of correlation in the return increments but high correlation in the absolute returns are found. However, compared with the daily open Bitcoin price data, the high-frequency Bitcoin data display stronger auto-correlation in the absolute return increments.

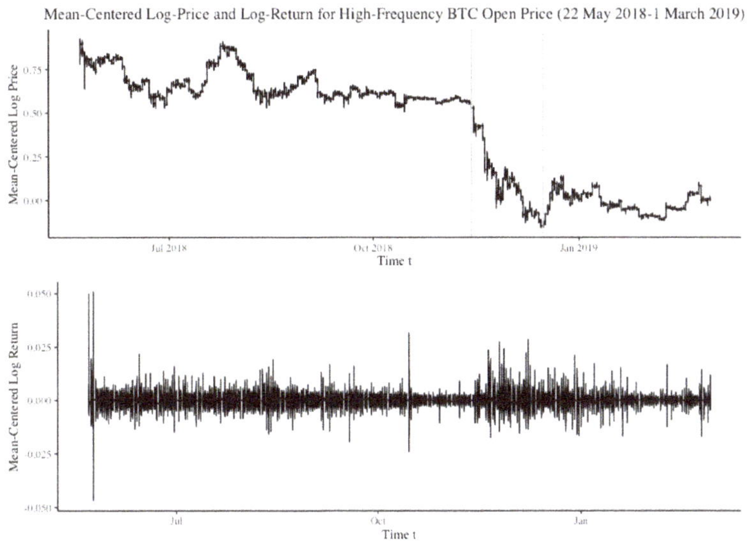

Figure 8. High frequency mean-centered log Bitcoin open price process (**top**) and mean-centered log returns process (**bottom**).

This data set covers approximately a one year period from May 2018 to March 2019. The two corresponding annual breakdown tests for daily Bitcoin open prices covering this period in Appendix B.1 in Appendix B do not indicate multifractal scaling, despite some evidence in Tables 1 and 3 for multifractality in daily data, generally.

The analysis of the high-frequency minute-by-minute data are broadly consistent with this result. With the estimated scaling function $\hat{\tau}(q)$ shown in Figure 9 and the test results in Table 4, there appears to be little evidence of multifractal scaling for the high frequency data. Nevertheless, as shown in Appendix B.2, multifractality can be detected in some cases if we partition the data into smaller subperiods.

Given these contradictory results and that the high-frequency data only spans one year, we are reluctant to infer at this stage that the Bitcoin time series scales in the same way over longer or shorter time intervals.

Overall, it is possible that multifractal scaling exists for Bitcoin prices; however, a longer time series is necessary to substantiate the use of a multifractal model and further tests are needed to discern between monofractal models as a parsimonious alternative. In the following section, we test for the presence of multifractal scaling in other financial assets. These assets have more established markets with a long history of price data. It is thus useful to compare their scaling properties to that of the Bitcoin and to identify any similarities.

Table 4. Hypothesis test results on high frequency Bitcoin open prices (22 May 2018–1 March 2019).

Tail Index	**2.7759**			
	Sample Size	**Test Statistic**	**Rejection Region**	**Test Result**
Localised Test	1682	0.2778	$[-1, -0.0556)$	Non-multifractal
Global Test	83	−0.2714	$[-1, -0.5049)$	Non-multifractal

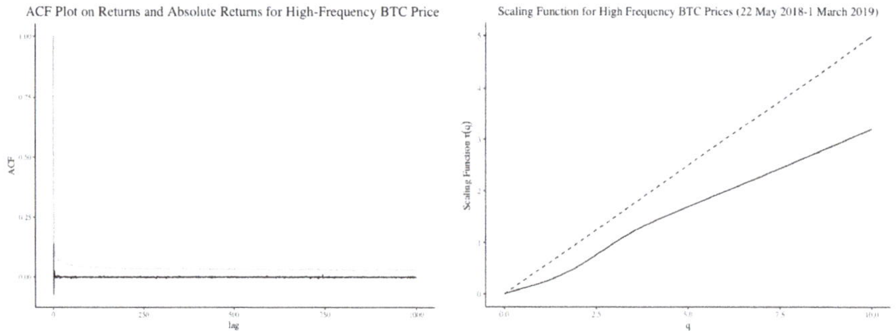

Figure 9. Left—Autocorrelations of mean-centered log returns (black) and absolute returns (grey) for high frequency Bitcoin open prices (22 May 2018–1 March 2019). **Right**—Scaling function for high frequency Bitcoin open prices (22 May 2018–01 March 2019).

3.2. Bitcoin Compared to Other Financial Assets

Cryptocurrencies are a new financial asset whose value depends upon the evolution of its underlying technology as well as the design of its economic model. Bitcoin in particular appears to have characteristics that span a commodity, medium of exchange and technology. As a result, it is unclear which asset class Bitcoin most resembles. In the previous section, we identified that Bitcoin's price dynamics could be characterised by multifractal scaling laws after accounting for heavy tails. In this section, we compare Bitcoin's scaling properties to other financial assets. Included in our set of comparable assets are stock indices, a foreign exchange rate series and gold futures. The S&P500 index[7] has been chosen to represent a large class of global equities; the Nasdaq Composite Index[8] illustrates the price behaviour of technology-stocks; the USD/JPY exchange rate[9] represents foreign currency; and gold futures prices[10] are also included in the comparison, as Bitcoin is often referred to as the digital version of gold.

The results of the hypothesis tests are summarised in Tables 5–7 and the associated scaling functions are depicted in Figures 10–12. Table 5 compares Bitcoin daily prices to other assets, over a short time period spanning Bitcoin's limited but available price history, from 2013–2019. We observe that the local and global results can produce conflicting evidence. The local test for the S&P500 marginally accepts the null hypothesis, where the global test result marginally accepts the alternative in favour of multifractality for BTC Daily. The global test statistic reveals that the greatest evidence for multifractal scaling is for the USD/JPY exchange series. The scaling functions for each asset class look visibly concave for all assets except the S&P 500; however, multifractality in the presence of heavy tails is only indicated for Bitcoin and the the USD/JPY, indicating on prima facie evidence that Bitcoin could share similar scaling properties to foreign exchange. However, Tables 6 and 7 reveal more compelling evidence given the larger data set spanning longer time periods. The lengthy time period is able to capture scaling behaviour for a wide range of time scales, as is necessary to establish a multifractal scaling relationship for an arbitrary set of rescaling factors. The results in Tables 6 and 7 indicate that both the NASDAQ and the USD/JPY foreign exchange series could share multifractal scaling properties along with Bitcoin. The scaling function of the Gold Futures series looks visibly concave; however, the hypothesis test accepts the null in the presence of heavy tails indicating that the concavity is a result of heavy tails as opposed to multifractal scaling.

---

7 Retrieved from Yahoo Finance (2019) for the period 30 December 1927 to 26 February 2020 with 23,147 observations.
8 Retrieved from Yahoo Finance (2020) for the period 5 February 1971 to 25 February 2020 with 12,372 observations.
9 Retrieved from investing.com Australia (2020b) for the period 4 March 1988 to 28 February 2020 with 8337 observations.
10 Retrieved from investing.com Australia (2020a) for the period 27 December 1979 to 28 February 2020 with 10,190 observations.

Table 5. Test results among different financial assets (28 April 2013–3 September 2019).

Financial Asset	Tail Index	Test	Test Statistics	Rejection Region	Test Result (Local)
BTC Daily	3.06	Local	−0.22	[−1, −0.06)	Multifractal
		Global	−0.63	[−1, −0.61)	Multifractal
S&P500	3.13	Local	−0.11	[−1, −0.11)	Non-Multifractal
		Global	−0.14	[−1, −0.66)	Non-Multifractal
NASDAQ	3.19	Local	0.11	[−1, −0.11)	Non-Multifractal
		Global	−0.44	[−1, −0.66)	Non-Multifractal
USD/JPY	2.69	Local	−0.28	[−1, −0.17)	Multifractal
		Global	−0.86	[−1, −0.49)	Multifractal
Gold Futures	1.35	Local	−0.67	[−1, −0.72)	Non-Multifractal
		Global	−0.89	[−1, −0.9979)	Non-Multifractal

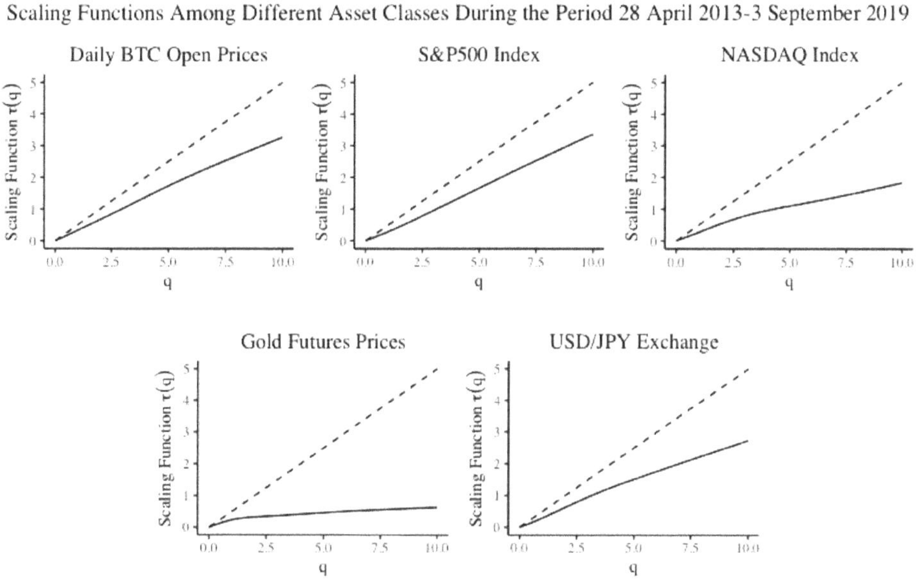

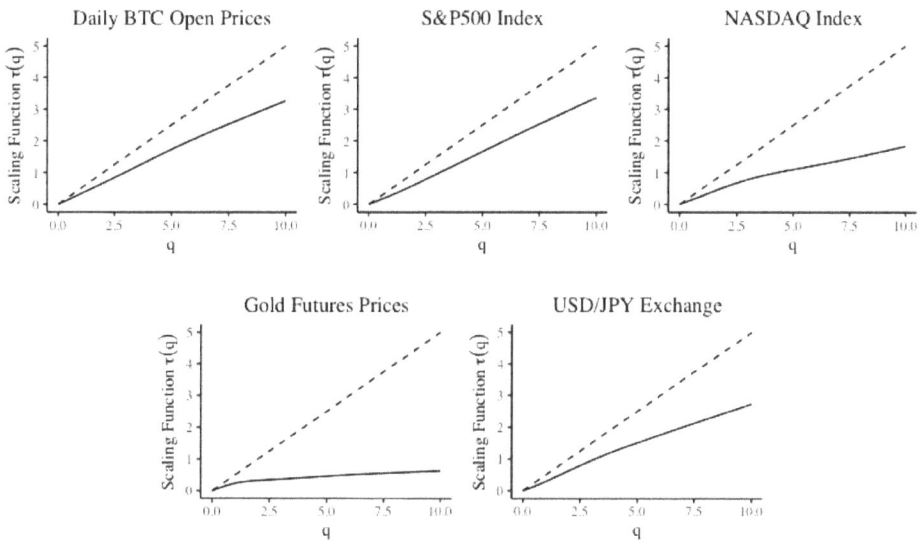

Figure 10. Scaling functions for S&P500, NASDAQ Index, USD/JPY Exchange and Gold Futures Prices the period 28 April 2013 to 3 September 2019.

Table 6. Test results among different financial assets during the dot-com bubble (3 January 1994–8 October 2004).

Financial Asset	Tail Index	Test	Test Statistics	Rejection Region	Test Result (Local)
S&P500	3.41	Local	−0.22	[−1, −0.17)	Multifractal
		Global	−0.40	[−1, −0.71)	Non-Multifractal
NASDAQ	2.81	Local	−0.44	[−1, −0.06)	Multifractal
		Global	−0.79	[−1, −0.52)	Multifractal
USD/JPY	3.50	Local	−0.33	[−1, −0.17)	Multifractal
		Global	−0.80	[−1, −0.76)	Multifractal
Gold Futures	3.48	Local	0.22	[−1, −0.17)	Non-Multifractal
		Global	−0.48	[−1, −0.71)	Non-Multifractal

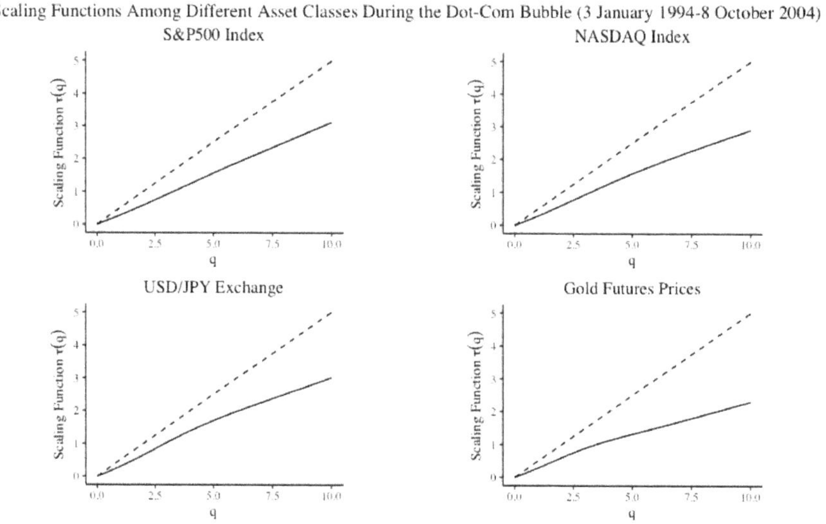

Figure 11. Scaling functions for S&P500, NASDAQ Index, USD/JPY Exchange and Gold Futures Prices during the dot-com bubble (3 January 1994–8 October 2004). The time period from 3 January 1994 to 8 October 2004 corresponds to the dot-com bubble and the dot-com crash.

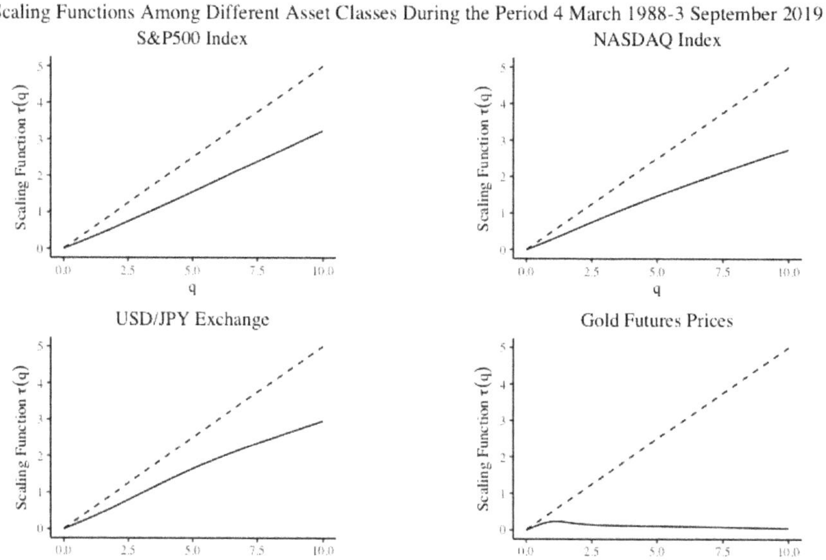

Figure 12. Scaling functions for S&P500, NASDAQ Index, USD/JPY Exchange and Gold Futures Prices the period 4 March 1988 to 3 September 2019.

Table 7. Test results among different financial assets (4 March 1988–3 September 2019).

Financial Asset	Tail Index	Test	Test Statistics	Rejection Region	Test Result (Local)
S&P500	3.20	Local	0.78	[−1, −0.11)	Non-Multifractal
		Global	0.93	[−1, −0.66)	Non-Multifractal
NASDAQ	3.84	Local	−0.61	[−1, −0.22)	Multifractal
		Global	−0.93	[−1, −0.84)	Multifractal
USD/JPY	3.33	Local	−0.28	[−1, −0.17)	Multifractal
		Global	−0.72	[−1, −0.70)	Multifractal
Gold Futures	1.36	Local	−0.11	[−1, −0.72)	Non-Multifractal
		Global	0.11	[−1, −0.9979)	Non-Multifractal

4. Conclusions

Multifractal scaling cannot be assumed to exist a priori, but instead should be established after accounting for the heavy tail effect on scaling functions. In this paper, we demonstrate how one can develop a multifractal scaling hypothesis test that accounts for the heavy tail effect on scaling functions. The test outlined in this paper doesn't incorporate the possibility of monofractal scaling, but it can be incorporated into the test in the future and we will undertake such an approach in further research. The hypothesis test presented in this paper distinguishes between the heavy tail effect that distorts a linear scaling function to look concave, and true multifractal scaling. To implement the test, a look-up table is employed to simplify the hypothesis test procedure. This makes it easy to implement the test on various time series with marginal distributions of varying tail indexes. Our test results are of course contingent upon the validity of the underlying distributional assumptions. While a sound statistical theory awaits further development, a thorough examination of the test properties by means of Monte Carlo simulation can be carried out straightforwardly, in future research.

We apply this hypothesis test to Bitcoin prices and reveal that Bitcoin exhibits scaling behaviour more similar to a multifractal model than to a heavy tail process. We then extend the test to a set of other financial assets to ascertain whether Bitcoin prices are likely to share multifractal scaling relationships akin to other financial time series. Our results show that Bitcoin, USD/JPY exchange rates, and the technology heavy NASDAQ could all share multifractal scaling properties, after accounting for heavy tails. The findings of this paper are that, while Bitcoin prices span a relatively short period, the hypothesis test indicates that multifractal scaling is plausible and such scaling could be a feature of foreign exchange markets and technology stocks as well. This indicates some helpful methodology for model selection in risk analysis. Furthermore, the research suggests that financial time series may be classified by their statistical scaling properties in addition to the asset class they belong to. This additional type of classification could allow practitioners to construct statistically diverse portfolios based on assets grouped by their scaling dynamics.

Author Contributions: Research and analysis, C.J.; Supervision, P.D. and R.A.M. All authors have read and agreed to the published version of the manuscript.

Funding: This research was partially funded by ARC grant DP160104737.

Conflicts of Interest: The authors declare no conflict of interest. The funders had no role in the design of the study; in the collection, analyses, or interpretation of data; in the writing of the manuscript, or in the decision to publish the results.

Appendix A. Look-Up Table

Table A1. Look-up tables for multifractality hypothesis test.

Localised Concavity Measure		**Global Concavity Measure**	
Tail Index	Critical Value	Tail Index	Critical Value
0.50	−0.8889	0.50	−0.9979
0.75	−0.8889	0.75	−0.9987
1.00	−0.8333	1.00	−0.9987
1.25	−0.7778	1.25	−0.9986
1.50	−0.6667	1.50	−0.9963
1.75	−0.5556	1.75	−0.8543
2.00	−0.3889	2.00	−0.7503
2.25	−0.3333	2.25	−0.5482
2.50	−0.2222	2.50	−0.5264
2.75	−0.1111	2.75	−0.4992
3.00	−0.0556	3.00	−0.6231
3.25	−0.1111	3.25	−0.7011
3.50	−0.1667	3.50	−0.7562
3.75	−0.2222	3.75	−0.8330
4.00	−0.2778	4.00	−0.8791
4.25	−0.3333	4.25	−0.9274
4.50	−0.3889	4.50	−0.9291
4.75	−0.5000	4.75	−0.9228
5.00	−0.5556	5.00	−0.9259
5.25	−0.5556	5.25	−0.9149
5.50	−0.5556	5.50	−0.9133
5.75	−0.5556	5.75	−0.9086
6.00	−0.5083	6.00	−0.9006
6.25	−0.5000	6.25	−0.8835
6.50	−0.4444	6.50	−0.8548
6.75	−0.4444	6.75	−0.8233
7.00	−0.4444	7.00	−0.8047
7.25	−0.3333	7.25	−0.7321
7.50	−0.3333	7.50	−0.7018
7.75	−0.2528	7.75	−0.6804
8.00	−0.2222	8.00	−0.6545
8.25	−0.2222	8.25	−0.6203
8.50	−0.2528	8.50	−0.5517
8.75	−0.2222	8.75	−0.4959
9.00	−0.2222	9.00	−0.4449
9.25	−0.2222	9.25	−0.4065
9.50	−0.2222	9.50	−0.3928
9.75	−0.1167	9.75	−0.3969
10.00	−0.1111	10.00	−0.3293

Appendix B. Multifractality Test Results

Appendix B.1. Hypothesis Test Results on Daily Bitcoin Open Price Data—Annual Breakdown

We explore for the existence of multifractality for each calendar year. The results are shown in Tables A2 and A3.

Table A2. Local hypothesis test results on daily Bitcoin open prices.

Time Period	Tail Index	Localised Measure	Sample Size	Test Result
28/04/2013–31/12/2013	2.0886	−0.5556	2026	Multifractal
01/01/2014–31/12/2014	1.4785	−0.3333	1904	Non-Multifractal
01/01/2015–31/12/2015	0.9464	0.2222	980	Non-Multifractal
01/01/2016–31/12/2016	1.7584	−0.7778	2036	Multifractal
01/01/2017–31/12/2017	2.2187	−0.6111	1997	Multifractal
01/01/2018–31/12/2018	1.6145	0.1667	1977	Non-Multifractal
01/01/2019–03/09/2019	1.4411	0.6111	1867	Non-Multifractal

Table A3. Global Hypothesis test results on daily Bitcoin open prices.

Time Period	Tail Index	Global Measure	Sample Size	Test Result
28/04/2013–31/12/2013	2.0886	−0.9260	72	Multifractal
01/01/2014–31/12/2014	1.4785	−0.7300	77	Non-Multifractal
01/01/2015–31/12/2015	0.9464	−0.0511	50	Non-Multifractal
01/01/2016–31/12/2016	1.7584	−0.9473	80	Multifractal
01/01/2017–31/12/2017	2.2187	−0.9551	70	Multifractal
01/01/2018–31/12/2018	1.6145	0.2706	74	Non-Multifractal
01/01/2019–03/09/2019	1.4411	0.8439	80	Non-Multifractal

Appendix B.2. Hypothesis Test Results on High Frequency Bitcoin Price Data

The high frequency Bitcoin price data are divided into 6 equal-length time periods with 67,681 observations in each time period. The results are presented as follows:

Table A4. Local hypothesis test results on high frequency Bitcoin open prices.

Time Period	Tail Index	Localised	Sample Size	Test Result
22/05/2018 14:01–08/07/2018 23:23	2.1226	0.0000	2015	Non-Multifractal
08/07/2018 23:24–24/08/2018 23:24	2.9599	−0.3333	1572	Multifractal
24/08/2018 23:25–11/10/2018 00:25	2.5649	−0.4444	1889	Multifractal
11/10/2018 00:26–27/11/2018 10:56	2.5984	−0.6667	1847	Multifractal
27/11/2018 10:57–13/01/2019 10:57	2.8381	−0.2778	1654	Multifractal
13/01/2019 10:58–01/03/2019 10:58	2.6245	−0.5000	1845	Multifractal

Table A5. Global Hypothesis test results on high frequency Bitcoin open prices.

Time Period	Tail Index	Global	Sample Size	Test Result
22/05/2018 14:01–08/07/2018 23:23	2.1226	−0.4811	72	Non-Multifractal
08/07/2018 23:24–24/08/2018 23:24	2.9599	−0.3872	96	Non-Multifractal
24/08/2018 23:25–11/10/2018 00:25	2.5649	−0.5587	74	Multifractal
11/10/2018 00:26–27/11/2018 10:56	2.5984	−0.8287	74	Multifractal
27/11/2018 10:57–13/01/2019 10:57	2.8381	−0.6690	88	Multifractal
13/01/2019 10:58–01/03/2019 10:58	2.6245	−0.4125	75	Non-Multifractal

References

Abrevaya, Jason, and Wei Jiang. 2005. A nonparametric approach to measuring and testing curvature. *Journal of Business & Economic Statistics* 23: 1–19.

Bariviera, Aurelio F. 2017. The inefficiency of bitcoin revisited: A dynamic approach. *Economics Letters* 161: 1–4. [CrossRef]

Bariviera, Aurelio F., María José Basgall, Waldo Hasperué, and Marcelo Naiouf. 2017. Some stylized facts of the bitcoin market. *Physica A: Statistical Mechanics and Its Applications* 484: 82–90. [CrossRef]

Binance. 2019. *BTC/USDT*. Available online: https://www.binance.com/en/trade/BTC_USDT (accessed on 20 March 2019).

Bouchaud, Jean-Philippe, Marc Potters, and Martin Meyer. 2000. Apparent multifractality in financial time series. *The European Physical Journal B-Condensed Matter and Complex Systems* 13: 595–99. [CrossRef]

Calvet, Laurent E., Adlai J. Fisher, and Benoit B. Mandelbrot. 1997. *Large Deviations and the Distribution of Price Changes*. Cowles Foundation Discussion Paper No. 1165. New Haven: Cowles Foundation for Research in Economics Yale University.

Chambers, Clem. 2019. Bitcoin Is Fractal. Available online: https://www.forbes.com/sites/investor/2019/01/23/bitcoin-is-fractal/#27bbcc49208d (accessed on 30 April 2019).

CoinMarketCap. 2019. Bitcoin (BTC) Price, Charts, Market Cap, and Other Metrics. Available online: https://coinmarketcap.com/currencies/bitcoin/ (accessed on 5 September 2019).

Embrechts, Paul, and Makoto Maejima. 2000. An introduction to the theory of self-similar stochastic processes. *International Journal of Modern Physics B* 14: 1399–420. [CrossRef]

Grahovac, Danijel, and Nikolai N. Leonenko. 2014. Detecting multifractal stochastic processes under heavy-tailed effects. *Chaos, Solitons & Fractals* 65: 78–89.

Heyde, Chris C. 2009. Scaling issues for risky asset modelling. *Mathematical Methods of Operations Research* 69: 593–603. [CrossRef]

investing.com Australia. 2020a. Gold Futures—Apr 20 (GCJ0). Available online: https://au.investing.com/commodities/gold-historical-data (accessed on 27 February 2020).

investing.com Australia. 2020b. USD JPY Historical Data—Investing.com AU. Available online:https://au.investing.com/currencies/usd-jpy-historical-data (accessed on 27 February 2020).

Kantelhardt, Jan W., Stephan A. Zschiegner, Eva Koscielny-Bunde, Shlomo Havlin, Armin Bunde, and H. Eugene Stanley. 2002. Multifractal detrended fluctuation analysis of nonstationary time series. *Physica A: Statistical Mechanics and Its Applications* 316: 87–114. [CrossRef]

Lahmiri, Salim, and Stelios Bekiros. 2018. Chaos, randomness and multi-fractality in bitcoin market. *Chaos, Solitons & Fractals* 106: 28–34.

Mandelbrot, Benoit B., Adlai J. Fisher, and Laurent E. Calvet. 1997. A multifractal model of asset returns. *Cowles Foundation Discussion Paper No. 1164*. New Haven: Cowles Foundation for Research in Economics Yale University.

Matia, Kaushik, Yosef Ashkenazy, and H. Eugene Stanley. 2003. Multifractal properties of price fluctuations of stocks and commodities. *EPL (Europhysics Letters)* 61: 422. [CrossRef]

Mensi, Walid, Yun-Jung Lee, Khamis Hamed Al-Yahyaee, Ahmet Sensoy, and Seong-Min Yoon. 2019. Intraday downward/upward multifractality and long memory in bitcoin and ethereum markets: An asymmetric multifractal detrended fluctuation analysis. *Finance Research Letters* 31: 19–25. [CrossRef]

Milutinović, Monia. 2018. Cryptocurrency. Економика-Часопис за економску теорију и праксу и друштвена питањаа 1: 105–122. [CrossRef]

Nadarajah, Saralees, and Jeffrey Chu. 2017. On the inefficiency of bitcoin. *Economics Letters* 150: 6–9. [CrossRef]

Nakamoto, Satoshi. 2009. Bitcoin: A Peer-to-Peer Electronic Cash System. Available online: https://bitcoin.org/bitcoin.pdf (accessed on 20 November 2018).

Patterson, Michael. 2018. Crypto's 80% Plunge Is Now Worse Than the Dot-Com Crash. Available online: https://www.bloomberg.com/news/articles/2018-09-12/crypto-s-crash-just-surpassed-dot-com-levels-as-losses-reach-80 (accessed on 7 August 2019).

Platen, Eckhard, and Renata Rendek. 2008. Empirical evidence on student-t log-returns of diversified world stock indices. *Journal of Statistical Theory and Practice* 2: 233–251. [CrossRef]

Popken, Ben. 2018. Bitcoin Loses More Than Half Its Value Amid Crypto Crash. Available online: https://www.nbcnews.com/tech/internet/bitcoin-loses-more-half-its-value-amid-crypto-crash-n844056 (accessed on 7 August 2019).

Salat, Hadrien, Roberto Murcio, and Elsa Arcaute. 2017. Multifractal methodology. *Physica A: Statistical Mechanics and Its Applications* 473: 467–487. [CrossRef]

Sly, Allan. 2006. Self-similarity, multifractionality and multifractality. Master's thesis, Australian National University, Canberra, Australia.

Sreenivasan, Katepalli. 1991. Fractals and multifractals in fluid turbulence. *Annual Review of Fluid Mechanics* 23: 539–604. [CrossRef]

Stavroyiannis, Stavros, Vassilios Babalos, Stelios Bekiros, Salim Lahmiri, and Gazi Salah Uddin. 2019. The high frequency multifractal properties of bitcoin. *Physica A: Statistical Mechanics and Its Applications* 520: 62–71. [CrossRef]

Yahoo Finance. 2019. S&P 500 (^GSPC) Historical Data. Available online: https://au.finance.yahoo.com/quote/^GSPC/history?p=^GSPC (accessed on 27 February 2020).

Yahoo Finance. 2020. NASDAQ Composite (^IXIC) Historical Data. Available online: https://finance.yahoo.com/quote/%5Eixic/history?ltr=1 (accessed on 27 February 2020).

Zhang, Wei, Pengfei Wang, Xiao Li, and Dehua Shen. 2018. The inefficiency of cryptocurrency and its cross-correlation with dow jones industrial average. *Physica A: Statistical Mechanics and Its Applications* 510: 658–670. [CrossRef]

Journal of
Risk and Financial Management

MDPI

Article

Robust Inference in the Capital Asset Pricing Model Using the Multivariate *t*-Distribution

Manuel Galea [1,*], David Cademartori [2], Roberto Curci [3] and Alonso Molina [1]

[1] Departamento de Estadística, Pontificia Universidad Católica de Chile, Avenida Vicuña Mackenna 4860, Santiago 7820436, Chile; aomolina@uc.cl
[2] Escuela de Comercio, Pontificia Universidad Católica de Valparaíso, Avenida Brasil 2830, Valparaíso 2340031, Chile; dcademar@gmail.com
[3] Brennan School of Business, Dominican University, River Forest, IL 60305, USA; rcurci@dom.edu
* Correspondence: mgalea@mat.uc.cl

Received: 1 May 2020; Accepted: 9 June 2020; Published: 13 June 2020

Abstract: In this paper, we consider asset pricing models under the multivariate *t*-distribution with finite second moment. Such a distribution, which contains the normal distribution, offers a more flexible framework for modeling asset returns. The main objective of this work is to develop statistical inference tools, such as parameter estimation and linear hypothesis tests in asset pricing models, with an emphasis on the Capital Asset Pricing Model (CAPM). An extension of the CAPM, the Multifactor Asset Pricing Model (MAPM), is also discussed. A simple algorithm to estimate the model parameters, including the kurtosis parameter, is implemented. Analytical expressions for the Score function and Fisher information matrix are provided. For linear hypothesis tests, the four most widely used tests (likelihood-ratio, Wald, score, and gradient statistics) are considered. In order to test the mean-variance efficiency, explicit expressions for these four statistical tests are also presented. The results are illustrated using two real data sets: the Chilean Stock Market data set and another from the New York Stock Exchange. The asset pricing model under the multivariate *t*-distribution presents a good fit, clearly better than the asset pricing model under the assumption of normality, in both data sets.

Keywords: capital asset pricing model; estimation of systematic risk; tests of mean-variance efficiency; *t*-distribution; generalized method of moments; multifactor asset pricing model

1. Introduction

The Capital Asset Pricing Model (CAPM) is one of the most important asset pricing models in financial economics. It is widely used in estimating the cost of capital for companies and measuring portfolio (or investment fund) performance, among others applications; see, for instance, Campbell et al. (1997), Amenc and Le Sourd (2003), Broquet et al. (2004), Levy (2012) and Ejara et al. (2019).

The CAPM framework provides financial practitioners with a measure of *beta* (or systematic risk) for entire stock markets, industry sub-sectors, and individual equities (Pereiro 2010).

The literature on the CAPM based on the multivariate normal distribution is vast, as seen, for instance, in the works published by Elton and Gruber (1995), Campbell et al. (1997), Broquet et al. (2004), Francis and Kim (2013), Johnson (2014), Brandimarte (2018) and Mazzoni (2018). However, multivariate normality is not required to ensure the validity of the CAPM. In fact, it is well known that the CAPM is still valid within the class of elliptical distributions, of which multivariate normal and multivariate *t*-distributions are special cases (see Chamberlain 1983; Hamada and Valdez 2008; Ingersoll 1987; Owen and Rabinovitch 1983). It is also well known that in practice, excess returns are not normally distributed. Most financial assets exhibit excess kurtosis, that is to say, returns having distributions whose tails are heavier than those of the normal distribution and present some degree of skewness; see Fama (1965), Blattberg and Gonedes (1974), Zhou (1993), Campbell et al. (1997), Bekaert and Wu (2000), Chen et al. (2001), Hodgson et al. (2002) and Vorknik (2003). Recently Bao et al. (2018) discuss estimation in the univariate CAPM with asymmetric power distributed errors. In this paper, the multivariate version of the CAPM is considered, primarily focusing on modeling non-normal returns due to excess kurtosis.

Within the class of elliptical distributions, the multivariate t-distribution has been widely used to model data with heavy tails. For instance, Lange et al. (1989) discuss the use of the t-distribution in regression and in problems related to multivariate analysis. Sutradhar (1993) has considered a score test aimed at testing if the covariance matrix is equal to some specified covariance matrix using the t-distribution; Bolfarine and Galea (1996) used the t-distribution in structural comparative calibration models, while Pinheiro et al. (2001) used the multivariate t-distribution for robust estimation in linear mixed-effects models. Cademartori et al. (2003), Fiorentini et al. (2003), Galea et al. (2008), Galea et al. (2010) and Kan and Zhou (2017) provide empirical evidence of the usefulness of t-distribution to model stock returns. In addition, statistical inference based on the t-distribution is simple to implement, and the computational cost is considerably low.

Following Kan and Zhou (2017), there are three main reasons for using the t-distribution in modeling returns of financial instruments. (i) empirical evidence shows that this distribution is appropriate for modeling non-normal returns in many situations, (ii) with the algorithms implemented in this paper, the t-distribution has become almost as tractable as the normal one, and (iii) the CAPM is still valid under t-distribution. It is clear that the t-distribution does not describe all the features of the return data. For instance, the volatility variation over time is one of them, for which the GARCH models are very useful. However, according to our experience (see Cademartori et al. 2003; Galea et al. 2008 2010; Galea and Giménez 2019), and as mentioned by Kan and Zhou (2017), there is little evidence of GARCH effects on the monthly data that are typically used for asset pricing and corporate studies. In addition, when we have a moderate number of assets, for example more than 10, the fit of the GARCH models requires an important computational effort, which limits its application to real data sets. For more details see Harvey and Zhou (1993) and Kan and Zhou (2017).

Thus, the main goal of this paper is to develop statistical inference tools, such as parameter estimation and hypothesis tests, in asset pricing models, with an emphasis on the CAPM, using the multivariate t-distribution. An extension of the CAPM, the multifactor asset pricing model (MAPM), is also discussed. The t-distribution incorporates an additional parameter, which allows modeling returns with high kurtosis. We consider a reparameterization of the multivariate t-distribution with a finite second moment. This enables a more direct comparison with the normal distribution (see Bolfarine and Galea 1996; Sutradhar 1993). Based on Fiorentini et al. (2003), who use the reparameterization of degrees of freedom suggested by Lange et al. (1989) to model financial data, this version of the multivariate t-distribution is adopted to test hypotheses of interest, such as the hypothesis of mean-variance efficiency. The three most widely used tests based on the likelihood function are considered; Wald tests, likelihood-ratio tests, and score tests (also known as Lagrange multiplier tests). Under the assumption of normality, these tests have been discussed in the literature, see for instance Campbell et al. (1997) and Chou and Lin (2002). Recently Kan and Zhou (2017) discuss the likelihood-ratio tests in the CAPM assuming that the excess returns follow a multivariate t-distribution. In this paper, the modeling of the asset returns conditional on market portfolios and the three most widely used tests are considered. Additionally, a fourth test statistic is considered, based on the likelihood proposed by Terrell (2002), the gradient test. To our knowledge this test has not been applied to test hypothesis in asset pricing models.

The article is developed as follows. In Section 2, the CAPM under the multivariate t-distribution, estimation of parameter and tests of mean-variance efficiency are briefly reviewed, and the Generalized Method of Moments is summarized for comparative purposes. In Section 3, the methodology developed in this paper is applied to two real data sets: the Chilean Stock Market data set and another from the New York Stock Exchange, USA. In Section 4, multifactor asset pricing models under the $\boldsymbol{t}$-distribution are discussed. In Section 5, a conclusion and final comments are included. The appendices contain technical details.

2. Methodology

2.1. The CAPM under the t-Distribution

First, a set of $p \geq 1$ assets of interest is considered, and let R_i denote the return for asset i, with $i = 1, \ldots, p$. CAPM specifies that the stock's expected return is equal to the risk-free rate return plus a risk premium; i.e.,

$$E(R_i) = R_f + \beta_i\{E(R_m) - R_f\}, \quad i = 1, \ldots, p, \tag{1}$$

where R_f is the risk-free interest rate, β_i is the systematic risk of the asset i, and R_m is the market return. This model was independently derived by Sharpe (1964), Lintner (1965) and Mossin (1966). For these p assets, the excess returns can be described using the following multivariate linear regression model; Gibbons et al. (1989), MacKinlay and Richardson (1991) and Campbell et al. (1997),

$$\boldsymbol{y}_t = \boldsymbol{\alpha} + \boldsymbol{\beta} x_t + \boldsymbol{\epsilon}_t, \quad t = 1, \ldots, n, \tag{2}$$

where $\boldsymbol{y}_t = (y_{1t}, \ldots, y_{pt})^T$ is a $p \times 1$ vector representing excess returns of the set of p assets of interest in period t such that, $y_{it} = R_{it} - R_{ft}$ denotes the excess return of asset i during period t, $\boldsymbol{\alpha} = (\alpha_1, \ldots, \alpha_p)^T$ is the intercept vector, $\boldsymbol{\beta} = (\beta_1, \ldots, \beta_p)^T$ is the slope vector that corresponds to the sensitivity of the portfolio return to changes in this benchmark return; $x_t = R_{mt} - R_{ft}$ represents the excess return of the market portfolio during period t and finally $\boldsymbol{\epsilon}_t$ is the errors vector during period t, with mean zero and variance-covariance matrix $\boldsymbol{\Sigma}$, independent of t, for $t = 1, \ldots, n$. If the CAPM holds for this set of assets and the benchmark portfolio is mean-variance efficient, the following restriction on the parameters of model (2) should hold $E(\boldsymbol{y}_t) = \boldsymbol{\beta} x_t$, for $t = 1, \ldots, n$. Hence, this restriction implies a testable hypothesis:

$$H_\alpha : \boldsymbol{\alpha} = \boldsymbol{0}. \tag{3}$$

Much of the theory of the CAPM is based on the assumption that excess returns follow a multivariate normal distribution; see for instance Campbell et al. (1997), Broquet et al. (2004), Johnson (2014), Brandimarte (2018), Mazzoni (2018) and Galea and Giménez (2019). However, it has been shown that although the assumption of normality is sufficient to generate the model (1), it is not necessary. Chamberlain (1983), Owen and Rabinovitch (1983), Ingersoll (1987), Berk (1997) and most recently Hamada and Valdez (2008) show that (1) can be obtained under the assumption of elliptically symmetric return distributions. In particular, Berk (1997) showed that when agents maximize the expected utility, elliptical symmetry is both necessary and sufficient for the CAPM.

In this paper, we are interested in develop statistical inference tools, estimation and hypothesis tests in asset pricing models supposing that $\boldsymbol{\epsilon}_t$, the random errors vector following a multivariate $\boldsymbol{t}$-distribution, has a mean zero and a covariance matrix $\boldsymbol{\Sigma}$. In effect, we supposed that the density function of $\boldsymbol{\epsilon}_t$ is given by

$$f(\boldsymbol{\epsilon}) = |\boldsymbol{\Sigma}|^{-1/2} g(\delta), \quad \delta \geq 0, \tag{4}$$

where

$$g(\delta) = k_p(\eta)\big(1 + c(\eta)\delta\big)^{-\frac{1}{2\eta}(1+\eta p)},$$

with $\delta = \boldsymbol{\epsilon}^T \boldsymbol{\Sigma}^{-1} \boldsymbol{\epsilon}$, $k_p(\eta) = (c(\eta)/\pi)^{p/2}\{\Gamma((1+\eta p)/2\eta)/\Gamma(1/2\eta)\}$ and $c(\eta) = \eta/(1-2\eta)$, $0 < \eta < 1/2$. In this case we wrote $\boldsymbol{\epsilon}_t \sim T_p(\boldsymbol{0}, \boldsymbol{\Sigma}, \eta)$. From properties of the $\boldsymbol{t}$-distribution (see Appendix A), we have, given x_t, that $\boldsymbol{y}_t \sim T_p(\boldsymbol{\alpha} + \boldsymbol{\beta} x_t, \boldsymbol{\Sigma}, \eta)$ independently, $t = 1, \ldots, n$. The $\boldsymbol{t}$-distribution offers a more flexible framework for modeling asset returns. In this distribution η is a shape parameter that can be used for adjusting the kurtosis distribution and for providing more robust procedures than the ones that use the normal distribution, with moderate additional computational effort.

Following Campbell et al. (1997), we consider the joint distribution of the excess returns given the excess return market. Specifically, we assume that the excess returns $\boldsymbol{y}_1, \ldots, \boldsymbol{y}_n$, given the excess return market, are independent random vectors with a multivariate t-distribution and common covariance matrix. Then, the probability density function of $\boldsymbol{y}_t$ takes the form of

$$f(\boldsymbol{y}_t|\boldsymbol{\theta}) = |\boldsymbol{\Sigma}|^{-1/2} g(\delta_t), \tag{5}$$

where, $\delta_t = (\boldsymbol{y}_t - \boldsymbol{\alpha} - \boldsymbol{\beta} x_t)^T \boldsymbol{\Sigma}^{-1} (\boldsymbol{y}_t - \boldsymbol{\alpha} - \boldsymbol{\beta} x_t)$, for $t = 1, \ldots, n$. Therefore, the density for a sample of n periods is given by

$$f(\boldsymbol{Y}|\boldsymbol{\theta}) = \prod_{t=1}^{n} f(\boldsymbol{y}_t|\boldsymbol{\theta}) = \prod_{t=1}^{n} |\boldsymbol{\Sigma}|^{-1/2} g(\delta_t), \tag{6}$$

with $\boldsymbol{Y} = (\boldsymbol{y}_1, \ldots, \boldsymbol{y}_n)$ and $\boldsymbol{\theta} = (\boldsymbol{\alpha}^T, \boldsymbol{\beta}^T, \boldsymbol{\sigma}^T, \eta)^T$, where $\boldsymbol{\sigma} = \text{vech}(\boldsymbol{\Sigma})$ is the $p(p+1)/2$ vector obtained from $\text{vec}(\boldsymbol{\Sigma})$ by deleting from it all of the elements that are above the diagonal of $\boldsymbol{\Sigma}$.

2.2. Maximum Likelihood Estimation

The logarithm of the likelihood function for the model (6) is given by

$$\mathcal{L}(\boldsymbol{\theta}) = \sum_{t=1}^{n} \mathcal{L}_t(\boldsymbol{\theta}), \tag{7}$$

where $\mathcal{L}_t(\boldsymbol{\theta}) = -\frac{1}{2} \log|\boldsymbol{\Sigma}| + \log\{g(\delta_t)\} = \log k_p(\eta) - \frac{1}{2} \log|\boldsymbol{\Sigma}| - \frac{1}{2\eta}(1 + \eta p) \log(1 + c(\eta)\delta_t)$ is the contribution from the tth return to the likelihood, $t = 1, 2, \ldots, n$.

From (7), the score function is given by

$$\mathcal{U}(\boldsymbol{\theta}) = \sum_{t=1}^{n} U_t(\boldsymbol{\theta}), \tag{8}$$

where $U_t(\boldsymbol{\theta}) = (U_{t\alpha}^T, U_{t\beta}^T, U_{t\sigma}^T, U_{t\eta})^T$ with

$$\begin{aligned}
U_{t\alpha} &= \omega_t \boldsymbol{\Sigma}^{-1} \boldsymbol{\epsilon}_t, \\
U_{t\beta} &= x_t U_{t\alpha}, \\
U_{t\sigma} &= -\frac{1}{2} \boldsymbol{D}_p^T \text{vec}\left(\boldsymbol{\Sigma}^{-1} - \omega_t \boldsymbol{\Sigma}^{-1} \boldsymbol{\epsilon}_t \boldsymbol{\epsilon}_t^T \boldsymbol{\Sigma}^{-1}\right), \quad \text{and} \\
U_{t\eta} &= \frac{1}{2\eta^2} \{c(\eta)p - \beta(\eta) - \omega_t c(\eta)\delta_t + \log(1 + c(\eta)\delta_t)\},
\end{aligned}$$

where $\omega_t = \left(\frac{1+\eta p}{\eta}\right)\left(\frac{c(\eta)}{1 + c(\eta)\delta_t}\right)$, for $t = 1, \ldots, n$; $\beta(\eta) = \psi\left(\frac{1}{2\eta}(1 + \eta p)\right) - \psi\left(\frac{1}{2\eta}\right)$; $\psi(x)$ is the digamma function and $\boldsymbol{D}_p$ is the duplication matrix; see Magnus and Neudecker (2007). It is difficult to obtain the maximum likelihood (ML) estimators from $\mathcal{U}(\boldsymbol{\theta}) = \boldsymbol{0}$. The EM algorithm has been suggested frequently to obtain ML estimators in statistical models under the t-distribution, mainly because it leads to a simple implementation of an iteratively weighted estimation procedure. As is well known, the t-distribution is a scale mixture of a normal distribution (see Lange et al. 1989), which facilitates the implementation of the EM algorithm considerably. Then, based on the complete-data log-likelihood function we obtained the expressions of ML estimates (see Liu and Rubin 1995; Shoham 2002; Xie et al.

2007). Thus, in our case, as shown in Appendix B, the ML estimates of $\boldsymbol{\alpha}$, $\boldsymbol{\beta}$, $\boldsymbol{\Sigma}$ and η are obtained as solution of the following equations:

$$\hat{\boldsymbol{\alpha}} = \bar{\boldsymbol{y}}_{\omega} - \hat{\boldsymbol{\beta}}\bar{x}_{\omega}, \qquad \hat{\boldsymbol{\beta}} = \frac{\sum_{t=1}^{n} \omega_t (x_t - \bar{x}_{\omega})(\boldsymbol{y}_t - \bar{\boldsymbol{y}}_{\omega})}{\sum_{t=1}^{n} \omega_t (x_t - \bar{x}_{\omega})^2}, \qquad \hat{\boldsymbol{\Sigma}} = \frac{1}{n}\sum_{t=1}^{n} \omega_t \hat{\boldsymbol{\epsilon}}_t \hat{\boldsymbol{\epsilon}}_t^T, \tag{9}$$

and

$$\hat{\eta}^{-1} = \frac{2}{a + \log a - 1} + 0.0416\Big\{1 + erf\Big(0.6594 \log\Big(\frac{2.1971}{a + \log a - 1}\Big)\Big)\Big\},$$

where $\hat{\boldsymbol{\epsilon}}_t = \boldsymbol{y}_t - \hat{\boldsymbol{\alpha}} - \hat{\boldsymbol{\beta}}x_t$; $\bar{\boldsymbol{y}}_{\omega} = \sum_{t=1}^{n} \omega_t \boldsymbol{y}_t / \sum_{t=1}^{n} \omega_t$; $\bar{x}_{\omega} = \sum_{t=1}^{n} \omega_t x_t / \sum_{t=1}^{n} \omega_t$; $erf(x) = \frac{2}{\sqrt{\pi}} \int_0^x \exp(-u^2)du$, $a = -(1/n)\sum_{t=1}^{n}(v_{t2} - v_{t1})$, with $v_{t1} = (1 + p\eta)/(1 + c(\eta)\delta_t)$ and $v_{t2} = \psi\Big(\frac{1 + p\eta}{2\eta}\Big) - \log\Big(\frac{1 + c(\eta)\delta_t}{2\eta}\Big)$, for $t = 1, \ldots, n$. The iterative process given by Equation (9) was implemented in **R** language. Note that the normal model $\omega_t = 1, t = 1, ..., n$ and the ML estimators of $\boldsymbol{\alpha}$, $\boldsymbol{\beta}$ and $\boldsymbol{\Sigma}$ correspond to the normal case. Under the *t*-model, the exact marginal distribution of $\hat{\boldsymbol{\alpha}}$, $\hat{\boldsymbol{\beta}}$ and $\hat{\boldsymbol{\Sigma}}$ are particularly difficult to obtain, but under normal distribution, the estimators of $\boldsymbol{\alpha}$, $\boldsymbol{\beta}$ and $\boldsymbol{\Sigma}$ have exact marginal distributions (see Campbell et al. 1997).

2.3. Asymptotic Standard Errors

The standard errors of the ML estimators can be estimated using the expected information matrix. For a multivariate elliptically symmetric distribution, Lange et al. (1989) indicated how to compute the expected information matrix. See also Mitchell (1989). In our case, by using score function (8), the Fisher information matrix for $\boldsymbol{\theta}$ in the log-likelihood function defined in (7) assumes the form

$$\boldsymbol{J} = E\{\mathcal{U}(\boldsymbol{\theta})\mathcal{U}^T(\boldsymbol{\theta})\} = \begin{pmatrix} \boldsymbol{J}_{11} & \boldsymbol{0} & \boldsymbol{0} \\ \boldsymbol{0} & \boldsymbol{J}_{22} & \boldsymbol{J}_{23} \\ \boldsymbol{0} & \boldsymbol{J}_{23}^T & J_{33} \end{pmatrix}, \tag{10}$$

where $\boldsymbol{J}_{11}$, $\boldsymbol{J}_{22}$, $\boldsymbol{J}_{23}$ and J_{33} denote information concerning $(\boldsymbol{\alpha}, \boldsymbol{\beta})$, $\boldsymbol{\sigma}$, $(\boldsymbol{\sigma}, \eta)$ and η, respectively, and are given by

$$\begin{aligned}
\boldsymbol{J}_{11} &= c_\alpha(\eta)(X^T X) \otimes \boldsymbol{\Sigma}^{-1}, \\
\boldsymbol{J}_{22} &= \frac{n}{4}\boldsymbol{D}_p^T\{2c_\sigma(\eta)(\boldsymbol{\Sigma}^{-1} \otimes \boldsymbol{\Sigma}^{-1})\boldsymbol{N}_p + (c_\sigma(\eta) - 1)(\operatorname{vec}\boldsymbol{\Sigma}^{-1})(\operatorname{vec}\boldsymbol{\Sigma}^{-1})^T\}\boldsymbol{D}_p, \\
\boldsymbol{J}_{23} &= -\frac{nc(\eta)c_\sigma(\eta)(p+2)}{(1+p\eta)^2}\boldsymbol{D}_p^T \operatorname{vec}\boldsymbol{\Sigma}^{-1}, \\
J_{33} &= -\frac{n}{2\eta^2}\Big\{\Big(\frac{p}{(1-2\eta)^2}\Big)\Big(\frac{1 + \eta p(1-4\eta) - 8\eta^2}{(1+\eta p)(1+\eta(p+2))}\Big) - \beta'(\eta)\Big\},
\end{aligned}$$

with $\boldsymbol{N}_p = \frac{1}{2}(\boldsymbol{I}_{p^2} + \boldsymbol{K}_p)$ where $\boldsymbol{K}_p$ is the commutation matrix of order $p^2 \times p^2$ (Magnus and Neudecker 2007); $c_\alpha(\eta) = c_\sigma(\eta)/(1 - 2\eta)$, $c_\sigma(\eta) = (1 + p\eta)/(1 + (p+2)\eta)$; and

$$\beta'(\eta) = -\frac{1}{2\eta^2}\Big\{\psi'\Big(\frac{1 + p\eta}{2\eta}\Big) - \psi'\Big(\frac{1}{2\eta}\Big)\Big\},$$

where $\psi'(z)$ denotes the trigamma function. Note that $c_\alpha(\eta) = c_\sigma(\eta) = 1$ when $\eta = 0$ and $\boldsymbol{N}_p\boldsymbol{D}_p = \boldsymbol{D}_p$ (see for instance Magnus and Neudecker 2007), we have to recover the expressions corresponding to the normal case. Here, X is an $n \times 2$ matrix such $X^T = \begin{pmatrix} 1 & \cdot & \cdot & \cdot & 1 \\ x_1 & \cdot & \cdot & \cdot & x_n \end{pmatrix}$ and $\otimes$ denotes the Kronecker product. The asymptotic sampling distribution of the ML estimator $\hat{\boldsymbol{\theta}}$ is given by

$$\sqrt{n}(\hat{\boldsymbol{\theta}} - \boldsymbol{\theta}) \overset{\mathcal{D}}{\mapsto} \mathcal{N}_r(0, \boldsymbol{V}^{-1}),$$

where $\boldsymbol{V} = \lim_{n\to\infty}(1/n)\boldsymbol{J}$ and $r = \{p(p+5)+2\}/2$ is the dimension of $\boldsymbol{\theta}$. To estimate $\boldsymbol{V}$, we use $\hat{\boldsymbol{V}} = \boldsymbol{J}(\hat{\boldsymbol{\theta}})/n$.

2.4. Test of Mean-Variance Efficiency

To test $H_\alpha : \boldsymbol{\alpha} = \boldsymbol{0}$ the three classic tests based on the likelihood function are considered, including the Wald test, likelihood-ratio test, and score test; see for instance Boos and Stefanski (2013). Let $\boldsymbol{\theta} = (\boldsymbol{\alpha}^T, \boldsymbol{\theta}_2^T)^T$, with $\boldsymbol{\theta}_2 = (\boldsymbol{\beta}^T, \boldsymbol{\sigma}^T, \eta)^T$ and $\mathcal{U}(\boldsymbol{\theta}) = (U_\alpha^T(\boldsymbol{\theta}), U_2^T(\boldsymbol{\theta}))^T$ the score function (8) partitioned following the partition of $\boldsymbol{\theta}$. In this case, after some algebraic manipulations, the test statistics are given by

$$\begin{aligned} Lr &= n\log\{|\tilde{\boldsymbol{\Sigma}}|/|\hat{\boldsymbol{\Sigma}}|\} + 2\textstyle\sum_{t=1}^n \log\{g(\hat{\delta}_t)/g(\tilde{\delta}_t)\}, \\ Wa &= nc_\alpha(\hat{\eta})(1+\bar{x}^2/s^2)^{-1}\hat{\boldsymbol{\alpha}}^T\hat{\boldsymbol{\Sigma}}^{-1}\hat{\boldsymbol{\alpha}}, \\ Sc &= \frac{1}{nc_\alpha^{-1}(\tilde{\eta})}(1+\bar{x}^2/s^2)\boldsymbol{d}^T\tilde{\boldsymbol{\Sigma}}^{-1}\boldsymbol{d}, \end{aligned}$$

where $\bar{x} = (1/n)\sum_{t=1}^n x_t$, $s^2 = (1/n)\sum_{t=1}^n(x_t - \bar{x})^2$, $\hat{\delta}_t = \hat{\boldsymbol{e}}_t^T\hat{\boldsymbol{\Sigma}}^{-1}\hat{\boldsymbol{e}}_t$, $\tilde{\delta}_t = (\boldsymbol{y}_t - \tilde{\boldsymbol{\beta}}x_t)^T\tilde{\boldsymbol{\Sigma}}^{-1}(\boldsymbol{y}_t - \tilde{\boldsymbol{\beta}}x_t)$; $\hat{\boldsymbol{\alpha}}$, $\hat{\boldsymbol{\beta}}$, $\hat{\boldsymbol{\Sigma}}$ and $\hat{\eta}$ are the ML estimators in the model (6); $\tilde{\boldsymbol{\beta}}$, $\tilde{\boldsymbol{\Sigma}}$ and $\tilde{\eta}$ are the ML estimators of $\boldsymbol{\beta}$, $\boldsymbol{\Sigma}$ and η under H_α, $\boldsymbol{d} = \sum_{t=1}^n \tilde{\omega}_t(\boldsymbol{y}_t - \tilde{\boldsymbol{\beta}}x_t)$, $\tilde{\boldsymbol{\theta}}$ and $\hat{\boldsymbol{\theta}}$ are the restricted and unrestricted ML estimators of $\boldsymbol{\theta}$, respectively. Under H_α, the asymptotic distribution of each of these test statistics is $\chi^2(p)$. Note that $c_\alpha(\eta) = 1$ when $\eta = 0$ and $Wa = n(1+\bar{x}^2/s^2)^{-1}\hat{\boldsymbol{\alpha}}^T\hat{\boldsymbol{\Sigma}}^{-1}\hat{\boldsymbol{\alpha}}$, which corresponds to the Wald test under normality; see, for instance, Campbell et al. (1997). In addition, under the assumption of multivariate normality, the likelihood-ratio test is given by $Lr = n\log(1 + Wa/n)$, and the score test takes the form $Sc = Wa/(1 + Wa/n)$. The gradient test Terrell (2002) is also discussed, defined as

$$Ga = \mathcal{U}^T(\tilde{\boldsymbol{\theta}})(\hat{\boldsymbol{\theta}} - \tilde{\boldsymbol{\theta}}). \tag{11}$$

Since $U_2(\tilde{\boldsymbol{\theta}}) = \boldsymbol{0}$, the gradient statistic in (11) can be written as $Ga = U_\alpha^T(\tilde{\boldsymbol{\theta}})\hat{\boldsymbol{\alpha}} = \boldsymbol{d}^T\tilde{\boldsymbol{\Sigma}}^{-1}\hat{\boldsymbol{\alpha}}$. Note that Ga is attractive, as it is simple to compute and does not involve knowledge of the Fisher information matrix (10), unlike Wa and Sc. Asymptotically, Ga has a chi-square distribution with p degrees of freedom under H_α. For more details and applications of this test, see Terrell (2002) and Lemonte (2016). However, in this case, under the normality assumption, the gradient statistic does not offer an alternative to test the hypothesis of mean-variance efficiency since $Sc = Ga$, see Appendix D.

To calculate the values of the statistics Lr, Sc and Ga, it is necessary to estimate $\boldsymbol{\theta}$ under H_α. The EM algorithm leads to the following equations to obtain the ML estimates of $\boldsymbol{\beta}$, $\boldsymbol{\Sigma}$ and η under H_α:

$$\tilde{\boldsymbol{\beta}} = \frac{\sum_{t=1}^n \omega_t x_t \boldsymbol{y}_t}{\sum_{t=1}^n \omega_t x_t^2}, \qquad \tilde{\boldsymbol{\Sigma}} = \frac{1}{n}\sum_{t=1}^n \omega_t(\boldsymbol{y}_t - \tilde{\boldsymbol{\beta}}x_t)(\boldsymbol{y}_t - \tilde{\boldsymbol{\beta}}x_t)^T$$

and

$$\tilde{\eta}^{-1} = \frac{2}{a + \log a - 1} + 0.0416\Big\{1 + erf\Big(0.6594\log\Big(\frac{2.1971}{a + \log a - 1}\Big)\Big)\Big\},$$

where $a = -(1/n)\sum_{t=1}^n(v_{t2} - v_{t1})$, with $v_{t1} = (1+p\eta)/(1+c(\eta)\tilde{\delta}_t)$ and $v_{t2} = \psi\Big(\frac{1+p\eta}{2\eta}\Big) - \log\Big(\frac{1+c(\eta)\tilde{\delta}_t}{2\eta}\Big)$, for $t = 1, \ldots, n$.

2.5. Model Assessment and Outlier Detection

Any statistical analysis should include a critical analysis of the model assumptions. Following Lange et al. (1989), in this work the Mahalanobis distance is used to assess the fit of the CAPM. In effect, the random variables

$$F_t = \left(\frac{1}{1-2\eta}\right)\frac{\delta_t}{p} \sim F(p, 1/\eta)$$

for $t = 1, \ldots, n$. Substituting the ML estimators yields $\hat{F}_t = F_t(\hat{\boldsymbol{\theta}})$, which has asymptotically the same F distribution as F_t, $t = 1, \ldots, n$. Using the Wilson-Hilferty approximation,

$$z_t = \frac{\left(1 - \frac{2\eta}{9}\right)\hat{F}_t^{1/3} - \left(1 - \frac{2}{9p}\right)}{\sqrt{\frac{2\eta}{9}\hat{F}_t^{2/3} + \frac{2}{9p}}} \tag{12}$$

for $t = 1, \ldots, n$, with an approximately standard normal distribution. Thus, a QQ-plot of the transformed distances $\{z_1, \ldots, z_n\}$ can be used to evaluate the fit of the CAPM under the multivariate t-distribution. For $\eta = 0$, the transformed distances are simplified to $z_t = \{\hat{F}_t^{1/3} - (1 - 2/9p)\}/\sqrt{2/9p}$ and can be used to assess of fit of the CAPM under the assumption of normality. Additionally, the Mahalanobis distance can be used for multivariate outlier detection. In effect, larger than expected values of the Mahalanobis distance, $\hat{F}_t$, $t = 1, \ldots, n$, identify outlying cases (see Lange et al. 1989).

2.6. Generalized Method of Moments Tests

If the iid multivariate $\boldsymbol{t}$ assumption of random errors is violated, hypothesis (3) can be tested using the Generalized Method of Moments (GMM) (see Hansen 1982). No distributional assumptions are needed other than the data being stationary and ergodic. With the GMM framework, the random errors can be both serially dependent and conditionally heteroskedastic. From (2), we have $\boldsymbol{\epsilon}_t = \boldsymbol{y}_t - \boldsymbol{\alpha} - \boldsymbol{\beta}x_t$, for $t = 1, \ldots, n$. The idea of the GMM approach (see Hansen 1982), is to use sample moments conditions to replace the population moment conditions of the model restrictions. The relevant population moment conditions are $E(\boldsymbol{\epsilon}_t) = \mathbf{0}$ and $E(x_t\boldsymbol{\epsilon}_t) = \mathbf{0}$, for $t = 1, \ldots, n$.

Define $2p \times 1$ vectors $f_t(\boldsymbol{\psi})$ and $\boldsymbol{g}_n(\boldsymbol{\psi})$ as follows,

$$f_t(\boldsymbol{\psi}) = (\epsilon_{t1}, x_t\epsilon_{t1}, \ldots, \epsilon_{tj}, x_t\epsilon_{tj}, \ldots, \epsilon_{tp}, x_t\epsilon_{tp})^T,$$

and

$$\boldsymbol{g}_n(\boldsymbol{\psi}) = \frac{1}{n}\sum_{t=1}^{n} f_t(\boldsymbol{\psi}) = \frac{1}{n}\sum_{t=1}^{n}(\boldsymbol{\epsilon}_t \otimes \boldsymbol{x}_t),$$

where, $\boldsymbol{\psi} = (\alpha_1, \beta_1, \ldots, \alpha_p, \beta_p)^T$, whose dimension is $2p \times 1$, where p is the number of assets and $\boldsymbol{x}_t = (1, x_t)^T$ for $t = 1, \ldots, n$. The GMM estimator is obtained by minimizing the quadratic form

$$Q(\boldsymbol{\psi}) = \boldsymbol{g}_n^T(\boldsymbol{\psi})W_n\boldsymbol{g}_n(\boldsymbol{\psi}),$$

where W_n, $2p \times 2p$, is the weighting matrix. As noted by MacKinlay and Richardson (1991), in this model the GMM estimator is independent of the weighting matrix and always coincides with the OLS estimators, which are given by

$$\hat{\boldsymbol{\alpha}} = \bar{\boldsymbol{y}} - \bar{x}\hat{\boldsymbol{\beta}}, \quad \text{and } \hat{\boldsymbol{\beta}} = \frac{\sum_{t=1}^{n}(x_t - \bar{x})(\boldsymbol{y}_t - \bar{\boldsymbol{y}})}{\sum_{t=1}^{n}(x_t - \bar{x})^2}, \tag{13}$$

where $\bar{\boldsymbol{y}} = \frac{1}{n}\sum_{t=1}^{n}\boldsymbol{y}_t$ and $\bar{x} = \frac{1}{n}\sum_{t=1}^{n}x_t$.

As we know, there are several versions of the GMM test, for simplicity, in this work the Wald-type GMM test is considered (see MacKinlay and Richardson 1991). It is well known that the GMM estimators (13) are normally distributed asymptotically. In effect, from MacKinlay and Richardson (1991) it follows that the asymptotic sampling distribution of the estimator $\hat{\boldsymbol{\psi}}$ is given by

$$\sqrt{n}(\hat{\boldsymbol{\psi}} - \boldsymbol{\psi}) \overset{\mathcal{D}}{\mapsto} \mathcal{N}_{2p}(0, \Psi)\,,$$

and a consistent estimator of Ψ is $\hat{\Psi} = (D_n^T S_n^{-1} D_n)^{-1}$ with $D_n = (1/n)\sum_{t=1}^{n}(\boldsymbol{I}_p \otimes \boldsymbol{x}_t \boldsymbol{x}_t^T) = (1/n)(\boldsymbol{I}_p \otimes X^T X)$ and $S_n = (1/n)\sum_{t=1}^{n}(\hat{\boldsymbol{\epsilon}}_t \hat{\boldsymbol{\epsilon}}_t^T \otimes \boldsymbol{x}_t \boldsymbol{x}_t^T)$. The Wald-type GMM test is given by

$$Wa = n\hat{\boldsymbol{\alpha}}^T (C\hat{\Psi}C^T)^{-1}\hat{\boldsymbol{\alpha}},$$

where $C = \boldsymbol{I}_p \otimes (1,0)$ such that $C\hat{\boldsymbol{\psi}} = \hat{\boldsymbol{\alpha}}$. This test has an asymptotic $\chi^2(p)$, a χ^2 distribution with degrees of freedom p. See MacKinlay and Richardson (1991) for more details.

For the development of the methodology proposed in this paper, the classical approach is used. Optionally, the Bayesian approach can be used. Two recent references are Barillas and Shanken (2018) and Borup (2019), who propose a Bayesian framework for asset pricing models. For applications of Bayesian inference using the Markov Chain Monte Carlo (MCMC) approach in Capital Asset Pricing Models, see Glabadanidis (2014).

3. Applications

3.1. The Chilean Stock Market Data Set

As an application of the methodology presented in this paper, monthly returns of shares from the Chilean Stock Market were analyzed. The data corresponded to the period from September, 2002 to March, 2020 and five companies: BSantander (one of the biggest banks in the country), ENEL (an electrical distribution company), Falabella (a retail company), LTM (an airline), and SQMB (a company from the chemical industry). The Selective Index of Share Prices (IPSA) was used as the return for the market and the 10-Years Bonds in UFs (BCU, BTU) of the Central Bank of Chile, was used as the risk-free rate, both monthly. This risk free rate is a long-rate, the trend of which is a smoother curve than that of a short-rate.

The means, standard deviations (SDs), Sharpe ratios (Sharpe), coefficients of skewness and kurtosis, and the Jarque-Bera test (JB Test) for normality of the monthly returns are presented in Table 1. SQMB had the highest mean return (1.19% per month), while ENEL had the lowest average return (0.13%). In addition, LTM had the highest volatility (11.21%), while BSantander had the lowest volatility (5.56%) among the five assets. Furthermore, the IPSA index had a standard deviation of 4.60%, which was less than the volatility of the five assets considered. With the exception of SQMB, a lithium-producing company, Sharpe ratios were close to zero.

Except for BSantander, which has a moderate positive asymmetry, the returns of the remaining assets had a moderately negative skew. Except for BSantander, the returns of the remaining assets had a highest kurtosis. LTM showed the highest kurtosis with an estimated coefficient of 22.7946, and BSantander showed the lowest kurtosis. These coefficients provide us initial evidence of the absence of normality in the monthly returns. In fact, with the exception of BSantander, the normality hypothesis was rejected in the other assets using the Jarque-Bera test (JB Test). In brief, the descriptive statistics summary reported in Table 1, confirmed the presence of low levels of skewness and high levels of kurtosis.

Table 1. Summary statistics for monthly log-returns of five assets and IPSA index, from the Chilean Stock Market data set. p-values are in parentheses.

Asset	Mean (%)	SD (%)	Sharpe	Skewness	Kurtosis	JB Test
BSantander	0.4590	5.5594	0.0480	0.1441	2.9212	0.7846 (0.6755)
ENEL	0.1311	7.4571	−0.0082	−1.3978	9.2396	410.9952 (0.0000)
Falabella	0.6296	7.3003	0.0601	−0.3574	5.9289	79.9115 (0.0000)
LTM	0.5687	11.2062	0.0336	−2.4017	22.7946	3647.6426 (0.0000)
SQMB	1.1889	9.4381	0.1057	−0.0603	5.5979	59.4642 (0.0000)
IPSA	0.5800	4.6000	0.0850	−0.1324	3.8769	7.3770 (0.0250)

Figure 1 shows scatter plots and estimated lines for the five assets, using the normal and t distributions. From this figure, it is possible to observe linear relationships between asset returns and IPSA returns, and potential outliers. The IPSA index returns explained between 28% and 51% of the variability of the five assets returns. The IPSA index explained 50.94% of the variability in the returns of the Falabella and 27.82% of the returns variability of SQMB.

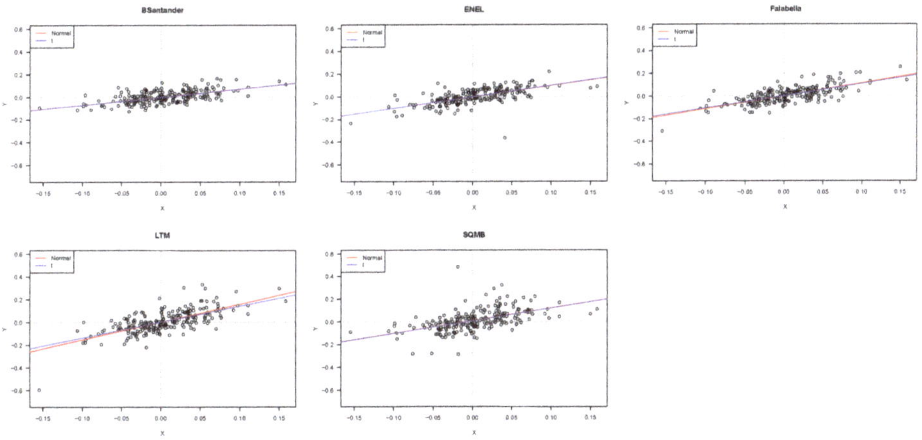

Figure 1. Scatter plots and estimated lines for five assets, using the normal and t distributions, for the Chilean Stock Market data set.

We also performed an analysis of the heteroscedasticity and autocorrelation of the returns of the five assets. Using the White test (see Lee 1991; Waldman 1983; White 1980) Falabella and LTM showed evidence of heteroscedasticity, while the Durbin-Watson test indicated evidence of first order autocorrelation only in the returns of LTM. Then, considering the significant departure from normality, high kurtosis (evidence that the returns had fat-tailed distributions), the moderate skewness, and the results of the tests for heteroscedasticity and autocorrelation of errors, it is assumed in this study that the random vectors $\{\epsilon_t, t = 1, \ldots, n\}$ were iid as a multivariate t-distribution, with zero mean and covariance matrix $\boldsymbol{\Sigma}$ and density given by (4). For illustrative purposes, the normal distribution and tests based on weaker distributional assumptions were used, such as the GMM tests, for testing hypothesis (3).

Table 2 presents the ML estimate for parameters of the CAPM using the normal and *t* distributions. The standards errors were estimated using the expected information matrix. The results in Table 2 show that the estimates of the coefficients α and β were very similar using both models (*N*CAPM and *T*CAPM), especially the systematic risk estimators ($\hat{\beta}$) of the assets considered.

Table 2. Adjustment results of Capital Asset Pricing Model (CAPM) using the multivariate normal and *t* distributions, standard errors are in parentheses, for the Chilean Stock Market data set.

Model	Asset	$\hat{\alpha}$	$\hat{\beta}$			$\hat{\Sigma}$		
Normal	BSantander	0.0007 (0.0032)	0.7105 (0.0685)	0.0021	−0.0001	−0.0003	−0.0001	−0.0003
	ENEL	−0.0028 (0.0038)	0.9901 (0.0830)		0.0030	−0.0003	0.0004	−0.0005
	Falabella	0.0014 (0.0035)	1.1298 (0.0767)			0.0026	−0.0001	−0.0007
	LTM	0.0019 (0.0052)	1.5608 (0.1124)				0.0056	−0.0004
	SQMB	0.0091 (0.0057)	1.1047 (0.1231)					0.0067
t ($\hat{\eta} = 0.135$)	BSantander	−0.0011 (0.0031)	0.7090 (0.0675)	0.0024	0.0000	−0.0003	−0.0001	−0.0001
	ENEL	−0.0010 (0.0032)	1.0039 (0.0700)		0.0026	−0.0004	0.0002	−0.0006
	Falabella	0.0026 (0.0034)	1.0623 (0.0727)			0.0028	−0.0004	−0.0003
	LTM	0.0014 (0.0047)	1.3873 (0.1011)				0.0054	−0.0002
	SQMB	0.0070 (0.0050)	1.1039 (0.1072)					0.0060

The following hypothesis test $H_0 : \eta = 0$ against $H_1 : \eta > 0$ was considered. In this case, it was found that $\hat{\eta} = 0.134926$. The asymptotic distribution of the LR test for the previous hypothesis corresponded to a 50:50 mixture of chi-squares with zero and one degree of freedom, whose critical value was 2.7055 at a significance level of 5% (see, for instance Song et al. 2007). In this case, the maximum log-likelihood for the *N*CAPM was 1481.39 and for the *T*CAPM, the maximum log-likelihood was 1524.06, which corresponded to a likelihood-ratio statistic of 85.34. This indicates that the *T*CAPM fit the data significantly better than the *N*CAPM. As suggested by a referee, for address the impact of finite samples on the *p*-values and on the standard errors of the parameter estimates, we also used a nonparametric bootstrap procedure (Chou and Zhou 2006; Efron and Tibshirani 1993). Nevertheless, the results were very similar to those obtained using the normal and *t*-distribution; therefore, they are not shown here. Figure 2 displays the transformed distance plots for the normal and *t* distributions, see Equation (12). These graphics confirm that the *T*CAPM presented the best fit.

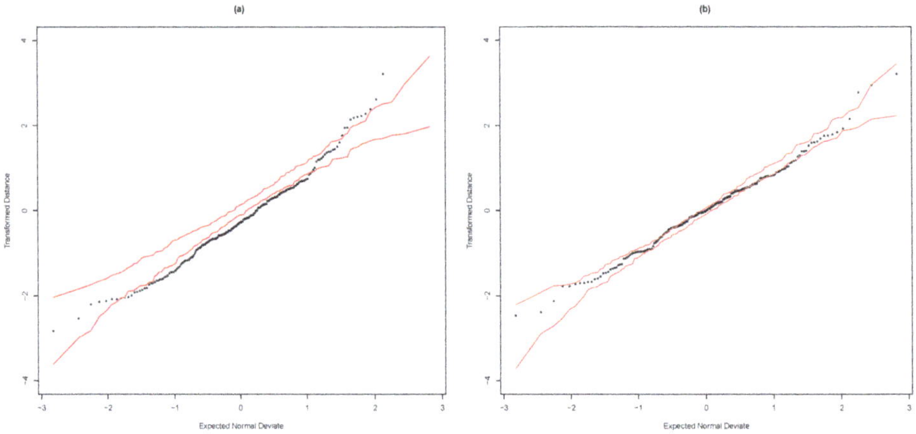

Figure 2. QQ-plot of transformed distances for the *N*CAPM (**a**) and *T*CAPM (**b**), for the Chilean Stock Market data set.

Table 3 presents tests results for hypothesis (3) based on the Wald, likelihood-ratio, score, and gradient tests. The results in Table 3 show that the mean-variance efficiency of the IPSA index is not rejected (p-values > 0.59), with any of the tests used for the three scenarios (normal, t-distributions and the GMM).

Table 3. Test of the mean-variance efficiency; p-values in parentheses, for the Chilean Stock Market data set.

Test	Normal Fit	Multivariate t Fit	GMM Fit
Wald	3.7243	3.0368	3.6917
	(0.5898)	(0.6943)	(0.5946)
Likelihood-ratio	3.6918	2.9712	-
	(0.5946)	(0.7044)	-
Score	3.6597	2.9508	-
	(0.5994)	(0.7076)	-
Gradient	-	2.9698	-
	-	(0.7046)	-

Figure 3 shows the Mahalanobis distances for the normal and t-distribution, for both data sets; the Chilean data set and the New York Stock Exchange data set. For the Chilean data set, under normality Figure 3a, we observe that the returns for 2008/Jun, 2009/Jul and 2020/Mar are possible outliers. For instance, in 2009/Jul, economic activity fell by 3.5%, when Chile entered a recession due to the global financial crisis, while in 2020/Mar, the fall in economic activity (initial) was due to the pandemic caused by Covid-19. Already in Figure 3b, we see as expected, that the $TCAPM$ reduced the possible effect of these returns.

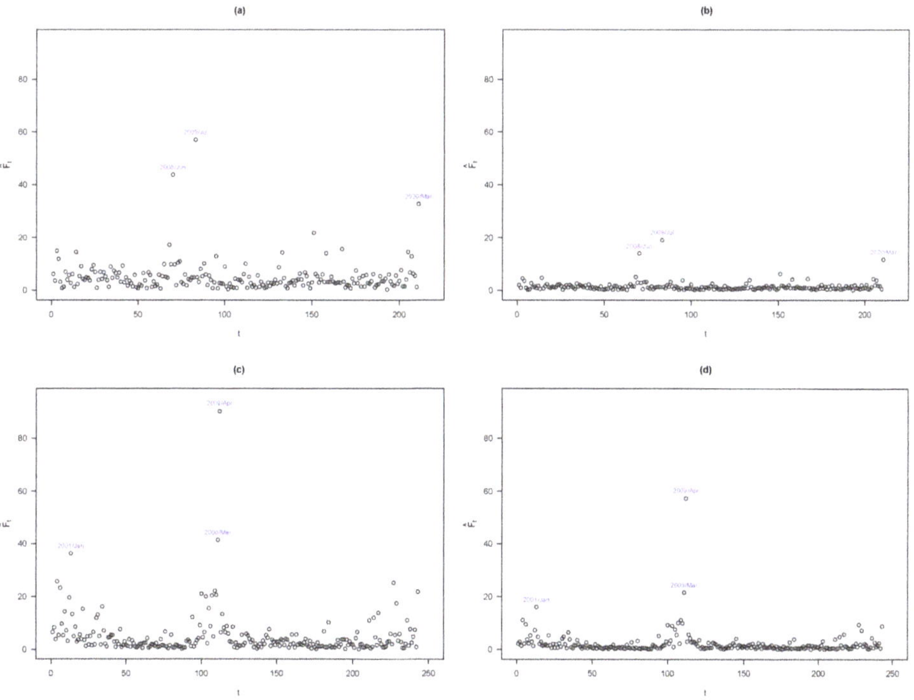

Figure 3. Mahalanobis distances ($\hat{F}_t$) for the $NCAPM$ (**a**) and $TCAPM$ (**b**), for the Chilean Stock Market data set, and $NCAPM$ (**c**) and $TCAPM$ (**d**) for the NYSE data set.

3.2. The New York Stock Exchange Data Set

We considered monthly returns of shares from five companies whose common stock shares trade on the New York Stock exchange, NYSE: Bank of America, Boeing, Ford Motor Company, General Electric Company and Microsoft. The S&P500 was taken as the market price. The 10-year bond yield was used as the risk-free returns; it is a long risk-free rate, similar to the one used for the Chilean data set. The excess returns were the returns minus the risk-free rate. The data corresponded to the period from January, 2000 to March, 2020.

The means, standard deviations (SD), Sharpe ratios (Sharpe), coefficients of skewness and kurtosis, and the Jarque-Bera test (JB Test) for normality of the monthly returns are presented in Table 4. Boeing had the highest mean return (0.53% per month), while General Electric Company had the lowest average return (−0.77%). In addition, Ford had the highest volatility (13.10%), while Microsoft had the lowest volatility (8.34%) among the five assets. Furthermore, the S&P500 index had a standard deviation of 4.34%, which was less than the volatility of the five assets considered. With the exception of General Electric Company, with a negative Sharpe ratio, the other Sharpe ratios were close to zero.

The assets had a moderate (positive and negative) asymmetry. Again, the returns of the assets had a highest kurtosis. The normality hypothesis was rejected in all the assets using the Jarque-Bera test (JB Test). In brief, the descriptive statistics summary reported in Table 4, confirmed the presence of low levels of skewness and high levels of kurtosis.

Table 4. Summary statistics for monthly log-returns of five assets and S&P500 index from the NYSE data set. p-values are in parentheses.

Asset	Mean (%)	SD (%)	Sharpe	Skewness	Kurtosis	JB Test
Bank of America	−0.0691	11.9324	−0.0281	−1.3041	12.6330	1008.4271 (0.0000)
Boeing	0.5269	9.2462	0.0282	−1.8571	12.0454	968.1001 (0.0000)
Ford	−0.7582	13.0995	−0.0782	0.0119	16.1538	1751.8490 (0.0000)
Gelectric	−0.7728	8.5741	−0.1212	−0.6836	5.9354	106.1649 (0.0000)
Microsoft	0.4093	8.3394	0.0171	−0.3767	6.7068	144.8702 (0.0000)
S&P500	0.2300	4.3400	−0.0077	−0.8143	4.4698	48.7262 (0.0000)

Figure 4 shows scatter plots and estimated lines of the five assets, using the normal and t distributions. From this figure, it is possible to observe linear relationships between asset returns and S&P500 returns, and potentials outliers. In this case, the S&P500 index returns explained between 27% and 45% of the variability of the five assets returns, similar to the Chilean Data Set.

The Whites test show evidence of heteroscedasticity in Bank of America, Boeing and Ford Motor Company. The Durbin-Watson test indicates no evidence of first order autocorrelation.

Table 5 presents the ML estimate for parameters of the CAPM using the normal and t distributions. The standards errors were estimated using the expected information matrix. Similar results to the Chilean data set were observed. For this data set, it was found that $\hat{\eta} = 0.276870$, indicating a greater departure from normality than the Chilean data set. The likelihood-ratio statistic value, for the hypothesis $H_0 : \eta = 0$ against $H_1 : \eta > 0$ was 285.8, which was highly significant. In this case, the maximum log-likelihood for the $NCAPM$ was 1361.2 and for the $TCAPM$ was 1504.1. Again, this indicates that the *T*CAPM fit the data significantly better than the *N*CAPM. This was also confirmed by the transformed distance plots displayed in Figure 5.

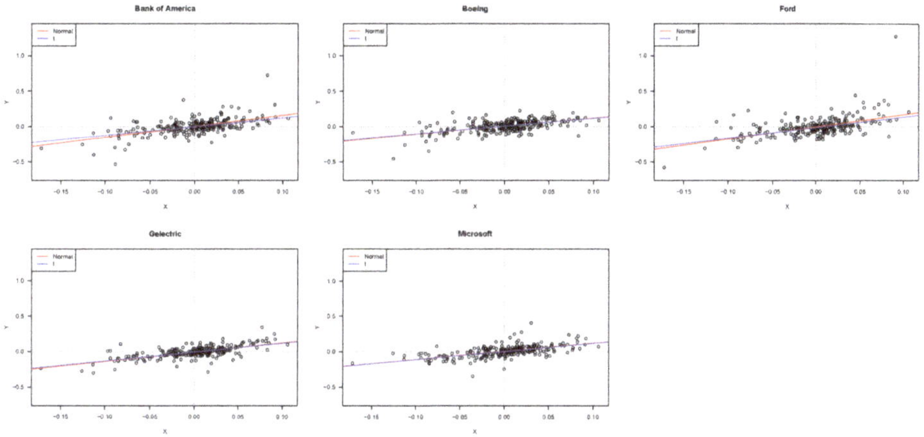

Figure 4. Scatter plots and estimated lines for five assets, using the normal and *t* distributions, for the NYSE data set.

Table 5. Adjustment results of CAPM using the multivariate normal and *t* distributions, standard errors are in parentheses, for the NYSE data set.

Model	Assets	$\hat{\alpha}$	$\hat{\beta}$	$\hat{\Sigma}$				
Normal	Bank of Am	0.0025 (0.0060)	1.5633 (0.1407)	0.0087	0.0002	0.0019	0.0013	−0.0004
	Boeing	0.0060 (0.0046)	1.1405 (0.1080)		0.0051	0.0007	0.0005	−0.0012
	Ford	−0.0026 (0.0077)	1.7125 (0.1802)			0.0143	0.0006	−0.0005
	Gelectric	−0.0076 (0.0040)	1.3070 (0.0931)				0.0038	−0.0003
	Microsoft	0.0042 (0.0043)	1.1518 (0.1013)					0.0045
t ($\hat{\eta} = 0.277$)	Bank of Am	−0.0017 (0.0044)	1.2387 (0.1036)	0.0087	0.0002	0.0008	0.0007	−0.0004
	Boeing	0.0065 (0.0039)	1.0935 (0.0908)		0.0067	0.0010	0.0004	−0.0011
	Ford	−0.0147 (0.0050)	1.4773 (0.1174)			0.0111	−0.0002	−0.0005
	Gelectric	−0.0074 (0.0032)	1.2406 (0.0747)				0.0045	0.0002
	Microsoft	0.0007 (0.0034)	1.1487 (0.0797)					0.0051

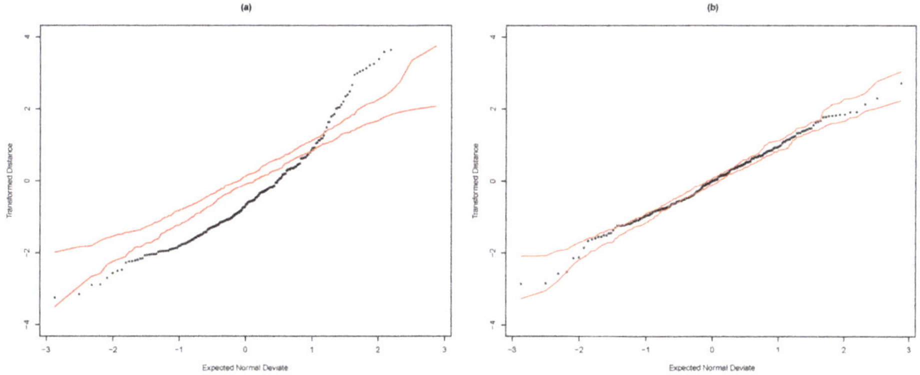

Figure 5. Plots of transformed distances for the *N*CAPM (**a**) and *T*CAPM (**b**), for the NYSE data set.

Table 6 presents tests results for hypothesis (3). The results in Table 6 show that the mean-variance efficiency of the S&P500 index could not be rejected (p-values > 0.1277), with any of the tests, if we used the NCAPM (or GMM test). However, if we used TCAPM, the hypothesis (3) was rejected ($0.0014 < p$-values < 0.0030) with any of the four tests. That is to say, there was a change in statistical inference.

Table 6. Test of the mean-variance efficiency; p-values in parentheses, for the NYSE data set.

Test	Normal Fit	Multivariate t Fit	GMM Fit
Wald	8.5507	19.7321	8.5664
	(0.1284)	(0.0014)	(0.1277)
Likelihood-ratio	8.4037	18.7816	-
	(0.1353)	(0.0021)	-
Score	8.2601	18.1012	-
	(0.1425)	(0.0028)	-
Gradient	-	17.9527	-
	-	(0.0030)	-

As suggested by a referee, it may also be of interest to test the hypotheses $H_\beta : \boldsymbol{\beta} = \mathbf{1}$ and $H_{\alpha\beta} : \boldsymbol{\alpha} = \mathbf{0},\ \boldsymbol{\beta} = \mathbf{1}$. The four tests were implemented to verify these hypotheses using the $\boldsymbol{t}$-distribution, see Appendix C. However, with the four tests statistics, we strongly rejected the null hypotheses, and therefore they are not shown in the present study. More details about this interesting topic can be found at Glabadanidis (2009, 2014, 2019).

Figure 3 show the Mahalanobis distances for the NCAPM and TCAPM models, showing results similar to the Chilean data set, except that the return corresponding to 2009/Apr for TCAPM (see Figure 3d) was a possible outlier. In April 2009, the five assets had high returns, highlighting Ford Motor Company, with a 127.4%. However, when deleting these returns, there were no changes in statistical inference. Once again, this suggests that the TCAPM provided an appropriate way for achieving robust inference.

3.3. Robustness

Aspects of the robustness of the TCAPM with respect to the NCAPM can be illustrated perturbing some observations in the original data. Changes in the ML estimates of $\boldsymbol{\beta}$ can be evaluated using the following procedure. First, an observation can be perturbed to create an outlier by $\boldsymbol{y}_n \leftarrow \boldsymbol{y}_n + \Delta\mathbf{1}_p$, for $\Delta = -0.20, -0.10, 0, 0.10, 0.20$. Then, we re-calculate the ML estimates of $\boldsymbol{\beta}$ under the TCAPM and under the NCAPM. Note that, for the NCAPM,

$$\hat{\beta}_{\Delta j} = \hat{\beta}_j + (x_n - \bar{x})\Delta / \sum_{t=1}^{n}(x_t - \bar{x})^2, \tag{14}$$

for $j = 1, \ldots, p$. Finally, a graph of $\hat{\beta}_{\Delta j}$, $j = 1, \ldots, p$ versus Δ for each of the p assets, is useful to visualize changes in the estimators. Figures 6 and 7 show the curves of the estimates of $\hat{\beta}_{\Delta j}$, $j = 1, \ldots, 5$ versus Δ for each of the 5 assets included in the two data sets considered in this paper. For this perturbation scheme, it can be observed that the influence on parameter estimation was unbounded in the NCAPM, see Equation (14), whereas it was obviously bounded in the TCAPM. This suggests that TCAPM provided an appropriate way for achieving robust statistical inference.

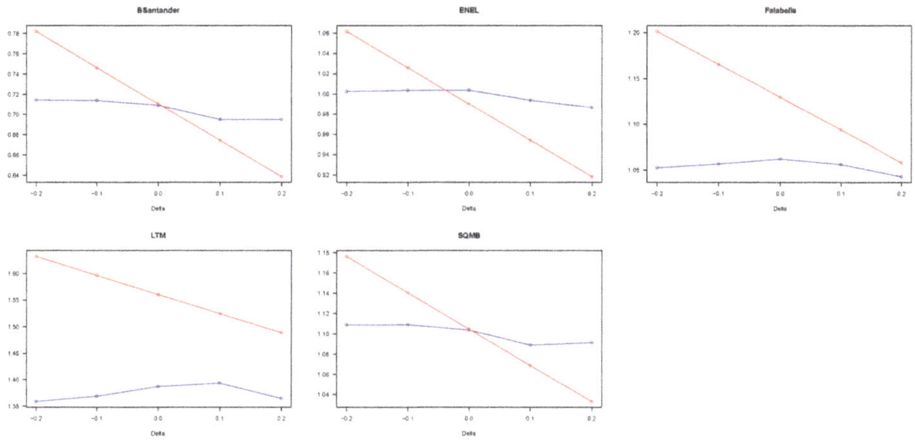

Figure 6. Perturbed ML estimates of $\boldsymbol{\beta}$ under the NCAPM (red line) and TCAPM (blue line), for the Chilean Stock Market data set.

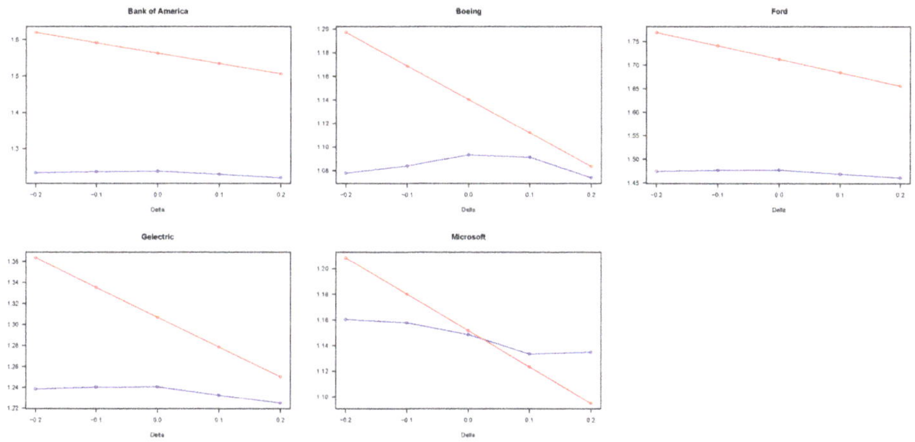

Figure 7. Perturbed maximum likelihood (ML) estimates of $\boldsymbol{\beta}$ under the NCAPM (red line) and TCAPM (blue line), for the NYSE data set.

4. Multifactor Asset Pricing Models under the *t*-Distribution

As suggested by a referee, in some cases it is necessary to use more than one factor to estimate the expected returns of the assets of interest. In this Section we briefly discuss an extension of the *TCAPM* that includes more than one factor. More details on estimation, hypothesis testing, and applications will be discussed in a separate paper. The multifactor model (MAPM) is a multivariate linear regression model with excess returns on p assets, as follows:

$$\boldsymbol{y}_t = \boldsymbol{\alpha} + \boldsymbol{\beta}_1 x_{t1} + \ldots + \boldsymbol{\beta}_q x_{tq} + \boldsymbol{\epsilon}_t, \quad t = 1, \ldots, n, \tag{15}$$

where $(x_1, \ldots, x_q)$ denotes the excess returns of q factors (benchmark assets), $\boldsymbol{\beta}_j$ is a $p \times 1$ parameter vector, $j = 1, \ldots, q$. The above regression model can be expressed as

$$\begin{aligned} \boldsymbol{y}_t &= \boldsymbol{\alpha} + \boldsymbol{B}_1 \boldsymbol{x}_t^f + \boldsymbol{\epsilon}_t, \\ \boldsymbol{y}_t &= \boldsymbol{B}\boldsymbol{x}_t + \boldsymbol{\epsilon}_t, \end{aligned} \tag{16}$$

where $\boldsymbol{B} = (\boldsymbol{\alpha}, \boldsymbol{B}_1)$, denotes the matrix $(p \times q+1)$ of regression coefficients, $\boldsymbol{B}_1 = (\boldsymbol{\beta}_1, \ldots, \boldsymbol{\beta}_q)$, $\boldsymbol{x}_t = (1, \boldsymbol{x}_t^f)^T$ and $\boldsymbol{x}_t^f = (x_{t1}, \ldots, x_{tq})^T$, $t = 1, \ldots, n$.

As in Section 2.1, we assume that the excess returns $\boldsymbol{y}_t$ follows an multivariate $\boldsymbol{t}$-distribution with mean vector $\boldsymbol{\mu}_t$ and variance-covariance matrix $\boldsymbol{\Sigma}$, named $\boldsymbol{y}_t \sim T_p(\boldsymbol{\mu}_t, \boldsymbol{\Sigma}, \eta)$, independent, $t = 1, \ldots, n$, whose density function takes the form,

$$f(\boldsymbol{y}_t|\boldsymbol{\theta}) = |\boldsymbol{\Sigma}|^{-1/2} g(\delta_t), \tag{17}$$

where, $\delta_t = (\boldsymbol{y}_t - \boldsymbol{\mu}_t)^T \boldsymbol{\Sigma}^{-1} (\boldsymbol{y}_t - \boldsymbol{\mu}_t)$ is the square of the Mahalanobis distance, with $\boldsymbol{\mu}_t = \boldsymbol{B}\boldsymbol{x}_t$, $\boldsymbol{x}_t = (1, x_{t1}, \ldots, x_{tq})^T$ denoting the t-th row of the matrix $(n \times q+1)$ $\boldsymbol{X} = (\boldsymbol{x}_1, \ldots, \boldsymbol{x}_n)^T$, for $t = 1, \ldots, n$.

Thus, in this case, the ML estimates of $\boldsymbol{B}$, $\boldsymbol{\Sigma}$ and η are obtained as solution of the following equations (see Equation (9)):

$$\hat{\boldsymbol{B}}^T = (\boldsymbol{X}^T \boldsymbol{W} \boldsymbol{X})^{-1} \boldsymbol{X}^T \boldsymbol{W} \boldsymbol{Y}, \qquad \hat{\boldsymbol{\Sigma}} = \frac{1}{n} \sum_{t=1}^{n} \omega_t \hat{\boldsymbol{\epsilon}}_t \hat{\boldsymbol{\epsilon}}_t^T, \tag{18}$$

and

$$\hat{\eta}^{-1} = \frac{2}{a + \log a - 1} + 0.0416 \Big\{ 1 + erf\Big(0.6594 \log \Big(\frac{2.1971}{a + \log a - 1} \Big) \Big) \Big\},$$

where $\hat{\boldsymbol{\epsilon}}_t = \boldsymbol{y}_t - \hat{\boldsymbol{B}}^T \boldsymbol{x}_t$ and $\boldsymbol{W} = \mathrm{diag}(\omega_1, \ldots, \omega_n)$ an $n \times n$ diagonal matrix with elements $\omega_t = \Big(\frac{1 + \eta p}{\eta} \Big) \Big(\frac{c(\eta)}{1 + c(\eta)\delta_t} \Big)$, for $t = 1, \ldots, n$, and the matrix $(n \times p)$ $\boldsymbol{Y} = (\boldsymbol{y}_1, \ldots, \boldsymbol{y}_n)^T$.

As in Section 2.3, the standard errors of the ML estimators $\hat{\boldsymbol{B}}$, $\hat{\boldsymbol{\Sigma}}$ and $\hat{\eta}$ can be estimated using the expected information matrix. In this case, the Fisher information matrix for $\boldsymbol{\theta} = (\boldsymbol{B}, \boldsymbol{\Sigma}, \eta)$ assumes the same form of the matrix $\boldsymbol{J}$ given in the Equation (10), but the information concerning to $\boldsymbol{B}$ is now $\boldsymbol{J}_{11} = c_\alpha(\eta)(\boldsymbol{X}^T \boldsymbol{X}) \otimes \boldsymbol{\Sigma}^{-1}$, with c_α as defined in Equation (10). To test linear hypotheses of interest, such as H_α, we can use the same four tests discussed in Section 2.4.

As a illustration we consider the NYSE data set. We fit the following three-factor model,

$$\boldsymbol{y}_t = \boldsymbol{\alpha} + \boldsymbol{\beta}_1 x_t + \boldsymbol{\beta}_2 \mathrm{SMB}_t + \boldsymbol{\beta}_3 \mathrm{HML}_t + \boldsymbol{\epsilon}_t, \quad k = 1, \ldots, n, \tag{19}$$

where, x is the excess return of the S&P500 index, used in the NYSE data set, while SMB and HML used in the Fama-French model were from the website of Prof. Kenneth French. For details on risk factors, SMB and HML see Fama and French (1995).

In this case, the three risk factors explained between 32% and 50% of the variability of the five assets' returns, which corresponded to an increase of approximately 5% with respect to the CAPM. From Table 7, wecan see that the values in $\hat{\boldsymbol{\alpha}}$ were very similar to those obtained using CAPM as presented in Table 5, while estimates in $\hat{\boldsymbol{\beta}}_1$ tended to be lower than estimates in $\hat{\boldsymbol{\beta}}$, in the case of CAPM (see Table 5).

Figure 8 displays the transformed distance plots for the normal and $\boldsymbol{t}$ distributions. Here NMAPM denotes the three risk factors under normality and TMAPM denotes the three risk factors under multivariate $\boldsymbol{t}$-distribution. These graphics show clear evidence that the TMAPM had a better fit than the NMAPM. Using the likelihood-ratio test, the hypothesis H_α could not be rejected (p-value $=$ 0.1277), if we used the NMAPM. However, if we used TMAPM, the hypothesis (3) was rejected (p-value $= 0.0011$). Once again, there was a change in statistical inference.

Table 7. Adjustment results of Multifactor Asset Pricing Model (MAPM) using the multivariate normal and t distributions from the NYSE data set and Fama-French data set. Standard errors are in parentheses.

Model	Asset	$\hat{\alpha}$	$\hat{\beta}_1$	$\hat{\beta}_2$	$\hat{\beta}_3$
Normal	Bank of Am	0.0006 (0.0052)	1.4698 (0.1237)	0.2059 (0.1656)	1.4310 (0.1624)
	Boeing	0.0052 (0.0044)	1.1015 (0.1042)	0.0557 (0.1395)	0.6612 (0.1367)
	Ford	−0.0041 (0.0075)	1.6341 (0.1765)	0.3050 (0.2363)	0.9135 (0.2317)
	Gelectric	−0.0081 (0.0038)	1.2836 (0.0910)	−0.0050 (0.1218)	0.4815 (0.1194)
	Microsoft	0.0051 (0.0041)	1.1967 (0.0970)	−0.1058 (0.1298)	−0.6713 (0.1273)
t ($\hat{\eta} = 0.27$)	Bank of Am	−0.0017 (0.0027)	1.1916 (0.0634)	0.1535 (0.0849)	1.2474 (0.0832)
	Boeing	0.0056 (0.0026)	1.1063 (0.0609)	−0.0279 (0.0815)	0.5455 (0.0799)
	Ford	−0.0149 (0.0033)	1.4170 (0.0780)	0.2127 (0.1045)	0.6901 (0.1024)
	Gelectric	−0.0081 (0.0021)	1.2611 (0.0497)	−0.1479 (0.0665)	0.3387 (0.0652)
	Microsoft	0.0017 (0.0022)	1.1636 (0.0524)	−0.3077 (0.0701)	−0.4498 (0.0688)

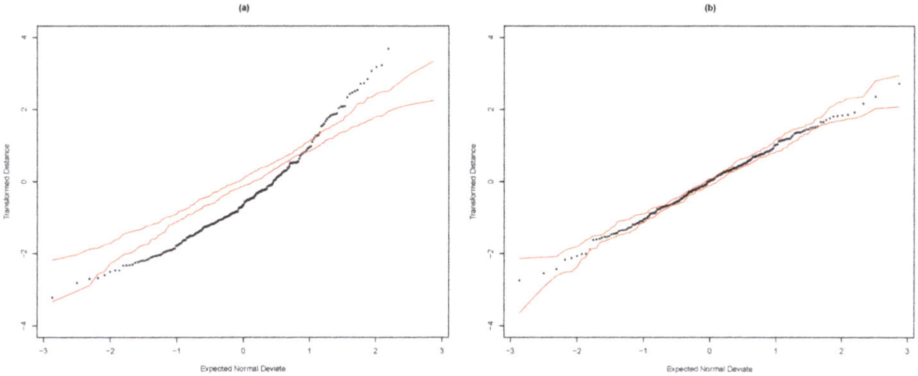

Figure 8. Plots of transformed distances for the $NMAPM$ (**a**) and $TMAPM$ (**b**), for the NYSE data set.

5. Conclusions

Since the pioneering work by Lange et al. (1989), the t-distribution has proved to be a versatile and robust modeling approach in many regression models. In fact, the t-distribution has a parameter (η) modeling kurtosis, which brings more flexibility than the normal distribution.

In this paper, robust methods for statistical inference in asset pricing models with emphasis on CAPM were developed. In effect, assuming a multivariate t-distribution for the stock returns, ML equations for parameters were derived and statistics were proposed to test linear hypotheses of interest, in particular the hypothesis of mean-variance efficiency. Simple expressions were provided in this study for the likelihood-ratio, Wald, score and gradient statistics and for the score function and Fisher information matrix. The proposed statistics generalized results from the literature, which considered tests for mean-variance efficiency under the assumption of multivariate normality (Brandimarte 2018; Campbell et al. 1997; Chou and Lin 2002; Gibbons et al. 1989; Mazzoni 2018). In addition, statistical inference based on the t-distribution is simple to implement, and the computational cost is considerably low.

A simple graphical device for checking the model was implemented, and the methodology developed in this paper was illustrated with two real data sets: the Chilean Stock Market data set (a developing country), and another from the New York Stock Exchange, USA (a developed country). In both data sets, the CAPM under the t-distribution clearly presents a better fit than under the normal distribution. Additionally, in the application of the multifactor asset pricing model to the NYSE data set, the multivariate t-distribution presents a better fit than the normal distribution.

This empirical study provides new evidence for the useful application of the t-distribution in modeling stock returns (Kan and Zhou 2017). As we have pointed out, the log-returns frequently present some degree of skewness. We are currently working on statistical inference in the asset pricing models under the multivariate skew-elliptical distributions. We understand that a skewed t-distribution of Branco and Dey (2001) may be useful for returns with high levels of skewness. For previous applications of the skew-elliptical distributions in finance and actuarial science, see Harvey et al. (2010) and Adcock et al. (2015). See also Paula et al. (2011).

Author Contributions: Conceptualization and investigation, M.G., D.C. and R.C.; methodology, M.G. and A.M.; software and validation, M.G., D.C. and A.M.; formal analysis, resources, data curation, M.G., D.C., R.C. and A.M.; writing—original draft preparation, M.G., D.C., and A.M.; writing—review and editing, M.G., D.C., R.C. and A.M.; visualization, M.G., D.C., R.C. and A.M.; supervision, M.G., D.C., R.C. and A.M.; project administration, M.G. and A.M. All authors have read and agreed to the published version of the manuscript.

Funding: This research received no external funding.

Acknowledgments: The first author acknowledges the partial financial support from Project Puente 001/2019, Dirección de Investigación de la Vicerrectoría de Investigación de la Pontificia Universidad Catlica de Chile, Chile. The authors are grateful to the editor and two reviewers for their helpful comments and suggestions.

Conflicts of Interest: The authors declare no conflict of interest.

Appendix A. The Multivariate t-Distribution

For completeness, we present some properties of the multivariate t-distribution, with finite second moment, based on the parameterization given in (5).

Property A1. *Let* $y \sim T_p(\mu, \Sigma, \eta)$, *with* $\eta < 1/2$.

(i) *Suppose that* $y|u \sim N_p(\mu, u^{-1}\Sigma)$, *and that* $u \sim G(1/2\eta, 1/2c(\eta))$, *then* $y \sim T_p(\mu, \Sigma, \eta)$

(ii) $E(y) = \mu$ *and* $\mathrm{Cov}(y) = \Sigma$

(iii) $u|y \sim G((1/\eta + p)/2, (1/c(\eta) + \delta)/2)$

(iv) *The random variable*

$$F = \left(\frac{1}{1-2\eta}\right)\frac{\delta}{p} \sim F(p, 1/\eta)$$

(v) *Let* $A(q \times p)$, $c \in \mathbb{R}^q$ *and* $q \leq p$, *then* $Ay + c \sim T_q(A\mu + c, A\Sigma A^T, \eta)$

(vi) *Let* $y = (y_1, y_2)^T$ *a partition of* y *with* y_1 *of dimension* $p_1 \leq p$, *and let*

$$\mu = \begin{pmatrix} \mu_1 \\ \mu_2 \end{pmatrix} \text{ and } \Sigma = \begin{pmatrix} \Sigma_{11} & \Sigma_{12} \\ \Sigma_{21} & \Sigma_{22} \end{pmatrix},$$

then $y_1 \sim T_{p_1}(\mu_1, \Sigma_{11}, \eta)$

(vii) *Using the same previous partition, the conditional distribution of* y_1 *given* y_2, $(y_1|y_2) \sim T_{p_1}(\mu_1 - \Sigma_{11}^{-1}\Sigma_{12}(\mu_2 - y_2), q(y_2, \eta)(\Sigma_{11} - \Sigma_{12}\Sigma_{22}^{-1}\Sigma_{21}), \eta)$,

where $\delta = (y-\mu)^T\Sigma^{-1}(y-\mu)$, $q(y_2, \eta) = \{c^{-1}(\eta) + (y_2 - \mu_2)^T\Sigma_{22}^{-1}(y_2 - \mu_2)\}/(\eta^{-1} + p_2)$, *and* $G(a, b)$ *denotes the gamma distribution with probability density function* $f(x) = b^a x^{a-1} exp\{-bx\}/\Gamma(a)$, *for* $x, a, b > 0$.

Appendix B. ML Estimation Using the EM Algorithm

To obtain the ML estimate using the EM algorithm, we augmented the observed data, Y, by incorporating latent variables to obtain $Y_{\text{com}} = \{(y_1^T, u_1), \ldots, (y_n^T, u_n)\}$. Thus, based on property $i)$ we can consider the following hierarchical model $y_t|u_t \overset{\text{ind}}{\sim} N_p(\alpha + \beta x_t, \Sigma/u_t)$, $u_t \overset{\text{ind}}{\sim} G(1/2\eta, 1/2c(\eta))$, for $t = 1, \ldots, n$. The log-likelihood function of complete data, is denoted by $\mathcal{L}_c(\theta) = \log f(Y_{\text{com}}|\theta)$.

By using Property A1, the conditional expectation of the complete-data log-likelihood function can be expressed as

$$E\{\mathcal{L}_c(\boldsymbol{\theta})|\boldsymbol{Y},\boldsymbol{\theta}^{(*)}\} = Q(\boldsymbol{\theta}|\boldsymbol{\theta}^{(*)}) = Q_1(\boldsymbol{\tau}|\boldsymbol{\theta}^{(*)}) + Q_2(\eta|\boldsymbol{\theta}^{(*)}), \tag{A1}$$

where $\boldsymbol{\tau} = (\boldsymbol{\alpha}^T, \boldsymbol{\beta}^T, \boldsymbol{\sigma}^T)^T$, and

$$Q_1(\boldsymbol{\tau}|\boldsymbol{\theta}^{(*)}) = -\frac{n}{2}\log|\boldsymbol{\Sigma}| - \frac{1}{2}\sum_{t=1}^{n}\omega_t^{(*)}(\boldsymbol{y}_t - \boldsymbol{\alpha} - \boldsymbol{\beta}x_t)^T\boldsymbol{\Sigma}^{-1}(\boldsymbol{y}_t - \boldsymbol{\alpha} - \boldsymbol{\beta}x_t),$$

$$Q_2(\eta|\boldsymbol{\theta}^{(*)}) = n\Big\{\frac{1}{2\eta}\log\Big(\frac{1}{2c(\eta)}\Big) - \log\Gamma\Big(\frac{1}{2\eta}\Big) + \frac{1}{2c(\eta)}\Big[\psi\Big(\frac{1/\eta^{(*)}+p}{2}\Big) - \log\Big(\frac{1/\eta^{(*)}+p}{2}\Big) + \frac{1}{n}\sum_{t=1}^{n}(\log\omega_t^{(*)} - \omega_t^{(*)})\Big]\Big\},$$

where $\omega_t^{(*)} = E\{u_t|\boldsymbol{y}_t, \boldsymbol{\theta}^{(*)}\}$ are the weights ω_t defined in (8) and evaluated at $\boldsymbol{\theta} = \boldsymbol{\theta}^{(*)}$, for $t = 1, \ldots, n$. Maximizing the Q-function (A1), we obtain the iterative process defined in Equation (9).

Appendix C. ML Estimation under H_β and $H_{\alpha\beta}$

In this case $H_\beta : \boldsymbol{\beta} = \mathbf{1}$. To calculate the values of the statistics Lr, Sc and Ga, we need to estimate $\boldsymbol{\theta}$ under H_β. The EM algorithm leads to the following equations to obtain the ML estimates of $\boldsymbol{\alpha}$, $\boldsymbol{\Sigma}$ and η under H_β:

$$\tilde{\boldsymbol{\alpha}} = \frac{\sum_{t=1}^{n}\tilde{\omega}_t(\boldsymbol{y}_t - \mathbf{1}_p x_t)}{\sum_{t=1}^{n}\tilde{\omega}_t}, \qquad \tilde{\boldsymbol{\Sigma}} = \frac{1}{n}\sum_{t=1}^{n}\tilde{\omega}_t(\boldsymbol{y}_t - \tilde{\boldsymbol{\alpha}} - \mathbf{1}_p x_t)(\boldsymbol{y}_t - \tilde{\boldsymbol{\alpha}} - \mathbf{1}_p x_t)^T \tag{A2}$$

and

$$\tilde{\eta}^{-1} = \frac{2}{a + \log a - 1} + 0.0416\Big\{1 + erf\Big(0.6594\log\Big(\frac{2.1971}{a + \log a - 1}\Big)\Big)\Big\},$$

where $a = -(1/n)\sum_{t=1}^{n}(v_{t2} - v_{t1})$, with $v_{t1} = (1 + p\eta)/(1 + c(\eta)\tilde{\delta}_t)$ and $v_{t2} = \psi\Big(\frac{1+p\eta}{2\eta}\Big) - \log\Big(\frac{1+c(\eta)\tilde{\delta}_t}{2\eta}\Big)$, $\tilde{\delta}_t = (\boldsymbol{y}_t - \tilde{\boldsymbol{\alpha}} - \mathbf{1}_p x_t)^T\tilde{\boldsymbol{\Sigma}}^{-1}(\boldsymbol{y}_t - \tilde{\boldsymbol{\alpha}} - \mathbf{1}_p x_t)$, $\tilde{\omega}_t = \Big(\frac{1+\eta p}{\eta}\Big)\Big(\frac{c(\eta)}{1+c(\eta)\tilde{\delta}_t}\Big)$, for $t = 1, \ldots, n$.

It may also be of interest to test the joint hypothesis $H_{\alpha\beta} : \alpha = \mathbf{0}$, $\boldsymbol{\beta} = \mathbf{1}$. Similarly, to calculate the values of the statistics Lr, Sc and Ga, we need to estimate $\boldsymbol{\Sigma}$ and η under $H_{\alpha\beta}$. The EM algorithm leads to the following equations to obtain the ML estimates of $\boldsymbol{\Sigma}$ and η under $H_{\alpha\beta}$:

$$\tilde{\boldsymbol{\Sigma}} = \frac{1}{n}\sum_{t=1}^{n}\tilde{\omega}_t(\boldsymbol{y}_t - \mathbf{1}_p x_t)(\boldsymbol{y}_t - \mathbf{1}_p x_t)^T \tag{A3}$$

and

$$\tilde{\eta}^{-1} = \frac{2}{a + \log a - 1} + 0.0416\Big\{1 + erf\Big(0.6594\log\Big(\frac{2.1971}{a + \log a - 1}\Big)\Big)\Big\},$$

where $a = -(1/n)\sum_{t=1}^{n}(v_{t2} - v_{t1})$, with $v_{t1} = (1 + p\eta)/(1 + c(\eta)\tilde{\delta}_t)$ and $v_{t2} = \psi\Big(\frac{1+p\eta}{2\eta}\Big) - \log\Big(\frac{1+c(\eta)\tilde{\delta}_t}{2\eta}\Big)$, $\tilde{\delta}_t = (\boldsymbol{y}_t - \mathbf{1}_p x_t)^T\tilde{\boldsymbol{\Sigma}}^{-1}(\boldsymbol{y}_t - \mathbf{1}_p x_t)$, $\tilde{\omega}_t = \Big(\frac{1+\eta p}{\eta}\Big)\Big(\frac{c(\eta)}{1+c(\eta)\tilde{\delta}_t}\Big)$, for $t = 1, \ldots, n$.

Appendix D. Equality of the Score and Gradient Tests under Normality

First, let us remember that the score tests, under normality, test for mean-variance efficiency can be written as (Campbell et al. 1997) $Sc = \dfrac{\mathcal{J}_0}{1+\mathcal{J}_0/n}$, where $\mathcal{J}_0 = nb\hat{\boldsymbol{\alpha}}^T\hat{\boldsymbol{\Sigma}}^{-1}\hat{\boldsymbol{\alpha}}$, with $b = s^2/(\bar{x}^2+s^2)$, which is the corresponding Wald tests. In this case, the Gradient test takes the form of $Ga = U_\alpha^T(\tilde{\boldsymbol{\theta}})\hat{\boldsymbol{\alpha}}$, where

$$U_\alpha(\tilde{\boldsymbol{\theta}}) = \tilde{\boldsymbol{\Sigma}}^{-1}\sum_{t=1}^{n}(\boldsymbol{y}_t - \tilde{\boldsymbol{\beta}}x_t), \tag{A4}$$

$\tilde{\boldsymbol{\beta}} = \hat{\boldsymbol{\beta}} + c\hat{\boldsymbol{\alpha}}$, $\tilde{\boldsymbol{\Sigma}} = \hat{\boldsymbol{\Sigma}} + b\hat{\boldsymbol{\alpha}}\hat{\boldsymbol{\alpha}}^T$ and $c = \bar{x}/(\bar{x}^2+s^2)$; see Campbell et al. (1997) for details on these results. Then, by replacing $\sum_{t=1}^{n}(\boldsymbol{y}_t - \tilde{\boldsymbol{\beta}}x_t) = nb\hat{\boldsymbol{\alpha}}$ in (A4) and using the Sherman-Morrison formula to invert the matrix $\tilde{\boldsymbol{\Sigma}}$, we obtain

$$\begin{aligned} Ga &= nb\hat{\boldsymbol{\alpha}}^T\tilde{\boldsymbol{\Sigma}}^{-1}\hat{\boldsymbol{\alpha}} \\ &= nb\hat{\boldsymbol{\alpha}}^T(\hat{\boldsymbol{\Sigma}} + b\hat{\boldsymbol{\alpha}}\hat{\boldsymbol{\alpha}}^T)^{-1}\hat{\boldsymbol{\alpha}} \\ &= \frac{\mathcal{J}_0}{1+\mathcal{J}_0/n} \\ &= Sc. \end{aligned}$$

References

Adcock, Christopher, Martin Eling, and Nicola Loperfido. 2015. Skewed distributions in finance and actuarial science: A review. *The European Journal of Finance* 21: 1253–81. [CrossRef]

Amenc, Noel, and Veronique Le Sourd. 2003. *Portfolio Theory and Performance Analysis*. New York: John Wiley.

Barillas, Francisco, and Jay Shanken. 2018. Comparing Asset Pricing Models. *The Journal of Finance* 73: 715–54. [CrossRef]

Bao, Te, Ceer Diks, and Hao Li. 2018. A generalized CAPM model with asymmetric power distributed errors with an application to portfolio construction. *Economic Modelling* 68: 611–21. [CrossRef]

Bekaert, Geer, and Guojun Wu. 2000. Asymmetric Volatility and Risk in Equity Markets. *The Review of Financial Studies* 13: 1–42. [CrossRef]

Berk, Jonathan. 1997. Necessary conditions for the CAPM. *Journal of Economic Theory* 73: 245–57. [CrossRef]

Blattberg, Robert C., and Nicholas J. Gonedes. 1974. A comparison of the stable and student distribution as statistical models for stock prices. *Journal of Business* 47: 244–80. [CrossRef]

Bolfarine, Heleno, and Manuel Galea. 1996. On structural Comparative Calibration under a *t*-model. *Computational Statistics* 11: 63–85.

Boos, Dannis D., and Leonard A. Stefanski. 2013. *Essential Statistical Inference, Theory and Methods*. New York: Springer.

Borup, Daniel. 2019. Asset pricing model uncertainty. *Journal of Empirical Finance* 54: 166–89. [CrossRef]

Branco, Marcia D., and Dipak K. Dey. 2001. A general class of multivariate skew-elliptical distributions. *Journal of Multivariate Analysis* 79: 99–113. [CrossRef]

Brandimarte, Paolo. 2018. *An Introduction to Financial Markets: A Quantitative Approach*. Hoboken: John Wiley.

Broquet, Claude, Robert Cobbaut, Roland Gillet, and Andre van den Berg. 2004. *Gestion de Portefeuille*, 4th ed. Louvain-la-Neuve: De Boeck Université. Bruxelles.

Cademartori, David, Cecilia Romo, Richardo Campos, and Manuel Galea. 2003. Robust estimation of systematic risk using the *t*-distribution in the Chilean Stock Markets. *Applied Economics Letters* 10: 447–53. [CrossRef]

Campbell, John, Andrew Lo, and A. Craig MacKinlay. 1997. *Econometrics of Financial Markets*. Princeton: Princeton University Press.

Chamberlain, Gary. 1983. A characterization of the distributions that imply mean-variance utility functions. *Journal of Economic Theory* 29: 185–201. [CrossRef]

Chen, Joseph, Harrison Hong, and Jeremy C. Stein. 2001. Forecasting crashes: Trading volume, past returns, and conditional skewness in stock prices. *Journal of Financial Economics* 61: 345–81. [CrossRef]

Chou, Pin-Huang, and Mei-Chen Lin. 2002. Tests of international asset pricing model with and without a riskless asset. *Applied Financial Economics* 12: 873–83. [CrossRef]

Chou, Ping-Huang, and Guofu Zhou. 2006. Using Bootstrap to Test Portfolio Efficiency. *Annals of Economics and Finance* 2: 217–49.

Efron, Bradley, and Robert J. Tibshirani. 1993. *An Introduction to the Bootstrap*. New York: Chapman and Hall.

Ejara, Demissew, Alain Krapl, Thomas J. O'Brien, and Santiago Ruiz de Vargas. 2019. Local, Global, and International CAPM: For Which Countries Does Model Choice Matter ? Available online: https://ssrn.com/abstract=3023501 (accessed on 24 January 2020).

Elton, Edwin and Martin Gruber. 1995. *Modern Portfolio Theory and Investment Analysis*. New York: John Wiley.

Fama, Eugene. 1965. The behavior of stock market prices. *Journal of Business* 38: 34–105. [CrossRef]

Fama, Eegene, and Kenneth R. French. 1995. Size and book-to-market factors in earnings and returns. *Journal of Finance* 50: 131–55. [CrossRef]

Fiorentini, Gabriele, Enriques Sentana, and Giorgio Calzolari. 2003. Maximum likelihood estimation and inference in multivariate conditionally heteroscedastic dynamic regression models with Student t innovations. *Journal of Business & Economic Statistics* 21: 532–46.

Francis, Jack Clark and Dongcheol Kim. 2013. *Modern Portfolio Theory: Foundation, Analysis, and New Dvelopments*. Hoboken: John Wiley.

Galea, Manuel, Jose A. Díaz-Garcá, and Filidor Vilca. 2008. Influence diagnostics in the capital asset pricing model under elliptical distributions. *Journal of Applied Statistics* 35: 179–92. [CrossRef]

Galea, Manuel, David Cademartori, and Filidor Vilca. 2010. The structural sharpe model under t-distributions. *Journal of Applied Statistics* 37: 1979–90. [CrossRef]

Galea, Manuel, and Patricia Giménez. 2019. Local influence diagnostics for the test of mean-variance efficiency and systematic risks in the Capital Asset Pricing Model. *Statistical Papers* 60: 293–312. [CrossRef]

Gibbons, Michael, Stephen Ross, and Jay Shanken. 1989. A test of the efficiency of a given portfolio. *Econometrica* 57: 1121–53. [CrossRef]

Glabadanidis, Paskalis. 2009. Measuring the economic significance of mean-variance spanning. *The Quarterly Review of Economics and Finance* 49: 596–616. [CrossRef]

Glabadanidis, Paskalis. 2014. What Difference Fat Tails Make: A Bayesian MCMC Estimation of Empirical Asset Pricing Models. In *Bayesian Inference in the Social Sciences*. Edited by Ivan Jeliazkov and Xin-She Yang. Hoboken: John Wiley.

Glabadanidis, Paskalis. 2019. An exact test of the improvement of the minimum variance portfolio. *International Review of Finance* 19: 45–82. [CrossRef]

Hamada, Mahmoud, and Emiliano A. Valdez. 2008. CAPM and option pricing with elliptically contoured distributions. *The Journal of Risk and Insurance* 75: 387–409. [CrossRef]

Hansen, Lars Peter. 1982. Large Sample Properties of Generalized Method of Moments Estimators. *Econometrica* 50: 1029–54. [CrossRef]

Harvey, Campbell, and Guofu Zhou. 1993. International asset pricing with alternative distributional specifications. *Journal of Empirical Finance* 1: 107–31. [CrossRef]

Harvey, Campbell R., John Liechty, M. Liechty, and P. M. Müller. 2010. Portfolio selection with higher moments. *Quantitative Finance* 10: 469–85. [CrossRef]

Hodgson, Douglas, Oliver Linton, and Keith Vorkink. 2002. Testing the capital asset pricing model efficiently under elliptical symmetry: A semiparametric approach. *Journal of Applied Econometrics* 17: 617–39. [CrossRef]

Ingersoll, Jonathan. 1987. *Theory of Financial Decision Making*. Lanham: Rowman and Littlefield.

Johnson, R. Stafford. 2014. *Equity Markets and Portfolio Analysis*. Hoboken: John Wiley.

Kan, Raymond, and Guofu Zhou. 2017. Modeling Non-normality Using Multivariate t: Implications for Asset Pricing. *China Finance Review International* 7: 2–32. [CrossRef]

Lange, Kenneth L., Roderick J. Little, and Jeremy Taylor. 1989. Robust statistical modelling using the t-distribution. *Journal of the American Statistical Association* 84: 881–96.

Lee, John. 1991. A Lagrange multiplier test for GARCH models. *Economics Letters* 37: 265–71. [CrossRef]

Lemonte, Artur. 2016. *The Gradient Test: Another Likelihood-Based Test*. London: Academic Press.

Levy, Haim. 2012. *The Capital Asset Pricing Model in the 21st Century: Analytical, Empirical, and Behavioral Perspectives*. New York: Cambridge University Press.

Lintner, John. 1965. The valuation of risk assets and the selection of risky investments in stock portfolios and capital budgets. *Review of Economics and Statistics* 41: 13–37. [CrossRef]

Liu, Chuanhai, and Donald B. Rubin. 1995. ML estimation of the t distribution using EM and its extensions, ECM and ECME. *Statistica Sinica* 5: 19–39.

MacKinlay, A. Craig, and Mathew P. Richardson. 1991. Using Generalized Method of Moments to Test Mean-Variance Efficiency. *The Journal of Finance* 46: 511–27. [CrossRef]

Magnus, Jan R., and Heinz Neudecker. 2007. *Matrix Differential Calculus with Applications in Statistics and Econometrics*, 3rd ed. New York: John Wiley.

Mazzoni, Thomas. 2018. *A First Course in Quantitative Finance*. New York: Cambridge University Press.

Mitchell, Ann. 1989. The information matrix, skewness tensor and α-connections for the general multivariate elliptic distributions. *Annals of the Institute of Statistical Mathematics* 41: 289–304. [CrossRef]

Mossin, Jan. 1966. Equilibrium in capital asset market. *Econometrica* 35: 768–83. [CrossRef]

Owen, Joel, and Ramon Rabinovitch. 1983. On the class of elliptical distributions and their applications to the theory of portfolio. *The Journal of Finance* 38: 745–52. [CrossRef]

Paula, Gilberto, Victor Leiva, Michelli Barros, and Shuangzhe Liu. 2011. Robust statistical modeling using the Birnbaum-Saunders−t distribution applied to insurance. *Applied Stochastic Models in Business and Industry* 28: 16–34. [CrossRef]

Pereiro, Luis E. 2010. The beta dilemma in emerging markets. *Journal of Applied Corporate Finance* 22: 110–22. [CrossRef]

Pinheiro, Jose C., Chuanhai Liu, and Ying Nian Wu. 2001. Efficient algorithms for robust estimation in linear mixed-effects models using the multivariate t distribution. *Journal of Computational and Graphical Statistics* 10: 249–76. [CrossRef]

Sharpe, William. 1964. Capital asset prices: A theory of markets equilibrium under conditions of risk. *Journal of Finance* 19: 425–42.

Shoham, Shy. 2002. Robust clustering by deterministic agglomeration EM of mixtures of multivariate t distribution. *Pattern Recognition* 35: 1127–42. [CrossRef]

Song, Peter. X. -K., Peng Zhang, and Annie Qu. 2007. Maximum likelihood inference in robust linear mixed-effects models using the multivariate t distributions. *Statistica Sinica* 17: 929–43.

Sutradhar, Brajendra C. 1993. Score test for the covariance matrix of elliptical t-distribution. *Journal of Multivariate Analysis* 46: 1–12. [CrossRef]

Terrell, George. 2002. The Gradient Statistic. *Computing Science and Statistics* 34: 206–15.

Vorkink, Keith. 2003. Return distributions and improved tests of asset pricing models. *The Review of Financial Studies* 16: 845–74. [CrossRef]

Waldman, Donald M. 1983. A note on algebraic equivalence of White's test and a variation of the Godfrey/Breusch-Pagan test for heteroscedasticity. *Economics Letters* 13: 197–200. [CrossRef]

White, Halbert. 1980. A Heteroskedasticity-Consistent Covariance Matrix Estimator and a Direct Test for Heteroskedasticity. *Econometrica* 48: 817–38. [CrossRef]

Xie, Feng-Chang, Bo-Cheng Wei, and Jin-Guan Lin. 2007. Case-deletion Influence Measures for the Data from Multivariate t Distributions. *Journal of Applied Statistics* 34: 907–21. [CrossRef]

Zhou, Guofu 1993. Asset-pricing test under alternative distributions. *The Journal of Finance* 48: 1927–42. [CrossRef]

Journal of
Risk and Financial Management

MDPI

Reply

Reply to "Remarks on Bank Competition and Convergence Dynamics"

Maria Karadima [1,*] and Helen Louri [1,2]

1. Department of Economics, Athens University of Economics and Business, 76 Patission Street, GR-10434 Athens, Greece; elouri@aueb.gr
2. European Institute/Hellenic Observatory, London School of Economics, Houghton Street, London WC2A 2AE, UK

* Correspondence: karadimam@aueb.gr

Received: 10 June 2020; Accepted: 11 June 2020; Published: 15 June 2020

Abstract: In this reply, we provide detailed answers to the remarks made by Tsionas on the use of stochastic frontier-based measures of market power in a part of our empirical study, which examines the fragmentation and convergence dynamics of market power, concentration and credit risk in the euro area banking sector during 2005–2017. Our answers clarify all the issues raised by Tsionas and show that the only challenging, in our opinion, point of the criticism has been based on a hypothesis that does not hold in the case of our study.

Keywords: Lerner index; stochastic frontiers; convergence analysis

---

1. Introduction

Recently, Tsionas (2020, MT) made some remarks regarding the use of stochastic frontier-based measures of market power in a part of our empirical study (Karadima and Louri 2020, KL), which examines the evolution, as well as the fragmentation and convergence dynamics, of market power, concentration and credit risk in the euro area banking sector during 2005–2017. To facilitate the comparison of the arguments of both sides, our answers are provided below in the same order as MT's remarks.

The present reply is organized as follows. In Section 2, we describe the context in which the term "profit maximization" is used in our research. In Section 3, we show that the calculation of the Lerner index, following the Kumbhakar et al. (2012) stochastic frontier methodology, does not involve the direct estimation of a translog cost function per se, but only the estimation of its partial derivative with respect to output. In Section 4, we explain why our basic equation cannot be considered as equivalent to the equation proposed by MT. In response to a general comment on output price, we take the opportunity in Section 5 to underline, using our own equations, one of the biggest innovations from Kumbhakar et al. (2012). As some auxiliary calculations had not been included for brevity in our research, we illustrate in Section 6 how we arrived at our Equation (5), starting from our Equation (4). In Section 7, we provide our answers to the criticism on the use of a single-output cost function. Finally, we show in Section 8 that the MT's criticism on our convergence analysis has been based on the incorrect hypothesis of the use of individual-bank data. Since our analysis has actually been based on country-level aggregated data, we consider that the criticism at this point is not relevant.

2. Calculation of a Lerner Index following a Stochastic Frontier Methodology

2.1. Point of Criticism

"KL state incorrectly that ... this assumption is, of course, fairly weak". (Page 1 of MT's remarks)

2.2. *Answer*

Our reference to a profit maximization behavioral assumption is exclusively related to the calculation of the Lerner index per se. This should not be confused with the cost minimization behavioral assumption, which is behind the estimation of a cost function.

As it is well known in the literature, the calculation of the Lerner index is based on the assumption of static profit maximization, hence the mark-up should always have to be non-negative. However, as Kumbhakar et al. (2012, p. 113) note, when the marginal cost (*MC*) is calculated through the estimation of a cost function there is no guarantee that it would take a non-negative value for each observation. In contrast, the Kumbhakar et al. (2012) stochastic frontier methodology, which we follow in our research, rectifies this problem by always producing non-negative values of the Lerner index.

3. The Reasons for Not Estimating the Translog Cost Function

3.1. *Point of Criticism*

> *"Clearly, KL did not estimate a cost function as claimed … half-normally distributed […] (page 9)". (Page 2 of MT's remarks)*

3.2. *Answer*

The above comment is apparently based on our phrase "so we derive its value from the estimation of the following translog cost function" (see Page 7 of our research), which should have rather been expressed in a more general manner (e.g., "so the most common approach is to derive its value from the estimation of a translog cost function"), since our only aim there was to show the steps that should have been followed if we had adopted the traditional approach.

In this context, we first state that the basis of our Lerner index estimations is our Equation (7) (see Figure 1).

Taking the partial derivative in (3), we get:

$$\frac{\partial lnTC_{it}}{\partial lnQ_{it}} = \alpha_Q + \alpha_{QQ} lnQ_{it} + \sum_{k=1}^{2} \alpha_{Qk} \ln\left(\frac{W_{k,it}}{W_{3,it}}\right) + \alpha_{EQ} lnE_{it} + \alpha_{TQ} T \quad (6)$$

Substituting (6) into (5), we get:

$$\frac{TR_{it}}{TC_{it}} = \alpha_Q + \alpha_{QQ} lnQ_{it} + \sum_{k=1}^{2} \alpha_{Qk} \ln\left(\frac{W_{k,it}}{W_{3,it}}\right) + \alpha_{EQ} lnE_{it} + \alpha_{TQ} T + v_{it} + u_{it} \quad (7)$$

Figure 1. A part of the Lerner index calculation process.

Second, we would like to emphasize that the Kumbhakar et al. (2012) stochastic frontier methodology does not require the estimation of a translog cost function per se, but only the estimation of its partial derivative with respect to output. As shown in Figure 1, we arrived at our Equation (7) after having taken the partial derivative of the translog cost function and "fitting" it into our Equation (5). This explains the reason why we have not included in our research any description at all, either in an equation or in a descriptive text form, of the calculation of marginal cost (*MC*).

4. Differences between Our Equation (7) and the Equation (7) in MT's Remarks

4.1. *Point of Criticism*

> *"It is not clear why one would want … is equivalent (up to statistical noise) to our Equation (7)". (Page 2 of MT's remarks)*

4.2. Answer

First, regarding the question why the Lerner index calculation is based on our Equation (7) (see Figure 2), instead of having been based on the cost function (our Equation (3)), the answer is that the direct estimation of our Equation (3) could not provide the residual term u (see our Equation (7)), which captures the mark-up. We have clearly stated that the methodology we have followed is that of Kumbhakar et al. (2012). The calculation of the residual term u is a very essential task in the implementation of their stochastic frontier methodology.

$$\frac{TR_{it}}{TC_{it}} = \alpha_Q + \alpha_{QQ} lnQ_{it} + \sum_{k=1}^{2} \alpha_{Qk} \ln\left(\frac{W_{k,it}}{W_{3,it}}\right) + \alpha_{EQ} lnE_{it} + \alpha_{TQ} T + v_{it} + u_{it} \quad (7)$$

Figure 2. KL's basic equation in the Lerner index calculation process.

Second, regarding the equation $\Theta = u/E_{CQ}$ (mentioned in the above MT's remark), we confirm that we have indeed used the "return-to-dollar" specification in our Equation (7) in order to calculate the term u, through which we first calculated Θ and then L (please note that the equation $\Theta = u/E_{CQ}$, mentioned in the above remark, is exactly the same as our Equation 8, although using different notation).

To summarize, we followed the steps below:

a. We defined the translog cost function (our Equation (3)).
b. We "fitted" its first derivative (our Equation (6)) into our Equation (5) in order to finally arrive at our Equation (7).
c. We estimated our Equation (7) to derive the value of the residual u, which captures the mark-up.
d. We used the value of u to calculate Θ and L.

All the above steps have been performed following the Kumbhakar et al. (2012) stochastic frontier methodology.

The alternative procedure proposed in the criticism (as we understand it) follows the steps below:

a. It estimates the translog cost function in order to calculate E_{cq}, where $E_{cq} = (\partial lnTC)/(\partial lnQ)$.
b. Based on the estimated value of Ecq, derived in step (a), it estimates either Equation (6) (in the criticism) in order to derive directly the value of L, or, alternatively, it estimates Equation (7) (in the criticism) in order to first derive Θ and then L.

First, it is clear that the alternative approach proposed by MT is the usual approach followed in the empirical literature.

Second, in response to the MT's comment regarding the statistical noise, we clarify that in the methodology of Kumbhakar et al. (2012) the term u is uniquely related to the mark-up. For further details about the term u, the reader can refer to Kumbhakar et al. (2012, p. 115). Regarding the statistical noise, it is captured by v, which is a symmetric two-sided noise term (Kumbhakar et al. (2012, p. 114)). We also take the opportunity here to explain that although the term u is calculated in a way that resembles the estimation of cost inefficiency in a cost frontier model, in Kumbhakar et al. (2012) the term u is uniquely related to the mark-up, leading Kumbhakar et al. (2012) to consider their approach as a non-standard application of stochastic frontier models. More precisely, their approach is not a cost frontier model, but a revenue share to total cost (TR/TC) frontier model. The bigger the distance between the observed TR/TC value from the minimum level it can reach (the frontier), the bigger the mark-up (and the market power).

5. The Innovation of Kumbhakar, Baardsen and Lien with Respect to the Output Price

5.1. Point of Criticism

"Moreover, KL use as a proxy for Q … is often not available". (Page 2 of MT's remarks)

5.2. Answer

Although Kumbhakar et al. (2012, p. 110) describe first the problem that the marginal cost (MC) is usually not observable, pointing out additional weaknesses of the traditional approaches in later pages, one of their innovations is indeed related to output price. As it can easily be seen in Figure 2, the estimation of our Equation (7) does not require the availability of separate information on output price, since information on total revenue is sufficient (Kumbhakar et al. 2012, p. 116).

6. Description of Some Auxiliary Equations

6.1. Point of Criticism

"Moreover, KL write that … in view of our (6) and (7)". (Page 2 of MT's remarks)

6.2. Answer

The fact that both P and $r = TR/TC$ are on the left side of our Equations (4) and (5), respectively, in no way means that $P = r$. In the Figure 3 below, we illustrate how we arrived at our Equation (5), starting from our Equation (4). In our paper, we have not included for brevity ("after doing some mathematics") the auxiliary calculations presented in Figure 3 (in which, for simplicity, we have not used subscripts).

$$P \geq MC \equiv \frac{\partial TC}{\partial Q} \qquad (4)$$

If we multiply both terms of (4) by Q/TC, we get:

$$P\frac{Q}{TC} \geq \frac{\partial TC}{\partial Q}\frac{Q}{TC} \qquad (4a)$$

from which we get

$$\frac{PQ}{TC} \geq \frac{\partial lnTC}{\partial lnQ} \qquad (4b)$$

From (4b) we get:

$$\frac{TR}{TC} = \frac{\partial lnTC}{\partial lnQ} + u + v \qquad (5)$$

where TR indicates total revenues.

Figure 3. Description of the intermediate steps between Equations (4) and (5).

7. Comments on the Use of a Single-Output Cost Function

7.1. Point of Criticism

"It must also be pointed out that … KL's (7) is better than (9)". (Pages 2–3 of MT's remarks)

7.2. Answer

The use of a single output (total assets) in our research is due to constrains on data availability with respect to the sub-period 2005–2010. For this reason, we preferred the use of total assets as our single aggregate output factor, following the most common strand in the empirical banking literature (e.g., Amidu and Wolf 2013; Angelini and Cetorelli 2003; Anginer et al. 2014; Berger et al. 2009; Carbó et al. 2009; Cruz-García et al. 2017; De-Ramon et al. 2018; Fernández and Garza-García 2015; Fernández de Guevara et al. 2007; Fu et al. 2014; Fungacova and Weill 2013; Leroy and Lucotte 2017; Liu and Wilson 2013; Sanya and Gaertner 2012; Turk-Ariss 2010; Weill 2013). In the opposite case, we would have preferred the use of an aggregated weighted-average Lerner index (e.g., Kick and Prieto 2015), as this could fit better to the goals of our study.

Regarding the remark on the use of the term u, see our answer in Section 4.

8. Convergence Analysis with Respect to Market Power

8.1. Point of Criticism

"However, there is an additional mistake … as they are all negative!". (Pages 3–4 of MT's remarks)

8.2. Answer

It is clear that the criticism has been based on the incorrect hypothesis that the underlying dataset of our Equation (14) contains raw data (i.e., a Lerner index for each bank).

Actually, the underlying dataset of our Equation (14) contains weighted data (in terms of total assets), which have been aggregated at the country level. The index ***i*** in Figure 4 explicitly refers to countries, not to individual banks.

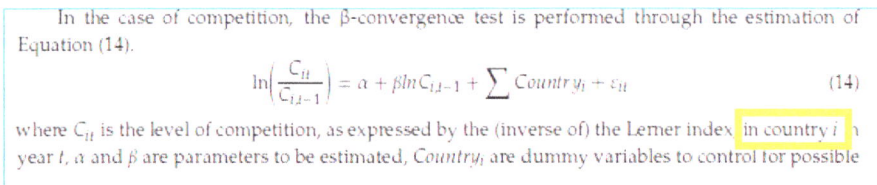

In the case of competition, the β-convergence test is performed through the estimation of Equation (14).

$$\ln\left(\frac{C_{it}}{C_{i,t-1}}\right) = \alpha + \beta \ln C_{i,t-1} + \sum Country_i + \varepsilon_{it} \tag{14}$$

where C_{it} is the level of competition, as expressed by the (inverse of) the Lerner index in country i in year t, α and β are parameters to be estimated, $Country_i$ are dummy variables to control for possible

Figure 4. The β-convergence test with respect to competition.

Besides, it is clear that Section 7 in our research investigates the existence of β-convergence (with respect to competition) of countries belonging to three euro area country groups (all 19 countries, core countries, and periphery countries, respectively). There is nowhere any reference to convergence of individual banks with respect to competition.

Based on the above, we consider that the criticism on our convergence analysis is not relevant.

Funding: Financial assistance from the Research Centre of the Athens University of Economics and Business.

Conflicts of Interest: The authors declare no conflict of interest.

References

Amidu, Mohammed, and Simon Wolf. 2013. Does bank competition and diversification lead to greater stability? Evidence from emerging markets. *Review of Development Finance* 3: 152–66. [CrossRef]

Angelini, Paolo, and Nicola Cetorelli. 2003. The Effects of Regulatory Reform on Competition in the Banking Industry. *Journal of Money, Credit and Banking* 35: 663–84. [CrossRef]

Anginer, Deniz, Asli Demirguc-Kunt, and Min Zhu. 2014. How does competition affect bank systemic risk? *Journal of Financial Intermediation* 23: 1–26. [CrossRef]

Berger, Allen, Leora Klapper, and Rima Turk-Ariss. 2009. Bank competition and financial stability. *Journal of Financial Services Research* 35: 99–118. [CrossRef]

Carbó, Santiago, David Humphrey, Joaquín Maudos, and Philip Molyneux. 2009. Cross-country comparisons of competition and pricing power in European banking. *Journal of International Money and Finance* 28: 115–34. [CrossRef]

Cruz-García, Paula, Juan Fernández de Guevara, and Joaquín Maudos. 2017. The evolution of market power in European banking. *Finance Research Letters* 23: 257–62. [CrossRef]

De-Ramon, Sebastian, William Francis, and Michael Straughan. 2018. *Bank Competition and Stability in the United Kingdom*. Staff Working Paper No. 748. London: Bank of England.

Fernández, Raúl Osvalso, and Jesús Garza-García. 2015. The relationship between bank competition and financial stability: A case study of the Mexican banking industry. *Ensayos Revista de Economía* 34: 103–20.

Fernández de Guevara, Juan, Joaquín Maudos, and Francisco Pérez. 2007. Integration and competition in the European financial markets. *Journal of International Money and Finance* 26: 26–45. [CrossRef]

Fu, Xiaoqing (Maggie), Yongjia (Rebecca) Lin, and Philip Molyneux. 2014. Bank Competition and Financial Stability in Asia Pacific. *Journal of Banking and Finance* 38: 64–77. [CrossRef]

Fungacova, Zuzana, and Laurent Weill. 2013. Does Competition Influence Bank Failures? Evidence from Russia. *Economics of Transition* 21: 301–22. [CrossRef]

Karadima, Maria, and Helen Louri. 2020. Bank Competition and Credit Risk in Euro Area Banking: Fragmentation and Convergence Dynamics. *Journal of Risk and Financial Management* 13: 57. [CrossRef]

Kick, Thomas, and Esteban Prieto. 2015. Bank Risk Taking and Competition: Evidence from Regional Banking Markets. *Review of Finance* 19: 1185–222. [CrossRef]

Kumbhakar, Subal C., Sjur Baardsen, and Gudbrand Lien. 2012. A new method for estimating market power with an application to Norwegian sawmilling. *Review of Industrial Organization* 40: 109–29. [CrossRef]

Leroy, Aurélien, and Yannick Lucotte. 2017. Is there a competition-stability trade-off in European banking? *Journal of International Financial Markets, Institutions & Money* 46: 199–215.

Liu, Hong, and John Wilson. 2013. Competition and risk in Japanese banking. *The European Journal of Finance* 19: 1–18. [CrossRef]

Sanya, Sarah, and Matthew Gaertner. 2012. *Competition in the EAC Banking System*. Working Paper No. 12/32. Washington, DC: International Monetary Fund.

Tsionas, Mike. 2020. Remarks on Bank Competition and Convergence Dynamics. *Journal of Risk and Financial Management* 13: 101. [CrossRef]

Turk-Ariss, Rima. 2010. On the Implication of Market Power in Banking: Evidence from Developing Countries. *Journal of Banking and Finance* 34: 765–75. [CrossRef]

Weill, Laurent. 2013. Bank competition in the EU: How has it evolved? *Journal of International Financial Markets, Institutions and Money* 26: 100–12. [CrossRef]

Journal of
Risk and Financial Management

MDPI

Article

Ridge Type Shrinkage Estimation of Seemingly Unrelated Regressions And Analytics of Economic and Financial Data from "Fragile Five" Countries

Bahadır Yüzbaşı [1,*] and S. Ejaz Ahmed [2]

[1] Department of Econometrics, Inonu University, 44280 Malatya, Turkey
[2] Department of Mathematics and Statistics, Brock University, St. Catharines, ON L2S 3A1, Canada; sahmed5@brocku.ca
* Correspondence: b.yzb@hotmail.com

Received: 26 April 2020; Accepted: 16 June 2020; Published: 18 June 2020

Abstract: In this paper, we suggest improved estimation strategies based on preliminarily test and shrinkage principles in a seemingly unrelated regression model when explanatory variables are affected by multicollinearity. To that end, we split the vector regression coefficient of each equation into two parts: one includes the coefficient vector for the main effects, and the other is a vector for nuisance effects, which could be close to zero. Therefore, two competing models per equation of the system regression model are obtained: one includes all the regression of coefficients (full model); the other (sub model) includes only the coefficients of the main effects based on the auxiliary information. The preliminarily test estimation improves the estimation procedure if there is evidence that the vector of nuisance parameters does not provide a useful contribution to the model. The shrinkage estimation method shrinks the full model estimator in the direction of the sub-model estimator. We conduct a Monte Carlo simulation study in order to examine the relative performance of the suggested estimation strategies. More importantly, we apply our methodology based on the preliminarily test and the shrinkage estimations to analyse economic data by investigating the relationship between foreign direct investment and several economic variables in the "Fragile Five" countries between 1983 and 2018.

Keywords: shrinkage estimator; seemingly unrelated regression model; multicollinearity; ridge regression

---

1. Introduction

A seemingly unrelated regression (SUR) system, originally proposed by Zellner (1962), comprises multiple individual regression equations that are correlated with each other. Zellner's idea was to improve estimation efficiency by combining several equations into a single system. Contrary to SUR estimation, the ordinary least squares (OLS) estimation loses its efficiency and will not produce best linear unbiased estimates (BLUE) when the error terms between the equations in the system are correlated. This method has a wide range of applications in economic and financial data and other similar areas (Shukur 2002; Srivastava and Giles 1987; Zellner 1962). For example, Dincer and Wang (2011) investigated the effects of ethnic diversity on economic growth. Williams (2013) studied the effects of financial crises on banks. Since it considers multiple related equations simultaneously, a generalized least squares (GLS) estimator is used to take into account the effect of errors in these equations. Barari and Kundu (2019) reexamined the role of the Federal Reserve in triggering the recent housing crisis with a vector autoregression (VAR) model, which is a special case of the SUR model with lagged variables and deterministic terms as common regressors. One might also consider the correlations of explanatory variables in SUR models. Alkhamisi and Shukur (2008) and Zeebari et al. (2012, 2018) considered a modified version of the ridge estimation proposed by

Hoerl and Kennard (1970) for these models. Alkhamisi (2010) proposed two SUR-type estimators by combining the SUR ridge regression and the restricted least squares methods. These recent studies demonstrated that the ridge SUR estimation is superior to classical estimation methods in the presence of multicollinearity. Srivastava and Wan (2002) considered the Stein-rule estimators from James and Stein (1961) in SUR models with two equations.

In our study, we consider preliminarily test and shrinkage estimation, more information on which can be found in Ahmed (2014), in ridge-type SUR models when the explanatory variables are affected by multicollinearity. In a previous paper, we combined penalized estimations in an optimal way to define shrinkage estimation (Ahmed and Yüzbaşı 2016). Gao et al. (2017) suggested the use of the weighted ridge regression model for post-selection shrinkage estimation. Yüzbaşı et al. (2020) gave detailed information about generalized ridge regression for a number of shrinkage estimation methods. Srivastava and Wan (2002) and Arashi and Roozbeh (2015) considered Stein-rule estimation for SUR models. Erdugan and Akdeniz (2016) proposed a restricted feasible SUR estimate of the regression coefficients.

The organization of this paper is as follows: In Section 2, we briefly review the SUR model and some estimation techniques, including the ridge type. In Section 3, we introduce our new estimation methodology. A Monte Carlo simulation is conducted in Section 4, and our economic data are analysed in Section 5. Finally, some concluding remarks are given in Section 6.

2. Methodology

Consider the following model:

$$\mathbf{Y}_i = \mathbf{X}_i\boldsymbol{\beta}_i + \boldsymbol{\varepsilon}_i, i = 1, 2, \ldots, M, \tag{1}$$

the ith equation of an M seemingly unrelated regression equation with T number of observations per equation. $\mathbf{Y}_i$ is a $T \times 1$ vector of T observations; $\mathbf{X}_i$ is a $T \times p_i$ full column rank matrix of T observations on p_i regressors; and $\boldsymbol{\beta}_i$ is a $p_i \times 1$ vector of unknown parameters.

Equation (1) can be rewritten as follows:

$$\mathbf{Y} = \mathbf{X}\boldsymbol{\beta} + \boldsymbol{\varepsilon}, \tag{2}$$

where $\mathbf{Y} = \left(\mathbf{Y}_1', \mathbf{Y}_2', \ldots, \mathbf{Y}_M'\right)'$ is the vector of responses and $\boldsymbol{\varepsilon} = \left(\boldsymbol{\varepsilon}_1', \boldsymbol{\varepsilon}_2', \ldots, \boldsymbol{\varepsilon}_M'\right)'$ is the vector of disturbances with dimension $TM \times 1$, $\mathbf{X} = diag\left(\mathbf{X}_1, \mathbf{X}_2, \ldots, \mathbf{X}_M\right)$ of dimension $TM \times p$, and $\boldsymbol{\beta} = \left(\boldsymbol{\beta}_1', \boldsymbol{\beta}_2', \ldots, \boldsymbol{\beta}_M'\right)'$ of dimension $p \times 1$, for $p = \sum_{i=1}^{M} p_i$.

The disturbances vector $\boldsymbol{\varepsilon}$ satisfies the properties:

$$E(\boldsymbol{\varepsilon}) = \mathbf{0}$$

and:

$$E(\boldsymbol{\varepsilon}\boldsymbol{\varepsilon}') = \begin{bmatrix} \sigma_{11}\mathbf{I} & \ldots & \sigma_{1M}\mathbf{I} \\ \vdots & \ddots & \\ \sigma_{M1}\mathbf{I} & \ldots & \sigma_{MM}\mathbf{I} \end{bmatrix} = \boldsymbol{\Sigma} \otimes \mathbf{I},$$

where $\boldsymbol{\Sigma} = [\sigma_{ij}], i, j = 1, 2, \ldots, M$ is an $M \times M$ positive definite symmetric matrix, $\otimes$ stands for the Kronecker product, and $\mathbf{I}$ is an identity matrix of order of $T \times T$. Following Greene (2019), we assume strict exogeneity of $\mathbf{X}_i$,

$$E\left[\boldsymbol{\varepsilon} | \mathbf{X}_1, \mathbf{X}_2, \ldots, \mathbf{X}_M\right] = \mathbf{0},$$

and homoscedasticity:

$$E\left[\boldsymbol{\varepsilon}_i\boldsymbol{\varepsilon}_i' | \mathbf{X}_1, \mathbf{X}_2, \ldots, \mathbf{X}_M\right] = \sigma_{ii}\mathbf{I}.$$

Therefore, it is assumed that disturbances are uncorrelated across observations, that is,

$$E\left[\varepsilon_{it}\varepsilon_{js} | \mathbf{X}_1, \mathbf{X}_2, \ldots, \mathbf{X}_M\right] = \sigma_{ij}, \text{ if } t = s \text{ and } 0 \text{ otherwise},$$

and it is assumed that disturbances are correlated across equations, that is,

$$E\left[\varepsilon_i\varepsilon_j'|\mathbf{X}_1,\mathbf{X}_2,\ldots,\mathbf{X}_M\right] = \sigma_{ij}\mathbf{I}.$$

The OLS and GLS estimator of model (2) are thus given as:

$$\widehat{\beta}^{\mathrm{OLS}} = (\mathbf{X}'\mathbf{X})^{-1}\mathbf{X}'\mathbf{Y}$$

and:

$$\widehat{\beta}^{\mathrm{GLS}} = (\mathbf{X}'(\mathbf{\Sigma}^{-1}\otimes\mathbf{I})\mathbf{X})^{-1}\mathbf{X}'(\mathbf{\Sigma}^{-1}\otimes\mathbf{I})\mathbf{Y}.$$

$\widehat{\beta}^{\mathrm{OLS}}$ simply consists of the OLS estimators computed separately from each equation and omits the correlations between equation, as can be seen in Kuan (2004). Hence, it should use the GLS estimator when correlations exist among equations. However, the true covariance matrix $\mathbf{\Sigma}$ is generally unknown. The solution for this problem is a feasible generalized least squares (FGLS) estimation, which uses covariance matrix $\widehat{\mathbf{\Sigma}}$ of $\mathbf{\Sigma}$ in the estimation of GLS. In many cases, the residual covariance matrix is calculated by:

$$\sigma_{ij} = \frac{\widehat{\varepsilon}_i'\widehat{\varepsilon}_j}{T - max(p_i, p_j)},\ i,j = 1,\ldots,M,$$

where $\widehat{\varepsilon}_i = \mathbf{Y}_i - \mathbf{X}_i\widehat{\beta}_i$ represents residuals from the ith equation and $\widehat{\beta}_i$ may be the OLS or ridge regression (RR) estimation such that $(\mathbf{X}_i'\mathbf{X}_i + \lambda\mathbf{I})^{-1}\mathbf{X}_i'\mathbf{Y}_i$ with the tuning parameter $\lambda \geq 0$. Note that we use the RR solution to estimate $\mathbf{\Sigma}$ in our numerical studies because we assume that two or more explanatory variables in each equation are linearly related. Therefore, $\widehat{\mathbf{\Omega}} = \widehat{\mathbf{\Sigma}}\otimes\mathbf{I}$, the FGLS of the SUR system, is:

$$\widehat{\beta}^{\mathrm{FGLS}} = (\mathbf{X}'\widehat{\mathbf{\Omega}}^{-1}\mathbf{X})^{-1}\mathbf{X}'\widehat{\mathbf{\Omega}}^{-1}\mathbf{Y}.$$

By following Srivastava and Giles (1987) and Zeebari et al. (2012), we first transform Equation (2) by using the following transformations, in order to retain the information included in the correlation matrix of cross equation errors:

$$\mathbf{Y}_* = \left(\widehat{\mathbf{\Sigma}}^{-1/2}\otimes\mathbf{I}\right)\mathbf{Y}, \mathbf{X}_* = \left(\widehat{\mathbf{\Sigma}}^{-1/2}\otimes\mathbf{I}\right)\mathbf{X} \text{ and } \varepsilon_* = \left(\widehat{\mathbf{\Sigma}}^{-1/2}\otimes\mathbf{I}\right)\varepsilon.$$

Hence, Model (2) turns into:

$$\mathbf{Y}_* = \mathbf{X}_*\beta + \varepsilon_*. \tag{3}$$

The spectral decomposition of the symmetric matrix $\mathbf{X}_*'\mathbf{X}_*$ is $\mathbf{X}_*'\mathbf{X}_* = \mathbf{P\Lambda P}'$ with $\mathbf{PP}' = \mathbf{I}$. Model (3) can then be written as:

$$\begin{aligned}\mathbf{Y}_* &= \mathbf{X}_*\mathbf{PP}'\beta + \varepsilon_* \\ &= \mathbf{Z}\alpha + \varepsilon_*,\end{aligned} \tag{4}$$

with $\mathbf{Z} = \mathbf{X}_*\mathbf{P}$, $\alpha = \mathbf{P}'\beta$ and $\mathbf{Z}'\mathbf{Z} = \mathbf{P}'\mathbf{X}_*'\mathbf{X}_*\mathbf{P} = \mathbf{\Lambda}$, so that $\mathbf{\Lambda}$ is a diagonal matrix of eigenvalues and $\mathbf{P}$ is a matrix whose columns are eigenvectors of $\mathbf{X}_*'\mathbf{X}_*$.

The OLS estimator of model (4) is:

$$\widehat{\alpha}^{\mathrm{OLS}} = (\mathbf{Z}'\mathbf{Z})^{-1}\mathbf{Z}'\mathbf{Y}_*.$$

The least squares estimates of β in model (2) can be obtained by an inverse linear transformation as:

$$\widehat{\beta}^{\mathrm{OLS}} = (\mathbf{P}')^{-1}\widehat{\alpha}^{\mathrm{OLS}} = \mathbf{P}\widehat{\alpha}^{\mathrm{OLS}}. \tag{5}$$

Furthermore, by following Alkhamisi and Shukur (2008), the full model ridge SUR regression parameter estimation is:

$$\widehat{\alpha}^{\mathrm{RR}} = (\mathbf{Z}'\mathbf{Z}+\mathbf{K})^{-1}\mathbf{Z}'\mathbf{Y}_*, \tag{6}$$

where $\mathbf{K} = diag(\mathbf{K}_1, \mathbf{K}_2, \ldots, \mathbf{K}_M)$, $\mathbf{K}_i = diag(k_{i1}, k_{i2}, \ldots, k_{ip_i})$ and $k_{ij} = \frac{1}{\left(\widehat{\alpha}^{\mathrm{OLS}}\right)^2_{ij}} > 0$ for $i = 1, 2, \ldots, M$ and $j = 1, 2, \ldots, p_i$.

Now let us assume that uncertain non-sample prior information (UNPI) on the vector of β parameters is available, either from previous studies, expert knowledge, or researcher's experience. This information might be of use for the estimation of parameters, in order to improve the quality of the estimators when the sample data have a low quality or may not be reliable Ahmed (2014). It is assumed that the UNPI on the vector of parameters will be restricted by the equation for Model (2),

$$\mathbf{R}\beta = \mathbf{r}, \tag{7}$$

where $\mathbf{R} = diag(\mathbf{R}_1, \mathbf{R}_2, \ldots, \mathbf{R}_M)$, $\mathbf{R}_i, i = 1, \ldots, M$ is a known $m_i \times p_i$ matrix of rank $m_i < p_i$ and $\mathbf{r}$ is a known $\sum_i^M m_i \times 1$ vector. In order to use restriction (7) in Equation (2), we transform it as follows:

$$\mathbf{R}\mathbf{P}\mathbf{P}'\beta = \mathbf{H}\alpha = \mathbf{r}, \tag{8}$$

where $\mathbf{H} = \mathbf{R}\mathbf{P}$ and $\alpha = \mathbf{P}'\beta$, which is defined above. Hence, the restricted ridge SUR regression estimation is obtained from the following objective function:

$$\begin{aligned}
\widetilde{\alpha}^{\mathrm{RR}} &= \arg\min_{\alpha} \left\{ (\mathbf{Y}_* - \mathbf{Z}\alpha)'(\mathbf{Y}_* - \mathbf{Z}\alpha) \right\} \text{ w.r.t } \mathbf{H}\alpha = \mathbf{r} \text{ and } \alpha\mathbf{K}\alpha' \leq \tau^2, \\
&= \widehat{\alpha}^{\mathrm{RR}} - \mathbf{Z}_{\mathbf{K}}^{-1}\mathbf{H}'(\mathbf{H}\mathbf{Z}_{\mathbf{K}}^{-1}\mathbf{H}')^{-1}(\mathbf{H}\widehat{\alpha}^{\mathrm{RR}} - \mathbf{r}),
\end{aligned} \tag{9}$$

where $\mathbf{Z}_{\mathbf{K}} = (\mathbf{Z}'\mathbf{Z} + \mathbf{K})$.

Theorem 1. *The risks of $\widehat{\alpha}^{\mathrm{RR}}$ and $\widetilde{\alpha}^{\mathrm{RR}}$ are given by:*

$$\begin{aligned}
R\left(\widehat{\alpha}^{\mathrm{RR}};\alpha\right) &= tr\left[(\Lambda+\mathbf{K})^{-1}\Lambda(\Lambda+\mathbf{K})^{-1}\right] + \alpha'\mathbf{K}'(\Lambda+\mathbf{K})^{-2}\mathbf{K}\alpha, \\
R\left(\widetilde{\alpha}^{\mathrm{RR}};\alpha\right) &= tr\left[(\Lambda+\mathbf{K})^{-1}\left(\Lambda - \mathbf{H}'\left(\mathbf{H}\Lambda^{-1}\mathbf{H}'\right)^{-1}\mathbf{H}\right)(\Lambda+\mathbf{K})^{-1}\right] \\
&+ \alpha'\mathbf{K}'(\Lambda+\mathbf{K})^{-2}\mathbf{K}\alpha + \delta'\Lambda(\Lambda+\mathbf{K})^{-2}\Lambda\delta \\
&+ 2\delta'\Lambda(\Lambda+\mathbf{K})^{-2}\mathbf{K}\alpha,
\end{aligned}$$

where $\delta = \Lambda^{-1}\mathbf{H}'\left(\mathbf{H}\Lambda^{-1}\mathbf{H}'\right)^{-1}(\mathbf{H}\alpha - \mathbf{r})$.

Proof. For the risk of the estimators $\widehat{\alpha}^{\mathrm{RR}}$ and $\widetilde{\alpha}^{\mathrm{RR}}$, we consider:

$$R(\alpha^*;\alpha) = E\left[(\alpha^* - \alpha)'(\alpha^* - \alpha)\right] = tr\left[\boldsymbol{M}(\alpha^*)\right],$$

where α^* is the one of the estimators $\widehat{\alpha}^{\mathrm{RR}}$ and $\widetilde{\alpha}^{\mathrm{RR}}$ and $\boldsymbol{M}(\alpha^*) = E\left[(\alpha^* - \alpha)(\alpha^* - \alpha)'\right]$. Since:

$$\begin{aligned}
\widehat{\alpha}^{\mathrm{RR}} &= (\Lambda+\mathbf{K})^{-1}\mathbf{Z}'\mathbf{Y}_* \\
&= (\Lambda+\mathbf{K})^{-1}\Lambda\widehat{\alpha}^{\mathrm{OLS}} \\
&= \left[\Lambda^{-1}(\Lambda+\mathbf{K})\right]^{-1}\widehat{\alpha}^{\mathrm{OLS}} \\
&= \left[\mathbf{I}+\Lambda^{-1}\mathbf{K}\right]^{-1}\widehat{\alpha}^{\mathrm{OLS}} \\
&= \Lambda(\mathbf{K})\widehat{\alpha}^{\mathrm{OLS}} \text{ and} \\
\widehat{\alpha}^{\mathrm{OLS}} &= \Lambda^{-1}\mathbf{Z}'\mathbf{Y}_* \\
&= \alpha + \Lambda^{-1}\mathbf{Z}'\varepsilon_*,
\end{aligned}$$

where $\mathbf{\Lambda} = \mathbf{Z}'\mathbf{Z}$.

$$\begin{aligned} E\left(\widehat{\boldsymbol{\alpha}}^{\mathrm{RR}} - \boldsymbol{\alpha}\right) &= E\left(\mathbf{\Lambda}(\mathbf{K})\widehat{\boldsymbol{\alpha}}^{\mathrm{OLS}} - \boldsymbol{\alpha}\right) \\ &= \left[\mathbf{\Lambda}(\mathbf{K}) - \mathbf{I}\right]\boldsymbol{\alpha}. \end{aligned}$$

Using $\mathbf{\Lambda}(\mathbf{K}) = \left[\mathbf{I} + \mathbf{\Lambda}^{-1}\mathbf{K}\right]^{-1}$, $k_{ij} \geq 0$, we get:

$$\begin{aligned} \mathbf{\Lambda}^{-1}(\mathbf{K}) &= \mathbf{I} + \mathbf{\Lambda}^{-1}\mathbf{K} \\ \mathbf{I} &= \mathbf{\Lambda}(\mathbf{K}) + \mathbf{\Lambda}(\mathbf{K})\mathbf{\Lambda}^{-1}\mathbf{K} \\ \mathbf{\Lambda}(\mathbf{K}) - \mathbf{I} &= -\mathbf{\Lambda}(\mathbf{K})\mathbf{\Lambda}^{-1}\mathbf{K} \\ &= -\left(\mathbf{\Lambda} + \mathbf{K}\right)^{-1}\mathbf{K}. \end{aligned}$$

Hence,

$$\begin{aligned} E\left(\widehat{\boldsymbol{\alpha}}^{\mathrm{RR}} - \boldsymbol{\alpha}\right) &= -\left(\mathbf{\Lambda} + \mathbf{K}\right)^{-1}\mathbf{K}\boldsymbol{\alpha} \\ Var\left(\widehat{\boldsymbol{\alpha}}^{\mathrm{RR}} - \boldsymbol{\alpha}\right) &= Var\left(\mathbf{\Lambda}(\mathbf{K})\widehat{\boldsymbol{\alpha}}^{\mathrm{OLS}}\right) \\ &= \left(\mathbf{\Lambda} + \mathbf{K}\right)^{-1}\mathbf{\Lambda}\left(\mathbf{\Lambda} + \mathbf{K}\right)^{-1}. \end{aligned}$$

Therefore, the risk of $\widehat{\boldsymbol{\alpha}}^{\mathrm{RR}}$ is directly obtained by definition. Similarly,

$$\begin{aligned} \widetilde{\boldsymbol{\alpha}}^{\mathrm{RR}} &= \mathbf{\Lambda}(\mathbf{K})\widetilde{\boldsymbol{\alpha}}^{\mathrm{OLS}} \\ &= \mathbf{\Lambda}(\mathbf{K})\left(\widehat{\boldsymbol{\alpha}}^{\mathrm{OLS}} - \mathbf{\Lambda}^{-1}\mathbf{H}'\left(\mathbf{H}\mathbf{\Lambda}^{-1}\mathbf{H}'\right)^{-1}\left(\mathbf{H}\widehat{\boldsymbol{\alpha}}^{\mathrm{OLS}} - \mathbf{r}\right)\right) \\ &= \mathbf{\Lambda}(\mathbf{K})\widehat{\boldsymbol{\alpha}}^{\mathrm{OLS}} - \left(\mathbf{\Lambda} + \mathbf{K}\right)^{-1}\mathbf{H}'\left(\mathbf{H}\mathbf{\Lambda}^{-1}\mathbf{H}'\right)^{-1}\left(\mathbf{H}\widehat{\boldsymbol{\alpha}}^{\mathrm{OLS}} - \mathbf{r}\right) \\ E\left(\widetilde{\boldsymbol{\alpha}}^{\mathrm{RR}} - \boldsymbol{\alpha}\right) &= E\left(\mathbf{\Lambda}(\mathbf{K})\widehat{\boldsymbol{\alpha}}^{\mathrm{OLS}} - \boldsymbol{\alpha}\right) - E\left(\left(\mathbf{\Lambda} + \mathbf{K}\right)^{-1}\mathbf{H}'\left(\mathbf{H}\mathbf{\Lambda}^{-1}\mathbf{H}'\right)^{-1}\left(\mathbf{H}\widehat{\boldsymbol{\alpha}}^{\mathrm{OLS}} - \mathbf{r}\right)\right) \\ &= -\left(\mathbf{\Lambda} + \mathbf{K}\right)^{-1}\mathbf{K}\boldsymbol{\alpha} - \mathbf{\Lambda}(\mathbf{K})\boldsymbol{\delta}, \end{aligned}$$

and,

$$\begin{aligned} Var\left(\widetilde{\boldsymbol{\alpha}}^{\mathrm{RR}} - \boldsymbol{\alpha}\right) &= Var\left(\mathbf{\Lambda}(\mathbf{K})\left(\widehat{\boldsymbol{\alpha}}^{\mathrm{OLS}} - \mathbf{\Lambda}^{-1}\mathbf{H}'\left(\mathbf{H}\mathbf{\Lambda}^{-1}\mathbf{H}'\right)^{-1}\left(\mathbf{H}\widehat{\boldsymbol{\alpha}}^{\mathrm{OLS}} - \mathbf{r}\right)\right)\right) \\ &= \mathbf{\Lambda}(\mathbf{K})\left(\mathbf{\Lambda}^{-1} - \mathbf{\Lambda}^{-1}\mathbf{H}'\left(\mathbf{H}\mathbf{\Lambda}^{-1}\mathbf{H}'\right)^{-1}\mathbf{H}\mathbf{\Lambda}^{-1}\mathbf{H}'\left(\mathbf{H}\mathbf{\Lambda}^{-1}\mathbf{H}'\right)^{-1}\mathbf{H}\mathbf{\Lambda}^{-1}\right)\mathbf{\Lambda}'(\mathbf{K}) \\ &= \left(\mathbf{\Lambda} + \mathbf{K}\right)^{-1}\left(\mathbf{\Lambda} - \mathbf{H}'\left(\mathbf{H}\mathbf{\Lambda}^{-1}\mathbf{H}'\right)^{-1}\mathbf{H}\right)\left(\mathbf{\Lambda} + \mathbf{K}\right)^{-1}. \end{aligned}$$

Thus, the risk of $\widetilde{\boldsymbol{\alpha}}^{\mathrm{RR}}$ is directly obtained by definition. □

3. Preliminary Test and Shrinkage Estimation

Researchers have determined that restricted estimation (RE) generally performs better than the full model estimator (FME) and leads to smaller sampling variance than the FME when the UNPI is correct. However, the RE might be a noteworthy competitor of FME even though the restrictions may, in fact, not be valid; we refer to Groß (2003) and Kaçıranlar et al. (2011). It is important that the consequences of incorporating UNPI in the estimation process depends on the usefulness of the information. The preliminary test estimator (PTE) uses UNPI, as well as the sample information. The PTE chooses between the RE and the FME through a pretest. We consider the SUR-PTE of $\boldsymbol{\alpha}$ as follows:

$$\widehat{\boldsymbol{\alpha}}^{\mathrm{PTE}} = \widetilde{\boldsymbol{\alpha}}^{\mathrm{RR}} I(F_n < F_{m,M \cdot T-p}(\alpha)) + \widehat{\boldsymbol{\alpha}}^{\mathrm{RR}} I(F_n \geq F_{m,M \cdot T-p}(\alpha)), \tag{10}$$

where $F_{m,M\cdot T-p}(\alpha)$ is the upper α-level critical value from the central F-distribution, $I(A)$ stands for the indicator function of the set A, and F_n is the F test for testing the null hypothesis of (8), given by:

$$F_n = \frac{\left(\mathbf{H}\widehat{\boldsymbol{\alpha}}^{\text{OLS}} - \mathbf{r}\right)' \left(\mathbf{H}\left(\mathbf{Z}'\mathbf{Z}\right)^{-1}\mathbf{H}'\right)^{-1} \left(\mathbf{H}\widehat{\boldsymbol{\alpha}}^{\text{OLS}} - \mathbf{r}\right)/m}{\widehat{\varepsilon_*}'\widehat{\varepsilon_*}/\left(M\cdot T - p\right)}, \tag{11}$$

where m is the number of restrictions and p is the total number of estimated coefficients. Under the null hypothesis (8), F_n is F distributed with n and $M\cdot T - p$ degrees of freedom (Henningsen et al. 2007). The PTE selects strictly between FME and RE and depends strongly on the level of significance. Later, we will define the Stein-type regression estimator (SE) of $\boldsymbol{\alpha}$. This estimator is the smooth version of PTE, given by,

$$\widehat{\boldsymbol{\alpha}}^{\text{SE}} = \widehat{\boldsymbol{\alpha}}^{\text{RR}} - d\left(\widehat{\boldsymbol{\alpha}}^{\text{RR}} - \widetilde{\boldsymbol{\alpha}}^{\text{RR}}\right)F_n^{-1}, \tag{12}$$

where $d = (m-2)(T-p)/m(T-p+2)$ is the optimum shrinkage constant. It is possible that the SE may have the opposite sign of the FME due to small values of F_n. To alleviate this problem, we consider the positive-rule Stein-type estimator (PSE) defined by:

$$\widehat{\boldsymbol{\alpha}}^{\text{PSE}} = \widetilde{\boldsymbol{\alpha}}^{\text{RR}} + \left(1 - dF_n^{-1}\right)I(F_n > d)\left(\widehat{\boldsymbol{\alpha}}^{\text{RR}} - \widetilde{\boldsymbol{\alpha}}^{\text{RR}}\right). \tag{13}$$

4. Simulation

In this section, the performance of the preliminary test and shrinkage SUR ridge estimators of $\boldsymbol{\beta}$ are investigated via Monte Carlo simulations. We generate the response from the following model:

$$\begin{pmatrix} \mathbf{Y}_1 \\ \mathbf{Y}_2 \\ \vdots \\ \mathbf{Y}_M \end{pmatrix} = \begin{pmatrix} \mathbf{X}_1 & \mathbf{0} & \dots & \mathbf{0} \\ \mathbf{0} & \mathbf{X}_2 & \dots & \mathbf{0} \\ \vdots & \vdots & \ddots & \vdots \\ \mathbf{0} & \mathbf{0} & \vdots & \mathbf{X}_M \end{pmatrix} \begin{pmatrix} \boldsymbol{\beta}_1 \\ \boldsymbol{\beta}_2 \\ \vdots \\ \boldsymbol{\beta}_M \end{pmatrix} + \begin{pmatrix} \boldsymbol{\varepsilon}_1 \\ \boldsymbol{\varepsilon}_2 \\ \vdots \\ \boldsymbol{\varepsilon}_M \end{pmatrix}.$$

The explanatory variables are generated from a multivariate normal distribution $\text{MVN}_{p_i}(\mathbf{0}, \boldsymbol{\Sigma}_x)$, and the random errors are generated from $\text{MVN}_M(\mathbf{0}, \boldsymbol{\Sigma}_\varepsilon)$. We summarize the simulation details as follows:

1. Generate the ith explanatory matrix $\mathbf{X}_i$ from $\text{MVN}_{p_i}(\mathbf{0}, \boldsymbol{\Sigma}_x)$ so that $\mathbf{X}_i$ is different from $\mathbf{X}_j$ for all $i, j = 1, 2, \ldots, M$, where $diag(\boldsymbol{\Sigma}_x) = 1$ and off $-$ $diag(\boldsymbol{\Sigma}_x) = \rho_x$. The ρ_x regulates the strength of collinearity among explanatory variables per equation. In this study, we consider $\rho_x = 0.5, 0.9$. Further, the response is centred, and the predictors are standardized for each equation.
2. The variance-covariance matrix of errors for interdependency among equations is defined by $diag(\boldsymbol{\Sigma}_\varepsilon) = 1$ and off $-$ $diag(\boldsymbol{\Sigma}_\varepsilon) = \rho_\varepsilon = 0.5, 0.9$, and the errors are generated from $\text{MVN}_M(\mathbf{0}, \boldsymbol{\Sigma}_\varepsilon)$ and $M = 2, 3$ for each replication.
3. We consider that an SUR regression model is assumed to be sparse. Hence, the vector of coefficients can be partitioned as $\boldsymbol{\beta}' = \left(\boldsymbol{\beta}_1', \boldsymbol{\beta}_2'\right)'$ where $\boldsymbol{\beta}_1$ is the the coefficient vector of the main effects, while $\boldsymbol{\beta}_2$ is the vector of nuisance, which means that it does not contribute to the model significantly. We set $\boldsymbol{\beta}_1 = (1, -3, 2)'$ and $\boldsymbol{\beta}_2 = \mathbf{0}$. For the suggested estimations, we consider the restriction of $\boldsymbol{\beta}_2 = \mathbf{0}$ and test it. We also investigate the behaviours of the estimators when the restriction is not true. To this end, we add a Δ value to one component of $\boldsymbol{\beta}_2$ so that it violates the null hypothesis.

Here, we use Δ values between zero and two and use $\alpha = 0.05$. We also consider that the lengths of the nuisance parameter $\boldsymbol{\beta}_2$ are two and four, respectively. Therefore, the restricted matrices are:

$$\mathbf{R}_i = \begin{bmatrix} 0 & 0 & 0 & 1 & 0 \\ 0 & 0 & 0 & 0 & 1 \end{bmatrix}, \mathbf{r}_i = \begin{bmatrix} 0 \\ 0 \end{bmatrix}, \text{ if } p_i = 5 \text{ and}$$

$$\mathbf{R}_i = \begin{bmatrix} 0 & 0 & 0 & 1 & 0 & 0 & 0 \\ 0 & 0 & 0 & 0 & 1 & 0 & 0 \\ 0 & 0 & 0 & 0 & 0 & 1 & 0 \\ 0 & 0 & 0 & 0 & 0 & 0 & 1 \end{bmatrix}, \mathbf{r}_i = \begin{bmatrix} 0 \\ 0 \\ 0 \\ 0 \end{bmatrix}, \text{ if } p_i = 7,$$

where $i = 2, 3$ are the number of equation. Hence, $\mathbf{R}$ will be $diag(\mathbf{R}_1, \mathbf{R}_2)$ and $diag(\mathbf{R}_1, \mathbf{R}_2, \mathbf{R}_3)$. Furthermore, $\mathbf{r}$ will be $(\mathbf{r}_1', \mathbf{r}_2')'$ and $(\mathbf{r}_1', \mathbf{r}_2', \mathbf{r}_3')'$.

4. The performance of an estimator is evaluated by using the relative mean squared error (RMSE) criterion. The RMSE of an estimator $\widehat{\boldsymbol{\alpha}}^*$ with respect to $\widehat{\boldsymbol{\alpha}}^{\text{RR}}$ is defined as follows:

$$\text{RMSE}\left(\widehat{\boldsymbol{\alpha}}^*\right) = \frac{\text{MSE}\left(\widehat{\boldsymbol{\alpha}}^{\text{RR}}\right)}{\text{MSE}\left(\widehat{\boldsymbol{\alpha}}^*\right)},$$

where $\widehat{\boldsymbol{\alpha}}^*$ is one of the listed estimators. If the RMSE of an estimator is larger than one, it indicates that it is superior to $\widehat{\boldsymbol{\alpha}}^{\text{RR}}$.

Table 1 provides notations and a symbol key for the benefit of the reader.

Table 1. Values and explanations of the symbols.

Symbol	Description	Design
M	the number of equations	2,3
T	the number of observations per equation	100
p_i	the number of covariates per equation	5,7
$\boldsymbol{\Sigma}_\varepsilon$	the variance–covariance matrix of errors	$diag(\boldsymbol{\Sigma}_\varepsilon) = 1$ and off $-$ $diag(\boldsymbol{\Sigma}_\varepsilon) = \rho_\varepsilon$
ρ_ε	off-diagonal elements of $\boldsymbol{\Sigma}_\varepsilon$	0.5,0.9
$\boldsymbol{\Sigma}_x$	the variance–covariance matrix of covariates	$diag(\boldsymbol{\Sigma}_\varepsilon) = 1$ and off $-$ $diag(\boldsymbol{\Sigma}_x) = \rho_x$
ρ_x	off-diagonal elements of $\boldsymbol{\Sigma}_x$	0.5,0.9
Δ	the magnitude of violation of the null hypothesis	$[0, 2]$

We plot the simulation results in Figures 1 and 2. The simulation results for some other parameter configurations were also obtained, but are not included here for the sake of brevity.

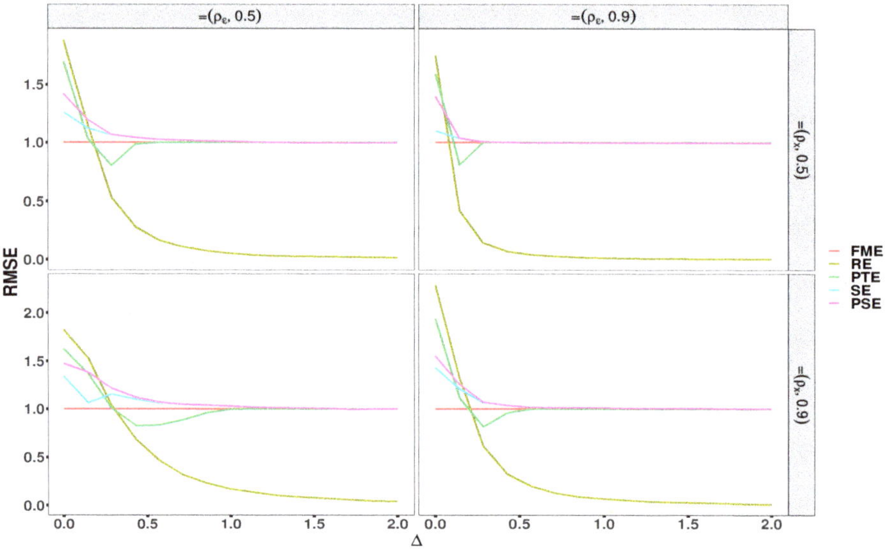

(**a**) As $p_i = 5, i = 1, 2$

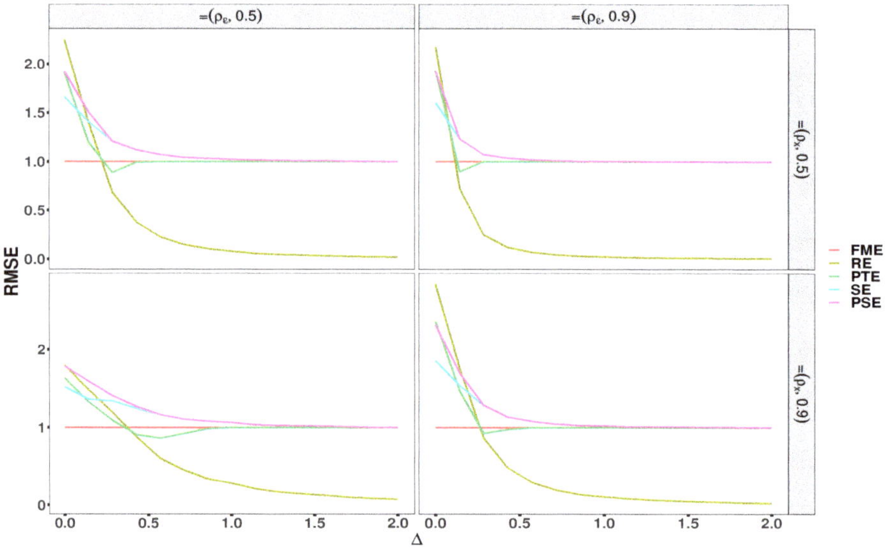

(**b**) As $p_i = 7, i = 1, 2$

Figure 1. RMSE of the estimators as a function of Δ when $M = 2$, $T = 100$, $\rho_x = 0.5, 0.9$, and $\rho_\varepsilon = 0.5, 0.9$. FME, full model estimator; RE, restricted estimation; PTE, preliminary test estimator; PSE, positive-rule Stein-type estimator.

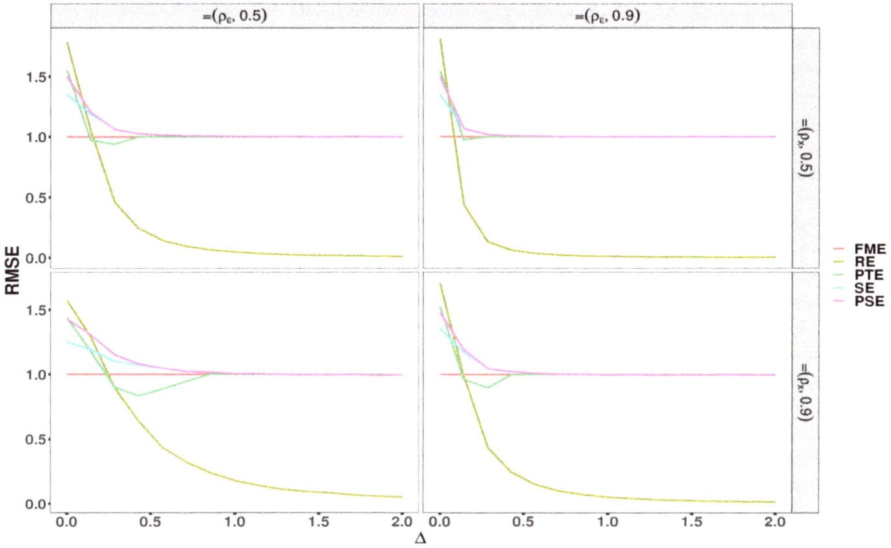

(**a**) As $p_i = 5, i = 1, 2$

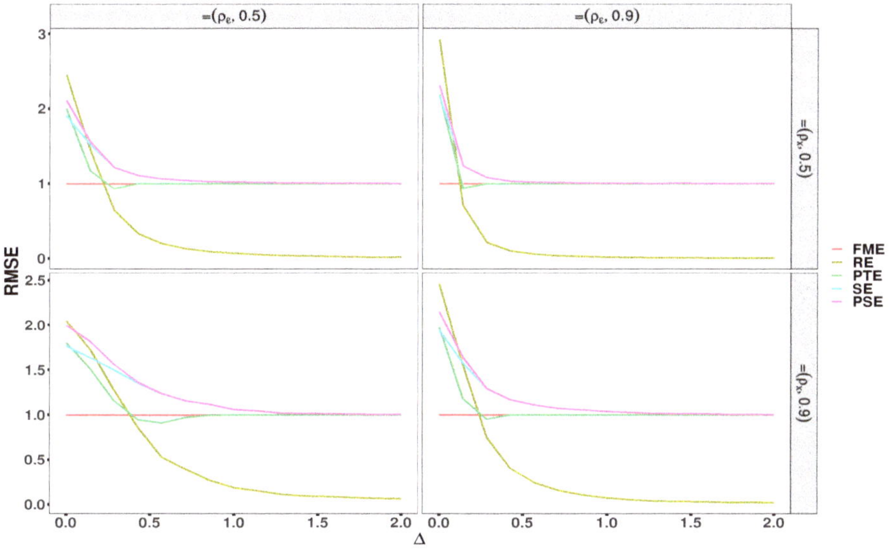

(**b**) As $p_i = 7, i = 1, 2$

Figure 2. RMSE of the estimators as a function of Δ when $M = 3$, $T = 100$, $\rho_x = 0.5, 0.9$, and $\rho_\varepsilon = 0.5, 0.9$.

According to these results:

1. When $\Delta = 0$, which means that the null hypothesis is true or that the restrictions are consistent, the RE estimator always performs competitively when compared to other estimators. The PTE mostly outperforms the SE and PSE when $p_i = 5$, while it looses its efficiency when $p_i = 7$ when compared to PSE. The SE may perform worse than the FME due its sign problem, as is indicated in Section 3.

2. When $\Delta > 0$, which means that the null hypothesis is violated or the restrictions are invalid, the RE looses its efficiency, and its RMSE goes to zero, meaning that it becomes inconsistent. The RMSE of PTE decreases and remains below one for some values of Δ, but approaches one for larger values of Δ. The performance of PSE decreases, but its efficiency remains above the FME, for intermediate values of Δ, while it acts as the FME for larger values of Δ. It can be concluded that the PSE is a robust estimator even if the restriction is not true.
3. We examined both medium and high correlation between disturbance terms. The results showed that the performance of suggested estimators was consistent with its theory; see Ahmed (2014).
4. We examined both medium and high correlation between regressors across different equations. The results showed that the performance of suggested estimators was consistent with its theory; see Yüzbası et al. (2017).

5. Application

In the following section, we will apply the proposed estimation strategies to a financial dataset to examine the relative performance of the listed estimators. To illustrate and compare the listed estimators, we will study the effect of several economic and financial variables on the performance of the "Fragile Five" countries (coined by Stanley 2013) in terms of their attraction of direct foreign investment (FDI) over the period between 1983 and 2018. The "Fragile Five" include Turkey (TUR), South Africa (ZAF), Brazil (BRA), India (IND), and Indonesia (IDN). Agiomirgianakis et al. (2003), Hubert et al. (2017), and Akın (2019) used the FDI as the dependent variable across countries. With five countries, we have $M = 5$ blocks in our SUR model, with measurements of $T = 36$ years per equation. Table 2 provides information about prediction variables, and the raw data are available from the World Bank[1].

Table 2. Descriptions of variables.

Variables	Descriptions
Dependent Variables	
FDI	Foreign direct investment, net inflows (% of GDP)
Covariates	
GROWTH	GDP per capita growth (annual %)
DEFLATOR	Inflation, GDP deflator (annual %)
EXPORTS	Exports of goods and services (% of GDP)
IMPORTS	Imports of goods and services (% of GDP)
GGFCE	General government final consumption expenditure (% of GDP)
RESERVES	Total reserves (includes gold, current US$)/GDP (current US$)
PREM	Personal remittances, received (% of GDP)
BALANCA	Current account balance (% of GDP)

We suggest the following model:

$$\begin{aligned} \mathrm{FDI}_{it} &= \beta_{0i} + \beta_{1i}\mathrm{GROWTH} + \beta_{2i}\mathrm{DEFLATOR} + \beta_{3i}\mathrm{EXPORTS} + \beta_{4i}\mathrm{IMPORTS} + \\ &\quad \beta_{5i}\mathrm{GGFCE} + \beta_{6i}\mathrm{RESERVES} + \beta_{7i}\mathrm{PREM} + \beta_{8i}\mathrm{BALANCE} + \epsilon_{it}, \end{aligned} \tag{14}$$

where i denotes countries ($i = \mathrm{TUR}, \mathrm{ZAF}, \mathrm{BRA}, \mathrm{IND}, \mathrm{IDN}$) and t is time ($t = 1, 2, \ldots, T$). Following Salman (2011), the errors of each equation are assumed to be normally distributed with mean zero, homoscedastic, and serially not autocorrelated. Furthermore, there is contemporaneous correlation between corresponding errors in different equations. We test these assumptions along with the assumptions in Section 2. We first check the following assumptions of each equation:

[1] https://data.worldbank.org.

Nonautocorrelation of errors: There are a number of viable tests in the reviewed literature for testing the autocorrelation. For example, the Ljung–Box test is widely used in applications of time series analysis, and a similar assessment may be obtained via the Breusch–Godfrey test and the Durbin–Watson test. We apply the Ljung–Box test of (Ljung and Box 1978). The null hypothesis of the Ljung–Box Test, H_0, is that the errors are random and independent. A significant *p*-value in this test rejects the null hypothesis that the time series is not autocorrelated. Results reported in Table 3 suggest a rejection of H_0 for the equations of both TUR and IND at any conventional significance level. Thus, the estimation results will be clearly unsatisfactory for these two equation models. To tackle this problem, we performed the first differences procedure to transform the variables. After transformation, the test statistics and *p*-values of the equation TUR and IND were $\chi^2_{(1)} = 1.379$, $p = 0.240$ and $\chi^2_{(1)} = 0.067$, $p = 0.794$, respectively. Hence, each equation satisfied the assumption of nonautocorrelation. We confirmed our result using the Durbin–Watson test.

Table 3. Ljung-Box test.

Equation	Test Statistic	*p*-Value
TUR	$\chi^2_{(1)} = 6.853$	0.008
ZAF	$\chi^2_{(1)} = 0.704$	0.401
BRA	$\chi^2_{(1)} = 0.489$	0.483
IND	$\chi^2_{(1)} = 6.301$	0.012
IDN	$\chi^2_{(1)} = 1.061$	0.302

Homoscedasticity of errors: To test for heteroscedasticity, we used the Breusch–Pagan test (Breusch and Pagan 1979). The results in Table 4 failed to reject the null hypothesis in each equation.

Table 4. Breusch–Pagan test.

Equation	Test Statistic	*p*-Value
TUR	$\chi^2_{(8)} = 3.686$	0.884
ZAF	$\chi^2_{(8)} = 10.003$	0.264
BRA	$\chi^2_{(8)} = 7.544$	0.479
IND	$\chi^2_{(8)} = 6.455$	0.596
IDN	$\chi^2_{(8)} = 8.328$	0.402

The assumption homoscedasticity in each equation was thus met.

Normality of errors: To test for normality, there are various tests such as Shapiro–Wilk, Anderson–Darling, Cramer–von Mises, Kolmogorov–Smirnov, and Jarque–Bera. In this study, we performed the Jarque–Bera goodness-of-fit test (Jarque and Bera 1980).

Table 5. Jarque–Bera test.

Equation	Test Statistic	*p*-Value
TUR	$\chi^2_{(2)} = 3.969$	0.137
ZAF	$\chi^2_{(2)} = 72.852$	0.000
BRA	$\chi^2_{(2)} = 2.355$	0.308
IND	$\chi^2_{(2)} = 1.815$	0.403
IDN	$\chi^2_{(2)} = 2.794$	0.247

The null hypothesis for the test is that the data are normally distributed. The results reported in Table 5 suggested a rejection of H_0 only for ZAF. We also performed the Kolmogorov–Smirnov test for

ZAF, and the results showed that the errors were normally distributed. Thus, each equation satisfied the assumption of normality.

Cross-sectional dependence: To test whether the estimated correlation between the sections was statistically significant, we applied the Breusch and Pagan (1980) Lagrange multiplier (LM) statistic and the Pesaran (2004) cross-section dependence (CD) tests. The null hypothesis of these tests claims there is no cross-section dependence. Both tests in Table 6 suggested a rejection of the null hypothesis that the residuals from each equation were significantly correlated with each other. Consequently, the SUR model would be the preferred technique, since this model assumed contemporaneous correlation across equations. Therefore, the joint estimation of all parameters rather than OLS, on each equation, was more efficient (Kleiber and Zeileis 2008).

Table 6. Cross-section dependence test results. LM, Lagrange multiplier; CD, cross-section dependence.

Correlation Matrix of Residuals				
	TUR	**ZAF**	**BRA**	**IND**
ZAF	−0.207			
BRA	0.066	−0.187		
IND	0.414	−0.107	−0.016	
IDN	0.128	−0.334	−0.064	0.235

Breusch and Pagan LM and Pesaran CD tests		
Test	**Test Statistic**	***p*-Value**
LM	$\chi^2_{(2)} = 29.516$	0.001
CD	$Z = -4.353$	0.000

Specification test: The regression equation specification error test (RESET) designed by Ramsey (1969) is a general specification test for the linear regression model. It tests the exogeneity of the independent variables, that is the null hypothesis is $E\left[\varepsilon_i|\mathbf{X}_i\right] = 0$. Thus, rejecting the null hypothesis indicates that there is a correlation between the error term and the regressors or that nonlinearities exist in the functional form of the regression. The results reported in Table 7 suggested a rejection of H_0 only for IDN.

Table 7. The regression equation specification error test (RESET) test.

Equation	Test Statistic	*p*-Value
TUR	$F(8,18) = 0.458$	0.869
ZAF	$F(8,19) = 1.185$	0.357
BRA	$F(8,19) = 1.062$	0.428
IND	$F(8,18) = 1.648$	0.180
IDN	$F(8,19) = 7.788$	0.000

Multicollinearity: We calculated the variance inflation factor (VIF) values among the predictors. A VIF value provides the user with a measure of how many times larger the $\text{Var}(\beta_j)$ will be for multicollinear data than for orthogonal data. Usually, the multicollinearity is not a problem, as the VIFs are generally not significantly larger than one (Mansfield and Helms 1982). In the literature, values of VIF that exceed 10 are often regarded as indicating multicollinearity, but in weaker models, values above 2.5 may be a cause for concern. Another measure of multicollinearity is to calculate the condition number (CN) of $\mathbf{X}_i'\mathbf{X}_i$, which is the square root of the ratio of the largest characteristic root of $\mathbf{X}_i'\mathbf{X}_i$ to the smallest. Belsley et al. (2005) suggested that a CN greater than fifteen poses a concern, a CN in excess of 20 is indicative of a problem, and a CN close to 30 represents a severe problem. Table 8 displays the results from a series of multicollinearity diagnostics. In general, EXPORTS, IMPORTS, and BALANCE were found to be problematic with regard to VIF values, while the others may be a little concerning. On the other hand, the results from the CN test suggested that there was a very serious concern about multicollinearity for the equations of ZAF, BRA, and IDN. In light of these results, it was clear that the problem of multicollinearity existed in the equations. According to Greene (2019), the SUR estimation is more efficient when the less correlation exists between covariates. Therefore, the ridge-type SUR estimation will be a good solution of this problem.

Table 8. Variance inflation factor (VIF) and CN values.

Equation	GROWTH	DEFLATOR	EXPORTS	IMPORTS	GGFCE	RESERVES	PREM	BALANCE	CN
TUR	4.039	2.638	16.289	13.959	2.055	1.791	1.462	19.073	11.122
ZAF	3.070	7.354	69.891	191.248	3.891	12.918	5.847	60.728	248.221
BRA	1.204	1.614	18.324	32.159	6.329	3.131	3.938	13.301	85.336
IND	1.745	1.757	6.545	6.653	1.517	1.527	1.378	2.712	6.535
IDN	7.835	7.786	44.842	34.152	5.564	8.274	3.072	15.022	127.099

Structural change: To investigate the stability of the coefficients in each equation, we used the CUSUM (cumulative sum) test of Brown et al. (1975) that checks for structural changes. The null hypothesis is that of coefficient constancy, while the alternative suggests inconsistent structural change in the model over time. The results in Table 9 suggested the stability of coefficients over time.

Table 9. CUSUM test.

Equation	Test Statistic	*p*-Value
TUR	$T = 0.734$	0.653
ZAF	$T = 0.417$	0.995
BRA	$T = 0.496$	0.966
IND	$T = 0.413$	0.995
IDN	$T = 0.401$	0.997

Following Lawal et al. (2019), we selected important variables in each equation of the SUR model and implemented the stepwise AIC forward regression by using the function **ols_step_forward_aic** from the **olsrr** package in the R project. The statistically significant variables are shown in Table 10. After that, the sub-models were constituted by using these variables per equation.

Table 10. Important variables per equation.

Equation	GROWTH	DEFLATOR	EXPORTS	IMPORTS	GGFCE	RESERVES	PREM	BALANCE
TUR			✓					
ZAF							✓	
BRA		✓		✓				✓
IND				✓			✓	✓
IDN			✓	✓			✓	

In light of the selected variables in Table 10, we construct the matrices of restrictions as follows:

$$\mathbf{R}_1 = \begin{bmatrix} 1 & 0 & 0 & 0 & 0 & 0 & 0 & 0 & 0 \\ 0 & 1 & 0 & 0 & 0 & 0 & 0 & 0 & 0 \\ 0 & 0 & 0 & 1 & 0 & 0 & 0 & 0 & 0 \\ 0 & 0 & 0 & 0 & 1 & 0 & 0 & 0 & 0 \\ 0 & 0 & 0 & 0 & 0 & 1 & 0 & 0 & 0 \\ 0 & 0 & 0 & 0 & 0 & 0 & 1 & 0 & 0 \\ 0 & 0 & 0 & 0 & 0 & 0 & 0 & 0 & 1 \end{bmatrix}, \mathbf{R}_2 = \begin{bmatrix} 1 & 0 & 0 & 0 & 0 & 0 & 0 & 0 & 0 \\ 0 & 1 & 0 & 0 & 0 & 0 & 0 & 0 & 0 \\ 0 & 0 & 1 & 0 & 0 & 0 & 0 & 0 & 0 \\ 0 & 0 & 0 & 1 & 0 & 0 & 0 & 0 & 0 \\ 0 & 0 & 0 & 0 & 1 & 0 & 0 & 0 & 0 \\ 0 & 0 & 0 & 0 & 0 & 1 & 0 & 0 & 0 \\ 0 & 0 & 0 & 0 & 0 & 0 & 0 & 0 & 1 \end{bmatrix}, \mathbf{r}_1 = \mathbf{r}_2 = \begin{bmatrix} 0 \\ 0 \\ 0 \\ 0 \\ 0 \\ 0 \\ 0 \end{bmatrix},$$

$$\mathbf{R}_3 = \begin{bmatrix} 1 & 0 & 0 & 0 & 0 & 0 & 0 & 0 \\ 0 & 0 & 1 & 0 & 0 & 0 & 0 & 0 \\ 0 & 0 & 0 & 0 & 1 & 0 & 0 & 0 \\ 0 & 0 & 0 & 0 & 0 & 1 & 0 & 0 \\ 0 & 0 & 0 & 0 & 0 & 0 & 1 & 0 \end{bmatrix}, \mathbf{R}_4 = \begin{bmatrix} 0 & 1 & 0 & 0 & 0 & 0 & 0 & 0 \\ 0 & 0 & 1 & 0 & 0 & 0 & 0 & 0 \\ 0 & 0 & 0 & 0 & 1 & 0 & 0 & 0 \\ 0 & 0 & 0 & 0 & 0 & 0 & 1 & 0 \\ 0 & 0 & 0 & 0 & 0 & 0 & 0 & 1 \end{bmatrix},$$

$$\mathbf{R}_5 = \begin{bmatrix} 1 & 0 & 0 & 0 & 0 & 0 & 0 & 0 \\ 0 & 1 & 0 & 0 & 0 & 0 & 0 & 0 \\ 0 & 0 & 0 & 0 & 1 & 0 & 0 & 0 \\ 0 & 0 & 0 & 0 & 0 & 1 & 0 & 0 \\ 0 & 0 & 0 & 0 & 0 & 0 & 0 & 1 \end{bmatrix} \text{ and } \mathbf{r}_3 = \mathbf{r}_4 = \mathbf{r}_5 = \begin{bmatrix} 0 \\ 0 \\ 0 \\ 0 \\ 0 \end{bmatrix};$$

thus, the reduced models are given by:

$$\text{TUR} : \text{FDI}_t = \beta_0 + \beta_3\text{EXPORTS} + \epsilon_t, \tag{15}$$

$$\text{ZAF} : \text{FDI}_t = \beta_0 + \beta_7\text{PREM} + \epsilon_t, \tag{16}$$

$$\text{BRA} : \text{FDI}_t = \beta_0 + \beta_2\text{DEFLATOR} + \beta_4\text{IMPORTS} + \beta_8\text{BALANCE} + \epsilon_t, \tag{17}$$

$$\text{IND} : \text{FDI}_t = \beta_0 + \beta_4\text{IMPORTS} + \beta_7\text{PREM} + \beta_8\text{BALANCE} + \epsilon_t, \tag{18}$$

$$\text{IDN} : \text{FDI}_t = \beta_0 + \beta_3\text{EXPORTS} + \beta_4\text{IMPORTS} + \beta_7\text{PREM} + \epsilon_t, \tag{19}$$

Next, we combined Model (14) and Models (15)–(19) using the shrinkage and preliminarily test strategies outlined in Section 3. Before we performed our analysis, the response was centred, and the predictors were standardized for each equation so that the intercept term was omitted. We then split the data by using the time series cross-validation technique of Hyndman and Athanasopoulos (2018) into a series of training sets and a series of testing sets. Each test set consisted of a single observation for the models that produced one step-ahead forecasts. In this procedure, the observations in the corresponding training sets occurred prior to the observation of the test sets. Hence, it was ensured that no future observations could be used in constructing the forecast. We used the function **createTimeSlices** from the **caret** package in the R project here. The listed models were applied to the data, and predictions were made based on the divided training and test sets. The process was repeated 15 times, and for each subset's prediction, the mean squared error (MSE) and the mean absolute error (MAE) were calculated. The means of the 15 MSEs and MAEs were then used to evaluate the performance for each method. We also report the relative performances (RMAE and RMSE) with respect to the full model estimator for easier comparison. If a relative value of an estimator is larger than one, it is superior to the full model estimator.

In Table 11, we report the MSE and MAE values and their standard errors to see the stability of the algorithm. Based on this table, as expected, the RE had the smallest measurement values since the insignificant variables were selected as close to correct as possible. We saw that the performance of the PSE after the RE was best by following the SE and the PTE. Moreover, the performance of the OLS was the worst due to the problem of multicollinearity.

Table 11. Comparison of forecasting performance.

	RE	**FME**	**PTE**	**SE**	**PSE**	**OLS**
MAE	0.572 (0.114)	1.076 (0.148)	0.656 (0.139)	0.649 (0.124)	0.646 (0.122)	1.166 (0.165)
RMAE	1.879	1	1.639	1.656	1.664	0.922
MSE	0.598 (0.061)	0.800 (0.062)	0.624 (0.067)	0.624 (0.069)	0.622 (0.068)	0.831 (0.064)
RMSE	1.338	1	1.283	1.282	1.287	0.963

The numbers in parenthesis are the corresponding standard errors of the MAE and MSE.

In order to test whether the two competing models had the same forecasting accuracy, we used the two-sided statistical Diebold–Mariano (DM) test (Diebold and Mariano 1995) when the forecasting horizon was extended to one year, and the loss functions were both squared errors and absolute errors. A significant p-value in this test rejected the null hypothesis that the models had different forecasting accuracy. The results based on the absolute-error loss in Table 12 suggested that the FME had different prediction accuracy with all methods except RE. Additionally, the forecasting accuracy of the OLS differed from the listed estimators. On the other hand, the results of the DM test based on the squared error loss suggested that the observed differences between the RE and shrinkage estimators were significant.

Table 12. Diebold–Mariano test for the forecasting results.

LF		FME	RE	PTE	SE	PSE
MAE	RE	−1.308 (0.191)				
	PTE	−2.601 (0.009 ***)	−0.608 (0.543)			
	SE	−2.146 (0.032 **)	−0.733 (0.463)	0.276 (0.783)		
	PSE	−2.163 (0.031 **)	−0.702 (0.483)	0.33 (0.741)	0.551 (0.582)	
	OLS	3.734 (0.000 ***)	1.700 (0.089 *)	2.972 (0.003 ***)	2.543 (0.011 **)	2.56 (0.010 **)
MSE	SM	−0.187 (0.852)				
	PTE	−1.968 (0.049 **)	−2.165 (0.030 **)			
	SE	−1.444 (0.149)	−2.392 (0.017 **)	1.443 (0.149)		
	PSE	−1.474 (0.140)	−2.374 (0.018 **)	1.436 (0.151)	−1.496 (0.135)	
	OLS	3.528 (0.000 ***)	0.691 (0.490)	2.379 (0.017 **)	1.904 (0.057 *)	1.933 (0.053 *)

The numbers in parenthesis are the corresponding p-values; LS is the "loss function" of the method to compute; * $p < 0.1$, ** $p < 0.05$, *** $p < 0.01$.

Finally, the estimates of coefficients of all countries are given in Table 13.

Table 13. Estimated coefficients.

Estimation	Country	GROWTH	DEFLATOR	EXPORTS	IMPORTS	GGFCE	RESERVES	PREM	BALANCE
RE	TUR	0 (0)	0 (0)	0.102 (0.003)	0 (0)	0 (0)	0 (0)	0 (0)	0 (0)
	ZAF	0 (0)	0 (0)	0 (0)	0 (0)	0 (0)	0 (0)	0.509 (0.007)	0 (0)
	BRA	0 (0)	−0.231 (0.005)	0 (0)	0.912 (0.005)	0 (0)	0 (0)	0 (0)	−0.377 (0.006)
	IND	−0.113 (0.002)	0 (0)	0 (0)	0.122 (0.003)	0 (0)	0.052 (0.002)	0 (0)	0 (0)
	IDN	0 (0)	0 (0)	−1.903 (0.015)	1.341 (0.014)	0 (0)	0 (0)	0.427 (0.004)	0 (0)
FME	TUR	−0.369 (0)	−0.064 (0)	0.327 (0.003)	−0.187 (0)	−0.140 (0)	0.036 (0)	0.061 (0)	−0.543 (0)
	ZAF	−0.120 (0)	−0.397 (0)	0.521 (0)	−0.139 (0)	0.012 (0)	−0.810 (0)	0.551 (0.007)	−0.420 (0)
	BRA	0.059 (0)	−0.18 (0.005)	0.999 (0)	−0.265 (0.005)	0.859 (0)	0.004 (0)	−0.210 (0)	−1.042 (0.006)
	IND	−0.071 (0.002)	0.018 (0)	−0.091 (0)	0.253 (0.003)	−0.002 (0)	−0.024 (0.002)	0.149 (0)	0.150 (0)
	IDN	0.280 (0)	0.177 (0)	−2.348 (0.015)	1.689 (0.014)	−0.009 (0)	−0.233 (0)	0.475 (0.004)	0.242 (0)
PTE	TUR	−0.151 (0)	−0.026 (0)	0.188 (0.003)	−0.072 (0)	−0.058 (0)	0.014 (0)	0.026 (0)	−0.219 (0)
	ZAF	−0.048 (0)	−0.140 (0)	0.184 (0)	−0.014 (0)	0.012 (0)	−0.318 (0)	0.514 (0.007)	−0.160 (0)
	BRA	0.024 (0)	−0.215 (0.005)	0.420 (0)	0.404 (0.005)	0.350 (0)	0.011 (0)	−0.073 (0)	−0.664 (0.006)
	IND	−0.094 (0.002)	0.006 (0)	−0.032 (0)	0.174 (0.003)	0.003 (0)	0.021 (0.002)	0.059 (0)	0.062 (0)
	IDN	0.126 (0)	0.064 (0)	−2.072 (0.015)	1.475 (0.014)	−0.002 (0)	−0.087 (0)	0.445 (0.004)	0.094 (0)
SE	TUR	−0.110 (0)	−0.019 (0)	0.166 (0.003)	−0.053 (0)	−0.042 (0)	0.010 (0)	0.018 (0)	−0.160 (0)
	ZAF	−0.036 (0)	−0.108 (0)	0.142 (0)	−0.022 (0)	0.006 (0)	−0.237 (0)	0.517 (0.007)	−0.119 (0)
	BRA	0.017 (0)	−0.218 (0.005)	0.299 (0)	0.554 (0.005)	0.253 (0)	0.005 (0)	−0.057 (0)	−0.579 (0.006)
	IND	−0.100 (0.002)	0.005 (0)	−0.025 (0)	0.160 (0.003)	0.001 (0)	0.029 (0.002)	0.043 (0)	0.045 (0)
	IDN	0.088 (0)	0.048 (0)	−2.031 (0.015)	1.442 (0.014)	−0.002 (0)	−0.065 (0)	0.440 (0.004)	0.070 (0)
PSE	TUR	−0.112 (0)	−0.019 (0)	0.168 (0.003)	−0.055 (0)	−0.043 (0)	0.010 (0)	0.019 (0)	−0.164 (0)
	ZAF	−0.037 (0)	−0.112 (0)	0.146 (0)	−0.023 (0)	0.006 (0)	−0.243 (0)	0.517 (0.007)	−0.122 (0)
	BRA	0.018 (0)	−0.217 (0.005)	0.307 (0)	0.546 (0.005)	0.260 (0)	0.005 (0)	−0.059 (0)	−0.584 (0.006)
	IND	−0.099 (0.002)	0.005 (0)	−0.026 (0)	0.161 (0.003)	0.001 (0)	0.029 (0.002)	0.044 (0)	0.046 (0)
	IDN	0.090 (0)	0.050 (0)	−2.033 (0.015)	1.444 (0.014)	−0.002 (0)	−0.067 (0)	0.441 (0.004)	0.071 (0)
OLS	TUR	−0.400 (0)	−0.071 (0)	0.379 (0.003)	−0.230 (0)	−0.147 (0)	0.042 (0)	0.066 (0)	−0.618 (0)
	ZAF	−0.142 (0)	−0.443 (0)	0.648 (0)	−0.291 (0)	0.007 (0)	−0.916 (0)	0.613 (0.007)	−0.515 (0)
	BRA	0.067 (0)	−0.171 (0.005)	1.078 (0)	−0.327 (0.005)	0.909 (0)	−0.018 (0)	−0.225 (0)	−1.110 (0.006)
	IND	−0.074 (0.002)	0.020 (0)	−0.105 (0)	0.275 (0.003)	−0.004 (0)	−0.029 (0.002)	0.156 (0)	0.163 (0)
	IDN	0.270 (0)	0.179 (0)	−2.468 (0.015)	1.768 (0.014)	−0.016 (0)	−0.246 (0)	0.478 (0.004)	0.281 (0)

The numbers in parenthesis are the corresponding standard errors.

6. Conclusions

In this paper, we proposed the shrinkage and preliminary test estimation methods in a system of regression models when the disturbances were dependent and correlations existed among regressors in each equation. To build the model, we first multiplied both sides of Model (1) by the inverse variance–covariance matrix of the disturbances and transformed the values using spectral decomposition. We defined the full model estimator by following Alkhamisi and Shukur (2008) and the restricted estimator by assuming a UNPI on the vector of parameters. Finally, we combined them in an optimal way by applying the shrinkage and preliminary test strategies. To illustrate and compare the relative performance of these methods, we conducted a Monte Carlo simulation. The simulated results demonstrated that the RE outperformed all other estimators when there was sufficient evidence that the vector nuisance parameters were a zero vector, that is $\Delta = 0$. However, the RE lost its efficiency as Δ increased and became unbounded when Δ was large. The PSE dominated the FME at the small values of Δ, while the SE and PSE outshone the FME in the entire parametric space. However, the PSE was better than the SE because it controlled for the over-shrinking problem in SE. We also investigated the performance of the suggested estimations via a real-world example using financial data for the "Fragile Five" countries. The results of our data analysis were consistent with the simulated results.

For further research, one can use the other penalized techniques for the SUR model such as the smoothly clipped absolute deviation (SCAD) by Fan and Li (2001), the least absolute shrinkage and selection operator (LASSO) by Tibshirani (1996), and the adaptive LASSO estimators by Zou (2006), as well as our preliminary and shrinkage estimations.

Author Contributions: Conceptualization, B.Y. and S.E.A.; methodology, S.E.A.; software, B.Y.; validation, B.Y. and S.E.A.; formal analysis, B.Y.; investigation, S.E.A.; resources, S.E.A; data curation, B.Y.; writing-original draft preparation, B.Y.; writing-review and editing, B.Y. and S.E.A.; visualization, B.Y.; supervision, S.E.A.; project administration, B.Y.; funding acquisition, S.E.A. All authors have read and agreed to the published version of the manuscript.

Funding: The research of S. Ejaz Ahmed is supported by the Natural Sciences and the Engineering Research Council of Canada (NSERC).

Acknowledgments: The authors thank Guest Editors Shuangzhe Liu and Milind Sathye and the three reviewers for their detailed reading of the manuscript and their valuable comments and suggestions that led to a considerable improvement of the paper.

Conflicts of Interest: The authors declare no conflict of interest.

References

Agiomirgianakis, George Myron, Dimitrios Asteriou, and Kalliroi Papathoma. 2003. *The Determinants of Foreign Direct Investment: A Panel Data Study for the Oecd Countries.* Monograph (Discussion Paper). London: Department of Economics, City University London.

Ahmed, S. Ejaz. 2014. *Penalty, Shrinkage and Pretest Strategies: Variable Selection and Estimation.* New York: Springer.

Ahmed, S. Ejaz, and Bahadır Yüzbaşı. 2016. Big data analytics: Integrating penalty strategies. *International Journal of Management Science and Engineering Management* 11: 105–15. [CrossRef]

Akın, Tuğba. 2019. The effects of political stability on foreign direct investment in fragile five countries. *Central European Journal of Economic Modelling and Econometrics* 11: 237–55.

Alkhamisi, M. A. 2010. Simulation study of new estimators combining the sur ridge regression and the restricted least squares methodologies. *Statistical Papers* 51: 651–72. [CrossRef]

Alkhamisi, M. A., and Ghazi Shukur. 2008. Developing ridge parameters for sur model. *Communications in Statistics—Theory and Methods* 37: 544–64. [CrossRef]

Arashi, Mohammad, and Mahdi Roozbeh. 2015. Shrinkage estimation in system regression model. *Computational Statistics* 30: 359–76. [CrossRef]

Barari, Mahua, and Srikanta Kundu. 2019. The role of the federal reserve in the us housing crisis: A var analysis with endogenous structural breaks. *Journal of Risk and Financial Management* 12: 125. [CrossRef]

Belsley, David A., Edwin Kuh, and Roy E. Welsch. 2005. *Regression Diagnostics: Identifying Influential Data and Sources of Collinearity.* Hoboken: John Wiley & Sons, vol. 571.

Breusch, Trevor S., and Adrian R. Pagan. 1979. A simple test for heteroscedasticity and random coefficient variation. *Econometrica: Journal of the Econometric Society* 47: 1287–94. [CrossRef]

Breusch, Trevor S., and Adrian R. Pagan. 1980. The lagrange multiplier test and its applications to model specification in econometrics. *The Review of Economic Studies* 47: 239–53. [CrossRef]

Brown, Robert L., James Durbin, and James M. Evans. 1975. Techniques for testing the constancy of regression relationships over time. *Journal of the Royal Statistical Society: Series B (Methodological)* 37: 149–63. [CrossRef]

Diebold, Francis X., and Robert S. Mariano. 1995. Comparing predictive accuracy. *Journal of Business & Economic Statistics* 20: 134–44.

Dincer, Oguzhan C., and Fan Wang. 2011. Ethnic diversity and economic growth in China. *Journal of Economic Policy Reform* 14: 1–10. [CrossRef]

Erdugan, Funda, and Fikri Akdeniz. 2016. Restricted estimator in two seemingly unrelated regression model. *Pakistan Journal of Statistics and Operation Research* 12: 579–88. [CrossRef]

Fan, Jianqing, and Runze Li. 2001. Variable selection via nonconcave penalized likelihood and its oracle properties. *Journal of the American Statistical Association* 96: 1348–60. [CrossRef]

Gao, Xiaoli, S. E. Ahmed, and Yang Feng. 2017. Post selection shrinkage estimation for high-dimensional data analysis. *Applied Stochastic Models in Business and Industry* 33: 97–120. [CrossRef]

Greene, William H. 2019. *Econometric Analysis*. Harlow: Pearson.

Groß, Jürgen. 2003. Restricted ridge estimation. *Statistics & Probability Letters* 65: 57–64.

Henningsen, Arne, and Jeff D. Hamann. 2007. Systemfit: A package for estimating systems of simultaneous equations in r. *Journal of Statistical Software* 23: 1–40. [CrossRef]

Hoerl, Arthur E., and Robert W. Kennard. 1970. Ridge regression: Biased estimation for nonorthogonal problems. *Technometrics* 12: 55–67. [CrossRef]

Hubert, Mia, Tim Verdonck, and Özlem Yorulmaz. 2017. Fast robust sur with economical and actuarial applications. *Statistical Analysis and Data Mining: The ASA Data Science Journal* 10: 77–88. [CrossRef]

Hyndman, Rob J., and George Athanasopoulos. 2018. *Forecasting: Principles and Practice*. Melbourne: OTexts.

James, W., and C. Stein. 1961. Proc. fourth berkeley symp. math. statist. probab. In *Estimation with Quadratic Loss*. Berkeley: University California Press, vol. 1, pp. 361–79.

Jarque, Carlos M., and Anil K. Bera. 1980. Efficient tests for normality, homoscedasticity and serial independence of regression residuals. *Economics Letters* 6: 255–59. [CrossRef]

Kaçıranlar, Selahattin, Sadullah Sakallıoğlu, M. Revan Özkale, and Hüseyin Güler. 2011. More on the restricted ridge regression estimation. *Journal of Statistical Computation and Simulation* 81: 1433–48. [CrossRef]

Kleiber, Christian, and Achim Zeileis. 2008. *Applied Econometrics with R*. Heidelberg: Springer Science & Business Media.

Kuan, C.-M. 2004. *Introduction to Econometric Theory*. Lecture Notes. Available online: ftp://nozdr.ru/biblio/kolxoz/G/GL/Kuan%20C.-M.%20Introduction%20to%20econometric%20theory%20(LN,%20Taipei,%202002)(202s)_GL_.pdf (accessed on 18 June 2020).

Lawal, Afeez Abolaji, and Oluwayemesi Oyeronke ALABA. 2019. Exploratory analysis of some sectors of the economy: A seemingly unrelated regression approach. *African Journal of Applied Statistics* 6: 649–61. [CrossRef]

Ljung, Greta M., and George E. P. Box. 1978. On a measure of lack of fit in time series models. *Biometrika* 65: 297–303. [CrossRef]

Mansfield, Edward R., and Billy P. Helms. 1982. Detecting multicollinearity. *The American Statistician* 36: 158–60.

Pesaran, M. Hashem. 2004. *General Diagnostic Tests for Cross Section Dependence in Panels*. CESifo Working Papers. Cambridge: University of Cambridge, Faculty of Economics. .

Ramsey, James Bernard. 1969. Tests for specification errors in classical linear least-squares regression analysis. *Journal of the Royal Statistical Society: Series B (Methodological)* 31: 350–71. [CrossRef]

Salman, A. Khalik. 2011. Using the sur model of tourism demand for neighbouring regions in sweden and norway. In *Advances in Econometrics-Theory and Applications*. London: IntechOpen, 98p.

Shukur, Ghazi. 2002. Dynamic specification and misspecification in systems of demand equations: A testing strategy for model selection. *Applied Economics* 34: 709–25. [CrossRef]

Srivastava, Virendera K., and David E. A. Giles. 1987. *Seemingly Unrelated Regression Equations Models: Estimation and Inference*. New York: CRC Press, vol. 80.

Srivastava, Viren K., and Alan T. K. Wan. 2002. Separate versus system methods of stein-rule estimation in seemingly unrelated regression models. *Communications in Statistics—Theory and Methods* 31: 2077–99. [CrossRef]

Stanley, Morgan. 2013. Fx pulse preparing for volatility. *Global Outlook* 1: 1–37.

Tibshirani, Robert. 1996. Regression shrinkage and selection via the lasso. *Journal of the Royal Statistical Society: Series B (Methodological)* 58: 267–88. [CrossRef]

Williams, Barry. 2013. Income volatility of indonesian banks after the asian financial crisis. *Journal of the Asia Pacific Economy* 18: 333–58. [CrossRef]

Yüzbası, Bahadır, S. Ejaz Ahmed, and Mehmet Güngör. 2017. Improved penalty strategies in linear regression models. *REVSTAT–Statistical Journal* 15: 251–76.

Yüzbaşı, Bahadır, Mohammad Arashi, and S. Ejaz Ahmed. 2020. Shrinkage estimation strategies in generalised ridge regression models: Low/high-dimension regime. *International Statistical Review* 88: 229–51. [CrossRef]

Zeebari, Zangin, B. M. Golam Kibria, and Ghazi Shukur. 2018. Seemingly unrelated regressions with covariance matrix of cross-equation ridge regression residuals. *Communications in Statistics-Theory and Methods* 47: 5029–53. [CrossRef]

Zeebari, Zangin, Ghazi Shukur, and B. M. G. Kibria. 2012. Modified ridge parameters for seemingly unrelated regression model. *Communications in Statistics-Theory and Methods* 41: 1675–91. [CrossRef]

Zellner, Arnold. 1962. An efficient method of estimating seemingly unrelated regressions and tests for aggregation bias. *Journal of the American statistical Association* 57: 348–68. [CrossRef]

Zou, Hui. 2006. The adaptive lasso and its oracle properties. *Journal of the American Statistical Association* 101: 1418–29. [CrossRef]

Journal of
Risk and Financial Management

MDPI

Article

Developing an Explanatory Risk Management Model to Comprehend the Employees' Intention to Leave Public Sector Organization

Carolina Prihandinisari [1,2], Azizur Rahman [3,*] and John Hicks [4]

[1] Section Head of Withholding Income Taxes at Directorate of Tax Regulations, Directorate General of Tax, Ministry of Finance, Jakarta 12190, Indonesia; carolina.prihandinisari@pajak.go.id

[2] School of Management and Marketing, Charles Sturt University, Wagga Wagga, NSW 2678, Australia

[3] School of Computing and Mathematics, Charles Sturt University, Wagga Wagga, NSW 2678, Australia

[4] School of Accounting and Finance, Charles Sturt University, Bathurst, NSW 2678, Australia; jhicks@csu.edu.au

* Correspondence: azrahman@csu.edu.au; Tel.: +61-2-69334744

Received: 10 July 2020; Accepted: 1 September 2020; Published: 4 September 2020

Abstract: This paper reviews research and theory on the important topic of labour turnover resulting from issues related to job performance and/or job satisfaction which have, in turn, been initiated by changes in work motivation. We focus on labour turnover in the public sector—a neglected area of public administration research—and propose an explanatory model of the development of the intention to leave an organization. The model first describes the relationships between work motivation and job performance and/or job satisfaction. It then explains how changes in performance and/or satisfaction result in the formation of an intention to leave public service employment. The paper concludes by identifying key areas for future research.

Keywords: financial incentives; public service motivation; job performance; job satisfaction; intention to leave

1. Introduction

There is an increasing financial risk management issue arising in many organizations due to a high level of employees' turnover. These organizations are typically suffering from significant costs for employee replacement as well as operational disruptions. There is a growing literature on the topic of employee turnover research (e.g., Tett and Meyer 1993; Griffeth et al. 2000; Podsakoff et al. 2007; Zimmerman and Darnold 2009; Van Iddekinge et al. 2011). Many researchers found that a range of issues are associated with employee overall behavioral aspects that could trigger resignation. This research provides an explicit account of how an employees' intention to leave an organization develops and the important factors that drive to leave the organization.

Over the last several decades, a number of employees' turnover models have been developed by researchers (see, e.g., Bluedorn 1982a; Hellman 1997; Allen and Griffeth 1999; Peterson 2004; Luna-Arocas and Camps 2008; Steel and Lounsbury 2009; Chen et al. 2011). These models range from a theoretical development of employees' turnover puzzles to turnover process modeling. Most of the studies also mainly focused on a typical standpoint of the human resource improvement, especially in the private sector organizations. However, it is significant to analyze an organizational risk management perspective as well, with a focus to the public sector organizations.

Bluedorn (1982a) developed a unified model of turnover which combined three previous models: (i) the casual turnover model (Price 1989), (ii) the intermediate linkages model (Mobley 1977), and (iii) the organizational commitment model (Porter et al. 1974). According to this study, employees' intention to quit from an organization is negatively associated with the level of commitment to organization and positively associated with active job searching status. Commitment to the organization is positively linked to both job satisfaction and promotion opportunity, but negatively associated with potential role of conflict, equity, education, or skill development, and routinization, etc. Ultimately, the decision to leave an organization is particularly impacted by some significant factors such as intention to leave, routinization, employee's age, and workplace environment and opportunity (Bluedorn 1982a).

Another model suggests that there have been three distinct routes which led employee to resign from an organization (Allen and Griffeth 1999). First, there was the route associated with a desire to move, as might arise as a result of issues related to job satisfaction, job commitment, or an option to move as appropriate for remuneration contingency. Second, there was the route that arose through the ease of movement as exemplified by the number and quality of alternatives in the job market and moderated by the visibility of those jobs. The final route was in reaction to performance-related shocks associated with, for example, salient performance feedback, or an unsolicited job offer.

In existing literature, most of the studies have primarily concentrated on finding key factors for employee turnover (Ellett et al. 2007; Luna-Arocas and Camps 2008), examining link between employees' work motivation and turnover (Maertz and Griffeth 2004), job performance, and turnover (Allen and Griffeth 1999; Nyberg 2010), public service motivation and turnover (Bright 2008), and employees' sex and turnover (Sousa-Poza and Sousa-Poza 2007; Rutherford et al. 2012). Some other research also compared the worker's turnover between the public sector and private sector organization (e.g., see Carmeli and Weisberg 2006; Wang et al. 2012). Moreover, many scholars have found that there is a significant association between employees' turnover and job satisfaction (Mobley 1977; Hellman 1997; Steel 2002; Chiu and Francesco 2003; Boswell et al. 2005; Carmeli and Weisberg 2006; Spector et al. 2007; Bright 2008; de Moura et al. 2009; Lambert and Hogan 2009; Liu et al. 2010; Chen et al. 2011; Delobelle et al. 2011; Grissom et al. 2012; Wang et al. 2012; Mihajlov and Mihajlov 2016). For example, a recent study in Serbia demonstrates that job satisfaction plays a significant role in the overall courses of turnover, and employees in the public sector have a higher level of extrinsic job satisfaction with a lower level of turnover intentions compared to employees in the private sector (Mihajlov and Mihajlov 2016).

With only a few exceptions, research on turnover has been undertaken exclusively in a business or private sector context as well as from an organizational human resource development perspective. Research on employee turnover in the public sector is still very rare (Meier and Hicklin 2008), especially in a viewpoint of risk management of public sector organizations. To fill this gap in the literature, this review paper proposes an explanatory risk management model to empirically examine the nexus between work motivation and job performance and job satisfaction, and then assesses the impact of job performance and job satisfaction on the intention to leave a public sector organization through the model to minimize effects and potential risk to the organization due to turnover. In this context we have adopted a different perspective in research. The key novelty of this study can be divided into two folds. Firstly, our proposed explanatory model is based on extensive literature review of various behavioral psychology theories from private sector research. As the public sector research, and specially risk management research in public sector is still rare, this paper will fill-in such a research lacuna by focusing on public organizations. Secondly, it adopts a conceptual nature of connecting both theoretical research and public sector organizational research with risk management perception by offering a contemporary organizational risk management model and detailed constituents of it with validation from important literature in one place. This will bring significant benefits to prospective empirical research in the domain of public sector risk management.

The paper is organised as follows. The next section presents an explanatory risk management model of the intention to leave public sector employment. The model is based on a review of the behavioral psychology literature from private sector research. This section also provides an account of various fundamental arguments around the concepts of work motivation. Section 3 considers the literature related to the establishment of relationships between work motivation, job satisfaction and job performance. Section 4 provides an assessment of significant determinants of intention to leave the organization with a particular focus on the public sector context. Finally, Section 5 provides a summary of the findings and suggests directions for future research.

2. An Explanatory Risk Management Model

Extensive research has linked job satisfaction to turnover intentions. Other variables, such as gender, work motivation, organizational factors, and job performance, have been considered in the literature as moderating or mediating factors. Our model describes the relationships between work motivation and each of job performance and job satisfaction. It also examines how employees' intention to leave public sector organizations can be influenced by their job performance and job satisfaction. Additionally, this research considers the work motivation which comprises the concepts of intrinsic and extrinsic work motivation as well as the public service work motivation. Based on these traditional and contemporary concepts in this research area, we propose an explanatory risk management model of the development of the intention to leave an organization which is illustrated in Figure 1.

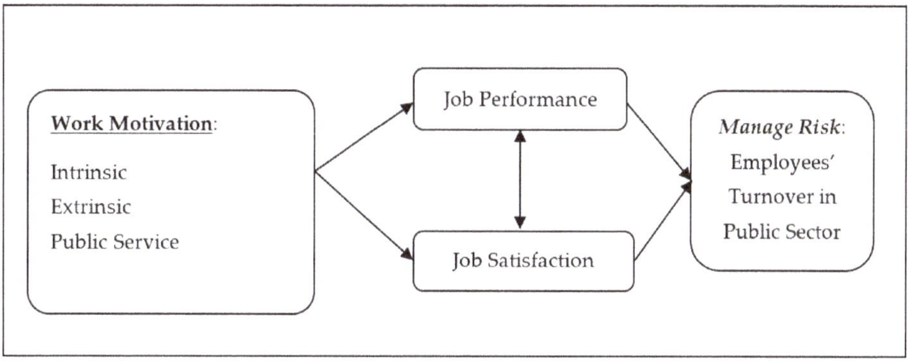

Figure 1. An explanatory risk management model depicting pathways of employee turnover in the public sector.

Work motivation drives employees to perform congruently with the organizations' objectives. It is obvious from the model that work motivation is a key factor influencing the employees' intention to leave organization through both job performance and job satisfaction. So, it is important to manage this growing risk of employee turnover in the public sector organization through assessing impacts of those factors. A range of research has been conducted to explore and model theories of work motivation. For example, the plethora of theories on motivation proposed an integrative context mainly based on a chronological order of motivation (e.g., see Locke 1991). While, some researchers considered the 1960s and 1970s to be the "golden age" of work motivation theory because of the considerable advances in our understanding of the concept that were made during this period (Steers et al. 2004).

According to the study by Locke (1991), motivational theories can be classified into a group of seven elements such as 'needs', 'values', 'goals', 'expectancy and self-efficacy', 'performance', 'rewards', and 'satisfaction'. Locke explained the elements as follows.

Needs: "The concept of need explains why living organism act". Theories of motivation based on needs include Maslow's hierarchy of needs theory and Deci's self-determination theory.

Values: In contrast to needs, which are innate, values are *in* consciousness and acquired. Values are the connection between needs and action. Locke included McClelland's need for achievement theory, Miner's role motivation theory, and Vroom's expectancy theory within this element.

Goals: The reflection of the person's values are found in the goals they set. Goals are defined as applications of values to specific situations. Goal theory (Locke and Latham 1990) explains how goals affect action by affecting the intensity, duration, and direction of action.

Expectancy and self-efficacy: These two concepts influence the process of setting up goals. The motivational theories which are included in this category are expectancy theory and social-cognitive theory (Locke 1991).

Performance: Goals and self-efficacy are considered as the most immediate and direct motivational determinants of performance. Typical attribution theory explains people's attribution on their performance and how such attributions affect subsequent passions and actions.

Rewards: People's action or performance are driven by rewards and therefore rewards can modify people's behaviour. Motivational theories which focused on rewards are behaviour modification theory and the equity theory.

Satisfaction: Some theories explain the relation between work and job satisfaction. These include Herzberg's two-factor (motivation–hygiene) theory, Hackman and Oldham's job characteristics theory, and Locke's satisfaction theory.

In the above framework, the researcher has emphasized values as the motivation core, because values are the keys that make every individual as unique and guide them to real choices and effective actions. Values and rewards has a strong correlation as well. Locke (1991) motivation sequence framework also indicates that goals, self-efficacy, and performance are important motivational core, which determines the individual's activities.

In an alternative review on motivational theories Steers et al. (2004) classified motivation theory into two groups: content theory and process theory. Factors that regulate and manage individual and social behaviour can be explained by content theory such as the motivation-hygiene theory (Herzberg et al. 1962). The motivation–hygiene theory proposes two types factors (Herzberg 1974) which are: (1) motivation factors such as achievement (i.e., a job itself will give an employee a sense of stimulated feeling of having done something worthwhile), recognition (i.e., an employee will be well recognized and/or praised for each of their successes by the supervisors and colleagues), responsibility (i.e., an employee must take responsibility of their job task with ownership to complete the task), growth (i.e., an employee should get opportunity to learn new skills through professional development and/or formal educational training), advancement (i.e., an employee should get an equal opportunity to be promoted at a higher level), and tasks in the occupation (i.e., everyday tasks in the work must be inspiring, diverse, and/or offer a good range of creative challenges); and (2) hygiene factors such as salary (i.e., a fair and reasonable salary structure which must be expediently competitive with other institutes within the same business domain), status and security (i.e., an employee should have a solid status in the organization and feel secure about their job without any significant risk of being jobless), supervision (i.e., an employee should get fair and appropriate supervision with their independence to do better and grow), relationship (i.e., an employee should work in a healthy, functional, and cooperative and collegial workplace without any bullying or cliques), work conditions (i.e., workplace environment and tools must be contemporary, safe, functional, and hygienic), and company policies (i.e., all policies need to be open, fair and equivalent for everyone within the company and their competitors). Over time, these concepts in motivation factors and hygiene factors have evolved into the terms "intrinsic motivation" and "extrinsic motivation", respectively. This theory and terms have been widely applied in many literature (e.g., Carmeli and Weisberg 2006; Furnham et al. 2009; Maidani 1991; Park et al. 1988; Sachau 2007; Smith and Shields 2013).

Typically, intrinsic motivation is related with job content, while later is correlated with extrinsic motivation. According to Herzberg (1974), achievement, recognition for achievement, job itself, responsibility, growth and advancement are intrinsic motivation factors, whereas, policy and administration of the organization, supervision strategies, interpersonal relationship between employees, workplace environments and conditions, job status, salary, and work security are extrinsic motivation factors. Given that intrinsic motivation was positively associated with job satisfaction, Herzberg proposed a technique of job enrichment through increasing intrinsic motivation to make jobs more interesting. Later on the work of Hackman and Oldham (1976), in developing the job characteristics model, which advocated work redesign or job enlargement, was strongly influenced by the motivation–hygiene theory.

Others argued that extrinsic motivation also contributes to job satisfaction. This debate gave rise to the initial use of the terms intrinsic motivation and extrinsic motivation as explained by Sachau (2007). When people work to fulfil hygiene needs they are responding to extrinsic motivation. That is, they are moved to act by life factors external to the job. Intrinsic motivation, on the other hand, refers to factors that influence work behaviour that are directly related to the nature of the work itself. Thus, when Herzberg controversially wrote that "money is not a motivator" (see p. 381), he was not saying that money could not move people to work. He was arguing that money was not an intrinsic motivator, but rather an extrinsic motivator as its value lay in its ability to acquire the goods and services on which life and life-style were based.

A similar distinction between intrinsic and extrinsic motivation was proposed by Ryan and Deci (2000) in developing their self-determination theory (SDT). Here, intrinsic motivation was defined as "the doing of an activity for its inherent satisfactions rather than for some separable consequences" (p. 56). Extrinsic motivation was defined as "a construct that pertains whenever an activity is done in order to attain some separable outcome" (p. 60). Moreover, their study identified four stages, external regulation, introjection, identification, and integration, though which extrinsic motivation is transformed into intrinsic motivation. The most autonomous form of extrinsic motivation is integration, i.e., a complete blending of external drivers and self-values for a particular action.

Debate has arisen over the potential impact of extrinsic rewards on intrinsic motivation with the view emerging that extrinsic rewards may weaken intrinsic motivation. Empirical research, however, is inconclusive. Following a meta-analytic study Wiersma (1992) noted that "it is not supported when task performance is measured while the extrinsic reward is in effect". On the other hand Deci et al. (1999), based on a meta-analysis of 128 past experiments, claimed that "tangible rewards tend to have a substantially negative effect on intrinsic motivation".

Finally, in considering work motivation for the public sector, we must ask if the motives that drive people to serve in public or community development are likely to be different to those in non-public sector occupations. Perry and Wise (1990) asserted that there exists a public service motivation (PSM) which can be defined as "an individual's predisposition to respond to motives grounded primarily or uniquely in public institutions and organizations" (see p. 368). Building on this, Perry and Hondeghem (2008) argued that public service motivation is composed of "individual motives that are largely, but not exclusively, altruistic and are grounded in public institutions" (refer to pp. 3–4). Perry (1997) also investigated the antecedents of public service administration, and proposed five sets of correlates: parental socialization, religious socialization, professional identification, political ideology, and individual demographics.

The work of Vandenabeele (2007, 2008, 2011) explained the theoretical framework of PSM, provided a measurement scale for PSM, and identified the antecedent of PSM which was related to the institutional development of PSM. Vandenabeele (2007) proposed a hypothetical framework that positioned PSM within the theories of institutionalism, SDT, and the person–organization fit theory. It assumed that "the degree of institutions respond to the individual psychological needs of relatedness, competence and autonomy, institutionalized public service values will be internalized more autonomously in the individual identity" (p. 553). Furthermore, he hypothesized "to the degree that a public service identity is more autonomous, it will result in a more consistent and intense public service behaviour, given that the institution in which the individual operates embraces the public service values" (p. 553). However, Vandenbeele acknowledged that further research was require to provide empirical validity to his theory.

In existing public administration literature, PSM has been considered as one of the key research topics at both national and international levels (Bright 2013). As the study of Pedersen (2013) confirmed that the PSM dimension of "public interest" was positively associated with attraction to public sector employment, as a support for one of Perry and Wise (1990) propositions.

3. Examining Relationship between Work Motivations and Job Performance and Job Satisfaction

The key three links between work motivation and job performance, work motivation and job satisfaction, and job performance and job satisfaction are examined in this section in line with the evidences from the literature. Although there is a range of studies available in this area of research which primarily focused on private sector, our focus here is on the public sector. Therefore, we will mainly rely on most of the resources from the public sector research which are consistent to validate our analysis.

3.1. Relationship between Work Motivations and Job Performance

Herzberg (1968) examined the relationship between work motivation and job performance by comparing a group of workers who had been enriched with motivator factors (intrinsic motivations which included achievement, responsibility, recognition, growth, and learning) with a control group. He observed that the test group had better performance and attitudes towards their job than the control group and concluded that motivator factors (intrinsic motivation) had a positive relationship to job performance.

With respect to extrinsic motivations, Sachau (2007) adopted Herzberg's notion that "hygiene factors have an escalating zero point" (see p. 386). That is "once a person has experienced a new higher level of a given hygiene factor, the new level becomes the minimal acceptable level".

Thus, both intrinsic and extrinsic motivations have been identified as critical factors driving job performance. Studies have consistently reported a positive relationship between job performance and intrinsic motivation (Dysvik and Kuvaas 2010, 2013; Grant 2008; Joo et al. 2010). Similarly, research generally supports the presumption that extrinsic rewards (a form of extrinsic motivators) will be positively related to job performance (Bonner and Sprinkle 2002; Condly et al. 2003; Dysvik and Kuvaas 2013; Garbers and Konradt 2014). However, some authors warn that findings with respect to extrinsic rewards should be used prudently—especially in relation to task complexity.

With respect to public service organizations, Perry and Wise (1990) proposed that

(1) A higher level of PSM of an individual is favourable to join a public sector organization;
(2) PSM is positively correlated with job performance; and
(3) Individual employees' performance can be easily managed if the public sector organizations appoint workforce having a higher level of PSM.

Subsequent studies have provided empirical validation of these hypotheses (see Naff and Crum 1999; Alonso and Lewis 2001; Bright 2007). While the first two of these three studies found a significantly positive relationship between PSM and job performance, the third study added to it by showing that the relationship was stronger when person–organization (P-O) fit was introduced as a mediating factor.

Vandenabeele (2009) undertaking research in public sector organizations in Belgium, confirmed that PSM was significantly related to job performance (as well as to both job satisfaction and organizational commitment). Further, research with Italian nurses (Bellé 2013) found that individuals with higher PSM had stronger job performance. Interestingly, Bellé (2013) also argued that "PSM is a dynamic state" and "the levels of PSM found among an organization's employees may be not wholly determined by attraction-selection-attrition mechanisms but may also be influenced by the organization to some extent".

3.2. Relationship between Work Motivation and Job Satisfaction

The motivation-hygiene theory is frequently used in contemporary research. Several studies have revealed that both work motivation and hygiene factors have positive relationship with employees' job satisfaction (e.g., Furnham et al. 2009; Islam et al. 2011; Sell and Cleal 2011; Smith and Shields 2013).

A sample of 107,292 observations from 49 countries has been used in a study by Huang and Vliert (2003), which reveals that various extrinsic job characteristics have a strong and significant relationship with job satisfaction in all countries. It also demonstrates that the strength of correlation is higher for data from richer countries, having better social security, more individualistic values, and relatively a less power distance culture.

Moreover, a study on job satisfaction in West Germany, Great Britain, the United States, Hungary, Norway, and Israel has revealed that there is a positive and statistically significant associations of both intrinsic and extrinsic rewards, relationships with administration and work-relations with colleagues to job satisfaction (Westover and Taylor 2010). However, intrinsic rewards were found to have the dominant influence. Furthermore, PSM was found to have an insignificant impact on job satisfaction, although PSM-fit proved to be significant. Counteracting this finding was the work of Taylor and Westover (2011). They used the same survey (the International Social Survey Program, ISSP), but chose different countries (the USA; Canada; Great Britain; Germany; France; Denmark; and Norway), and found that PSM was significantly related to job satisfaction in government employees.

3.3. *Relationship between Job Satisfaction and Job Performance*

The relationship between employees' job satisfaction and job performance remains a very important topic in organizational risk management processes. It is generally held that job satisfaction has an insignificant impact on job performance. Lawler and Porter (1967) cite the Brayfield and Crockett (1955) review study on this issue in which they conclude "there is little evidence in the available literature that employee attitudes bear any simple relationship to performance on the job" (see p. 21). This conclusion has resulted in the issue being frequently re-examined.

Lawler and Porter (1967) demonstrate that there is a positive and persistent relationship between job satisfaction and job performance. They stated that "satisfaction is an important variable from both a theoretical and a practical point of view despite its low relationship to performance" (see p. 24). Locke (1970), who took into consideration motivational theories (including expectancy theory, goal-setting theory, and achievement theory) inferred that "the effect of performance on satisfaction is viewed as a function of the degree to which performance entails or leads to the attainment of the individual's important job values".

Iaffaldano and Muchinsky (1985) concluded that job satisfaction had an insignificant impact on job performance. Judge et al. (2001), on the other hand, found a high and significant correlation and declared that it was "premature to dismiss the relationship" (see p. 389). They encouraged future research on the issue—proposing an integrative model of the relationship between job satisfaction and job performance (see p. 390).

This call was answered by Schleicher et al. (2004) who found a larger and significant correlation had existed between job satisfaction and job performance when moderated by affective-cognitive consistency. Subsequently Borgogni et al. (2010) confirmed "job satisfaction affects job performance, along with the organizational tenure" (refer to p. 288). Finally, Nyberg (2010) concluded that "performance was statistically significant and positively associated with job satisfaction". Therefore, our proposed model considers these two factors as the mediating factors of the development of the intention to leave an organization from the overall work motivation.

4. Determinants of the Intention to Leave an Organization

It can be very costly for an organization when its highly competent employees may have voluntary disengagement to the organization's perspectives. So, this organizational risk to me managed effectively specially in the public sector as it is a growing concern for many countries. According to a study by Hellman (1997), typical risks include employee replacement costs as well as operational disruptions. Often the individuals' perception of their prospects for generating a higher level income from private sector organizations can drive to leaving a public sector organizations. There is extensive research into turnover intentions, (e.g., see Bluedorn 1982b; Swailes and Fahdi 2011; Carmeli and Weisberg 2006; Nyberg 2010).

A meta-analysis by Zimmerman and Darnold (2009) concluded that the relationship between job performance and intention to quit is "both negative and modest". It was also recognized that the relationship could be mediated by other factors, such as job satisfaction. Nyberg (2010) on the other hand, concluded "the negative relationship between performance and voluntary turnover was stronger when pay growth was high than when pay growth was low" (see p. 449). This result implied that the high performers were more likely to stay within the organization when pay growth was high. A similar finding was associated with the prevalence of promotion prospects. High performing employees were found to have a higher propensity to voluntarily resign when the unemployment rate rose, as they believed that they could seize the better opportunities in a competitive labour market than the lower performing employees.

Typically, a low level job satisfaction is connected to a turnover intention. For instances, A recent study by Mihajlov and Mihajlov (2016) has revealed that public sector employees have higher extrinsic job satisfaction and lower turnover intentions compared to their counterparts in the private sector. Job satisfaction affects organizational commitment, which then successively effects intention to leave organization (Bluedorn 1982b), and job satisfaction and affective commitment have been significantly related to turnover intentions (Carmeli and Weisberg 2006). Another research also demonstrates that job satisfaction was a statistically significant mediator of performance–voluntary turnover relationship (Nyberg 2010, p. 449). These findings are repeated in several studies (Hellman 1997; Tett and Meyer 1993; Griffeth et al. 2000; Hom and Kinicki 2001; Chen et al. 2011).

Finally, Tett and Meyer (1993) conducted a path analyses based on meta-analytic findings of the relationships between job satisfaction, organizational commitment, and turnover. They found that job satisfaction had a high negative correlation with turnover intention and that this impact was stronger than that of organization commitment. So, the overall findings suggest that job satisfaction is one of the best predictive measurement of employees' intention to leave the organization, which is in consistent with the funding in other research (e.g., Griffeth et al. 2000).

4.1. The Public Sector Context

Our goal in this paper is to examine the influence of work motivation, job performance, and job satisfaction on the intention to leave an organization—especially in the contexts of the public sector organizations and the risk management in public sector. Employee voluntary turnover has been an important issue of both practical and theoretical significance. Voluntary turnover could be driven by many factors, such as low job satisfaction, poor individual or organizational performance, or external factors (i.e., unemployment rate).

Public sector management has evolved over the last three decades. In this 21st century's business environment, the public sector organization need a higher level of accountability and transparency than in the past century. Research and innovations in public administration and new public management concepts can be useful to meet this progressive demand. A relevant example could be the Organization for Economic Co-operation Development (OECD), which has pushed reform agendas to its member countries. Moreover, governments in many countries have already launched public sector organizational reform to tackle their internal social and economic crises or meet to international demand and standards.

Therefore, in the globalized services providing environments public sectors' financial organizations are in a huge challenge to reform and provide better outcomes and performance to local, national and international communities. When an organization is under reform, it employees not only face with changes related to their job design, salary arrangements, and performance appraisal system, but also they must meet specific performance target at individual and organizational levels. They require appropriate professional developments to equip themselves with high levels of work motivations to accomplish and align themselves to their organizational targets. The professional development opportunities may be limited in many public sector organization. As a result, a high proportion of employees may consider voluntary turnover, which will eventually disrupt performance of the organization to meet its functional objectives.

Highly motivated employees are valuable assets for organizations. Employees could be motivated by intrinsic and extrinsic factors. Interestingly, comparison studies on motivation and job satisfaction between public and private sectors have shown mixed results. Some have resulted in no significant differences in intrinsic motivation in either sector, but an important impact in the public sector for extrinsic motivation (Maidani 1991). Other researchers have found no significant disparities between private and public sectors (DeSantis and Durst 1996). While, a study of data from 51 countries revealed that employees of 21 countries (out of the 51 countries) have a higher intrinsic motivation in the public sector than the private sector (Cowley and Smith 2014). Table 1 presents the results of a comparative research between the public sector and private sector organizations on the topic of work motivation, job performance, job satisfaction, and intention to leave the organization. Although the table includes several selected studies from the public sector context, our discussion covers other relevant research which follows.

Table 1. A comparative study between public sector and private sector research on work motivation, job performance, job satisfaction, and turnover intention.

Author(s)	Objectives	Method	Major Findings
Maidani (1991)	Compare public and private sector job satisfaction using Herzberg's Two-Factor Theory	It used a survey of 173 and 177 respondents from private and public sector data, with staffs' work factor importance and job satisfaction measurement (Rosenfeld and Zdep 1971; Warr et al. 1979).	Motivators and hygiene factors were sources of satisfaction for both sectors. Employee in public sector had a higher level of job satisfaction than private sector. Moreover, public sector employees recognized higher value on the hygiene factors.
DeSantis and Durst (1996)	Test differences in job satisfaction between public and private sector.	The study utilized a panel data from the National Longitudinal Surveys of Youth (NLSY) in the US. The survey collected 12,686 respondents' data yearly from 1979–1985.	In general, both public and private sector showed similar perception in JS. Regarding salary, private staffs recognized it as key factor, and young employees considered the actual level of income is important.
Carmeli and Weisberg (2006)	Assess the effects of key factors on turnover intention on public sector (social workers and financial officers) and private sector (lawyers).	A study in Israel with the data from social workers (228) and financial officers (98), and professional lawyers (183). A structured questionnaire survey was conducted to collect the data, and it employed two hierarchical regressions analyses.	Affective commitment and intrinsic job satisfaction (IJS) were negatively linked to turnover, but no link between IJS and turnover. IJS had more impact on turnover than extrinsic job satisfaction (EJS). No link between job performance and turnover. Private sector had lower turnover than public sector.
Markovits et al. (2010)	Examine the effects of organizational commitment and JS on public and private sectors.	A sample of 257 private and 360 public sector staffs data by the MSQ (Warr et al. 1979) and a scale by Tett and Meyer (1993) were employed.	Extrinsic and intrinsic satisfactions were more strongly related to affective and normative commitment for public sector employees than for private sector.
Wang et al. (2012)	Compare job satisfaction and turnover intentions of public and private sector in Taiwan.	The study involved 243 public employees and 240 private employees (overall return rate of 48.3%) in Taiwan. The Chinese version of the MSQ was used as measurement.	Public employees had higher IJS, but lower EJS and turnover intent than private sector. The negative relationship between EJS and turnover intention is weaker in public than in private employees.
Cowley and Smith (2014)	Compare intrinsic motivation of public and private sector.	The study used data from the World Values Survey and used 51 countries.	A higher level of corruption in a country had negative effect on the proportion of intrinsically motivated public sector staffs.
Mihajlov and Mihajlov (2016)	Compare job satisfaction and turnover intentions of private and public sector in Serbia	The study used questionnaires based survey data from a random sample of 234 people of which 166 and 68 employees were from public and private sectors respectively.	Staff in public sector showed much higher level of JS and much lower level of turnover against private sector. Also public employees have a higher level of EJS but a lower level of IJS than their counterparts in private sector.

Findings reveal that intrinsic motivation has a statistically significant and positive link to an employee's job satisfaction (Carmeli and Weisberg 2006; Markovits et al. 2010; Cho and Perry 2012). Extrinsic motivation has also a positive relationship to the public sector motivation (Wang et al. 2012; Taylor and Taylor 2011). Additionally, people are attracted to the public sector organizations by their intrinsic rewards rather than their extrinsic rewards (Markovits et al. 2010; Georgellis et al. 2011). In other words, a higher level of extrinsic gains reduce the propensity of intrinsically motivated employees to involve in public sector organization (Mihajlov and Mihajlov 2016).

Additionally, in line with the sector characteristics, individuals might consider public sector occupation if they have high public service motivation (Perry and Wise 1990). Anderfuhren-Biget et al. (2010) examined the influence of PSM on work motivation in the public sector in Switzerland. Their study convincingly supported the inclusion of PSM as an important motivational factor in the public sector. Another study of PSM in the Australian public sector (Taylor 2007) confirmed that employees with higher levels of the four dimensions of PSM were more likely to show higher levels of organizational commitment, job motivation, and job satisfaction. Taylor and Westover (2011) investigated and compared the effects of a selection of antecedents related to job satisfaction in government employees in the USA; Canada; Great Britain; Germany; France; Denmark; and Norway. They reported that job satisfaction was significantly related to PSM, extrinsic workplace attributes, intrinsic workplace attributes, work relations with managers and work relations with co-workers. A more recent study by Taylor (2014) examined the relationship between PSM, job design, and job satisfaction in Australian local government, and concluded that government employees with a high level of PSM were more satisfied, particularly when they could observe the positive impact of their job to the community. Mihajlov and Mihajlov (2016) found somewhat a consistent finding in Serbia that a high level of PSM including extrinsic satisfaction can be derived from fundamental cultural values, close and harmonious relationships with supervisors and peers, and open information sharing within the corporation which reducing their fear and insecurity, and nurture strong bond with the corporation. Other studies also examined PSM in a non-western cultural context (Prihandinisari et al. 2016) and analyzed the effects of knowledge management (KM) and human resource management (HRM) processes to the performance organization and employee's job satisfaction (Rahman and Hasan 2017).

To conclude, these findings demonstrate that public sector context is an important area of research due to ever changing globally connected business environment, and demand for a higher level of accountability and transparency which must be competitive to the advanced private sector. It is interesting to note that in addition to the public sector motivation, both intrinsic and extrinsic motivation of public sector employees are crucial to maintain satisfactory levels of job performance and job satisfaction. These will ultimately contribute to employees' turnover intention including voluntary turnover from the public sector.

4.2. Turnover Intention in the Public Sector

It is only in the last few years that public administration scholars have begun exploring the question of job turnover in the public sector. The issues considered in these research have included the determinants of employee turnover (Bertelli 2007), administrative employees turnover (Bertelli 2007; Boyne et al. 2010; Bertelli and Lewis 2013), comparison of public and private sectors employees turnover (Carmeli and Weisberg 2006; Wang et al. 2012), examining link between employees turnover and their gender (Moynihan and Landuyt 2008; Grissom et al. 2012), individual and organization fit (Moynihan and Pandey 2008), analyzing organizational goals (Jung 2014), and employees and organization performance (Meier and Hicklin 2008; Lee and Jimenez 2011). Moreover, there are many research studies on turnover intention are related to job satisfaction though (e.g., Carmeli and Weisberg 2006; Bright 2008; Liu et al. 2010; Pitts et al. 2011; Grissom et al. 2012; Wang et al. 2012). Table 2 presents a summary of the findings from relevant research.

Table 2. Summary of research on turnover intention in public sector.

Author(s)	Objectives	Method	Major Findings
Bertelli (2007)	Examine the determinants of turnover intention in government service.	The study used the 2002 Federal Human Capital Survey (FHCS, USA). The targeted organizations were the Internal Revenue Service (IRS) and the Office of the Comptroller of the Currency (OCC) both are under the U.S. Treasury.	It found that job involvement and intrinsic motivations vs friendship solidarity with co-workers and supervisors both decrease the likelihood of turnover. Subordinates' turnover were not influenced by perceived rewards.
Bertelli and Lewis (2013)	Analyze turnover intention among federal executives, USA. Their model also considered agency-specific human capital and out-side options (labor market).	It used data from the 2007–2008 Survey on the Future of Government Service, a survey conducted by the Princeton Survey Research Center. The overall response rate for the survey is 34% (2398/7151) with 2069 completed the full survey.	The perceived availability of outside options increases probability of executive turnover. The influence of outside options on turnover is conditional on the presence of agency-specific human capital.
Boyne et al. (2010)	Explore whether public service performance makes a difference to the turnover of top managers in public organizations.	The study used 4 years (2002–2006) of panel data on all 148 English principal local governments (London boroughs, metropolitan boroughs, unitary authorities, and county councils).	Managers were more likely to leave for poor performance. The negative link between performance and turnover was weaker for chief executives than senior managements.
Grissom et al. (2012)	Assess the impact of manager gender on the job satisfaction and turnover of public sector workers.	The data on public school teachers used in this study were obtained from the National Center for Education Statistics (NCES) in the US.	Teachers preferred male principals. Gender incongruent more likely influenced job satisfaction and turnover intention for men, than women.
Moynihan and Landuyt (2008)	Test a turnover model focusing on life cycle stability, gender, organizational loyalty, diversity policy.	A total of 62,628 staff was surveyed in 53 different state agencies in Texas, US, resulting in 34,668 usable responses, a response rate of more than 55%.	Employees reached life cycle stability, were less likely to quit. Females were less likely to quit public sector. From HRM view, IJS and salary had big effects on turnover.
Moynihan and Pandey (2008)	Examine the role of social networks on turnover intention, and to examine how employee values shaped turnover intention.	Data used in this study were collected from 12 organizations in the northeastern part of the US in 2005; include private nonprofit (5) and public service organization (7). Of the 531 comprising the sample, 326 responded for a response rate of 61.4%.	Staff turnover affected by internal network. Staff who had a sense of obligation toward co-workers were less likely to leave in the short and long term. JS and years in position were key turnover factors. P-O fit negatively affected long-term turnover.
Jung (2014)	Explore the influence of goal clarity on turnover intentions in public organizations.	The main data sources for this analysis were the 2005 MPS and the 2005 PART, the samples comprised 18,242 US federal employees.	Goal specificity and goal importance, pay, promotion, and training showed negative links to turnover. Internal alliance had negative effect on turnover, at both personal and organizational level.
Lee and Jimenez (2011)	Examine the influence of performance management on turnover intention in federal employees.	The study used data from the 2005 Merit Principles Survey conducted by the Merit Systems Protection Board (MSPB). The total number of federal employees who completed the survey was 36,926 or a response rate of 49.9%.	Performance-based reward system and supporting supervision were significantly and negatively related to JS and turnover. Job position had positive link with turnover, and a U-shape relation found between age and turnover.
Meier and Hicklin (2008)	Study the relations between staff turnover and organizational performance in public sector.	It used a database of the 1000+ Texas school districts for the academic years 1994 through 2002. The data set was a panel data set that includes nine years data on each school district.	In higher task difficulties, an inverted U-shaped link existed between turnover and performance. At some point higher level turnover had detrimental effects on performance.
Bright (2008)	Investigate the relationship among PSM, job satisfaction, and the turnover intentions mediated by P-O fit.	The sample of 205 employees from three public organizations in states of Oregon, Indiana, and Kentucky was analysed.	PSM showed a big and positive link to P-O fit, but P-O fit had a negative link to turnover. If P-O fit was taken into account, PSM showed relation to JS and turnover.
Liu et al. (2010)	Investigate the relationship among P-O fit, job satisfaction, and turnover intentions in China public sector.	The study used a survey data from 259 part-time Master in Public Administration (MPA) program student but also full-time public sector employees.	P-O fit had noticeable positive link to JS, and negative link to turnover. Age and tenure had a strongly negative effect on turnover. JS mediates P-O fit and turnover intentions.
Pitts et al. (2011)	Explore key factors (e.g., demographic, organizational and satisfaction, workplace) that affected turnover.	The 2006 Federal Human Capital Survey (FHCS) data was used which consists a sample of more than 200,000 US federal government employees.	The most significant factors that affect turnover intentions of federal employees were job satisfaction, satisfaction with progress, and age.

Results demonstrate that the employee turnover intention might have a negative or positive impacts on organizational performances (Bluedorn 1982b; Meier and Hicklin 2008; Lee and Jimenez 2011). Typically, the negative effects encompass expenditures related to new staff recruitment, drop in productivity and reduced self-esteem in existing workers. There is also a functional impacts which imply the positive values of employee turnover intention, especially when the leaving workers are a low level performers. In such situations, the organization can get advantage from appointing some highly skilled new employees. In most cases, a new staff will usually come advanced ideas and bring better innovations in the organization.

The relationship between job performance and intention to leave could be positive, negative, a non-linear relationship, or not significant (Allen and Griffeth 1999; Carmeli and Weisberg 2006; Meier and Hicklin 2008; Zimmerman and Darnold 2009). The mixed findings in the literature on the relationship between job performance and turnover intention leaves a gap that should be addressed empirically to gain a better understanding and validation of the issue. By gaining better knowledge around these factors, public sector organization should be able to manage the employee turnover risk effectively.

As already mentioned above, most studies of turnover intention are related to job satisfaction. Hellman (1997) meta-analysis reported that "the relationship between job satisfaction and intention to leave was significantly different from zero and consistently negative". This conclusion was reached following the analysis of 50 studies between 1983 and 1993. The study took into consideration the relations of the variables amongst federal government employees. The study also revealed that federal government employees were less likely to leave the organizations than the private sector employees. However, the meta-analysis is limited to studies in the USA context.

Naff and Crum (1999) found that government employees with high PSM had higher job satisfaction and were less likely to leave their organizations. However, the PSM-job satisfaction-turnover intention relationships became insignificant when person–organization fit was introduced as a mediating factor (Bright 2008). Again, however, both studies were conducted in the USA. The studies of job satisfaction relationship to turnover intention in the public sector outside of those conducted in the USA include Liu et al. (2010) for China, Wang et al. (2012) for Taiwan, Carmeli and Weisberg (2006) for Israel; and Hwang and Chang (2008) for Korea.

The apparent mixed results concerning the relationship between turnover intention and both job satisfaction and job performance must be given serious consideration. Additional considerations that need to be addressed are whether higher performing employees have higher job satisfaction; whether or not high job satisfaction leads to high performance; and, if so, whether their high satisfaction rates result in the high performing employees staying in their organizations.

Additionally, as we observe, most of the public administration literature considers only developed western countries (mainly in the US context). It will therefore be interesting to study how work motivation, job performance and job satisfaction influence the employees' turnover intention in a recently reformed public sector financial organization of a developing country in Asia.

5. Conclusions

This paper has reviewed both organizational literature and public administration literature on turnover intention, and its relationship to both job performance and job satisfaction. It has also considered the impact of work motivations—including theoretical framework and empirical findings. The paper has offerred a explanatory risk management model which integrates work motivations (intrinsic and extrinsic motivations, and public service motivation), job satisfaction, and job performance, and the interplay between those factors in shaping public sector employee's turnover intention. Findings reveal that employee turnover is a considerable risk to manage in the public sector in many countries including developing countries in Asia.

It is evidenced in the findings that job satisfaction has a negative and significant relationship with the intention to leave an organization. Subsequently, employees' satisfaction is more likely built up from intrinsic and extrinsic motivation factors, as positive correlations have shown in most of the findings. This relation is also found in most PSM studies. Interestingly, the relationship between job performance and intention to leave has been diversely reported, as it could be positive, negative, a non-linear relationship, or not significant. However, research generally confirms a positive relationship between job performance and work motivations, including intrinsic motivation, extrinsic motivation, and PSM.

Another key point emanating from the results is the interplay between job performance and job satisfaction. Again, mixed results are reported. Some research indicates that employee satisfaction leads to better job performance On the other hand, other research suggests that higher job satisfaction was caused by higher levels of performance. Nevertheless, both groups agree that positive correlations exist.

It is important to note that most of the research on the public sector turnover intention has been from developed-western countries (the USA and European countries); or developed and non-western countries (Australia, New Zealand, and China). Some of the studies also employed a pre-existing data set derived from governmental survey or international survey organizations, leaving a question of reliability.

In conclusion, as the paper aimed to empirically examine the nexus between three key factors and their influences on employees' turnover intention in order to effectively manage this organizational risk, there was no specific methodology section provided. Our proposed explanatory risk management model is based on both traditional and contemporary concepts in the research though which has been descriptively validated with the existing research. Our motivation was to develop this conceptual risk management model for advancing it to a further application paper which will provide details of mixed methods, i.e., both qualitative and quantitative approaches to validate our model further with application to real world data from an Asian country. Moreover, considering many mixed research outputs in the topics, the proposed model could serve as a guideline for future research in public sector research. Further research should be directed at answering the questions such as to what extent do work motivation, job performance, and job satisfaction influences the intention to leave the public service? In this setting, PSM should be considered a critical work motivation in the public sector along with intrinsic and extrinsic motivations. Future research on these topic should also take into account the context of the study, such as in a developing and non-western country, a reformed organization, and possibly experiencing a high voluntary turnover. Studies of this type should be addressed to clarify our understanding of the importance of turnover intention in the public sector.

Author Contributions: Conceptualization, C.P.; A.R.; Methodology, A.R.; Formal Analysis, C.P.; Data Curation, C.P.; A.R.; Writing—Early Draft Preparation, C.P.; Writing—Review and Editing, A.R.; J.H. Supervision, A.R.; J.H. Project Administration, A.R. All authors have read and agreed to the published version of the manuscript.

Funding: This research received no external funding.

Acknowledgments: The authors would like to thanks the editors and three anonymous reviewers for their valuable insightful comments and stimulus which were used to form this final version. We would also like to acknowledge the editing support provided by the Data Science Research Unit at the Charles Sturt University, Australia.

Conflicts of Interest: The authors declare no conflict of interest.

References

Allen, David, and Rodger Griffeth. 1999. Job Performance and Turnover: A Review and Integrative Multi-Route Model. *Human Resource Management Review* 9: 525–48. [CrossRef]

Alonso, Pablo, and Gregory Lewis. 2001. Public Service Motivation and Job Performance: Evidence from the Federal Sector. *The American Review of Public Administration* 31: 363–80. [CrossRef]

Anderfuhren-Biget, Simon Varone, Frederic Giauque David, and Adrian Ritz. 2010. Motivating Employees of the Public Sector: Does Public Service Motivation Matter? *International Public Management Journal* 13: 213–46. [CrossRef]

Bellé, Nicola. 2013. Experimental Evidence on the Relationship between Public Service Motivation and Job Performance. *Public Administration Review* 73: 143–53. [CrossRef]

Bertelli, Anthony. 2007. Determinants of Bureaucratic Turnover Intention: Evidence from the Department of the Treasury. *Journal of Public Administration Research and Theory* 17: 235–58. [CrossRef]

Bertelli, Anthony, and David Lewis. 2013. Policy Influence, Agency-Specific Expertise, and Exit in the Federal Service. *Journal of Public Administration Research and Theory* 23: 223–45. [CrossRef]

Bluedorn, Allen. 1982a. A unified model of turnover from organizations. *Human Relations* 35: 135–53. [CrossRef]

Bluedorn, Allen. 1982b. Managing turnover strategically. *Business Horizons* 25: 6–12. [CrossRef]

Bonner, Sarah, and Geoffrey Sprinkle. 2002. The effects of monetary incentives on effort and task performance: Theories, evidence, and a framework for research. *Accounting, Organizations and Society* 27: 303–45. [CrossRef]

Borgogni, Laura, Dello Russo Salvia, Laura Petitta, and Michele Vecchione. 2010. Predicting job satisfaction and job performance in a privatized organization. *International Public Management Journal* 13: 275–96. [CrossRef]

Boswell, Wendy, John Boudreau, and Jan Tichy. 2005. The relationship between employee job change and job satisfaction: The honeymoon-hangover effect. *Journal of Applied Psychology* 90: 882–92. [CrossRef]

Boyne, George, Oliver James, Peter John, and Nicolai Petrovsky. 2010. Does Public Service Performance Affect Top Management Turnover? *Journal of Public Administration Research and Theory* 20: i261–i279.

Brayfield, Arthur, and Walter Crockett. 1955. Employee attitudes and employee performance. *Psychological Bulletin* 52: 396–424. [CrossRef] [PubMed]

Bright, Leonard. 2007. Does Person-Organization Fit Mediate the Relationship Between Public Service Motivation and the Job Performance of Public Employees? *Review of Public Personnel Administration* 27: 361–79. [CrossRef]

Bright, Leonard. 2008. Does public service motivation really make a difference on the job satisfaction and turnover intentions of public employees? *The American Review of Public Administration* 38: 149–66. [CrossRef]

Bright, Leonard. 2013. Where Does Public Service Motivation Count the Most in Government Work Environments? A Preliminary Empirical Investigation and Hypotheses. *Public Personnel Management* 42: 5–26. [CrossRef]

Carmeli, Abraham, and Jacob Weisberg. 2006. Exploring turnover intentions among three professional groups of employees. *Human Resource Development International* 9: 191–206. [CrossRef]

Chen, Gilad, Robert Ployhart, Helena Cooper Thomas, Neil Anderson, and Paul Bliese. 2011. The power of momentum: A new model of dynamic relationships between job satisfaction change and turnover intentions. *Academy of Management Journal* 54: 159–81. [CrossRef]

Chiu, Randy, and Anne Marie Francesco. 2003. Dispositional traits and turnover intention. Examining the mediating role of job satisfaction and affective commitment. *International Journal of Manpower* 24: 284–98. [CrossRef]

Cho, Yoon Jik, and James Perry. 2012. Intrinsic motivation and employee attitudes: Role of managerial trustworthiness, goal directedness, and extrinsic reward expectancy. *Review of Public Personnel Administration* 32: 382–406. [CrossRef]

Condly, Steven, Richard Clark, and Harold Stolovitch. 2003. The Effects of Incentives on Workplace Performance: A Meta-analytic Review of Research Studies. *Performance Improvement Quarterly* 16: 46–63. [CrossRef]

Cowley, Edd, and Sarah Smith. 2014. Motivation and mission in the public sector: Evidence from the World Values Survey. *Theory and Decision* 76: 241–63. [CrossRef]

de Moura, Georgina Randsley, Dominic Abrams, Carina Retter, Sigridur Gunnarsdottir, and Kaori Ando. 2009. Identification as an organizational anchor: How identification and job satisfaction combine to predict turnover intention. *European Journal of Social Psychology* 39: 540–57. [CrossRef]

Deci, Edward, Richard Ryan, and Richard Koestner. 1999. A meta-analytic review of experiments examining the effects of extrinsic rewards on intrinsic motivation. *Psychological Bulletin* 125: 627–68. [CrossRef] [PubMed]

Delobelle, Peter, Jakes Rawlinson, Sam Ntuli, Inah Malatsi, Rika Decock, and Anne Marie Depoorter. 2011. Job satisfaction and turnover intent of primary healthcare nurses in rural south africa: A questionnaire survey. *Journal of Advanced Nursing* 67: 371–83. [CrossRef] [PubMed]

DeSantis, Victor, and Samantha Durst. 1996. Comparing job satisfaction among public- and private-sector employees. *The American Review of Public Administration* 26: 327–43. [CrossRef]

Dysvik, Anders, and Bard Kuvaas. 2010. Intrinsic motivation as a moderator on the relationship between perceived job autonomy and work performance. *European Journal of Work and Organizational Psychology* 20: 367–87. [CrossRef]

Dysvik, Anders, and Bard Kuvaas. 2013. Intrinsic and extrinsic motivation as predictors of work effort: The moderating role of achievement goals. *British Journal of Social Psychology* 52: 412–30. [CrossRef]

Ellett, Alberta, Jacquelyn Ellis, Tonya Westbrook, and Denise Dews. 2007. A qualitative study of 369 child welfare professionals' perspectives about factors contributing to employee retention and turnover. *Children and Youth Services Review* 29: 264–81. [CrossRef]

Furnham, Adrian, Andreas Eracleous, and Tomas Chamorro-Premuzic. 2009. Personality, motivation and job satisfaction: Hertzberg meets the Big Five. *Journal of Managerial Psychology* 24: 765–79. [CrossRef]

Garbers, Yvonne, and Udo Konradt. 2014. The effect of financial incentives on performance: A quantitative review of individual and team-based financial incentives. *Journal of Occupational and Organizational Psychology* 87: 102–37. [CrossRef]

Georgellis, Yannis, Elisabetta Iossa, and Vurain Tabvuma. 2011. Crowding Out Intrinsic Motivation in the Public Sector. *Journal of Public Administration Research and Theory* 21: 473–93. [CrossRef]

Grant, Adam. 2008. Does Intrinsic Motivation Fuel the Prosocial Fire? Motivational Synergy in Predicting Persistence, Performance, and Productivity. *Journal of Applied Psychology* 93: 48–58. [CrossRef] [PubMed]

Griffeth, Rodger, Peter Hom, and Stefan Gaertner. 2000. A meta-analysis of antecedents and correlates of employee turnover: Update, moderator tests, and research implications for the next millennium. *Journal of Management* 26: 463–88. [CrossRef]

Grissom, Jason, Jill Nicholson-Crotty, and Lael Keiser. 2012. Does my boss's gender matter? Explaining job satisfaction and employee turnover in the public sector. *Journal of Public Administration Research and Theory* 22: 649–73. [CrossRef]

Hackman, Richard, and Greg Oldham. 1976. Motivation through the design of work: Test of a theory. *Organizational Behavior and Human Performance* 16: 250–79. [CrossRef]

Hellman, Chan. 1997. Job satisfaction and intent to leave. *The Journal of Social Psychology* 137: 677–89. [CrossRef]

Herzberg, Frederick. 1968. One more time: How do you motivate employees? *Harvard Business Review* 81: 87–96.

Herzberg, Frederick. 1974. Motivation-hygiene profiles: Pinpointing what ails the organization. *Organizational Dynamics* 3: 18–29. [CrossRef]

Herzberg, Frederick, Bernard Mausner, and Barbara Bloch Snyderman. 1962. *The Motivation to Work*, 2nd ed. New York: Wiley.

Hom, Peter, and Angelo Kinicki. 2001. Toward a greater understanding of how dissatisfaction drives employee turnover. *Academy of Management Journal* 44: 975–87. [CrossRef]

Huang, Xu, and Evert Van De Vliert. 2003. Where intrinsic job satisfaction fails to work: National moderators of intrinsic motivation. *Journal of Organizational Behavior* 24: 159–79. [CrossRef]

Hwang, Jee-In, and Hyejung Chang. 2008. Explaining turnover intention in Korean public community hospitals: Occupational differences. *The International Journal of Health Planning and Management* 23: 119–38. [CrossRef]

Iaffaldano, Michelle, and Paul Muchinsky. 1985. Job Satisfaction and Job Performance. A Meta-Analysis. *Psychological Bulletin* 97: 251–73. [CrossRef]

Islam, Jesmin, Quazi Ali, and Azizur Rahman. 2011. Nexus between cultural dissonance, management accounting systems, and managerial effectiveness: Evidence from an asian developing country. *Journal of Asia-Pacific Business* 12: 280–303. [CrossRef]

Joo, Baek-kyoo, Chang-Wook Jeung, and Hea Jun Yoon. 2010. Investigating the influences of core self-evaluations, job autonomy, and intrinsic motivation on in-role job performance. *Human Resource Development Quarterly* 21: 353–71. [CrossRef]

Judge, Timothy, Carl Thoresen, Joyce Bono, and Gregory Patton. 2001. The job satisfaction-job performance relationship: A qualitative and quantitative review. *Psychological Bulletin* 127: 376–407. [CrossRef] [PubMed]

Jung, Chan Su. 2014. Why Are Goals Important in the Public Sector? Exploring the Benefits of Goal Clarity for Reducing Turnover Intention. *Journal of Public Administration Research and Theory* 24: 209–34. [CrossRef]

Lambert, Eric, and Nancy Hogan. 2009. The Importance of Job Satisfaction and Organizational Commitment in Shaping Turnover Intent: A Test of a Causal Model. *Criminal Justice Review* 34: 96–118. [CrossRef]

Lawler, Edward, and Lyman William Porter. 1967. The effect of performance on job satisfaction. *Industrial Relations: A Journal of Economy and Society* 7: 20–28. [CrossRef]

Lee, Geon, and Benedict Jimenez. 2011. Does Performance Management Affect Job Turnover Intention in the Federal Government? *The American Review of Public Administration* 41: 168–84. [CrossRef]

Liu, Bangcheng, Jianxin Liu, and Jin Hu. 2010. Person-organization fit, job satisfaction, and turnover intention: An empirical study in the chinese public sector. *Social Behavior and Personality: An International Journal* 38: 615–25. [CrossRef]

Locke, Edwin. 1970. Job satisfaction and job performance: A theoretical analysis. *Organizational Behavior and Human Performance* 5: 484–500. [CrossRef]

Locke, Edwin. 1991. The motivation sequence, the motivation hub, and the motivation core. *Organizational Behavior and Human Decision Processes* 50: 288–99. [CrossRef]

Locke, Edwin, and Gray Latham. 1990. Work motivation and satisfaction: Light at the end of the tunnel. *Psychological Science* 4: 240–46. [CrossRef]

Luna-Arocas, Roberto, and Joaquin Camps. 2008. A model of high performance work practices and turnover intentions. *Personnel Review* 37: 26–46. [CrossRef]

Maertz, Carl, and Rodger Griffeth. 2004. Eight Motivational Forces and Voluntary Turnover: A Theoretical Synthesis with Implications for Research. *Journal of Management* 30: 667–83. [CrossRef]

Maidani, Ebrahim. 1991. Comparative study of Herzberg's two-factor theory of job satisfaction among public and private. *Public Personnel Management* 20: 441. [CrossRef]

Markovits, Yannis, Ann Davis, Doris Fay, and Rolf van Dick. 2010. The link between job satisfaction and organizational commitment: Differences between public and private sector employees. *International Public Management Journal* 13: 177–96. [CrossRef]

Meier, Kenneth, and Alisa Hicklin. 2008. Employee Turnover and Organizational Performance: Testing a Hypothesis from Classical Public Administration. *Journal of Public Administration Research and Theory* 18: 573–90. [CrossRef]

Mihajlov, Snezana, and Nenad Mihajlov. 2016. Comparing public and private employees' job satisfication and turnover intention. *MEST Journal* 4: 75–86. [CrossRef]

Mobley, William. 1977. Intermediate linkages in the relationship between job satisfaction and employee turnover. *Journal of Applied Psychology* 62: 237–40. [CrossRef]

Moynihan, Donald, and Noel Landuyt. 2008. Explaining Turnover Intention in State Government: Examining the Roles of Gender, Life Cycle, and Loyalty. *Review of Public Personnel Administration* 28: 120–43. [CrossRef]

Moynihan, Donald, and Sanjay Pandey. 2008. The Ties that Bind: Social Networks, Person-Organization Value Fit, and Turnover Intention. *Journal of Public Administration Research and Theory* 18: 205–27. [CrossRef]

Naff, Katherine, and John Crum. 1999. Working for America: Does public service motivation make a difference? *Review of Public Personnel Administration* 19: 5–16. [CrossRef]

Nyberg, Aanthony. 2010. Retaining your high performers: Moderators of the performance—job satisfaction—voluntary turnover relationship. *Journal of Applied Psychology* 95: 440–53. [CrossRef] [PubMed]

Park, Chunoh, Nicholas Lovrich, and Dennis Soden. 1988. Testing Herzberg's Motivation Theory in a Comparative Study of U.S. and Korean Public Employees. *Review of Public Personnel Administration* 8: 40–60. [CrossRef]

Pedersen, Mogens Jin. 2013. Public Service Motivation and Attraction to Public Versus Private Sector Employment: Academic Field of Study as Moderator? *International Public Management Journal* 16: 357–85. [CrossRef]

Perry, James. 1997. Antecedents of Public Service Motivation. *Journal of Public Administration Research and Theory* 7: 181–97. [CrossRef]

Perry, James, and Annie Hondeghem. 2008. Building theory and empirical evidence about public service motivation. *International Public Management Journal* 11: 3–12. [CrossRef]

Perry, James, and Lois Recascino Wise. 1990. The motivational bases of public service. *Public Administration Review* 50: 367–73. [CrossRef]

Peterson, Shari. 2004. Toward a Theoretical Model of Employee Turnover: A Human Resource Development Perspective. *Human Resource Development Review* 3: 209–27. [CrossRef]

Pitts, David, Marvel John, and Sergio Fernandez. 2011. So Hard to Say Goodbye? Turnover Intention among U.S. Federal Employees. *Public Administration Review* 71: 751–60. [CrossRef]

Podsakoff, Nathan, Jeffery LePine, and Marcie LePine. 2007. Differential challenge stressor-hindrance stressor relationships with job attitudes, turnover intentions, turnover, and withdrawal behavior: A meta-analysis. *Journal of Applied Psychology* 92: 438–54. [CrossRef] [PubMed]

Porter, Lyman William, Richard M. Steers, Richard T. Mowday, and Paul V. Boulian. 1974. Organizational Commitment, Job-Satisfaction, and Turnover among Psychiatric Technicians. *Journal of Applied Psychology* 59: 603–9. [CrossRef]

Price, James. 1989. The impact of turnover on the organization. *Work and Occupations* 16: 461–73. [CrossRef]

Prihandinisari, Carolina, Azizur Rahman, and John Hicks. 2016. What Motivate Individuals to Join Public Service? Examining Public Service Motivation in a Non-Western Cultural Context. In *5th Global Business and Finance Research Conference*. Berwick: World Business Institute, pp. 1–13.

Rahman, Azizur, and Najmul Hasan. 2017. Modeling Effects of KM and HRM Processes to the Organizational Performance and Employee's Job Satisfaction. *International Journal of Business and Management* 12: 35–45. [CrossRef]

Rosenfeld, Michael, and Steve Zdep. 1971. Instrinsic-extrinsic aspects of work and their demographic correlates. *Psychological Reports* 28: 359–62. [CrossRef]

Rutherford, Brian, Yujie Wei, JungKun Park, and Won-Moo Hur. 2012. Increasing job performance and reducing turnover: An examination of female Chinese salespeople. *Journal of Marketing Theory and Practice* 20: 423–36. [CrossRef]

Ryan, Richard, and Edward Deci. 2000. Intrinsic and extrinsic motivations: Classic definitions and new directions. *Contemporary Educational Psychology* 25: 54–67. [CrossRef]

Sachau, Daniel. 2007. Resurrecting the motivation-hygiene theory: Herzberg and the positive psychology movement. *Human Resource Development Review* 6: 377–93. [CrossRef]

Schleicher, Deidra, John Watt, and Gary Greguras. 2004. Reexamining the job satisfaction-performance relationship: The complexity of attitudes. *Journal of Applied Psychology* 89: 165–77. [CrossRef]

Sell, Lea, and Bryan Cleal. 2011. Job Satisfaction, Work Environment, and Rewards: Motivational Theory Revisited. *LABOUR* 25: 1–23. [CrossRef]

Smith, Deborah, and Joel Shields. 2013. Factors Related to Social Service Workers' Job Satisfaction: Revisiting Herzberg's Motivation to Work. *Administration in Social Work* 37: 189–98. [CrossRef]

Sousa-Poza, Alfonso, and Andres Sousa-Poza. 2007. The effect of job satisfaction on labor turnover by gender: An analysis for Switzerland. *The Journal of Socio-Economics* 36: 895–913. [CrossRef]

Spector, Paul, Tammy Allen, Steven Poelmans, Laurent Lapierre, Cary Cooper, Michael O'Driscoll, Juan Sanchez, Nureya Abarca, Matilda Alexandrova, Barbara Beham, and et al. 2007. Cross-national differences in relationships of work demands, job satisfaction, and turnover intentions with work–family conflict. *Personnel Psychology* 60: 805–35. [CrossRef]

Steel, Robert. 2002. Turnover theory at the empirical interface: Problems of fit and function. *Academy of Management Review* 27: 346–60. [CrossRef]

Steel, Robert, and John Lounsbury. 2009. Turnover process models: Review and synthesis of a conceptual literature. *Human Resource Management Review* 19: 271–82. [CrossRef]

Steers, Richard, Richard Mowday, and Debra Shapiro. 2004. The future of work motivation theory. *Academy of Management Review* 29: 379–87. [CrossRef]

Swailes, Stephen, and Saleh Al Fahdi. 2011. Voluntary turnover in the Omani public sector: An Islamic values perspective. *International Journal of Public Administration* 34: 682–92. [CrossRef]

Taylor, Jeannette. 2007. The impact of public service motives on work outcomes in Australia: A comparative multi-dimensional analysis. *Public Administration* 85: 931–59. [CrossRef]

Taylor, Jeannette. 2014. Public service motivation, relational job design, and job satisfaction in local government. *Public Administration* 92: 902–18. [CrossRef]

Taylor, Jeannette, and Ranald Taylor. 2011. Working hard for more money or working hard to make a difference? Efficiency wages, public service motivation, and effort. *Review of Public Personnel Administration* 31: 67–86. [CrossRef]

Taylor, Jeannette, and Janathan Westover. 2011. Job satisfaction in the public service. *Public Management Review* 13: 731–51. [CrossRef]

Tett, Robert, and John Meyer. 1993. Job satisfaction, organizational commitment, turnover intention, and turnover: Path analyses based on meta-analytic findings. *Personnel Psychology* 46: 259–93. [CrossRef]

Van Iddekinge, Chad, Philip Roth, Dan Putka, and Stephen Lanivich. 2011. Are you interested? A meta-analysis of relations between vocational interests and employee performance and turnover. *Journal of Applied Psychology* 96: 1167–94. [CrossRef] [PubMed]

Vandenabeele, Wouter. 2007. Toward a public administration theory of public service motivation. *Public Management Review* 9: 545–56. [CrossRef]

Vandenabeele, Wouter. 2008. Development of a public service motivation measurement scale: Corroborating and extending perry's measurement instrument. *International Public Management Journal* 11: 143–67. [CrossRef]

Vandenabeele, Wouter. 2009. The mediating effect of job satisfaction and organizational commitment on self-reported performance: More robust evidence of the PSM—Performance relationship. *International Review of Administrative Sciences* 75: 11–34. [CrossRef]

Vandenabeele, Wouter. 2011. Who Wants to Deliver Public Service? Do Institutional Antecedents of Public Service Motivation Provide an Answer? *Review of Public Personnel Administration* 31: 87–107. [CrossRef]

Wang, Yau-De, Chyan Yang, and Kuei-Ying Wang. 2012. Comparing Public and Private Employees' Job Satisfaction and Turnover. *Public Personnel Management* 41: 557–73. [CrossRef]

Warr, Peter, John Cook, and Toby Wall. 1979. Scales for the measurement of some work attitudes and aspects of psychological well-being. *Journal of Occupational Psychology* 52: 129–48. [CrossRef]

Westover, Jonathan, and Jeannette Taylor. 2010. International differences in job satisfaction. *International Journal of Productivity and Performance Management* 59: 811–28. [CrossRef]

Wiersma, Uco Jillert. 1992. The effects of extrinsic rewards in intrinsic motivation: A meta-analysis. *Journal of Occupational and Organizational Psychology* 65: 101–14. [CrossRef]

Zimmerman, Ryan, and Todd Darnold. 2009. The impact of job performance on employee turnover intentions and the voluntary turnover process. A meta-analysis and path model. *Personnel Review* 38: 142–58. [CrossRef]

MDPI
St. Alban-Anlage 66
4052 Basel
Switzerland
Tel. +41 61 683 77 34
Fax +41 61 302 89 18
www.mdpi.com

Journal of Risk and Financial Management Editorial Office
E-mail: jrfm@mdpi.com
www.mdpi.com/journal/jrfm

www.ingramcontent.com/pod-product-compliance
Lightning Source LLC
Chambersburg PA
CBHW051921190326
41458CB00026B/6367